WRITING
NOW

A College Handbook

WRITING NOW

A College Handbook

FRANCIS L. FENNELL
Loyola University of Chicago

SCIENCE RESEARCH ASSOCIATES, INC.
Chicago, Palo Alto, Toronto, Henley-on-Thames, Sydney, Paris
A Subsidiary of IBM

Credits

The selections that appear in this text are reprinted from the following sources:

Entry for *punish*. With permission. From *Webster's New World Dictionary*, Second College Edition. Copyright © 1978 by William Collins Publishers, Inc.

Entry for *punish*. © 1969 by Houghton Mifflin Company. Reprinted by permission from *The American Heritage Dictionary of the English Language*.

Entries for *jubilee*, *troll*, *punish*, and *odds*. By permission. From *Webster's New Collegiate Dictionary* © 1979 by G. & C. Merriam Co., Publishers of the Merriam-Webster Dictionaries.

Grin and Bear It by George Lichty. © Field Enterprises, Inc., 1978. Courtesy of Field Newspaper Syndicate.

List of 100 frequently misspelled words from Thomas Clark Pollock and William D. Baker: *The University Spelling Book*, © 1955 by Prentice-Hall, Inc. Reprinted by permission.

List of difficult words to spell from William Drake's *The Way to Spell: A Guide for the Hesitant Speller*.

Excerpt from "For the New Railway Station in Rome" from *Things of This World* by Richard Wilbur reprinted by permission from Harcourt Brace Jovanovich, Inc.

continued on page vi

Compositor	Graphic Typesetting Service
Designer	Judith Olson
Acquisition Editor	Phil Gerould
Project Editor	Mary McVey Gill

Library of Congress Cataloging in Publication Data

Fennell, Francis L.
Writing now.

Includes index.
1. English language—Rhetoric. I. Title.
PE1408.F445   808'.042   79-9249
ISBN 0-574-22050-X

180192

10   9   8   7   6   5   4   3   2   1

for Kay
and for Monica, Claire, and Mark
all of whom love good writing

Contents

Preface

TO THE INSTRUCTOR

Every spring I rip open dozens of those "Jiffy" mailing envelopes. In almost every case, out comes an English composition text whose advertising blurb promises that it is "different" and "better." Because that claim is so often made and so seldom fulfilled, I would rather not make it now, although I happen to believe it shelters a measure of truth for this handbook. In any event you will make your own comparisons. Here let me simply list what seem to me the most important advantages the book offers to you as the instructor.

First, *Writing Now* is a teaching handbook. Its goal is to offer the same practical advice an instructor would offer during an office conference. Each section has been written with one principle in mind: is this explanation detailed enough so that a student can understand it and use it? That is not to say the writing is below college level. Rather the effort is to take into account the student's perspective and background and then to make the explanations as clear as possible. Macaulay's dictum that "nothing is so useless as a general maxim" ought to have special application to handbooks. There are no big red-letter RULES here. In their place are attempts to discuss writing, with an emphasis on understanding why mistakes are made —no one makes them on purpose—and what can be done about them.

Second, I have tried to give this book both a logical structure and clear transitions. Deliberately absent is the bewildering and discouraging chemistry-text appearance that handbooks so often adopt. Consequently you can assign it to a class the way you would any other textbook—working from the first chapter to the last, for example, using the exercises to strengthen the student's mastery of each skill. Yet the chapter subsections and other signposts also allow students to use the book conveniently as a reference work, if you or they prefer. A special feature is the listing of all of the alternative correction symbols that might apply to a particular topic or section. Thus if you use symbols you can continue with whatever system you find natural, without having to adopt the chart used in this book unless you wish to do so.

Third, the advice this handbook offers is as sensible and up-to-date as possible. It distinguishes between severe faults and less grievous ones, between genuine errors and matters of taste. Whenever it is practical this advice reflects recent research in stylistics and in the composing process. Guidance is desirable, but it need not be prescriptive or pontifical. *Writing Now* respects the diversity and flexibility of modern English, summarizing the practice of good writers rather than simply issuing orders, like *Do not do Y* or *A writer should never use Z.*

Fourth, this handbook gives lengthier treatment to the problems students encounter more often. Research into student error patterns gives us the data needed for proportioning the emphasis according to the frequency or severity of the problem. Concretely, this means relatively more intensive discussions of such matters as run-on sentences, sentence fragments, subject-verb agreement, and even spelling. It means a lesser emphasis on mistakes that occur less often, like capitalization errors or confusing *like* for *as*, although these matters are of course included for those who need them.

Fifth, the examples, the exercises, and the sample assignments are drawn from student and professional writing and from actual writing assignments given in a wide variety of courses (not just composition courses). Therefore they have the flavor of "real" writing. Because they are words that somebody somewhere really did put down on paper, they will not be dismissed as easily as those contrived "Sue-and-John-(is) (are)-going-to-the-store" example sentences that many books use. Furthermore the experience of professional writers engaged in their craft is enlisted wherever it seems appropriate.

Sixth, and perhaps most noticeably, the tone of this handbook is different. Textbooks do not come from God and they need not sound like the Ten Commandments. The tone here is more informal, less didactic, reflecting the fact that one human being is speaking to others. Complementing the tone are numerous interpositions: jokes, aphorisms, cartoons, *obiter dicta*, whatever makes a relevant comment. They offer a respite, but more importantly they remind all of us that writing is indeed part of a larger world "out there." They also help to restore perspective, to make us aware again of the fact that writing is after all an art, not a science. Such material is common enough elsewhere, but somehow it has been excluded from handbooks, precisely the works most in need of some leavening.

I would return in the end to the point I made first. *Writing Now* will succeed or fail on the strength of its ability to teach students what they need to know in terms they can understand. If teaching does not take place in this book—real teaching, not just rule-making—then it loses its reason for existence. For unless we see handbooks as more than just compendiums of rules, unless we see how they can be made to both delight and instruct, we ought not write them or publish them or ask students to buy them.

F. L. F.

Preface

This book assumes you want to learn how to write better. Not that you are especially cheerful about it, mind you—few people like tasks that have no clearly defined beginning or end and for which progress is so hard to measure. But in my experience most students really do recognize the need to be able to write better than they do. Their attitude is usually a kind of resigned willingness.

If you have that resigned willingness, you are on solid ground. "Writing is an important skill"—you've heard the cliché countless times. Like so many clichés, it just happens to be true. A recent study by the National Institute of Education, for example, examined the careers of about four thousand people who graduated from college in 1961. The study uncovered the surprising fact that one-half of the women and two-thirds of the men chose their present careers only *after* leaving college, so that much of their undergraduate training had little direct relevance to what they were doing later. Translated into terms applicable to you, and taking into account the fact that over half of all college students change their major at least once *before* graduation, there is less than one chance in four that fifteen years from now you will actually be doing what you are now planning to do. This study then went one step further and asked these graduates what courses they would have taken in college if they had known then what they know now in their new careers. Heading the list: more courses in writing.

So improving your writing is an eminently practical step. The problem is, most students spend more energy yearning for it than they do acquiring it. They substitute the wish for the work.

The reason is that writing, unlike most other subjects, makes elastic requirements on your time. Twenty math problems take a certain number of hours. But when you're finished you're really finished. A writing assignment, on the other hand, is often given in terms of a word or page limit. When the five hundred words are on paper, it might seem like you are really finished here too. But you're not—if you want to write well, that is. Those five hundred words need to be gone over a second time, a third time, a fourth time, whatever it takes to make it the best writing you can produce. The difference between students who improve during a composition course and those who don't lies not so much in their desire as in their willingness to stretch that elastic time limit—to write a third draft, or proofread, or revise a graded paper. If you make that second effort, your writing can and will improve.

> What is written without effort is in general read without pleasure.
>
> *Samuel Johnson*

Let's assume you possess this second kind of willingness, as well as the resigned willingness that almost all students have. Here is how this book can help:

1. Your instructor may assign *Writing Now* as he or she would assign any other textbook. In other words, you may be asked to read certain chapters or sections of chapters. This book can be read continuously, one section or chapter leading into another. It is also, I hope, written so you can understand it. Exercises occur at the end of the major parts of each chapter and give you an important chance to test yourself on the skills you have been taught. Notice, by the way, that the example sentences, both in the exercises and in the text itself, are taken from selections by professional writers and by student writers like yourself.

2. Your instructor may ask you to use *Writing Now* as a resource book. When your papers show certain weaknesses, you will be asked to consult the appropriate section in this handbook and make whatever changes are necessary. If you will be using *Writing Now* this way, remember that every problem covered in the text is listed in the index. For further help in

locating the section you want, notice that each section lists the many possible abbreviations, symbols, or code words your instructor might use on your paper. These symbols, along with the numbered chapter sections and the list of symbols on the inside back cover of this book, should make it easy for you to find what you need. The exercises at the end of the major parts of each chapter can help you test your knowledge.

3. You may use *Writing Now* as a reference book. In fact, after your composition course is over you might be keeping the book for just that purpose. Here again the index and the symbols will be important location aids. But probably the sections you will find especially valuable are Chapter 5 on research papers and essay exams, Chapter 6 on grammar, Chapter 7 on conventions such as punctuation and capitalization, the Glossary of Usage, and the Glossary of Grammatical Terms.

One more thing: writing is important and practical, yes. But it need not be approached in hushed tones, as if we were conversing in an operating room during open-heart surgery. In this book you will find a more personal style than you may be accustomed to in most textbooks. You will also find some cartoons and some apt quotations. We have an important subject, but I hope it will never appear to be a grim one.

F.L.F.

Acknowledgments

The author is grateful to the many people whose sympathetic criticism has made this book a better one and whose support has made it a joyous one to write. Particularly, I want to thank: the student reviewers (Raymond Bilodeau, Marla Friedman, and Virginia Krause), who lent their own special expertise; Harry Burke, Victoria Hughes, Laurel Meredith, Deborah Skozek, and Ellen Titra, who provided valuable material; Rita Lynam and Sheryl Hansen, who typed the manuscript; and Robert Cummings, who did the proofreading and indexing. And I have benefited immensely from the suggestions of colleagues at other institutions who have commented so helpfully on the manuscript:

Tommy J. Boley, University of Texas, El Paso

Gary J. Cummings, De Anza College, Cupertino, California

Robert M. Frew, American River College, Sacramento, California

Winifred B. Horner, University of Missouri, Columbia

Richard L. Larson, Lehman College, City University of New York

Arnold R. Oliver, North Virginia Community College, Manassas, Virginia

James O'Malley, Triton College, River Grove, Illinois

Dwain Preston, Western Illinois University, Macomb, Illinois

David Rankin, California State University at Dominguez Hills, California

Donald Toburen, Butler County Community College, El Dorado, Kansas

I am especially grateful to Phil Gerould of SRA Inc., who encouraged this project back when it was a conviction rather than a book, and to Mary McVey Gill, who edited the manuscript so wisely and patiently that I became convinced she should write the next one herself.

F. L. F.

1

HOW WE WRITE: WORDS

Polonius: What do you read, my lord?
Hamlet: Words, words, words.
William Shakespeare

When meddlesome old Polonius asks Hamlet what he is reading, Hamlet's reply is so literally true as to seem foolish: "Words, words, words." We all use words every day, and yet how difficult it is to use them with meaning, precision, and grace.

Good writing involves taking a very familiar item, the word—staple of our daily conversation and of all our reading and writing—and employing it with uncommon skill. Excellent writing could be compared to the performance of a tennis star, a gymnast, or a dancer—these people take that most familiar of all objects, the human body, and perform feats requiring immense control and skill. We marvel at the performance of a good athlete because we know from our own experiences how difficult such feats must be. Similarly, when words are used with skill and agility we can appreciate this use of the familiar in an unfamiliar way.

Words are the building blocks of language, whether we speak or write. To use them well takes patience and concentration, just as in gymnastics or any other physical skill. Practice over an extended period of time is indispensable.

That's the bad news. The good news is that words *are* subject to your control; they *can* be made to do your bidding; real improvement *is* possible. Some people may have a natural flair for writing, just as some people have natural athletic ability. But everyone can make noticeable progress if he or she takes sufficient care and practices. To be a great writer requires innate talent and a lifetime of dedication to the craft. Most of us, however, are satisfied with competence, the ability to write clearly and persuasively. The goal lies quite within your range if you are willing to strive for it.

Even if we grant that such competency can be attained, you might still wonder why you should make such an effort. After all, few of us who watch an expert gymnast feel compelled to go into training the next morning. But the time you spend learning to write well has a practical value that should make acquiring such a skill very important to you. If you think about it for a

3

moment, you will realize that ours is a society that more often respects mental rather than physical attainments. A prospective employer, for example, will probably not care how strong or how swift you are. But he or she will be very interested in the strength and agility of your mind, and one of the ways a mind can be assessed is by its ability to use language skillfully. The same standard holds true in the professions as well.

I am not saying that everyone who succeeds always writes well. Of course that's not true. Marrying the boss's daughter, inheriting money from a rich aunt, being 7'2" with a devastating hook shot—all of these will do quite well. But if you lack such unusual assets, then you need every other advantage you can get. Perhaps the best of these advantages is the ability to manipulate words, the ability to make language do what you want it to do.

"You majored in English, Brinwell. Write us up a nice little request for higher appropriations."

Drawing by Mort Gerberg; © 1975 The New Yorker Magazine, Inc.

So that's what this chapter is all about—words, and increasing your ability to use them well. You will learn about the most effective ways to put language to work and also about how your choice of words can sometimes hinder you from communicating with others. Knowing more about words helps you use them, if you then put your knowledge to work through practice.

Let's begin with a common classroom situation: one of your instructors is handing back papers to the class. If you have word problems marked on your paper, they will usually be one of two types. The first type is what we might call an active misuse of words—something that you have written was not worded properly. These difficulties might be called to your attention by notes in the margin or elsewhere, perhaps by means of symbols. The most common such symbols are *d, w,* or *ww* (diction, word choice, wrong word); *wdy* (wordy); *big w* (unnecessarily big word), or *e* (exactness).

The second type of problem is a more general one: it deals not so much with commission (what you have done) as with omission (what you have not done). Your language in the paper might be technically correct, but also vapid, colorless, uninspiring. Here what is needed is for you to become more aware of the resources that the English language makes available to you, so that you can make use of a wider variety of skills, a greater repertoire.

This chapter will offer strategies for dealing with both types of problems. The first type, faults of commission, often responds to a direct application of the first strategy, "looking it up," which is discussed in detail in Part A of this chapter. Some problems of this type, however, require use of one or more of several alternative strategies. These alternative strategies are explored in Part B. Difficulties of the second type, faults of omission, usually do not occur singly—a writer who employs euphemism, for example, is very likely to use jargon as well. So the best strategy here is to cover all of Part B. Then in the last section of the chapter, Part C, we consider what might be the most frustrating problem of all: the fact that it is possible to make an excellent choice of words and still diminish their power by misspelling them. Each of the three chapter sections is followed by exercises to test and improve your knowledge of the material.

A. LOOKING IT UP

A powerful agent is the right word. Whenever we come upon one of those intensely right words in a book or in a newspaper the resulting effect is physical as well as spiritual, and electrically prompt.

Mark Twain

Chances are you were given a dictionary by Aunt Martha when you graduated from high school, or maybe you bought one yourself in anticipation of college work. If you haven't gotten one yet, better do it. A dictionary is to an aspiring writer what a fielder's mitt is to baseball player: you can play the game without it, but it sure will be a lot more painful.

Trouble is, most people use a dictionary for only two things: finding out what a word means and checking up on spelling. These are exemplary uses, of course, but dictionaries can teach us much more. The purpose of this section is, first, to make you better acquainted with your own dictionary, and then secondly to show you how this greater familiarity enables you to correct many of the unintentional mistakes you may have made with words. For a student of words, as all writers must be, the dictionary is your encyclopedia.

A1. Using the Dictionary

To begin, I would like you to get your dictionary and open it to a simple everyday word. Let's start with *punish*. Compare the entry in your dictionary for *punish* with the following entry, from *Webster's New Collegiate Dictionary* (Springfield, Mass.: G. & C. Merriam Co., 1976).

> **pun·ish** \\'pən-ish*vb* [ME *punisshen,* fr. MF *puniss-,* stem of *punir,* fr. L *punire.* fr. *poena* penalty — more at PAIN]. *vt* **1 a :** to impose a penalty on for a fault, offense, or violation **b :** to inflict a penalty for the commission of (an offense) in retribution or retaliation **2 a :** to deal with roughly or harshly **b :** to inflict injury on : HURT ~ *vt :* to inflict punishment — **pun·ish·abil·i·ty** \\ ,pən-ish-ə-'bil-ət-ē*n* — **pun· ish·able** \\ 'pən-ish-ə-bəl\\ *adj* — **pun·ish·er** *n syn* PUNISH, CHASTISE, CASTIGATE, CHASTEN, DISCIPLINE, CORRECT *shared meaning element* : to inflict a penalty on in requital for wrongdoing *ant* excuse, pardon.

There is a whole lot more information here than simply spelling and meaning. If you proceed through the entry from beginning to end, that information can be decoded as follows:

1. **Syllabication (pun·ish).** The word is composed of two three-letter syllables, as indicated by the dot between the *n* and the *i*. This information is especially helpful for telling when to break the word if you are typing and must finish the word on the next line.

2. **Pronunciation** (\'pən-ish\). Obvious in this case maybe. But not so obvious with hundreds of other words. How do you pronounce *Mackinac* as in *Mackinac Island*? (Not how you probably think.) What are the *four* acceptable pronunciations of *renaissance*? What about a word like *synechdoche*? Even this entry for *punish* may not be so obvious if English is not your native language. By the way, to use an entry successfully you need to know the pronunciation guide for your particular dictionary, since these guides vary.

3. **Word origin** (*vb* [ME *punisshen* . . . PAIN]). Translate the section with brackets as follows: *punish* derives from the Middle English word *punisshen*, which in turn comes from the Middle French *puniss;* the French word can then be traced back to the Latin *punire* and *poena;* finally, still more information about this derivation can be found under the entry for *pain*.

4. **Definition** (*vt* **1 a:** to impose . . . to inflict punishment). Here two essential meanings are given—either to inflict a penalty in response to an offense, or else, in a more general sense, simply to inflict pain of any sort. Further discriminations are then made; the second definition, for example, can mean either to treat roughly (a) or to actually injure (b).

> As sheer casual reading matter, I still find the English dictionary the most interesting book in our language.
>
> *Albert Nock*

If a word is used under more than one part of speech, each use must be listed separately, the change being called to your attention by the mark ~. Since *punish* can be a verb used intransitively (*vi*) as well as transitively (*vt*), this fact is noted and a definition provided ("to inflict punishment").

5. **Derived words** (—**pun·ish·abil·i·ty** ... **pun·ish·er** *n*). Three other words, marked by dashes and printed in boldface, can be said to derive from *punish* without need of further definition. Two of them, *punishability* and *punisher*, are nouns; the other is the adjective *punishable*. Suitable pronunciations are also given.

6. **Synonyms** (*syn* ... wrongdoing). This dictionary lists six other words as having meanings similar to *punish*. Notice that word *similar*. Synonyms, contrary to popular belief, do *not* mean the same thing. There are shades of difference, nuances, as a check of their respective definitions would show. But all the synonyms do have a "shared element of meaning," identified here as "to inflict a penalty on in requital for wrongdoing."

7. **Antonyms** (*ant* excuse, pardon). Two words are given as having meanings quite the opposite of *punish*.

One myth about dictionaries we ought to clear up right away is the idea that all dictionaries are alike. Just isn't so. For example, you have seen how *punish* is treated by *Webster's New Collegiate Dictionary*. First compare it with the entry in your own dictionary. Does your entry differ, and if so, how? Then compare *Webster's New Collegiate* with the treatments of the word given in two other equally reputable dictionaries. The first entry is from the *New World Dictionary* (Cleveland: Collins-World, 1976); the second is from the *American Heritage Dictionary of the English Language* (Boston: Houghton-Mifflin, 1969).

---

pun·ish (pun'ish) *vt*. [ME. *punischen* < extended stem of OFr. *punir* < L. *punire*, to punish < *poena*, punishment, penalty: see PENAL] **1.** to cause to undergo pain, loss, or suffering for a crime or wrongdoing **2.** to impose a penalty on a wrongdoer for (an offense) **3.** to treat harshly or injuriously /the *punishing* rays of the sun/ **4.** [Colloq.] to consume or use up —*vi*. to deal out punishment — **pun'ish·er** *n*.

SYN.—**punish** implies the infliction of some penalty on a wrongdoer and generally connotes retribution rather than correction /to *punish* a murderer by hanging him/; **discipline** supports punishment that is in-

tended to control or to establish habits of self-control
[to *discipline* a naughty child]; **correct** suggests
punishment for the purpose of overcoming faults [to
correct unruly pupils]; **chastise** implies usually corporal punishment and connotes both retribution and
correction; **castigate** now implies punishment by severe public criticism or censure [to *castigate* a corrupt
official]; **chasten** implies the infliction of tribulation in
order to make obedient, meek, etc. and is used especially in a theological sense ["He *chastens* and hastens
His will to make known"]

pun·ish (pun'ish) *tr. v.* **-ished, -ishing, -ishes. 1.** To
subject (someone) to penalty for a crime, fault, or
misbehavior. **2.** To inflict a penalty on a criminal or
wrongdoer for (an offense). **3.** To handle roughly; injure; hurt: *"the October wind / with frosty fingers
punishes my hair"* (Dylan Thomas). **4.** *Informal.* To deplete (a stock or supply) heavily. *—intr.* To give
punishment. [Middle English *punissen, punyschen,*
from Old French *punir* (stem *puniss*-), from Latin
punire, poenire, from *poena,* penalty, punishment,
from Greek *poinē.* See **kwei-**[1] in Appendix.*]
—pun'ish·er *n.*
  Synonyms: punish, chastise, discipline, castigate,
penalize. These verbs refer to different ways of causing
pain or loss to someone for wrong behavior. *Punish*
usually means subjecting someone to loss of freedom
or money or to physical pain for wrongdoing. *Chastise*
usually refers to corporal punishment as a means of
improving behavior. *Discipline* stresses punishment
designed to control an offender and to eliminate or
reform unacceptable conduct. *Castigate,* now always
verbal, means to berate or censure, often in public.
Penalize, weaker than *punish,* usually involves a demand for money or forfeiture of a privilege or gain
because the rules of fair play or established conduct
have been broken: *penalized for late payment of taxes.*

There are important similarities among these three entries. All
of them, for example, agree on syllabication, on pronunciation
(although they use different phonetic systems), and on derivation. All agree on a definition that stresses the imposition of a
penalty in response to wrongdoing and on a definition that
stresses the infliction of pain or injury. All of them find a single
definition for the word when it is used intransitively, and all cite
the verbs *chastise, castigate,* and *discipline* as synonyms.

But look at the differences too. Some are minor, like the four variant spellings of the Middle English root verb, each dictionary providing a different one. Others are much more significant. For example, *N.W.D.* and *A.H.D.* (let's make it easier by using abbreviations) are in substantial agreement on definitions. But *N.C.D.* sees the first two definitions provided by the others as really just different aspects of what is basically one meaning, hence the designation **1 a** and **1 b.** The third definition for the others is subdivided by *N.C.D.* into **2 a** and **2 b.** Most important of all, the definition of *punish* as "consume" or "deplete" puts them all at odds: *N.W.D.* and *A.H.D.* come to somewhat different conclusions about when it is proper to use the word this way, while *N.C.D.* by its omission of it claims the word is not used this way at all!

There are more differences. All three dictionaries agree on *chastise*, *castigate*, and *discipline* as synonyms, but *A.H.D.* drops *chasten* and *correct*, which the other two include, and adds one of its own: *penalize*. The section on synonyms is much larger and more detailed in *N.W.D.* and *A.H.D.* than in *N.C.D.*, but *N.C.D.* includes antonyms while the others do not. *A.H.D.* offers the verb ending transformations (**-ished, -ishing, -ishes**); the others do not. *N.C.D.* lists three derived words, *N.W.D.* one, and *A.H.D.* none.

These discrepancies are pointed out, not to praise one dictionary at the expense of another, but rather to show that good, well-respected reference books can differ. This is especially true in the matter of usage labels, like the "Colloq." of *N.W.D.* or the "Informal" of *A.H.D.* that we saw assigned to *punish*. (For the meanings of these labels see pp. 14–16.) If they differ so much on a word like *punish*, which we all "know," you can imagine what will happen on more controversial words. So when people try to resolve an argument about words by saying, "Look it up in the dictionary," the only sensible reply is *"Which* dictionary?"

Another advantage of noting these differences among dictionaries is the realization that each dictionary has its own special features, its own strengths and weaknesses. Looking again at those three entries for *punish*, *A.H.D.* seems to have the clearest definitions, *N.W.D.* the best treatment of synonyms, and *N.C.D.* the best description of the word's origin and its derived forms. These relative advantages will of course vary from entry to entry, so before you buy a dictionary, compare the ones available to you. Read the prefaces, look up a few test words, see which book you can use most quickly and comfortably. Then examine the special features of each: which ones have proper names and place names in the text, which place them separately at the end; which ones discuss the history of the language (and how important is that to you?); which ones include symbol charts or advice on form and style. No dictionary will fit your preferences exactly, but some will come closer than others.

> Dictionaries are like watches: the worst is better than none, and the best cannot be expected to go quite true.
>
> *Samuel Johnson*

One last point about dictionaries: don't buy a cheap paperback. It just won't tell you enough to do the job. To show you what I mean, take *punish* again. Here is the definition, word-for-word, as given in a cheap paperback I bought at Kresge's:

> **pun·ish** (pun'·ish) *vt.* *[<L. punire]* 1. to cause to undergo pain, loss, etc. as for a crime 2. to impose a penalty for (an offense) — **pun·ish·a·ble** *adj.*

That's all. So much is left out that might be important to you, like the discussion of synonyms. And what is left *in* is so shortened that it falsifies unconscionably: *punish* does not come directly from the Latin, *punish* does not have only two definitions, *punish* is not always used transitively. So when you shop for a dictionary, think in terms of the reputable hardcovers: either the three we have used so far *(N.C.D., N.W.D., A.H.D.)*; or *Funk and Wagnalls Standard College Dictionary* (New York: Harcourt Brace Jovanovich, 1968), or the *Random House College Dictionary* (New York: Random House, 1975). If cost has to be a factor, get the paperback version of one of these hardcovers. It will cost you only a dollar or so more than a cheap paperback and will provide much more information.

Now that you are familiar with a dictionary and how to use it, let's consider three specific ways in which the "looking it up" strategy can help you determine where your use of words went astray.

A2. Tone and Language Level

Usage is simply the ways words and phrases are actually used in our language. If a paper comes back to you with comments or symbols that suggest you have misused a word or phrase, the dictionary is your best resource for a solution to the problem (assuming, of course, that this handbook itself, especially the glossary, doesn't answer it). The comments or symbols might be any one of the following: *use* or *usage; d* (diction); *e* or *ex* (exactness); *loc* (localism); *reg* (regionalism); *colloq* (colloquialism); *sl* (slang); *glos* (glossary); *arch* (archaic); *dict* (dictionary); *approp* (appropriateness); *id* (idiom). And that's only a partial list! You and I might agree that it would be desirable for all teachers and books to use the same symbols, but it's not done that way. So your first step ought to be finding out what words and symbols your instructor will be using and what he or she means by them. Any one of these terms could be referring to a problem with your usage—or, more specifically, the level of your usage.

To understand usage level better, let's begin with the spoken word rather than the written word. Suppose you have an examination scheduled for a Tuesday morning, but on the same day at the same hour you have a court date to answer a summons for a speeding ticket. To your roommate you might say: "I've gotta be in court at nine on Tuesday. For sure I won't be back in time for Walker's bio test. Hope the old guy lets me take a makeup." But when you approach the venerable Dr. Walker himself, you unconsciously adjust your language: "Excuse me, sir, I have to be in court next Tuesday and so I must be absent from the midterm. Would it be possible for me to take the examination at some later time?"

Your adjustment is a recognition of the fact that each situation has a level of language appropriate to it. In conversation with a friend you use the appropriate language: contractions ("bio"), informal terms ("old guy"), and idioms ("for sure"). But when the situation calls for more formal language you use that instead. Otherwise you would run the risk of not persuading your listener. Dr. Walker probably would not be surprised to hear that he is sometimes called an "old guy." But he might not respond well if you call him that directly.

Writing is like speaking. Each writing situation has a language appropriate to it, depending in large part on the writer's expectations about what the reader wants to hear. Two key terms often used to describe these levels of language are *formal* and *informal*.

Formal language is the language of the public situation, when the writer's intended audience is not someone he or she knows personally. In such circumstances writers tend to be more careful, choosing words and arranging sentences to show an acknowledged lack of intimacy between themselves and their readers. They would probably also use fewer contractions and avoid certain words or phrases that might seem inappropriate (or put them in quotation marks to show an awareness that they have a nonliteral value or slang tone). For an example of formal writing, you often need go no further than your nearest textbook.

Informal language, on the other hand, presupposes an intimacy between author and reader, like the letters exchanged by old friends; it makes use of more contractions, more of the unbuttoned language usually found in everyday conversation. This is a good example:

> . . . I got so depressed and fed up with the Rev and his Holy Bobble that I swung with the collection one night (a cool 83¢) and went out looking for trouble.
>
> I figured I'd given the Rev more than 83¢ worth of happiness. Twofold happiness, in fact. When he first saw me, he thought he'd found the 13th Disciple. Later, when the true nature of the beast became apparent, he was able to say he had personally encountered the Anti-Christ. So it was kicks coming and going.

Contractions ("I'd," "the Rev"), slang ("swung," "cool"), and plays on words ("Holy Bobble") characterize this writing as very informal.

Formal and informal writing should not be thought of as two distinct categories, all writing being clearly one or the other. Instead you can visualize them as overlapping:

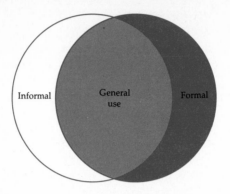

In the shaded area, where the overlap occurs, we find the great majority of words and phrases. These words are for general use in both formal and informal writing. The dark area represents those words usually found only in formal writing. These are often words with specialized meanings, like *dichotomous* or *serotinal,* that are not normally part of our conversation or writing but that in certain circumstances have a legitimate purpose. The white area represents those words that ordinarily do not find their way into our prose except in our most informal moments. This includes slang, nonstandard usage, localisms—many of the very things called to your attention by those words and symbols we discussed earlier. Here is where your dictionary can make an important contribution to your writing.

I said before that you have to know the set of symbols your instructor is using. The second thing you have to know is the terminology used by your dictionary to describe usage levels. These terms are called *restrictive labels* or *usage labels.* After your paper has been returned to you with a symbol placed next to a word you have used, look up the word in the dictionary. Most probably, at least one of its definitions will be accompanied by a restrictive label that will give you an idea of why your use of the word was not a desirable one. Here are some of the most important restrictive labels currently in use, along with their customary meanings:

1. **Slang.** Slang is a way of speaking or writing that often involves the use of exaggeration to produce a special effect. Old

words can be given new meanings—*rap* to describe talking, for example, or *high* to describe being intoxicated by drugs or alcohol. New words can also be created—*dude*, for example, to describe an attractive male. Everybody uses slang. It gives language much of its verve and its humor. But slang is much more common in speaking than in writing, and much more common in informal writing than in formal. So the more formal your writing situation, the more sparing you have to be in your use of slang and the more careful you have to be in following the old adage "when in doubt, don't."

Slang of course is quick-changing, ephemeral. Just a few years ago it was "hip" to call someone a "square," but now only "squares" would use either word. Slang can become more formal with time (dignity comes with age for words too) and therefore cease to be slang. Some people have the erroneous idea that slang is bad. Because it is sometimes ephemeral and inappropriate, they mistakenly believe that it is always harmful. "A pox on them," as Shakespeare would have said in his best Elizabethan slang, and he did not mean chicken pox. (Look it up in the dictionary.)

2. **Informal, Colloquial.** The line that separates words in this category from slang is a hazy one at best. "Informal" words (the term *colloquial* is fast disappearing because it was found to be misleading) are just what you might expect: words that are found much more often in speech and informal writing than in the more formal contexts. They differ from slang insofar as they lack some of the exaggeration usually characteristic of good slang. Take the word *wiseacre*, meaning an annoying know-it-all. It lacks the dramatic extension of meaning found in a word like *rap*, but at the same time it is perhaps out of place in very formal situations, so *A.H.D.* terms it "informal."

I think you can see that these distinctions are hard to make. *A.H.D.* calls *wiseacre* informal but *wise guy* slang; I'm hard pressed to see the difference. Because of these problems, some dictionaries—most notably *N.C.D.*—refuse to use *informal* or *colloquial*, preferring instead simply to give a definition without a usage label except in case of the most obvious slang.

The same cautions that were mentioned about slang words

can also be applied to informal words. These words are acceptable in themselves. But the more formal the writing situation, the more removed you are from intimate conversation, the less likely it is that such words will be effective. It's like a man arriving for dinner at an expensive restaurant without a coat and tie; there's nothing morally superior about a coat and tie instead of jeans and a tee shirt—it's just a matter of appropriateness.

3. **Obsolete, Archaic.** These are sometimes called temporal (i.e., time-related) labels, because they describe different degrees of being outdated. An *obsolete* word (or one meaning of that word) is one that was once used in a certain way but is no longer. *Archaic* applies to a word that is fast becoming obsolete—it now is rarely used with a certain meaning, and then only in unusual contexts. An example of an obsolete word is the verb *cope* used to mean *meet (someone) in combat. Cope* does not have that meaning any more (it has others, of course). Compare it with a word like *withal,* which is still in use but is swiftly becoming archaic, or at least some of its meanings are. You are not likely to use obsolete words, but you might occasionally stray into an archaicism, especially when you are trying too hard to sound impressive in highly formal writing.

4. **Vulgar.** I don't suppose I need to do much explaining here. A *vulgar* word is one that is taboo, at least in polite circles, whether in speech or in writing. Some dictionaries solve the problem in a simple way: they just don't include them. Others label them *vulgar,* to indicate the taboo, or else include them with those termed *slang.* In any event I assume it is clear that you would not use vulgarity in any situation except a highly informal one—perhaps when you are using dialogue in a personal-experience paper.

5. **Nonstandard, Substandard.** Both of these terms imply the existence of standard English, the language of educated speakers when they are being conscious of what and how they speak. *Nonstandard* is a deliberately bloodless term used by dictionaries to describe what some people would call "bad English." It includes words almost everybody uses—a familiar example is *ain't*—and some that are used by some and not

others, like *learn* meaning *teach: I'll learn him not to contradict me. N.C.D.* likes to make the distinction between words disapproved of by many but occasionally acceptable *(nonstandard)* and words that are always thought to lack prestige *(substandard)*.

Most of us make frequent use of nonstandard words and forms. But in writing we recognize that such words give offense to many readers and therefore hinder communication with them. Since other alternatives are available, it is best to avoid nonstandard usages whenever possible. Again dialogue might be a necessary exception.

If you have inadvertently used a nonstandard word or phrase, an excellent first resource is a glossary of usage like the one in this handbook (see page 413). But if a glossary is not handy, the dictionary will give a helpful albeit briefer explanation . It just ain't true that *ain't* ain't in the dictionary.

Since each dictionary has its own set of usage labels, it is a good idea to familiarize yourself with the particular terms used in your own dictionary. Remember too that restrictive labels are only opinions, reflecting the convictions of the makers of the dictionary. God does not make restrictive labels—editors do. Like all matters of opinion, judgments about words can be different. Some editors are more conservative than others about what is or is not slang, what is or is not taboo (nonstandard). If you are in doubt about the proper use of a certain word, and if the issue is important to you, check another dictionary before making up your mind.

A3. Denotation and Connotation

Here is another possible use for your dictionary in improving your writing. Your paper has come back with a word or phrase underlined, and your instructor says the problem is in your choice of words. You know the word has an acceptable usage, so at first you are puzzled. But when you look the word up, you discover that it has the wrong **connotation** (implied meaning) when used in the way you have used it.

Connotation has to be understood in comparison with its companion term, **denotation**. Denotation is the kernel of meaning that remains when a word is stripped of any emotional associations we might bring to it. Denotation is the technical meaning, the clinical meaning. Some words carry no emotional freight with them at all and have only a denotative value. Take a word like *farad*, for example. A farad is defined as "the unit of capacitance equal to the capacitance of a capacitator between whose plates there appears a potential of one volt when it is charged by one coulomb of electricity" *(N.C.D.).* No, I don't understand it either. The point is simply that *farad* is a technical term. It does not have emotional significance for us, even if we know something about electricity. It remains, and should remain, neutral.

But other words, while they do possess a core of denotative meaning, can never be used successfully without an awareness of their connotation, their power to suggest or imply. These words stimulate emotional reactions. We don't just understand, we respond. And most of the time we don't need a dictionary to tell us the connotation of a word either. If someone calls you an "idiot," you will not assume that he or she has measured your IQ and determined that your mental age is less than three years, a condition to which psychologists assign the technical term idiocy. You will ignore the denotation and respond directly to the connotation, which is that you are silly and foolish.

However, there are other words for which the connotations are more subtle, less readily apparent. Here the dictionary can help. Consider the word *opportunist.* In the strict sense it might seem to mean any person who takes advantage of his or her opportunities. But in actuality the word has bad connotations: opportunists are disreputable, they care more for success than for principle, and we do not trust them. To call someone an opportunist is usually not a compliment, except maybe in sports. A good dictionary will make you aware of this connotative value. The *Standard College Dictionary,* for example, defines an opportunist as one "who uses every opportunity to contribute to the achievement of some end, and who is relatively uninfluenced by moral principles or sentiment."

> Without knowing the force of words, it is impossible to know men.
>
> *Confucius*

Definitions are not the only means for becoming aware of connotation. Check on a word's synonyms, because they often provide clues. The discussion of synonyms for *punish* (p. 8), could be described as telling us about a denotative core meaning (the "shared element of meaning"), and then about the connotations of the various synonyms associated with that core meaning.

So in your writing, if a word is noted by your instructor as improperly used, check the dictionary to make sure you did not use the word in such a way as to allow its connotation to obstruct your intended meaning. You might use *opportunist* and intend it as a compliment. But your reader can hardly be blamed for not taking it that way.

The word saloon *is legalized in Wisconsin after 42 years*

MADISON, Wis. (AP) — Taverns in Wisconsin may now call themselves *saloons* under a court ruling being hailed as a victory for free speech and unpretentious drinking.

Circuit Judge Richard Bardwell struck down a state law yesterday that prohibited establishments from billing themselves as *saloons*.

"It is time we realized that this is 1975, not 1919," Bardwell said. "There is no longer anything opprobrious or disdainful about the word *saloon*."

The Wisconsin suit challenging the legal ban against the forbidden word was filed by Jack McManus, an attorney who rents part of a building he owns to a tavern. McManus hailed the decision, saying it "struck a blow for the working man who wants to do his drinking in a place other than a lounge."

The city attorney's office in Madison fought to keep the ban, arguing that the word *saloon* had been barred from tavern names in the wake of repeal of prohibition in 1933.

City officials said the law was enacted to protect the image of taverns. They said that to many persons a saloon was a wide-open, swinging-door establishment.

"At the time, the word *saloon* apparently had a connotation which was unappealing to many people," Bardwell said. "I take notice of the fact there no longer exists any negative connotation." *Philadelphia Enquirer*, 6 June 1975.

Of course the dictionary cannot solve all problems related to connotation. Some words, for example, have both good and bad connotations, and only the context enables us to tell whether the word conveys what it should. Other words have connotations known only to a certain group, or maybe only to a certain person. These words may have rich emotional associations for the select few, but these associations will not be found in a dictionary for general use. Finally, a dictionary can only describe connotation in a very basic and approximate way. It cannot suggest the fantastic richness of association that clings to some words and gives them their special power. Only by reading more can you begin to appreciate that wealth and to understand how connotation, far from being something to avoid, is rather one of the chief glories of our language.

A4. Shades of Meaning

Dictionaries are also useful in helping you separate the various **shades of meaning** words can have, in other words the small but important distinctions between a word and its synonyms. Then you will know which word is exactly the right one to express your meaning.

Let's go back to the *punish* example. Suppose for a moment you are a grade school teacher, and you are asked by the principal to file a written report on your handling of an unruly child who disrupted the class. Will you write that you *punished* the child, *disciplined* him, or merely *corrected* him? These words are listed by the dictionary as synonyms, but there are differences in their meanings. The first suggests that you inflicted some sort of penalty on the child, perhaps by depriving him of a privilege, perhaps even by corporal punishment (euphemism for spanking). *Disciplined,* on the other hand, is more vague—you brought him under control and attempted to reform his conduct, but the means you used are not specified. To *correct* implies that you simply pointed out to him the ways in which he should amend his conduct. The impact of your report on his mama and papa will vary considerably depending on the word chosen. The dictionary's discussion of synonyms for *punish* could help you avoid an unnecessary blunder.

Here is another example. Suppose a personal-experience paper were to begin with this sentence: "According to my remembrance, it was a day in late November." An instructor might very well underline the word *remembrance* and label it a diction problem. If the writer then turns to the *American Heritage Dictionary* he or she finds that *remembrance* does indeed refer to the memory of a specific past event, the intended meaning. But the dictionary adds the proviso that this memory is usually of a sentimental nature, and the writer did not mean to imply sentimentality at all. Reading further, the writer would discover that the word *recollection*, given as a synonym of *remembrance*, also refers to the memory of a specific past event, but an event that is deliberate or practical rather than sentimental. So *recollection* becomes a better choice for the sentence in question.

> How forcible are right words!
> *Job 6:25*

EXERCISES

1. Interpret the following entries from *Webster's New Collegiate Dictionary*. You can probably accomplish this best by reading aloud your own "translation" or decoding of what the entry is saying about the word. Be sure that your interpretation includes something about: a. syllabication, b. pronunciation, c. origin (if known), d. part of speech (i.e., noun, verb, etc.), e. possible definitions, f. usage labels, if any, and g. synonyms.

> **ju·bi·lee**\'jü-bə-(')lē,\'jü-bə-'lē \ *n* [ME, fr. MF & LL; MF *jubilé*, fr. LL *jubilaeus*, modif. of LGk *tōbelaios*, fr. Heb *yobhel* ram's horn, jubilee] **1** *often cap:* a year of emancipation and restoration provided by ancient Hebrew law to be kept every 50 years by the emancipation of Hebrew slaves, restoration of alienated lands to their former owners, and omission of all cultivation of the land **2 a:** a special anniversary, *esp:* a 50th anniversary **b:** a celebration of such an anniversary **3 a:** a period of time proclaimed by the Roman Catholic pope ordinarily every 25 years as a time of special solemnity **b:** a special plenary indulgence granted during a year of jubilee to Roman Catholics who perform certain specified works of repentance

and piety **4 a:** JUBILATION **b:** a season of celebration **5:** a Negro folk song with references to a future happy time

¹**troll** \'trol\ *vb* [ME *trollen*] *vt* **1:** to cause to move round and round: ROLL **2 a:** to sing the parts of (as a round or catch) in succession **b:** to sing loudly **c:** to celebrate in song **3:** to speak or recite in a rolling voice **4** *obs:* to move rapidly: WAG **5 a:** to angle for with a hook and line drawn through the water **b:** to angle in <~lakes> **c:** to pull through the water in angling <~a lure>~ *vi* **1:** to move around: RAMBLE **2:** to fish esp. by trolling a hook **3:** to sing or play in a jovial manner **4:** to speak rapidly — **troll·er** *n.*

odds\ ädz \ *n pl but sing or pl in constr* **1 a** *archaic* : INEQUALITIES **b** *obs* : degree of unlikeness **2 a** : an amount by which one thing exceeds or falls short of another <won the election by considerable ~> **b** (1) : a difference favoring one of two opposed things <the overwhelming ~ it affords the sportsman over bird and animal — Richard Jefferies> (2) : a difference in terms of advantage or disadvantage <what's the ~, if thinking so makes them happy — Flora Thompson> **c** (1) : the probability that one thing is so or will happen rather than another : CHANCES <the ~ are against it> (2) : the ratio of the probability of one event to that of an alternative event <it is even ~ which makes the more noise — Claudia Cassidy> **3** : DISAGREEMENT, VARIANCE — usu. used with *at* <faculty and administration often are at ~ on everything — W. E. Brock *b*1930> **4 a** : special favor : PARTIALITY **b** : an allowance granted by one making a bet to one accepting the bet and designed to equalize the chances favoring one of the bettors **c** : the ratio between the amount to be paid off for a winning bet and the amount of the bet — **by all odds** : in every way : without question <*by all odds* the best book of the year>

2. Look up these words in your dictionary, then answer the following questions:

rat	set	deal	plain
joint	come	spice	fry
pump	mouth	catch	junk

What is the history (origin) of each word? What definitions seem to you to be the most important? What synonyms are given for each word? What shared element of meaning do the synonyms have? How do they differ? Create a sentence for each definition of each word.

3. What restrictive labels, if any, does your dictionary supply for the following words? What do these restrictive labels tell you?

jaw *(as a verb)*	hornswoggle
ain't	jerk *(applied to a person)*
sap *(applied to a person)*	freak
gas	gig *(musician's engagement)*
stinker	bastard

4. The following passage is from Frank D'Angelo's *A Conceptual Theory of Rhetoric*. What words in the passage allow us to describe the passage as *formal* writing? Why?

This book attempts to explore the relationships that exist between thinking and writing, within the framework of a coherent theoretical system of rhetoric. Its principal features might be described as follows:

1. Invention, arrangement, and style are connected to each other and to underlying thought processes in important ways.
2. The process of invention continues throughout the composing process.
3. The topics of invention are symbolic manifestations of underlying thought processes, and they are essentially relational.
4. Nonlogical thought processes are important in the composing process.
5. The composing process is holistic and organic.
6. The composing process is a movement from an undifferentiated whole to a differentiated whole and repeats in microcosm larger evolutionary processes.
7. The overall shape of a discourse is more important than its parts.
8. Form consciousness is essential to good writing.
9. Syntagmatic and paradigmatic analyses of structure in discourse can be useful in developing a sense of form consciousness and in producing discourse.
10. Rhetoric is by its very nature interdisciplinary. Therefore, studies in cognitive psychology, psychoneurology, psychotherapy, linguistics, psycholinguistics, and anthropology, for example, may contribute important insights to the study of rhetoric.

5. What words in the following student-written passage allow us to describe the passage as *informal* writing? Why?

I knew the minute he walked in the door that we had a live one on our hands. He tried to look around the lobby casually, but he caught me watching him, so he made a bee line right for my counter. Obviously he was checking us out for an alarm system.

He came slowly toward me with a half-smile on his face. Trying to cover up his nervousness, I thought. Well at least he isn't a pro. That's all we needed. Our Holiday Inn had been operating for only six months, but already five color tv sets had been ripped off. So I was determined to get this guy.

6. Here are two passages by professional writers. The first one is from a newspaper article by Art Buchwald; the second is from *To Abolish Children*, by Karl Shapiro. What relative degrees of formality or informality do you find in each?

a. At the University Club the other day I was having a brandy and cigar with some very nice chaps when the question of student demonstrations came up.

"I see where they still haven't solved the problem of Columbia," Liverwhistle said.

"It's appalling, absolutely appalling," Cartwright sputtered.

"The students should all be booted out on their ears. You can't have a university if you're going to have children running around locking up the faculty."

Conrad said, "Did you see what's going on in Paris? The French students have tied up the city."

"Ah, yes," said Cartwright. "One can't help admiring the French students' gumption. They've certainly put De Gaulle in his place."

"You have to respect their attitude," Liverwhistle said. "At least the students can see through De Gaulle, if the rest of the French people can't."

"I don't think things have cooled off at Stanford." Scarsdale commented. "They're still holding the administration building."

"If you ask me," said Cartwright, "it's a Communist plot. These things don't just happen. There's nothing the Communists wouldn't do to shut down the schools in this country. The only answer is force. It will make those radicals sing another tune."

"Did you read where the students of Czechoslovakia not only demonstrated, but caused the downfall of the Soviet-backed regime?"

"God bless them," said Conrad. "If we're ever going to see the end of tyranny behind the Iron Curtain, it's going to be the students who accomplish it."

b. Betrayal is an act of vengeance, obviously. But in an age of betrayal, when men of authority traduce their office and violate the trust placed in their hands, betrayal becomes the official morality. "Official morality" shortly becomes "public immorality"; whereupon the fabric of a society rots before one's eyes. In the years since the end of the Second World War, announced by the drop of the first Ultimate Weapon, the world has been stunned, horrified, and ultimately cajoled and won over to the official morality of America and its corollary of public immorality and anarchy. Hardly a leader, whether President, general, public-relations man, professor, publisher, or poet, can be held to be honorable in his intentions. Everywhere lies the hidden premise and the calculated betrayal, the secret and chauvinistic lie.

7. What connotations do the following word pairs have? Under what circumstances might you choose one or the other?

cheap / economical   beautiful / gorgeous
skinny / thin   stubborn / high-principled
leader / commander   overweight / fat
bar / cocktail lounge   recent / new

8. Both members of the following word pairs have the same root word, but they have different meanings. Use your dictionary to isolate those differences in meaning. Then write a sentence using each member of the pair.

painful / painstaking   trend / trendy
infidel / infidelity   defensible / defensive
nauseous / nauseating

B. CHOOSING EFFECTIVE WORDS

Apt words have powers to suage
The tumors of a troubled mind.
John Milton

It would be nice if "looking it up" would solve all the problems you encounter in writing. Life is never that simple, I'm afraid. In this section we will consider other kinds of problems and solutions.

In the preceding section we discussed ways of using the dictionary to sharpen your sense for how words differ and what they imply. The assumption was that we could deal with something you had written, perhaps an essay that had some flaw to be identified and corrected (remember that *D* for diction). We were answering the question "What's wrong with my use of this word?" At the very least we could assume that, even if you hadn't written anything yet, you were faced with a problem you knew you had—like "What verb should I choose for this sentence?"

In some parts of this section we will continue to examine concrete problems of this sort. The discussions of jargon, euphemisms, and triteness are examples. The difference here will be that these problems in most cases cannot be resolved by a dictionary.

There is another part of writing that this section must also explore. Using words properly is an important first step, but developing control over language is not just a matter of avoiding mistakes. Your sentences might be error-free and still lifeless, dull. What's needed is a conscious effort to widen the word choices available to you as a writer. Good writing is vital, engaging, dramatic. Otherwise you will sound like a bureaucrat at a news conference and get just about as much attention.

"Widen the choices." Easy enough to say, but how can it be done? Changing what is already written is a lot less difficult than proceeding toward a vaguely defined goal, no matter how valuable that goal might be. Difficulty is not the same as impossibility. There *are* things that can be done to improve your grasp of the language and make it serve your purposes in writing.

The first suggestion is at once the most obvious and the most difficult: read more. There is no surer way to develop sensitivity to words. The more you read the wider your vocabulary becomes, and therefore the easier it is for the "right" words to slip into your consciousness when you write.

> Reading isn't fun;
> it's indispensable.
> *Woody Allen*

As you read, there is a second step you can take: observe carefully how the piece is written. Note good words and new words. Don't just note them mentally either. If it is at all possible, write down what you observe, maybe even copy down some phrases or sentences that catch your eye.

What should you look for? Try the following five questions. See if the prose you are reading would justify a yes answer to each question.

Then, more importantly, apply the questions to your own writing. The answers you get, either from your own analysis or from your instructor's, will go a long way towards telling you what kind of work you need to do. The effectiveness of any piece of writing depends on the writer's sensitivity to words. Part B is designed to increase both your sensitivity towards words and your skill in using them.

B1. Is the Language Direct?

Good writing does not belabor the obvious, does not use six words where four will do. And no phoniness either—we like a writer who is blunt, who comes right to the point rather than talking like a witness at a Watergate hearing. Here is an example from Tom Wolfe's *The Kandy-Kolored Tangerine-Flake Streamline Baby*, about the New York subway:

> In a way, of course, the subway is the living symbol of all that adds up to lack of status in New York. . . . The whole place is a gross assault on the senses. The noise of the trains stopping or rounding curves has a high-pitched harshness that is difficult to describe. People feel no qualms about pushing whenever it becomes crowded. Your tactile sense takes a crucifying you never dreamed possible. The odors become unbearable when the weather is warm. Between platforms, record shops broadcast 45 r.p.m. records with metallic tones and lunch counters serve the kind of hot dogs in which you bite through a tensile, rubbery surface and then hit a soft, oleaginous center like cottonseed meal, and the customers sit there with pastry and bread flakes caked around their mouths, belching to themselves so that their cheeks pop out flatulently now and then.

Not a wasted word. The writing is crisp, lively, frank—just like good conversation—and we appreciate Wolfe's directness.

For another example, here is a student paper. The writer recalls the first time he met his scuba-diving instructor and the instructor's girl friend.

Mike was about 24 years old, had blond hair, and wore white swim trunks to accentuate his rich tan. He originally came from Indiana. After graduating from a west coast diving school, he decided to come here, to the Virgin Islands, to teach. Felicia had a picture-book body—I couldn't make up my mind whether to watch Mike's daredevil driving or her belly button. She looked like a California blonde: straight waves of hair bleached by the sun, falling gently on her bronzed shoulders, turquoise eyes surrounded by long jet black lashes, moist lips hiding her shell white teeth until she smiled. Surf spray beaded her long slender legs, giving her a clean, wet look. When she rested her head on Mike's shoulder, while he was trying to drive, and gently caressed his arm, I would have given anything to trade places with him.

Again we appreciate the writer's directness, the confidence we feel that he is making every word count, holding nothing back.

What can happen when a writer is not direct? A lot of things, but unfortunately none of them is good.

One possibility is that the writer falls victim to that most dreadful of all diseases, verbal diarrhea. The words just come and come, copiously, and the reader slowly despairs. Take this example of the fault we call **wordiness:**

For over eighteen years the city of Chicago has been under the grip of Mayor Richard J. Daley and his Democratic machine. Although quite a few scandals have come up in that time, the mayor himself has kept himself, as far as one can tell, above suspicion. The mayor has always been known as working hard to clean up the scandals of Chicago politics, rather than being responsible for them. But there are two areas with which he is connected which are overtly corrupt—the patronage system and the Democratic machine.

That was written by a student in a composition class. After some work she was able to shorten it to half its original length—forty-six words instead of ninety—and improve it in the process:

For eighteen years Chicago has been ruled by Richard J. Daley and his machine. Despite frequent scandals, the mayor himself avoids suspicion. He always appears to be cleaning up scandals rather than causing them. But he cannot duck responsibility for one overt corruption: the machine's patronage system.

Check some of your own writing. Does every word carry its own weight? Go over what you have written sentence by sentence. What words or phrases or even whole sentences can you cut without diminishing your meaning? It's like pruning a shrub—the more you trim it back, assuming you don't harm an essential part, the better and more luxuriantly it will grow. Be a word ecologist; don't waste a single one. And you needn't worry that your writing will look skimpy or bare, because in a later section we will be discussing how the addition of more details will make your prose still more effective. Cut now so you can add later: it's like tightening your belt at lunchtime so you can enjoy a big steak at dinner.

Another type of wordiness is needless repetition. Here are two examples:

> Even though the idea of paddling the kayak scared me, I was still fascinated by the idea.

> The decision that we ought not go was one that we all agreed had to be made.

Such repetitions are annoying and lessen the impact of your sentences. This is true even when the repetition involves the use of different words:

> The frantic pace of life today is characteristic of the modern world.

"The real cause of inflation is things go up because everything else goes up."

Better to ease such repetitions out of your writing:

> Even though the idea of paddling a kayak scared me, I was still fascinated.

> The decision not to go was one that we all agreed had to be made.

> A frantic pace of life is characteristic of the modern world.

Wordiness does not always manifest itself in such obvious ways. Many writers are so addicted to wordiness that they fail to realize its grip on them. They don't just *decide*, they *arrive at a decision*. They don't *try*, they *make an attempt*. Richard Altick has drawn up a list of some of his favorite examples, together with their simpler alternatives; here are some of them:

in an efficient manner	efficiently
in the matter of (in respect to)	about
in many instances	often
avail oneself of	use
is in the process of being	is being
inform us of the reason	tell us why

There are many others: *subject matter* rather than *subject*, *prior to* rather than *before*, *undertake* rather than *do*. . . .

The cause of this disease is unknown. I suspect it comes from the very natural desire to impress the reader. *Make an attempt* somehow sounds more impressive than *try*. But it won't fool thoughtful readers—in fact, it will only annoy them. And remember that whatever annoys a good reader interferes with communication, simply by calling attention to itself rather than to the message.

This same cause might be responsible for another symptom: what I call the **big-word syndrome.** Many writers can't resist the temptation to offer a two-bit word when a nickel one is all that is needed. I had a friend in high school who spent ten minutes every day ransacking the dictionary, laying rough hands on whatever big words he could find and then using them indiscriminately in everything he said or wrote. Thus every old lady became a *dowager*, every place a *locality*, every statement a *pronunciamento*. It didn't matter to him if he had the wrong context or the wrong connotation—the fun was in using the biggest words in the humblest places.

This fondness for the big word is becoming all-pervasive in our society. If I look around the city where I live, for example, I find that where once we had dogcatchers, now we have *canine control officers;* where once you could hire a gardener, now you must *contract with a landscape service;* where once refuse was picked up by a garbage collector, now you call a firm that bills itself as *solid state ecologists* (it's true, so help me God!). Or take the university where I work. The night watchman has been replaced by a *security officer,* the maintenance people have become *physical plant personnel,* the lunchroom is now a *food service area.* Even my own English department is not immune, now that the freshman English director has become the *Director of Instruction in Writing* and the tutoring office is renamed *The Clinical Assistance Program in English.*

The reason for this galloping word inflation? Often just harmless vanity. You feel better about yourself if you can say you are a *building superintendent* rather than a janitor or if you work in a *health care delivery system* rather than a hospital. But good writers are aware of these evasions and shun them, because they deaden the impact of the message. Good writers are properly fearful that while bathing their egos in the warm waters of their own words, they risk drowning the suffering readers.

> I am a Bear of Very Little Brain, and Long words Bother me.
> *Winnie-the-Pooh*

Allied with the big-word syndrome is another ailment, **jargon.** Because language is so powerful (remember what we said earlier about connotation), it often seems to be at cross-purposes with the needs of scientists and others who use the language to convey the results of scholarly investigations. If you study a subject scientifically, emotions and value judgments often interfere with arriving at truth. You must be precise and dispassionate both in your investigations and in your statements of results. Yet simple, everyday words are often words with strong connotations. Therefore some writers have gotten into the habit of dealing with this fact by replacing simple words with complicated but neutral words known only to other people working in a certain field. The outcome is often jargon, as in a paragraph like the following:

Obligation was induced in two-man work groups by arranging for one member to contribute more to a common task which resulted in a higher joint reward. Friends responded to such obligation by deferring to their benefactors in a second interaction session while strangers who were obligated repaid through greater effort and the assumption of leadership. Self-esteem was positively related to deference.

That's from a sociology journal. Almost impossible to understand, right? But if you cut out the jargon terms like "interaction session" and "positively related to," and if you cure the bigword syndrome, this is what it says in simple English:

Suppose two people are working together on a project and both are given equal rewards even though one contributed more than the other. In such cases we found that if the two workers were friends, the lesser contributor was likely to let his friend be the leader in any future work sessions; but if the two were strangers, the lesser contributor would "repay" by assuming leadership and doing extra work. In either case, if your co-worker defers to you, it makes you feel good about yourself.

We need not pick on sociologists either. Jargon is in the vocabulary of nearly all professions, from police officers *(the suspects were apprehended leaving the premises)* to truck drivers *(that's a big ten-four, good buddy)* to sportscasters *(looks like this new pitcher has a real hummer)*. Anywhere a specific group develops its own specialized vocabulary you've probably got jargon. When speaking, you have immediate clues about whether your listener is following you, so jargon is usually harmless. But keep it out of your writing.

Analogous to jargon is the **euphemism.** Some words seem too painful, too emotionally loaded, so other words are substituted for them to disguise or hide the true meaning of what is being said. These disguising words are called euphemisms. Dying, for example. Our society does not like to face death, so we have devised numerous euphemisms to wall ourselves off from that experience. Some are harmless, gentle euphemisms like *pass away, enter into rest*, or *go to one's eternal reward*, whose principal purpose is to comfort the bereaved. Others are humorous, like *croak* or *kick off*, which allow a comfortable emotional distancing to those not immediately involved. Sometimes people use euphemisms out of politeness, when what they say may be unpleasant to some readers. An example is the school board that instructed teachers to describe pupil behavior to parents by such phrases as "resorts to physical means of winning his point" (i.e., hits other kids) and "shows difficulty in distinguishing between imaginative and factual material" (i.e., lies). Maybe the parents were mollified, but they probably got the message eventually anyway, and it was probably no more palatable later than earlier. Despite the good motives that prompt them, euphemisms ought to be avoided. Put it to your reader straight, using words to communicate rather than evade.

So what does it mean to be *direct* in your writing? In summary, it means making sure that your words are neither too many, too big, too specialized, or too evasive. After all, that's just the short way of saying you must avoid wordiness, the big-word syndrome, jargon, and euphemisms. Too many, too big, too specialized, too evasive—keep them in mind.

B2. Is the Language Fresh?

If one of your primary duties as a writer is to fasten the attention of your readers on what you say, make sure that what you say is new to them. Even when the subject is familiar, you have to jolt them into new ways of seeing or feeling. Readers must sense that your writing is original, the product of a mind dealing actively and intelligently with the world around it, rather than "just more of the same old stuff." Your choice of words will show whether you have kept out of the well-worn grooves of the familiar.

Take this brief passage in which L. Rust Hills describes an ice cream cone:

> It is a huge, irregular mass of ice cream, faintly domed at the top from the metal scoop, which has first produced it and then insecurely balanced it on the uneven top edge of a hollow inverted cone made out of the most brittle and fragile of materials. Clumps of ice cream hang over the side, very loosely attached to the main body. There is always much more ice cream than the cone could hold, even if the ice cream were tamped down. . . .

Hills describes a most familiar object, yet his choice of words lets us see it in a new way. He achieves this effect by words like "mass," "domed," "hollow," "inverted," "brittle," "fragile," "clumps," "tamped." None of these are unusual words, none of them are the kind of big words I was cautioning you about earlier. But how many of us would have thought to use them had we been describing an ice cream cone? Probably we would have settled for easy choices, like "cold" or "smooth." Hills' willingness to seek out better, fresher words gives his writing an edge and makes us want to read more.

I will be frank: there is no simple way to cure the language blahs. If your prose is often lifeless because the words are too easy, too familiar, the problem is usually one of vocabulary. You may know a great number of words but actively use a much smaller number. To enlarge both the number of words you know and the number you use, the best long-range program is the one I mentioned before—reading.

> I would sooner read a timetable or a catalogue
> than nothing at all.
> *W. Somerset Maugham*

In the meantime, however, there is one very important step you can take, and that is to examine your writing carefully to see if you have unintentionally fallen victim to **triteness** or the **cliché.** These are phrases or expressions that are worn out from too much use. They should be discarded, not because they are "wrong" but because their very familiarity allows a reader to tune out momentarily when he sees them. The reader whose attention is periodically disengaged quickly stops being a reader at all. Holding a reader is like landing a battling game fish—you must keep him hooked at all times while you reel him in, because once lost he may be gone forever.

Why does a reader tune out momentarily when he or she encounters a cliché? Put simply, the problem is that the reader knows in advance what the next few words will be and subconsciously skips over them. For example, if a friend moans to you about her chemistry midterm tomorrow and starts to say that she is going to have to "burn the . . . ," you know that "midnight oil" is coming next. The phrase is a cliché. Here are some others:

the crack of dawn	till hell freezes over
hotter than a firecracker	keeping up with the Joneses
meet the acid test	Don't rock the boat.
the long and short of it	All's well that ends well.
last but not least	Look before you leap.
it goes without saying	

When readers slide over clichés like these, they have every right to do so. The writer obviously did not think them up, and if the words do not represent the writer's own thinking, why should the reader give serious attention to them?

Of course the matter of triteness is more subtle than the list given in the preceding paragraph would suggest. Those phrases are obvious; we all recognize them, and for that reason we are not so often tempted to use them. The more serious temptation is the little two- or three-word combination that also recurs frequently but just does not have the status of being a cliché or a stock phrase. Consider this paragraph from a student's paper:

> *Well* now Anna is dead. She died slowly and painfully, but *for the first time in months* Anna *knows peace.* When I saw her lying on the bed *breathing her last,* I *couldn't help but think* that I had helped *put her through this.* If we would have *let nature take its course,* Anna would have *been in peace* much sooner. But we didn't and *nature took her revenge.*

The paragraph is as dead as Anna because almost all of it seems overused. The most obviously well-worn parts are in italics. We feel that the writer puts words down like a computer: push a button for *dying* and out comes some variant of *knows peace,* automatically. Only a few of the italicized phrases are genuine, four-star clichés ("let nature take its course" would qualify). But a concern for fresh language makes us realize that the whole paragraph needs to be thought through again and then rewritten. Compare the original with this possible revision:

> Anna is dead now. She died slowly and painfully, but at last her months of torment are over. When I saw her lying in that grim steel bed, her lungs straining for the few last breaths that remained to her, I was stricken with the realization that I was partly responsible for her agony. If we had not interfered, nature would have given her body rest long before. But we didn't, or couldn't, and the revenge of an outraged nature had been terrible to see.

I think you will agree that this version is fresher.

This last point about the dangers of habitual two- or three-word combinations cannot be emphasized too strongly. Dead writing rarely has more than a few scattered clichés, but it always has lots of these simple plug-in phrases. To make sure you understand what I mean, underline the tired language in the following student paragraph:

> Christmas shopping has always been a highlight of the year for me. It's always a great challenge to find that certain gift for that special person. A lot of people couldn't be bothered or simply don't care to do all the legwork; instead they take the easy way out and give money. When I'm ready to go shopping, I always drive to a big shopping center. Here there is every store imaginable, readily waiting at your fingertips. Of course this doesn't mean you won't have to fight your way through the crowds.

What words did you underline? Let's compare lists. There is always some room for disagreement in matters of this sort, but your list ought to include at least several of the following over-used phrases:

> a highlight of the (year)
> it's a great challenge
> that certain gift
> that special person
> can't be bothered
> do all the legwork
> take the easy way out
> every (thing) imaginable
> waiting at your fingertips
> fight your way through the crowds

Tired language, all of it. Puts readers to sleep very quickly.

So for an apprentice writer, the simplest rule of thumb (another cliché) is this: if the phrase or expression is familiar to you, don't use it, unless you can establish an excellent reason for doing so.

B3. Is the Language Concrete?

Concrete words refer to objects we can touch or see. *Baseball* qualifies. So do *lawns, books, peaches, giraffes* and *submarines.*

These words are often contrasted with **abstract words** like *democracy, experience,* and *bountiful* that name concepts or qualities (*democracy* and *experience* are concepts, while *bountiful* is a quality).

Now the usual advice is to use as many concrete words as possible rather than abstract ones. Good advice it is, too. The difficulty is that such a recommendation runs counter to a central fact about human beings, namely that mental growth can be defined as an increase in the ability to understand and use abstractions. In other words, the more your intellect matures, the more you will want to generalize, to abstract (in the sense of thinking about universals rather than the particular examples that give rise to the universals). Writers quite naturally will find themselves using abstract words to represent this kind of abstract thinking. Unconsciously they may even seek out abstract words as a way of showing that they have arrived at full intellectual maturity.

> There is one stylistic development which most people seldom notice in themselves or others, but which should be watched. As we grow older, we use more and more abstract nouns and adjectives: we move up the semantic ladder. The man who at 25 would have said "tough nut to crack" will when he is 55 say: "Conceivably that might be a problem which admits no solution."
>
> *Gilbert Highet*

Fight that tendency. The abstract thought is good, but present it as concretely as possible. Thinking may be a generalizing process, but perception—and perceiving is what readers do—begins with the real world. Don't write: *Experience teaches us to exercise care when driving an automobile.* Instead write, *Two dented fenders and a cracked front grille have taught me that you don't argue the right-of-way with a gravel truck.* Both sentences may have originated from the same collision, but dented fenders and cracked grilles are concrete objects, while "experience" is an abstraction. The second of those two sentences is far more graphic and therefore less likely to slip by the reader unnoticed.

Another way to make language concrete besides replacing abstract words with concrete ones is to be specific. Replace highly abstract words with words that while technically still abstract, exist on a much lower level of abstraction. *Colorful,* for example, is an abstract word describing a quality; *vermilion* still describes a quality, but is much more specific than merely being *colorful.* So if you cannot use concrete words, be as specific as possible in your choice of abstract words.

Both levels of the process of making language concrete can be illustrated by the following student paragraph:

> Since I am living on campus, I want to make my room feel like it's home to me. I would prefer if the wall opposite my desk had a bright, cheerful color. In a sense a wall can speak. It seems to me that if there was a cheerful color, it would respond with the utmost welcome for me when I came into the room. So what I'll do to remedy this problem is decorate it.

After rewriting, which included pruning the wordiness and then putting flesh on the abstractions, the paragraph looked like this:

> Now that I am living here in Stebler Hall, I want my room to feel like home. The wall opposite my desk, for example: it ought to be orange like October sunsets or yellow like May dandelions, rather than the mud brown which the housing office slops on everything. If a wall can speak, I want this one to shout "HEY! AIN'T IT JUST A SUPER DAY!" So I'm going to paint and then hang up my Frodo doll and my Wings posters. And next Saturday I'll be sure to bring my king-size cork bulletin board from home.

Notice the direction of the revision. Instead of "color," we have "sunset orange," "dandelion yellow," "mud brown." The vague "responding with the utmost welcome" becomes a joyous shout about "A SUPER DAY!" The abstract verb "decorate" is replaced by concrete objects like dolls, posters, and bulletin boards. Not just *any* dolls or posters either—again the attempt is to be as specific as possible.

Of course you cannot avoid abstractions. If you want to talk about *socialism* or *existentialism,* you probably must use those words. If you say that a friend of yours is *talkative* or *sensible* or *fractious,* you are assigning qualities. The point is that one ought to be as concrete as the context allows. We will see more on this subject in Chapters 3 and 4.

B4. Is the Language Colorful?

We human beings are sensuous creatures, no doubt about it. From our very first moments we live by responding to what our senses tell us. And we often enjoy most those pleasures that gratify as many of our five senses as possible. If you need confirmation of this, think about the way a successful rock group appeals to sight, touch, and smell as well as sound. Or think of an auto race: the shattering roar of the unmuffled engines, the odor of gasoline and burning rubber, the kaleidoscopic colors, the palpable tension in the pit of your stomach. We enjoy more delicate pleasures too, but the senses always play a dominant role.

Good writing, especially good narrative and descriptive writing, is often like Elton John or the Daytona 500—it draws upon your senses. Such writing is dramatic, detailed, **colorful.** Here is an example of what I mean. Norman Mailer describes Chicago:

> A great city, a strong city with faces tough as leather hide and pavement, it was also a city where the faces took on the broad beastiness of ears which were dull enough to ignore the bleatings of the doomed, noses battered enough to smell no more the stench of every unhappy end, mouths—fat mouths or slit mouths—ready to taste the gravies which were the reward of every massacre. . . .

It's all there in that one sentence: sight ("faces tough as leather hide"), sound ("bleatings of the doomed"), smell ("the stench of every unhappy end"), taste ("gravies"). That's what real color, real sensory appeal, means.

> Memorable sentences are memorable on account of some single irradiating word.
>
> *Alexander Smith*

Student writing can have the same appeal. Consider this student's description of a high school classmate eating lunch:

> Her favorite method of eating her eggs was to split them apart by sticking her thumbs through the unshelled surface and then tearing them in two. The yolk was still quite fluid and would trickle down her fingers. She licked her fingers, moaning as she tried to catch each

drop with her tongue. An odor of eggs, mingled with whatever chemical we had been using in lab the period before, impregnated the air as she stuffed the speckled mass into her mouth.

You can see the "speckled mass," hear the moan, smell the chemicals, feel the yolk trickling down the fingers.

We object to clothes that are pale, drab, uninviting. The same applies to what we read, even if we are not so conscious of what it is we don't like. When you describe or narrate, try to give pictures that can evoke sensory responses in your readers. And capture these pictures in color, not black and white.

B5. Is the Language Figurative?

You will recall my saying earlier that a writer must choose words as precisely as possible in order to convey meaning accurately. Finding the right word, the best possible word, is one way of reaching that goal. Another good way is to use comparisons. Of course you use comparisons quite often when you talk: a building will be described as *taller than Marina Towers;* your friend Jody might be identified as *the one with the short blond hair cut sort of like Ellen's;* a new car is *faster than my old Camaro.* But somehow comparisons get forgotten when we write. To neglect them is to pass up one of the simplest ways of clarifying your meaning.

When comparisons are used in writing, we call it **figurative language.** Here are some good comparisons from student writing:

Jeanie always ripped her food apart with a twisting motion of her wrists, as if she was wringing a chicken's neck.

I looked up in awe, like a country boy from Peoria looks up at the Sears Tower.

Breathing under water was like trying to suck a McDonald's milkshake through a thin straw.

Everyone agreed that Laurie was the fruitcake of our high school.

I tried to swallow, but my mouth was burlap dry.

The first three are more explicit as comparisons. They use "as if" or "like" to draw attention to the comparison, and because of their explicitness they are called **similes.** The last two are more implicit and can be termed **metaphors.** Even though there is no "as" or "like," the comparing process—of eccentricity to fruit-cake, of dryness to burlap—is still quite evident.

> The metaphor is probably the most fertile
> power possessed by man.
> *José Ortega y Gasset*

Sometimes an apprentice writer can give us too much of a good thing. Comparisons are good. But comparisons that are too extravagant begin to try the reader's patience, especially if combined (as they often are) with the "big-word syndrome." The result is what we call **flowery writing,** a term that is itself a comparison. Here, for example, is a student-written sentence with enough floweriness to make us choke on the sweetness:

> After years of self-love worthy of the immortal Narcissus, now the swelling tides of devotion, the swirling waves of loyalty, and the infinitely deep fathoms of love bring Tom to a realization of the majestic current which is Maggie's soul.

Floweriness is not found only in student writing. Advertising prose is often fertile ground for such blossoms:

> The light falls differently now. Behind the scent of woodsmoke there's a hint of snow. How will you dress for the new season? Wouldn't it be lovely to put on these new colors of Highland heathers, blued, greyed, softened with hints of autumn's mists? Singularly "Ultima II" [lipstick].

Two added points about figurative language. The first is to avoid what are called **mixed metaphors.** These metaphors are ones that begin with one comparison and then add another, incongruous to the first. In a sentence like *He put his nose to the grindstone and dug into the subject*, it is hard to imagine someone digging very well with his nose in such an awkward position. The surest way to avoid mixed metaphors is to avoid clichés, as the writer of the example sentence would have discovered had he eliminated the two cliché phrases "put his nose to the grind-stone" and "dug into." But even if you have not used clichés, it is still good to check your metaphors to make sure they are consistent.

The second point is that you should stay clear of comparisons that are too far-fetched to be convincing or illuminating. This sentence, for example:

> She could often be heard serenading herself in the halls and bathrooms, her distorted echoes leading me to compare her mouth to the Grand Canyon.

We grant that the girl is a poor singer. But comparing her mouth to the Grand Canyon is too extravagant. It just does not do the job that a comparison should do here, which is to tell us something about the quality of her voice or the size of her mouth (we're not sure which). Compare her voice to a screechy phonograph, maybe, or her mouth to a guitar amplifier; but keep the comparison within the range of credibility.

EXERCISES

1. Eliminate all unnecessary words in the following passages and then write your own tightened versions.

a. Most people detest storms but there's a lot to be said for a good storm once in a while. Besides the fact that it's good for the environment and helps the grass grow, it serves another purpose. Right now, in the study room of the library, I can hear the rain falling on the roof. At first one notices it, like when I entered the room, but after a while it becomes inaudible and fades into the background. All this sort of creates a peaceful and tranquil atmosphere around here. The upper half of the room is dark like that of a cathedral. The dark, wooden tables and chairs are lined up like pews, each side separated by a large aisle. Along with all this there is a strange silence broken only by a cough or a squeak of a chair. Suddenly the mood of the whole place changes. There is a great crash of thunder, and streaks of lightning illuminate the room through the now-bright stained glass windows. The lake can be heard dashing against the shoreline. Outside it is not yet dark, but a black line of clouds hovers above the horizon. The lake too is black and violent. Between the clashing waves and the dormant clouds is this sort of grey mist. The whole picture seems to depict that second before the judgment day when the world will end. . . .

b. The mechanical workings of the car are extremely interesting. Those all important air shocks are of little or no good, and after riding in the crazy car, you're not quite sure all of your body is still with you or if it got bounced off and fell out the window somewhere. The brake linings are so worn that you literally come to a screeching halt. The linkage is such that when you try to shift gears you are stopped halfway in between gears and are forced to coast until you lift up the guard plate on the shifter and manipulate the rods with a screwdriver, which can really shock someone who has never seen the process before. Sometimes that doesn't work, so all you have to do is talk to it a little and give the shifter a good swift kick and off you go. It's really a fantastic little automobile, after you get used to it.

2. Reduce the following to a single word or a shorter phrase:

meet with the approbation of	resembling in nature
a long period of time	it is the belief of
making a judgment	each and every one of us
subject matter	as of right now
subsequent to	thunderstorm activity
prior to	

3. What simpler words could replace these big words, assuming the context allows it? Your dictionary can be helpful.

exacerbate	obfuscate
pejorative	incarcerate
paradigmatic	valetudinarian

4. Do you know what the following jargon terms mean? Can you think of other simpler ways to explain or define them?

From education:	*From football:*
accountability	fly pattern
language arts	ring your bell
individualized instruction	get burned
compensatory education	blitz
heterogeneous grouping	bomb

From management:
bottom-line consciousness
go on-line
growth potential
impact study
systems capabilities
product development

5. What are some common euphemisms or slang words for the following?

sleep	love *(verb)*
get drunk	get angry
drive a car	tired
kill	hate *(verb)*
crazy	old person
policeman	movie

6. What is the meaning and function of these euphemisms?

military incursion	stonewall *(verb)*
backburner *(verb)*	countertherapeutic
internment	culturally deprived
pacification project	dentifrice
ex-offender	join your forefathers
antiperspirant	feeling indisposed
mentally incompetent	rip off

7. Create a metaphor or simile using each of the following:

wet	ached
mansion	shrub
dark green	old
laughing	horror-stricken

8. The following statement was issued by a school administrator. Examine the use of language in the statement. Where do you find unnecessary words? Jargon? The "big-word syndrome"? Leaving aside these cumbersome uses of language, what—if anything—is this "statement" really saying?

PRINCIPAL'S PROGRAM DESCRIPTION
FOR MIDDLE SCHOOL

Philosophy

The program will be governed by district policies and general procedures. It will strive toward the realization of the districtwide goals derived from the Board of Education policy statement. We believe that children are most helped toward the achievement of success in a school atmosphere in which teachers work constructively together. We believe in the concept "Middle School." We believe that humanness makes all human beings equal. We believe that each individual is unique. We believe that we help all pupils develop positive self-concepts. We believe in meeting the individual needs of each pupil. We believe in helping pupils experience success. We believe in the long range goal of individualization through flexibility within a heterogeneous setting.

[Note the following news item—maybe the principal should let his students write the statement!]

Plain English? It's child's play

By Robert Young
Chicago Tribune Press Service

WASHINGTON — A "think tank" of 7th graders finally has helped develop what a team of high-priced federal bureaucrats could not — a questionnaire the average American gas station owner can understand.

Frustrated by his staff's inability to write an easily digestible survey for gas station owners, a federal energy official turned to a group of 7th graders from Ellicott City, Md., to do the job.

And the kiddie braintrust came through.

"We're sure we've solved a lot of our problems," said Albert Linden, assistant administrator of the Energy Information Administration. "The kids were a great help."

What the kids did was take a two-page, 40-question survey chock full of bureaucratic gobbledygook and translate it into plain English.

They turned thumbs down on such technical terms as "volatile hydrocarbon mixture," which is a fancy way of saying gasoline.

They scoffed at such dandies as "weighted averages," and suggested that the word "sanctions" be shelved where "penalties" would do just fine.

They asked for shorter words and sentences, simpler instructions, and larger type.

"We missed the first time because we thought that if we could understand it, everybody could," Linden said. *Chicago Tribune*, 19 June 1978, p. 8 of section 5.

9. Write a short (one- or two-paragraph) essay on how Flannery O'Connor uses language in the following passage, from the book *Three by Flannery O'Connor*. Pay special attention to the use of concrete words, fresh and colorful words, and figurative language (metaphors and similes).

Ruby came in the front door of the apartment building and lowered the paper sack with the four cans of number three beans in it onto the hall table. She was too tired to take her arms from around it or to straighten up and she hung there collapsed from the hips, her head balanced like a big florid vegetable at the top of the sack. She gazed with stony unrecognition at the face that confronted her in the dark yellow-spotted mirror over the table. Against her right cheek was a gritty collard leaf that had been stuck there half the way home. She gave it a vicious swipe with her arm and straightened up, muttering, "Collards, collards," in a voice of sultry subdued wrath. Standing up straight, she was a short woman, shaped nearly like a funeral urn. She had mulberry-colored hair stacked in sausage rolls around her head but some of these had come loose with the heat and the long walk from the grocery store and pointed frantically in various directions. "Collard greens!" she said, spitting the word from her mouth this time as if it were a poisonous seed.

10. Many public figures in this country are known for their fascination with words: comedians like George Carlin ("the seven words you can't say on television"), politicians like former Vice-president Agnew ("nattering nabobs of negativism"), tv commentators like Edwin Newman (author of *Strictly Speaking*) or William F. Buckley, Jr., and newspaper columnists like Theodore Bernstein. Choose one of these figures, investigate their interest in and use of language, then write a brief description of what you have discovered.

11. Write a short essay that builds upon this statement by novelist Joseph Conrad: "There must be a wonderful soothing power in mere words since so many men have used them for self-communion." Use your own experiences in the essay wherever possible.

C. SPELLING

'Students to Site Grievances at National Conference,' the press release was headed, thereby suggesting that the students in the National Students Lobby might be wise to lobby for courses in spelling, if, as appears, it is not part of their curriculums.

Edwin Newman

Now for a final word about words: spelling. No matter how successful you are in choosing the best possible words for saying what you want to say, you can blow the whole game by misspelling them. Actually, spelling is more a matter of convention than anything else—we could consider it in Chapter 7 just as easily. But in most people's minds spelling a word properly is intimately connected with using it properly. So you cannot afford to overlook the final strategy for ensuring that your words have the best possible impact on your reader, and that strategy is to make sure your spelling is as good as it can be.

If you already spell with reasonable accuracy, you probably don't need any special work. Perhaps you should not even read any further in this section. The most you have to remember are the two rules that apply to any writer: 1. when in doubt, look it up, and 2. when not in doubt but later proven wrong (e.g., your paper comes back with a spelling error circled), memorize the corrected spelling. That would suffice.

However, there is another large group of people who do have trouble—sometimes small trouble, sometimes big—with spelling. (Want a quick way to know who you are? In a typical passage of 500 words, if you misspell more than two or three, I'd say you have at least a small problem. If you miss more than five or six, call it a big problem.) If you have spelling problems, the remainder of this chapter is designed to help you.

And the first question you should ask yourself is also perhaps the most important: are you ready to make the sacrifices of time and energy necessary for improving your spelling?

After all, there are some very plausible arguments for *not* working much on spelling. These are a few of them:

1. Spelling is only a convention, an agreement for the sake of convenience. Alternative spellings usually do not affect meaning. If you were to see the sentence *I went to there house today*, you would know that *there* is a possessive pronoun even though it is not spelled *t-h-e-i-r*. What is most important in any piece of writing is content, what the words say rather than how the words are spelled.

2. Spelling in the past was very flexible. The great Elizabethan writers, including Shakespeare, often spelled in whatever way seemed best at the time, so that the same word might be spelled several ways even by the same writer. There were no dictionaries or other authorities around to contradict them.

3. Even in our present, less flexible times, variant spellings exist for many words. We know that the British have *labour* to our *labor, centre* to our *center*. We know too that we can *surprise* or *surprize* someone, that we can accept or ignore *judgments (judgements)*, even when made by *archaeologists (archeologists)*. There are numerous other examples.

4. Some great writers are horrible spellers. F. Scott Fitzgerald wrote the following three sentences in a letter to his editor Max Perkins. I have taken the liberty of marking them up as if they had appeared in a freshman paper.

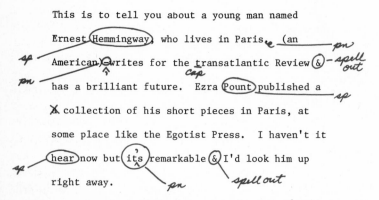

The punctuation problems are bad enough, but there is no excuse for the three spelling errors that mar this passage. Fitzgerald knew Hemingway and Pound personally, and surely he ought not have been so careless as to confuse *h-e-a-r* and *h-e-r-e*. Yet he did, and he made similar mistakes quite often. If one of the greatest twentieth-century American novelists can misspell so easily, why should *we* be fussy?

5. Spelling in the English language is often illogical, quirky, even downright ridiculous. Why we have *neighbors* rather than *naybors* I have never understood. Ditto for *lieutenant (lootenent?), scheme (skeem?),* and *foreign (forin?).* If spelling is so difficult, if it *requires (rekwires?) knowledge (nollidge?)* of so many *exceptions (eksepshuns?),* why *should (shood?)* we be so *conscious (conshus?)* of it?

> They spell it Vinci and pronounce it Vinchy; foreigners always spell better than they pronounce.
>
> *Mark Twain*

Yes, you could make these arguments. They would be true, every one of them. Also, I'm afraid, totally irrelevant. The fact is that most people expect a writer to spell with reasonable accuracy. The person who dismisses your job application by saying, "Why doesn't she learn to spell?" might be blind to historical process and contemporary vagaries, might not agree with you about the primacy of content over convention. No matter—your application is just as dead. Correct spelling is taken as one of the marks of an educated person. This opinion is probably based on a *non sequitur:* good spellers are often good writers; therefore bad spellers are bad writers. But the belief is a prevalent one, even—especially?—among college teachers, and you cannot wish it away.

So spelling is important. That brings us back to the original question: are you willing to sacrifice time and energy to improve yours? Because that's what it takes—your effort and your determination. With those qualities you are ready to make significant improvement. No one misspells on purpose. The task is to find out why and where you usually make mistakes—in other words to discover the patterns in your errors and then to systematically begin the work of curing them.

To improve your spelling, I recommend a four-stage process. These stages are in an order of decreasing severity, and you enter the process at the stage most appropriate for you. Thus if you have a severe spelling problem, follow all four steps, beginning with the first. If your problem is less severe, you can begin with the second or perhaps even the third, and then follow through to the end.

C1. Spelling Patterns

No one can memorize the spelling for each and every word of the thousands of words used in everyday speaking and writing. Fortunately most spelling is systematic, although there are exceptions to every pattern. It is one of the conventions of our language, for example, to spell the plural of most nouns by adding -*s* on the end: *boat, boats.* Learning to spell is really just a matter of learning the conventions used in English and then memorizing the few balky words that do not fit conveniently.

Learning spelling patterns is a large task, too large to cover in detail here. But if you are a "terable speler," there is no other way. Go out and buy yourself a good short guide to English spelling. (The best one I know is William Drake's *The Way to Spell: A Guide for the Hesitant Speller,* published by the Chandler Publishing Company. If your bookstore cannot get you a copy, send a request directly to the distributor, Dun-Donnelley Publishing Company, 666 Fifth Avenue, New York, New York 10019.) Then work right through the book, cover to cover. Allot maybe fifteen minutes a day to it, for about three months. At the end of that time you ought to be a much improved speller. Then you can go on to the next stage.

C2. Problem Areas

Experience shows us that six problem areas are involved in a disproportionate share of spelling errors. The reason these six are special plagues is that in many cases the pronunciation gives no clue as to proper spelling. In other words, the proper spelling and the most common improper one can both be pronounced exactly the same way. Therefore you have to rely on knowledge of the system, because both spelling versions are often going to "sound right" and perhaps even "look right."

Here are the six areas:

1. **Doubling a final consonant before adding a suffix (ending).** Why is it that when we have two simple verbs like *saunter* and

prefer, we spell their past-tense forms as *sauntered* (*r* not doubled) in the first case but *preferred* (*r* doubled) in the second?
After all, these words are quite similar—verbs of two syllables
ending in *-er*. If you are going to put an ending on words like
these, how do you know whether or not to double the final
consonant before adding the ending?

The secret is to concentrate, not on similarities in words like
these, but rather on differences. In the two words used as
examples in the preceding paragraph, notice that in *saunter* the
accent is on the first syllable, while in *prefer* it falls on the second. On the basis of distinctions like this a system has been
devised that provides guidance for what to do with words that
end in a single consonant.

The system works like this: when adding an ending to these
words, you do *not* double the final consonant, except in those
cases that meet *all three* of the following requirements: the base
word must end in a single consonant preceded by a single
vowel, the base word must be accented on the last syllable, and
the suffix must begin with a vowel. In these cases, and in these
cases only, the final consonant of the base word is doubled.

Examples of words that meet all three of these requirements
include the following:

referred	permitting
submitted	running
fattest	sadder
sledding	quipped

Using *referred* as a particular instance of this rule, note that the
base word *(refer)* ends with a consonant *(-r)* preceded by a vowel
(-e), that the base word is accented on the last syllable, and that
the suffix *(-ed)* begins with a vowel. If the base word ends with
two consonants, like *hard*, its final consonant is not doubled:
harder, hardest. If the accent falls on any syllable but the last, as in
the word *saunter* mentioned earlier, the final consonant is not
doubled: *sauntered, sauntering*. If the suffix begins with a consonant rather than a vowel, like *-ness*, again the final consonant
would not be doubled: *tenderness, resourcefulness*. (Incidentally,
quipped makes the preceding list because the *-ui-* combination
counts as only one vowel.)

So if a word meets *all three* of these requirements, you can

180192

double its final consonant. If it fails on any one of them, the final consonant will not be doubled. Simple enough?

Of course such a description cannot cover the many words where our confusion about whether or not to double the consonant does not center on the final consonant. If you spell *apologize* as *appologize*, there is no simple rule that will tell you why you have erred. The problem here is with the base word itself, and if a larger amount of reading does not help you "intuit" the correct spelling for words like these, the only other remedy is simply looking them up when you are in doubt or when you unintentionally misspell them. The system just described applies only to final consonants, but it is still quite useful, because final consonants are frequent sources of error.

2. Adding a prefix. In adding a prefix like *mis-* or *un-* to a base word that begins with a consonant, do not double the last consonant of the prefix: *misdirect* (not *missdirect*), *undoing* (not *unndoing*). A possible confusion arises, however, when the consonant that ends the prefix and the consonant that begins the base word are the same: *misspell, unnatural.* It *seems* like you are doubling the last consonant of the prefix and it looks "wrong" because we are so familiar with the procedure of not doubling these consonants. Therefore, many writers are sorely tempted to use *mispell* or *unatural*, to give us *ireconcilable* instead of *irreconcilable*, *nonuclear* instead of *nonnuclear.* This temptation must be resisted. The system is always uniform; prefix plus base word; never any doubling, and never any reduction to a single consonant either.

3. Silent -e. Again one of those seemingly mysterious contrasts: when a suffix beginning with a vowel, for example *-able*, is added to base words that end in a silent *-e*, sometimes the silent *-e* is dropped, but sometimes it is not. Thus *resolve* becomes *resolvable* but *replace* becomes *replaceable*. What gives here?

The answer this time is rooted in how we pronounce those words (how would you say *resolveable? replacable?*). We need not go into the intricacies of it. All you must do is keep one principle in mind: if the suffix begins with a vowel, drop the silent *e* at the end of the base word unless: 1. the silent *e* follows a *c* and the suffix is *-able*, or 2. the silent *e* follows a *g* and the suffix is *-able*, *-ance*, or *-ous*. Many words have the silent *e* dropped in this way:

dare → daring   dance → dancing
type → typical   pale → palest
move → moving   resolve → resolvable

The exceptions include words like *displaceable,* where the silent *e* follows a *c* and the ending is *-able.* They also include words like *knowledgeable* and *outrageous,* where the base words end in *g* and a silent *e* and the suffixes are *-able* and *-ous,* respectively. Of course, if the suffix begins with a consonant, the silent *e* always remains, as in words like *careful* or *niceness.*

> People do not realize that spelling misteaks
> are easily made.
>
> *student paper*

4. ei or ie? The woes caused by *i*'s going before *e*'s when it should be the other way around—or vice versa, *e*'s before *i*'s—have been experienced by every writer.

My sainted fourth-grade teacher used to give us the first rule for solving these dilemmas: "Children, it's *i* before *e* except after *c.*" Of course we would then ask her about *weigh* and she would glower. Still, she was on the right track: *i* does go before *e,* so long as the *-ie-* combination is pronounced like a long *e* (i.e., the vowel sound in a word like *she*). Thus *i* precedes *e* in words like *piece, believe,* or *chief.* And the rule does not hold when the preceding consonant is a *c,* as in *receive.*

What my teacher's formula could not cover was the occasions when the *ei/ie* combination was not pronounced as a long *e* but rather as a long *a,* the *a* sound of words like *male.* That's where *weigh* comes in. Also *neighborhood, veins,* and other words where the *e* comes before the *i* because the pronunciation is a long *a.*

(That puts us one step up on my fourth-grade teacher, right? Then how come we spell *weird* the way we do, or *either*? It turns out she was pretty shrewd after all, because she had another bit of advice that covers these words, and a few others like them, perfectly: "Children, there are exceptions to every rule.")

5. A final y becomes i. If you are adding a suffix to a base word that ends in *-y,* and if the letter that comes before the *-y* is a consonant, change -*y* to *i*. Otherwise, don't. So we have *silly, silliness* and *hoary, hoariest,* because in these and similar cases the letters that come before the -*y* (*l* and *r* here) are consonants. This is true for any suffix, by the way, even a simple -*s*, as when the verb *dry* becomes *dries* or the noun *gully* becomes *gullies*. An example of a word where the -*y* is preceded by a vowel and therefore does not change would be *delay*, thus *delays, delaying*.

So how come *dry* doesn't become *driness* instead of *dryness;* why doesn't *say* become *sayed* instead of *said*? "Children, there are exceptions to every rule."

6. Noun plurals. Most noun plurals are formed by adding an -*s* to the singular: *pencil, pencils; theme, themes*. If the noun ends in -*s*, -*z*, -*ch*, -*sh*, or -*x*, however, -*es* is added.

boss, bosses	church, churches
lass, lasses	ash, ashes
buzz, buzzes	ax, axes
arch, arches	tax, taxes

Some words that end in -*f* or -*fe* have plurals ending in -*ves*.

wife, wives	leaf, leaves
wharf, wharves	thief, thieves

But: *chief, chiefs; roof, roofs; belief, beliefs*.

A final -*y* preceded by a consonant must be changed to *i* before an -*es* is added to form the plural.

lady, ladies	reply, replies
tragedy, tragedies	berry, berries

However, words ending in a -*y* preceded by a vowel are made plural by just adding -*s*.

journey, journeys	ray, rays
attorney, attorneys	boy, boys

Some plurals are formed irregularly *(mouse, mice)* and some have foreign plurals *(alumnus, alumni; curriculum, curricula)*. If you are not sure how to form the plural of a noun, check your dictionary.

C3. Problem Words

If your spelling problems are minor but annoying, you might be able to cover most of them by studying the following list of one hundred most frequently misspelled words, from *The University Spelling Book*, by Thomas Clark Pollock and William D. Baker. Check your papers and see if a good proportion of your spelling errors appear on this list. If they do, close application to the list might be all that is necessary to cure most of what ails you. Underline the ones that you don't "know you know," then memorize them.

1. accommodate	29. existence	57. precede
2. achievement	30. existent	58. prejudice
3. acquire	31. experience	59. prepare
4. all right	32. explanation	60. prevalent
5. among	33. fascinate	61. principal
6. apparent	34. height	62. principle
7. argument	35. interest	63. privilege
8. arguing	36. its, it's	64. probably
9. belief	37. led	65. proceed
10. believe	38. lose	66. procedure
11. beneficial	39. losing	67. professor
12. benefited	40. marriage	68. profession
13. category	41. mere	69. prominent
14. coming	42. necessary	70. pursue
15. comparative	43. occasion	71. quiet
16. conscious	44. occurred	72. receive
17. controversy	45. occurring	73. receiving
18. controversial	46. occurrence	74. recommend
19. definitely	47. opinion	75. referring
20. definition	48. opportunity	76. repetition
21. define	49. paid	77. rhythm
22. describe	50. particular	78. sense
23. description	51. performance	79. separate
24. disastrous	52. personal	80. separation
25. effect	53. personnel	81. shining
26. embarrass	54. possession	82. similar
27. environment	55. possible	83. studying
28. exaggerate	56. practical	84. succeed

85. succession
86. surprise
87. technique
88. than
89. then
90. their

91. there
92. they're
93. thorough
94. to, too, two
95. transferred

96. unnecessary
97. villain
98. woman
99. write
100. writing

"The Presedency"
background sign used on ABC Evening News

Actually the preceding list "cheats" because it gives separate listings for words that are often confused—for example, *their / there / they're*. So just to play square I will add some other favorites, words which in my experience seem to cause students unusual hardship.

absence
accept, except
acquaintance
actually
adolescent
advice, advise
affect, effect
already, all ready
altogether, all together
attendance
breath, breathe
capital, capitol
challenge
cite, site, sight
cloths, clothes
complement, compliment
condemn
conscience
definitely
desirable
dessert, desert
dining
grammar
guarantee

hypocrisy
irresistible
knowledge
later, latter
maneuver
moral, morale
nickel
none, no one
parallel
precede, proceed
principle, principal
right, rite, write
roommate
sergeant
sincerely
skiing
sponsor
susceptible
therefore
truly
unusually
visible
weather, whether
yield

C4. A Reminder

I'm sorry if this sounds anticlimactic, but we must go back to something that was said earlier and that applies to all writers in all places:

1. If you are in doubt about how to spell a word, use your dictionary—that's partly what it is for. Before you begin a writing assignment, make sure the dictionary is nearby. Most people don't have the fortitude to go down three flights of stairs to consult it, but they will look up a word if the means for doing so is right at hand.

2. If you are not in doubt about how to spell a word, but when your assignment is returned you discover that you mis-spelled it after all, take note of the word and look up its proper spelling as soon as possible. Concentrate especially hard on such a word, because you have to erase from your mind your previous impression of the correct spelling.

This advice applies to all writers, good spellers and bad. Practically no one can do without it. Take this very chapter you are reading now. I'm a fairly good speller, but as I wrote I found myself unsure of the spelling of several words. I looked them up, and most of the time my initial impression was right. But three times that impression was wrong: *colloquial* (I had *colloqial*), *misspelling* (I had *mispelling*), and *anticlimactic (anticlimatic)*. I did my penance by looking them up and thus you are able to read them in their proper form. What's sauce for this gander. . . .

✻ ✻ ✻

How is yoor speling?!?

(CPS)-Everyone knows that students can't read or write as well as they used to, but what about spelling? Has the often Byzantine art of spelling the English language gone the way of the McGuffey's Reader?

Marygrove College in Detroit thinks so, and in response it has started a class in spelling that quickly became so popular it is know offered as a correspondence course.

I'm glad to now that this problem is know being taken care of.

EXERCISES

1. Study the following list of irregular words. As you do, you might circle the letter or letters that are most likely to cause misspellings. The list is from William Drake's *The Way to Spell: A Guide for the Hesitant Speller.*

hoarse	avalanche	aviary
gruesome	vanquish	municipal
biscuit	soliloquy	argument
eager	jewelry	fluorine
speak	dilapidated	verbatim
speech	exorbitant	medieval
view	affidavit	moccasin
aerial	derogatory	piety
superfluous	menagerie	assassin
intravenous	demagogue	traceable
nuisance	dungeon	initiative
poignant	diagnostician	ingredient
innuendo	flagrant	miniature
accessory	demerit	parliament
insipid	vigil	differential
linen	tacit	quotient
denim	material	peculiar
ancient	maniacal	erratic
enervate	esteem	appetite
auxiliary	curiosity	ricochet
prosaic	vineyard	amethyst
carburetor	hiatus	lecherous
trauma	cocoa	jeopardy
essential	punctual	reconnoiter
anxious	wondrous	repugnant
conscious	covet	vagrant
conscience	scoundrel	embarrass
fascinate	quantity	frightening
separate	definite	lightning
amateur	except	familiar
similar	suppress	existence
meant	discoveries	forward
roommate	influential	marriage
colossal	acknowledge	initiate

2. Find the spelling error in each of the sentences below:

a. Now that charter fairs are lower, a lot more people are travel-ing to Europe.
b. It was all ready after midnight and Deb still hadn't shown up.
c. "Women's liberation" is a misnomer, for it effects men as well as women.
d. People use to meet at church socials; now they go to singles' bars.
e. The judge illuded to the story of King Solomon.
f. The affects of nuclear testing have not been completely de-termined.
g. We haven't seen one another since we were altogether at Christmas.
h. The Swansons lived in a motel until there new house was ready.
i. The kidnappers alluded police for nearly three days.
j. Economists say that to much government control is worse than to little.
k. I was led to believe that the accident occured yesterday.

3. Combine the base words and suffixes or prefixes.

> EXAMPLES: ir / responsible
> **irresponsible**
>
> debate / able
> **debatable**

a. courage / ous
b. notice / able
c. lovely / ness
d. un / natural
e. funny / er
f. change / able
g. ski / ing
h. mis / state
i. permit / ed
j. stare / ing
k. sad / est
l. stubborn / ness
m. occur / ing
n. dip / ed
o. replace / able

4. Choose the correct word(s) to complete each sentence.

a. What were they (referring/refering) to?
b. What an (embarassing/embarrassing) situation!

c. Despite our arguments, they remain (unyeilding/unyielding).

d. I can't (accept/except) your point of view, nor can I follow your (advise/advice).

e. Has the building (site/sight) been chosen (all ready/already)?

f. The (preceding/preceeding) message was brought to you by General Motors.

g. It's (unbelieveable/unbelievable) that the problem of nuclear power generation should not be (resolvable/resolveable).

h. Follow this general (principal/principle) and you will always (sucede/succeed) in business.

5. Give the plurals of the following nouns.

a. balcony
b. thief
c. fox
d. penny
e. alloy

f. chief
g. speech
h. journey
i. cross
j. belief

2

SENTENCES

> It is my ambition to say in ten sentences what everyone else
> says in a whole book.
>
> *Nietzsche*

People communicate in many different ways. Words are only part of that process. Hand gestures, for example, convey a rich assortment of meanings depending on the culture. In Jordan a street vendor might ball up his fist and thrust it upward in the general direction of a customer. He means that the offer he has just received is much too low and the customer can go to blazes for all he cares. In Vietnam if you beckon a child toward you with your palm upward, as we might do, you would be insulting the child, because only animals are summoned that way. Of course we are more familiar with our own system of gestures: thumbs-up to show "everything's okay," for example, or a shrug of the shoulders to convey indifference.

We communicate with our bodies in other ways besides gestures. Posture can speak volumes, from the folded arms that tell of authority to the careless slouch that means defiance of that authority. Eyes speak too, like the familiar wink that suggests intimacy. We even structure the space around us to send messages to others. For most Americans the proper conversational distance is about three feet, and we show our interest in others by looking directly at them. Other cultures define space differently. The Latin American prefers standing much closer, even for ordinary conversation; proximity need not mean aggressiveness, as it would to a North American. In Asian cultures you express interest and respect by lowering the eyes, not by looking at someone squarely, as we would do; Asians interpret directness as boldness.

When speech is added to movement and gesture, our communication becomes still more complex. Yet even here we do not rely solely on words. Grunts, "hmm" noises, signs—these and dozens of other sounds punctuate every conversation, and we complement them with countless pauses and repetitions. Furthermore we quite often do not organize our speech into neat, clear, and coherent sentences, precisely because we can make use of these other devices for conveying meaning. Instead we spill out our words in an untidy, imprecise, confusing rush.

Of course speech may not seem so disorganized to you. Before you doubt too much, however, consider the following excerpt from the Watergate tapes.

EHRLICHMAN: You see . . .
PRESIDENT: You expect anyone . . . I was cogitating last night, and we've got the people that can—I mean on the obstruction of justice thing, which I think is our main problem at this time—well of course it is the main problem because it involved the other people.
EHRLICHMAN: Yeah.
PRESIDENT: Otherwise it's just Chapin.
EHRLICHMAN: Yes, Chapin.
PRESIDENT: And Mitchell.
EHRLICHMAN: Yeah.
PRESIDENT: Magruder.
EHRLICHMAN: Yeah.
PRESIDENT: Possibly Dean, but a . . .

Not a single complete sentence is spoken, not a single speech continues uninterrupted. These are well-educated men, occupying positions of immense power and prestige. If their conversation is sometimes gibberish to us, it is not because they failed to communicate—bribes were paid, lies were told, evidence was suppressed as a result of such conversations. The reason it might seem gibberish is simply that we are cut off from that rich assortment of looks, nods, and gestures which in real life were the necessary complements of these words and which "filled in the gaps" for those who were present. If someone made a tape of your conversation with family or friends, the tape would be just as mysterious to an outsider.

So words are only part of our communication in everyday life, and words often are not ordered into complete sentences. Then why are complete sentences so important a part of writing? The answer perhaps occurs to you already. Precisely because writing does not offer the props we rely upon during conversation, we must give it a special order and clarity. Only then can it be understood by someone distant from us both in space and in time. Sentences impose this order, they make us understood, they fill in the gaps of our tapes.

Using sentences effectively is therefore just as essential as using words effectively. Reading the work of a writer who has poor sentence structure is like listening to a tape rather than participating in the conversation: everything comes out half-garbled.

This chapter, which deals with writing effective sentences, is divided into two sections. In the first section, we will consider what a sentence is, how sentences can be described, how using a variety of types of sentences can improve your writing. Often poor sentences are correct in form but ineffective due to lack of variety or effective emphasis. In the second part of the chapter, we will examine the "faults of commission," ways to make your writing more cohesive by closely examining the structure of your sentences. If your papers come back to you with symbols on them like *frag, shift, awk, confus, f s,* or *coh,* Part B should be an important resource for you. Both of these sections contain exercises to help you refine and strengthen your writing skills.

A. GOOD SENTENCES—AND BETTER ONES

> What is our praise or pride
> But to imagine excellence, and try to make it?
> *Richard Wilbur*

The playwright Ben Jonson once claimed that a writer's "reason (cannot) be in frame whose sentence is preposterous." Jonson was putting it a bit strongly, perhaps. But surely he was right in finding a close relationship between the structure of a writer's sentences and the clear statement of the writer's ideas. Part A will help you understand sentences, first by describing what sentences are, then by explaining their structure and the various ways you can improve your use of them.

A1. What Is a Sentence?

Of course everybody knows what a sentence is. Of course. Then how about a quick definition? Suddenly we all pause, hem a bit, offer one or two possibilities, and then retract them. If you define a sentence as something made up of a subject and verb, for example, where is the subject in a sentence like *Stop it!*? If you define it more generally as the basic unit of communication, what makes sentences more basic than words? Even if we separate speech from writing, don't we recognize that there are obvious connections between how we organize at least some of our speech and how we organize writing as sentences?

In other words just about every formal definition we might construct would be open to one or more exceptions. The perfect definition would be harder to achieve than the perfect cup of coffee. It is not important that you have a definition. But what *is* important is knowing the *signs* or *clues* that signal the presence of a sentence:

- In speech, the signal usually is a falling pitch at the end of a group of words (you might say we "hear the period").
- In writing, the signals are capitalization at the beginning, a punctuation mark at the end, and the presence of both a subject (even if only understood) and a complete verb.

Let's be a little more specific. The first description, the one based on speech, relies on the verbal clues we give each other when we talk. Read *aloud* the following three lines:

You are coming home now.

Are you coming home now?

If you are coming home now . . .

The words used are almost identical in each case. Yet when you read them aloud, another person could recognize the first line as a complete declarative sentence, the second as a complete question, and the third as only part of a sentence. He or she would be able to make this distinction easily because of the way we let the pitch of our voice rise or fall to show the completion of a sentence unit. As noted before, much of our speech has no complete sentence structure at all. But when sentences are used, we know how to interpret these changes in pitch as markers for sentence units.

In writing, we can rely on capitalization of the first word and on some kind of end punctuation (period, question mark, exclamation point) as the easiest clues to sentences. However, while each sentence must have these signals, the converse is not true—i.e., the mere presence of such clues does not guarantee a sentence. A proper name, for example, is always capitalized, and a mid-sentence interjection might be followed by an exclamation point *(but oh! what a difference)*. Neither of these would be sentences by themselves.

110—HELP WANTED
Downtown Inn

Is now accepting applications for executive secretary to general manager. We are looking for someone highly efficient in typing and shorthand skills and preferably speaks with a British accent.

100 S. North Ave.

555-1000

It's not only what you say, it's how you say it.

What does guarantee a complete sentence is the presence of a subject, even if it is only an understood subject, and a complete verb. Each of these two elements deserves a closer examination.

The word *subject* has two relevant meanings. The one most familiar to us is subject as a word occupying a certain place in a sentence. Consider the word "woman" in this sentence by Edmund Wilson:

The woman behind me in the train talks to the conductor with a German accent.

"Woman" fills the subject place. To find the word filling the subject place in this or any sentence, perform a simple test: locate the verb, then ask *who?* or *what?* Here the verb is "talks." Who or what "talks"? Clearly, "woman talks." So "woman" fills the subject place.

But subject can also mean not just one word but rather a whole group of words, in fact all the words in a sentence that are not part of the predicate. (The predicate includes the verb and the words associated with or modifying the verb—more on this in a moment.) In the Wilson sentence, the full subject includes "woman" and all the words that explain it. Thus "The woman behind me in the train" is the full subject.

To keep these two meanings of *subject* distinct, and to make clear which meaning I intend each time I use the word, I would like to borrow a device from arithmetic. If you recall, numbers represented by the same letter are distinguished from each other by the use of a small number called a subscript written below and to the right of the letter, thus x_1 and x_2. In our case, when the word *subject* means a word filling the subject place, like "woman" in our example sentence, then it will be written *subject$_1$*. When *subject* means a whole group of words, everything in the sentence that is not the predicate, then it will be written *subject$_2$*.

We said earlier that sentences must have a complete verb (what is sometimes called a *finite verb*). First you must identify the verb before you can tell whether or not it is complete. To find the verb, locate the word or words in the sentence that would change if the time of the sentence changed. For example, suppose a sentence refers to the present time:

> I show my true feelings only to my family and close friends.   *student paper*

Change it to the past or future:

> I showed my true feelings only to my family and close friends.

> I will show my true feelings only to my family and close friends.

Clearly, "show" is the verb in the original sentence, because it is the only word that changes when the time changes *(showed, will show)*. Every sentence has a word (like *show, shows, showed*) or a group of words (like *was showing, are showing, will have been showing*) that changes to show time.

Remember that a key word in this description is *changes*. Some words do show time but are not verbs—*yesterday*, for example, or *today, tomorrow, then*, or *now*. None of these words can be verbs because none changes its form to show a change in time.

This test will locate the verbs in a sentence. However, you also need to determine if the verb you have identified is the complete verb the sentence needs. This means keeping in mind two other principles:

1. A verb with an *-ing* ending cannot be the complete verb unless accompanied by another word that shows time.

2. A verb preceded by a pronoun like *who, which,* or *that* or by a conjunction like *if, although,* or *since* cannot be the complete verb.

Let me explain how the first principle works. Verbs with an *-ing* ending, i.e., with a suffix added to a complete verb *(seeing, ringing, being),* must be accompanied by other words that can change as the time changes in order to constitute a complete verb. Thus:

> My hands were trembling as I removed the cap from the bottle.
>
> The organ is playing quietly but sonorously.

"Trembling" and "playing" need "were" and "is" to complete them, because "were" and "is" can change to show a change in time *(are trembling, will be playing).* By themselves they cannot form sentences:

> My hands trembling as I removed the cap from the bottle. [not a sentence]
>
> The organ playing quietly but sonorously. [not a sentence]

These *-ing* words can appear by themselves in sentences, but when they do there will always be a complete verb somewhere else in the sentence. For example:

> The crackling of some twigs gave away my presence.   *student paper*

"Crackling" we know cannot be the verb because it is not accompanied by another verb that changes to show time changes. So we look elsewhere, and sure enough we come across "gave." "Gave" can change *(gives, will give)* and is therefore the complete verb for the sentence.

As we said earlier, a verb preceded by a pronoun like *who, which,* or *that* or by a conjunction like *if, although,* or *since* cannot be a complete verb. Look at the following example:

> I do not know what I said to him when he came to my room that night.   *James Baldwin*

When you read this sentence you encounter three verbs that might be the complete verb. "Do (not) know," "said," and "came" all are verbs that can change as the time changes (for example, *will know, says, comes*). But "said" is ineligible because it is preceded by the pronoun "what." "Came" is ineligible because it is preceded by the conjunction "when." So "do (not) know" remains the only verb that can be the complete verb for the sentence. The other two, "said" and "came," are the verbs for the dependent clauses in the sentence. We will take up dependent clauses in the next section.

A complete verb is essential for a sentence. But a verb, just like a subject$_1$, can be accompanied by a large number of words that modify or explain it. These other words together with the verb itself can be termed collectively the **predicate.** The example sentence we used before was this one:

> The woman behind me in the train talks to the conductor with a German accent.

We agreed that "woman" was the subject$_1$ and that "The woman behind me in the train" forms the subject$_2$. So now "talks" is the complete verb and "talks to the conductor with a German accent" forms the complete predicate, because these last words help describe how and to whom the woman talks.

By now you should understand what a sentence is, whether or not you can offer a quick definition. To summarize: you should be able to find subjects—subject$_1$ and subject$_2$ (subject$_1$ plus any modifiers); you should be able to find complete verbs and complete predicates (complete verbs plus any modifiers); you should further understand that sentences consist of at least subject$_1$ + complete verb, and usually of subject$_2$ + complete predicate.

A few descriptive terms for sentences can be especially helpful in showing ways to give more maturity to your sentence structure. These terms can be grouped under three headings: simple-compound-complex; coordinate-subordinate; and cumulative-periodic. We will see how they apply in sections A2.–A4.

A2. Sentence Types and Sentence Variety

Three terms—simple, compound, complex—allow us to categorize sentences according to the number and types of clauses they contain.

A **clause** is any group of words that has a subject and a predicate. If a clause has a complete verb, it can form a sentence by

"I know that's the correct term, Finley, but couldn't we call them something else beside 'Sinking Fund Bonds'?"

Terms are important . . .

itself, as we saw earlier. Therefore it is called an *independent* or *main clause*. On the other hand, if a clause is introduced by a pronoun like *who, which,* or *that* or by a conjunction like *if, although,* or *since,* it cannot form a sentence by itself and is called a *dependent* or *subordinate clause*.

When a sentence has only one independent clause, and therefore only one subject$_2$-predicate combination, it is called a **simple sentence:**

Procrastination can endanger your academic health.   *pamphlet*

The first word is the subject$_1$; the remaining group of words is the predicate. Note that it is quite possible to have two subject$_1$ words and still have a simple sentence:

Procrastination and *inattention* can endanger your academic health.

The two italicized words are both examples of subject$_1$. Together, however, they form only one subject$_2$, and this is the crucial test. Two or more subject$_1$ words, by the way, form what is called a compound subject. Similarly, the predicate can contain two verbs (thus being termed a compound predicate) and still make only a simple sentence:

Procrastination *can endanger* your academic health *and destroy* your peace of mind.

Since you have just learned that two subject₁ words together make a compound subject, and two complete verbs make a compound predicate, perhaps you can deduce what a **compound sentence** might be. If there are two or more independent clauses in a sentence, in other words two or more clauses that by themselves can form separate sentences, the result is called a compound sentence.

Unions must represent all hourly employees in labor negotiations, and therefore they resent and lobby against right-to-work laws.   *student exam*

If you replace the comma in this sentence with a period and capitalize the first letter of the "and" that follows, the two independent clauses would then become two simple sentences. Because they are joined by the comma and the "and" conjunction, the clauses form not two separate sentences but rather one compound sentence. Observe too that this particular compound sentence has a compound predicate ("resent and lobby") in the second of its two independent clauses.

Every sentence has one independent clause (simple) or more than one (compound). In addition many sentences contain a dependent clause, one that has a subject and a predicate but cannot form a sentence on its own. When one or more of these dependent clauses are present, the sentence is said to be a **complex sentence.** Consider this example:

Few people realize the horrendous odds against them when they play the state lottery.   *tv editorial*

The clause "when they play the state lottery" is a dependent clause, because it begins with the conjunction "when" and therefore cannot form a sentence on its own. The inclusion of this clause in the example sentence allows us to term the example a complex sentence.

Furthermore if a sentence has two or more independent clauses (thus compound), and one or more dependent clauses (thus complex), the resulting hybrid can be termed a **compound-complex sentence.** Here is one:

> Artists have rarely been well paid for their labors, and now as our economy declines their future looks even bleaker.   *student paper*

Two independent clauses are joined by the conjunction "and," forming a compound sentence. The second independent clause includes within it the dependent clause "as our economy declines," so the full sentence becomes compound-complex.

To clarify these differences in your mind, use this diagram to chart what has just been said about categorizing sentences.

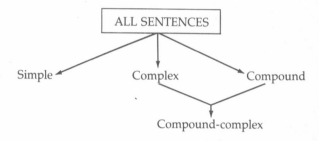

Simple enough? Complex enough?

The importance of knowing how to categorize sentences is simply this: you now have a good way of finding out why and how your sentences might be too monotonous.

Consider this example paragraph:

> It took a good deal of courage to register for class on June 11. But I am pleased I decided to take the step. On that day I purchased all the textbooks I would need for this class. I wanted to be sure that I would have all the material I needed. Then I got my bill, both for this course and for the textbooks. I realized I'd better get serious about returning to school if I was going to spend my hard-earned money. I also realized that I was going to have to start saying no to social invitations. It is going to be very hard, but I am determined to do well.

The paragraph is made up of eight sentences. Notice the sources of monotony:

1. Almost every sentence—six of eight—is a complex sentence following the formula of main clause + dependent clause. Only one sentence (fifth) is simple; only one (the last) is compound; none is compound-complex.

2. Almost every sentence—again six of the eight—has *I* as the subject$_1$; the other two have *it*.

3. Every sentence begins with the same pattern of subject$_1$ + verb, with perhaps at most a conjunction or brief phrase intervening. Compare them:

> It took. . . .
> But I'm pleased. . . .
> On that day I purchased. . . .
> I wanted. . . .
> Then I got. . . .
> I realized. . . .
> I also realized. . . .
> It is going to be. . . .

In other words, this paragraph shows almost no variety in sentence type or in choice of subject$_1$. And within the one type of sentence that does predominate (complex), the same pattern is used over and over, main clause + dependent clause, main clause + dependent clause, clackety-clack, clackety-clack, like the railroad cars of a fast passenger train. It's as if the writer has one formula for making sentences and cannot think of breaking free of it.

> The world's a scene of changes, and to be
> Constant, in Nature were inconstancy.
> *Abraham Cowley*

Suppose the paragraph were rewritten to use a greater variety of sentence patterns. It might read like this:

> Although it took courage to register for class on June 11, I'm pleased I decided to take the step. On that day I also purchased all the textbooks I would need for class, so that I would have the necessary material, and then got my bills both for the course and for the books. Suddenly I realized that if I was going to spend my hard-earned money, I had better get serious about school and start saying no to social invitations. It's going to be hard—but I'm determined to do well.

Eight sentences have been pared to four, monotonous patterns have been broken up, and some ideas have been emphasized more than others. The paragraph still needs much work, especially on word choice and level of detail, but at least a first step has been taken.

Here is a paragraph that illustrates the variety of sentence structures a good writer can produce. The novelist Eudora Welty is describing for us a scene in a Ross Macdonald detective story; the sentences are numbered so that they can be discussed in the paragraph that follows. The paragraph is from a review of *The Underground Man*.

(1) Fairy tale and living reality alternate on one current to pulse together in this remarkable scene. (2) The woman is a pivotal character, and Archer has caught up with her; they are face to face, and there comes a moment's embrace. (3) Of the many brilliant ways Mr. Macdonald has put his motif to use, I believe this is the touch that delighted me most. (4) For of course Archer, this middle-aging Californian who has seen everything in a career of going into impossible trouble with his eyes open, who has always been the protector of the weak and the rescuer of the helpless, is a born romantic. (5) Here he meets his introverted and ailing counterpart—this lady is the chatelaine of the romantic-gone-wrong. (6) He is not by nature immune, especially to what is lovely or was lovely once. (7) At a given moment, they may brush close—as Archer, the only one with insight into himself, is aware.

Notice the immense variety in the structure of the seven sentences that make up the paragraph. We could sum up our observations on them like this:

(1) complex sentence (compound subject$_1$); main clause + dependent clause

(2) two compound sentences, joined by a semicolon (four simple clauses in all)

(3) complex sentence; dependent clause + main clause + dependent clause

(4) complex sentence; subject$_1$ + dependent clause (with two other dependent clauses embedded within it) + dependent clause + verb and complement

(5) compound sentence; two independent clauses

(6) complex sentence; main clause + dependent clause

(7) complex sentence; main clause + dependent clause (with another dependent clause embedded within it).

How do you learn to write sentences with the variety of Eudora Welty's rather than the monotony of our first writer's? The first step is increasing your awareness of sentence patterns. Notice what sentence patterns you habitually use. Employ terms like *complex* or *compound* to characterize your own writing. Take a few paragraphs from something you have written recently and analyze them the way we have just analyzed Ms. Welty's paragraph.

Then, having determined the patterns you use most often, ask yourself some questions. Begin with asking the questions about what you have already written, trying to revise a couple of paragraphs according to the answers you receive. Then start a new writing project—perhaps a freshman English paper—and ask the questions *while you write*, incorporating the answers as you go along. Here are the questions:

1. Do your sentences begin the same way too often? For example, do they almost all begin with a noun subject, with a conjunction like *but*, with a personal pronoun like *I*, or with the indefinite *there (There is . . .)*? If so, try sometimes to begin with a phrase or a dependent clause. And sometimes vary your subject$_1$, especially if that subject$_1$ is too often a personal pronoun or the indefinite *there*.

2. Do you almost always use the same subject-verb-object (S-V-O) pattern in your sentences? Remember that occasionally it is permissible to invert the usual word order, either by a question or—every once in a great while—by putting the subject last (O-V-S) or perhaps even in the middle (O-S-V), thus throwing special emphasis on the words that stand in the subject's usual place. Here is an example:

   Glorious islets, too, I have seen rise out of the haze.   *Thomas Carlyle*

   The O ("islets")-S ("I")-V ("have seen") pattern focuses our attention on "islets."

3. Do you almost always use simple sentences? Or compound sentences? Or complex sentences of a certain predictable pattern? If so, try to find ways to break out of those confining patterns. Perhaps you also need to examine more carefully the relationships among your ideas, so that you can learn to subordinate some ideas to others (in other words, put some

ideas into phrases or dependent clauses rather than leaving them as independent clauses). Effective subordination enables you to clarify your meaning by showing which ideas are more important and which less, which ideas are conditioned upon others and which are not. We'll discuss this further in the next section.

Variety in the type of sentences you use is an important goal. It has a complementary goal: variety in sentence length.

Each time I teach a writing course I run a little experiment near the beginning of each semester. When the first batch of papers is about to be turned in, I ask the writers to do some counting. First I pick a paragraph, quite arbitrarily—let's say the third paragraph. Then I have them count the number of words in their third paragraph and divide by the number of sentences. The result is the average number of words per sentence. Having secured this figure from each writer, I can go on to establish an average number of words per sentence for the entire class. I write that average on the board, along with the shortest sentence written by anyone in the class and also the longest. The results for a three-year period are as follows:

year	*average words/sentence*	*shortest*	*longest*
1976	14.8	7 words	26 words
1977	14.5	8 words	31 words
1978	15.2	7 words	28 words

While my experiment can hardly be called scientific, the pattern is always very consistent, as these statistics show. Most of these beginning college students write sentences averaging fourteen or fifteen words in length and showing very little variation from that average. Never has a writer averaged fewer than ten words or more than eighteen. The shortest sentences are never less than six words and the longest rarely exceed thirty.

Compare these figures with comparable figures for professional writers. Although there may be considerable variation from author to author, most professionals average between twenty and twenty-five words per sentence. Furthermore they show greater extremes, from the really short two-or-three word sentence to the long fifty-word unit. My favorite example is a paragraph written by Norman Mailer that averages thirty-nine words per sentence, the shortest being three words and the longest, 103!

> The joy of life is variety.
> *Samuel Johnson*

What happens if your sentences don't vary in length? Let's go back to the example paragraph we used earlier. Its original version went like this:

It took a good deal of courage to register for class on June 11. But I am pleased I decided to take the step. On that day I purchased all the textbooks I would need for this class. I wanted to be sure that I would have all the material I needed. Then I got my bill, both for this course and for the textbooks. I realized I'd better get serious about returning to school if I was going to spend my hard-earned money. I also realized that I was going to have to start saying no to social invitations. It is going to be very hard, but I am determined to do well.

We agreed this is a pretty dull paragraph, despite the fact that each sentence is technically "correct." Part of the dullness comes from monotony in sentence length. The shortest sentence here is ten words, the longest nineteen, the average fourteen. Again we are reminded of the clickety-clack of the train wheels. After a few pages of such a monotonous pattern, you're fighting off sleep.

Suppose we agree that variation in sentence length is desirable—what then? You can't just go out and stitch a few sentences together, or chop off a few words here and add a few there. After all, the length of a sentence must relate to and, in fact, is determined by, its meaning.

The process of achieving greater variety in sentence length is a gradual one that, again, depends upon *increased awareness*. So long as you keep yourself aware of the goal, you can make progress toward it. A good yoga teacher would tell you that, if you cannot do a particular exercise at first, you should be content with picturing the exercise in your mind, going through it in your imagination; in time the muscles will relax and stretch and attune themselves to the new demands you wish to make on them. So too with writing.

Besides keeping the general goal in mind, it may also be helpful to remember a few principles:

1. A series of short sentences often gives the effect of speed and is therefore appropriate for describing tense or dramatic moments in a story. Otherwise such a series might make your prose seem choppy, almost childish.

2. A single short sentence is a valuable way to give emphasis. It allows you to offer a pithy summation of the preceding sentences, especially if it comes at the end of the paragraph.

3. Longer sentences are often appropriate for detailed description and for more leisurely explanations and arguments. But these longer sentences are always achieved by adding new, more precise details or by pushing the ideas to a still deeper and more thoughtful level. It is never done by yoking two separate sentences (unless they are closely related in meaning) or by "padding" with filler words.

To get a better grasp of the importance of variety in sentence length, compare the student paragraph on the previous page with the following paragraph by Lewis Thomas, director of the Sloan-Kettering Cancer Center in New York City. The paragraph is from *Lives of a Cell: Notes of a Biology Watcher*. Dr. Thomas describes his reaction to the idea that humans might have a temporary but important role to play in the drama of evolution:

> I would much prefer this useful role, if I had any say, to the essentially unearthly creature we seem otherwise on the way to becoming. It would mean making some quite fundamental changes in our attitudes toward each other, if we were really to think of ourselves as indispensable elements of nature. We would surely become the environment to worry about the most. We would discover, in ourselves, the sources of wonderment and delight that we have discerned in all other manifestations of nature. Who knows, we might even acknowledge the fragility and vulnerability that always accompany high specialization in biology, and movements might start up for the protection of ourselves as a valuable, endangered species. We couldn't lose.

Notice how Thomas exemplifies the principles we have been discussing. His sentences range from three words to thirty-two, with an average of twenty, six more than our typical freshman writer. The longer sentences result from his elaboration of an idea—for example, the idea that we are an endangered species, which he develops in the fifth sentence. Yet this longest sentence is juxtaposed against the shortest, sentence six; the sharp, colloquial, emphatic "We couldn't lose" summarizes his reaction and makes for a dramatic conclusion.

Some other practical hints:

1. Analyze a representative sample of your own prose to see how it compares to the statistics reported earlier.

2. Remember that the goal is greater *variety* in length, which means shorter as well as longer sentences.

3. Coordinate this section with the preceding pages on greater variety of sentence *types*.

A3. Coordination and Subordination of Clauses

These two terms are closely related to the three we just discussed. **Coordination** means linking independent clauses together by coordinating conjunctions, such as *but, and, or, nor, yet, for,* and *so.* When these conjunctions are used, they give equal status to each of the clauses they join. In other words, like any good *coordinator* they simply bring individuals together—in this case individual clauses—without asserting the superiority of one to another.

Look, for example, at this short passage:

> We are in a world of facts, *and* we use them, *for* there is nothing else to use. We do not quarrel with them, *but* we take them as they are, *and* avail ourselves of what they can do for us. *J. H. Newman* [italics added]

There are four coordinating conjunctions linking the separate-but-equal clauses that make up this passage.

Subordination, by contrast, does just what its name implies—it subordinates one clause to another. In order for one clause to be subordinate to another, it must depend upon the other. So subordination means making a clause dependent and therefore of lesser importance grammatically. Writing that is rich in subordination is therefore rich in dependent clauses and thus rich in complex sentences.

Subordination is usually achieved in one of two ways. The first is by using one of the subordinating conjunctions. These include:

if, as if	after	while
that, so that	as long as	because
although	until	unless
since	when, whenever	how
before	where, wherever	whether

The second way to subordinate is to use relative pronouns like *who, whoever, whose, that, which, what,* and *whatever.* Here are examples of both methods of subordination:

> We may all be transcendental yet, *whether we like it or not.   E. B. White*

> The main answer, I suppose, is *that I was born that way.   F. L. Lucas*

The italicized dependent clauses are introduced by the subordinating conjunction "whether" and the relative pronoun "that," respectively.

An important fact about dependent clauses is that they act as replacements for three and only three kinds of words: nouns, adjectives, and adverbs. The reason we use clauses is a simple one: the alternative (using nouns, adjectives, or adverbs alone) would be infinitely more cumbersome. Instead of saying *an old man who walks slowly and with great dignity,* for example, we would have to say *a slow-and-greatly-dignified-walking old man.*

Naturally enough, when clauses replace nouns they are termed *noun clauses* and do a noun's work. For example, they can act as:

1. a subject$_2$

   What she wanted was not help but confirmation.   *A. Alvarez*

2. the object of a verb

   Many think *that seeds improve with age.   H. D. Thoreau*

3. a complement (a word or words that complete the predicate, often following a form of the verb *to be*)

   The trouble is, in general, *that there is nobody at home.   C. H. Cooley*

Noun clauses most often begin with *that, what, whatever, whether, who, why, when,* and *where*.

When a clause modifies a noun or pronoun like an adjective does, it is called an *adjective clause:*

Doctors *who charge $40 for a ten-minute office visit* cannot expect much sympathy from their patients.   *newspaper item*

Here the italicized clause modifies the noun "doctors." Such clauses are usually introduced by relative pronouns, especially *who, which,* and *that,* but *when, where,* and *why* sometimes appear. Quite often the relative pronoun is understood, or omitted:

The car *(that) I would most like to have* is a Datsun 280-Z.   *student paper*

Adverb clauses are just as important. An adverb clause can modify:

1. a verb

We undoubtedly scavenged *whenever we could.*   *Robert Ardrey*

2. an adjective

He was as tired *as he had been those nights on the graveyard shift.*
student paper

3. an adverb

Darkness arrived more quickly *than we thought possible.*
student paper

4. a main clause

If the scheme of things is purposeless and meaningless, then the life of man is purposeless and meaningless too.   *W. T. Stace*

Several conjunctions can introduce adverb clauses. Among the most common ones are *after, although, as, because, before, if, since, so, than, though, unless, until, when, whenever, where,* and *while*.

Why should you be aware of these types of dependent clauses and their possible uses? The sole purpose is to help you practice effective subordination. And effective subordination in turn is necessary for two reasons.

First, subordination enables you to make your reader aware of the relative importance of your various ideas. Some ideas deserve greater emphasis than others. Those of lesser importance should be made subordinate to, dependent upon, the main ideas, as a signal to the reader of the proper weights to assign to them. If you do not subordinate, you imply that all ideas have equal importance, which in most cases is not true. Consider this sentence:

> Samuelson's theory simply cannot be accepted, but Samuelson's theory is persuasive in many ways.

This sentence is poor because it implies absolute equality between these two ideas. Consider two possible revisions:

> Samuelson's theory, *although persuasive in many ways,* simply cannot be accepted.

> Samuelson's theory, *although it cannot be accepted,* is persuasive in many ways.

The two revisions of course differ in meaning. The first, by subordinating the favorable comment, makes what is basically a negative judgment of Samuelson's theory. The second, on the other hand, subordinates the negative comment and thus offers a more favorable judgment. As these examples indicate, the use of dependent clauses allows you to distinguish major ideas from minor ones. It is up to you as the writer, of course, to decide which ideas are major and which minor.

Secondly, effective subordination enables you to be more exact in expressing your meaning, because you can show the precise relationship between major and minor ideas. Did the minor idea occur before or after the major one? Is the minor idea a cause or effect of the major one? Does the dependent clause particularize a noun in the main clause—does it define or give emphasis to the noun?

As an example of precise subordination, examine this sentence by the noted columnist Walter Lippmann:

> And so, if we truly wish to understand why freedom is necessary in a civilized society, we must begin by realizing that, because freedom of discussion improves our own opinions, the liberties of other men are our own vital necessity.

This sentence contains four dependent clauses:

if we truly wish to understand

why freedom is necessary in a civilized society

that . . . the liberties of other men are our own vital necessity

because freedom of discussion improves our own opinions

The third clause is structurally the most important because it is an indispensable part of the main, independent clause. Without the third clause the sentence would be incomplete. This structural importance mirrors the fact that the idea that it offers is also the most important. The first clause is introduced by "if" and therefore expresses *condition*, the condition under which the main clause can be realized. The second and fourth clauses, also of lesser importance, raise the question of reasons ("why. . . ," "because . . ."). Together these four clauses express a very complex idea, but Lippmann is able to be clear in expressing it because he has mastered the art of effective subordination.

What practical steps can you take to improve your use of subordination? I would make three suggestions.

First, check your recent papers to see how often and in what ways you have been using dependent clauses. Do you find them to be comparatively scarce—say, an average of fewer than one per sentence? Do you find any sentences where the relative importance of various ideas could be emphasized by subordinating some ideas to others? Locate the conjunctions that begin your dependent clauses. Are they precisely the right conjunctions to express your meaning? As an example of what to look for, read this paragraph from a student paper:

The Food Additives Amendment to the Food, Drug, and Cosmetic Act was passed in 1958. This act gave the FDA the authority to regulate the use of all food additives. The agency made up a list of all additives and circulated it among food technologists, biochemists, nutritionists, and medical people. Each one was asked for his or her evaluation of the safety of these substances. Some additives were considered harmful. These were tested at once and the bad ones were prohibited. Those additives to which the experts did not object were placed on an official roster, the Generally Recognized As Safe (GRAS) list. Such additives had not been proven safe. Since 1958 some substances have been removed from the GRAS list and others have been restricted to specific foods or specific quantities. These additives caused problems.

The paragraph is not a bad one. But if you examine it closely, you will see that it has almost no subordinate clauses. Consequently the author has missed several opportunities to make her meaning more precise by subordinating some ideas to other ideas. Notice how both the relative importance and the precise relationship of her ideas is made clear in this revised version:

> The Food Additives Amendment to the Food, Drug, and Cosmetic Act, passed in 1958, gave the FDA the authority to regulate the use of all food additives. The agency made up a list of additives and circulated it among food technologists, biochemists, nutritionists, and medical people. Each was asked for his or her evaluation of the safety of these substances. Those that were considered harmful were tested at once and then prohibited if necessary. Those additives to which the experts did not object were placed on an official roster, the Generally Recognized As Safe (GRAS) list, although they had never been proven safe. Since 1958 some substances have been removed from the GRAS list or restricted to specific foods or specific quantities because they were found to cause problems.

Notice how ten sentences have been cut to six, how ideas of lesser importance have been subordinated, how one idea has been contrasted to another ("although . . ."), how one idea has been identified as the reason for another ("because . . ."). This is the kind of analysis and the kind of revision you need to apply to your own completed papers.

> The scientist . . . shows his intelligence, if any, by his ability
> to discriminate between the important and the negligible.
> *Hans Zinsser*

A second practical step in this direction is to evaluate each paragraph *before* you write it, trying to sort out in your own mind which ideas are more important. Consider also how your ideas relate to one another and how those relationships can be expressed by the right conjunctions. Above all, try to have an awareness of the need to make subordinate clauses an integral part of your style. On the average a professional writer uses about two subordinate clauses per sentence. Please note this is an average figure and says nothing about whether any particular sentence should have dependent clauses. But how close to this average do you come?

The third practical step is to learn to recognize the two most common pitfalls writers might encounter when using subordinate clauses. One of them is the temptation to be so concerned with using dependent clauses that you unintentionally confuse your reader. If dependent clauses are put together in a close series, especially if they also begin with similar conjunctions, the result can be a sentence like this one:

> The test which a child is given that determines if he has any learning disabilities which need attention is one that is quite easy to administer. *student paper*

By the time the reader sorts out all the *which*'s and *that*'s, he or she is hopelessly lost. Better to simplify the construction:

> It is quite easy to administer the test that determines if a child has significant learning disabilities.

The other pitfall is the inexact and/or overfrequent use of *and* and *as*. *And* is a conjunction that gives equal status to two words or ideas, expressing no meaning of its own. Whenever possible replace it with more definite subordinating words like *because, when,* or *where:*

WEAK: I like Dr. Silverman very much and calculus is now one of my favorite courses. *student paper*

REVISION: Because I like Dr. Silverman very much, calculus is now one of my favorite courses.

Note that the revision is more precise, because it shows cause and effect. Another overused construction is the adverb clause beginning with *as,* when a more precise word would be better:

WEAK: As I had not come home by the time he went to bed, Dad left the porch light on. *student paper*

REVISION: Because I had not come home by the time he went to bed, Dad left the porch light on.

A4. Cumulative and Periodic Sentences

These two terms describe, or categorize, sentences and also the process of writing sentences. The **cumulative sentence** begins with the subject-predicate combination, the grammatical heart of the sentence. Then, once the essentials of the main clause have been stated, the writer adds details in much the same way a painter might add details to an initial sketch. These details can be considered further refinements of the main idea. They are provided in numerous ways, principally by adding phrases and dependent clauses. Consider these two examples from student writing:

> Her hands were always moving, pushing her glasses back up her slim nose, patting her hair into place, tapping a nonexistent ash off the end of her cigarette.

> I lied, which was probably a foolish thing to do, especially since I knew the truth could not be hidden much longer.

The first sentence shows the cumulative process by having its independent clause—"Her hands were always moving"— followed by three phrases. The second sentence also begins with the main clause ("I lied"), followed by two dependent clauses.

The process of writing a **periodic sentence** is different because some or all of the main independent clause is held back until the very end of the sentence. While both cumulative and periodic sentences contain descriptive phrases and dependent clauses, a cumulative sentence can be cut short after the main clause and be grammatically complete, while a periodic sentence cannot, since part of its main clause is at the end. Here are two student-written examples of periodic sentences:

> When my father had been wheeled into the recovery room, and the heart monitor and the glucose tubes had been disconnected, I finally relaxed.

> At last she had found, in a small insignificant-looking pamphlet, a pamphlet that seemed to promise nothing very special, the real answer.

In the first example, dependent clauses precede the main clause that ends the sentence ("I finally relaxed"). In the second, a portion of the main clause begins the sentence, but an essential part—the object of the verb—is postponed until the end, after the completion of a phrase and a clause.

> I attribute such success as I have had to the periodic
> sentence.
>
>   *Edmund Wilson*

Periodic sentences are fairly rare, although it is good to know what they are and to be able to use them. Cumulative sentences are not rare at all; in fact some people contend that cumulative sentences are the typical sentences of modern writing, especially of narrative and descriptive writing. Practice in creating effective cumulative sentences can be very important in developing your writing skills.

Here are some good examples of cumulative sentences:

> There is nothing about the way she (Ava Gardner) looks, up close, to suggest the life she has led: press conferences accompanied by dim lights and an orchestra; bullfighters writing poems about her in the press; rubbing Vaseline between her bosoms to emphasize the cleavage; roaming restlessly around Europe like a woman without a country, a Pandora with her suitcases full of cognac and Hershey bars ("for quick energy").   *Rex Reed*

> January 11, 1965, was a bright warm day in Southern California, the kind of day when Catalina floats on the Pacific horizon and the air smells of orange blossoms and it is a long way from the bleak and difficult East, a long way from the cold, a long way from the past.   *Joan Didion*

> Suddenly the briefcase fell open, spilling out not a sheaf of papers but rather a bottle of aftershave, a shoebrush, deodorant, and two pairs of sky-blue underwear.   *student writer*

Perhaps a question might occur to you: how is writing a cumulative sentence different from the subordinating process we discussed in the previous section? You would be correct in observing some overlap, because a cumulative sentence often involves adding dependent clauses. One difference, however, is that the cumulative process can also involve single words or phrases as well as clauses. A second difference is that the cumulative process always means having the main clause at or near the beginning and then adding modifiers to it, while the subordinating process is not limited to this form.

You can understand more about the process of writing cumulative sentences by looking at this example:

> We walked on toward the prison, coming as near as we could, for the crowd was enormous and in the dim light silent, almost motionless, like crowds seen in a dream.   *Katherine Anne Porter*

The main clause can be stated easily: "We walked on toward the prison." The next clause adds details about that walk. It could therefore be said to be at a lower level of generality, because it modifies the main clause. The second clause in turn is modified by still another clause: "for [because] the crowd was enormous and . . . silent, almost motionless. . . ." This third clause explains why they could not come nearer and works on a still lower level of generality. Another detail about the crowd itself is added by the phrase "in the dim light," which therefore works on the fourth, lowest level of generality, as does the remaining descriptive phrase "like crowds seen in a dream."

So we could schematize the whole sentence by printing it this way:

  (1) We walked on toward the prison,
      (2) coming as near as we could,
          (3) for the crowd was enormous and . . . silent, almost motionless,
             (4) in the dim light
             (4) like crowds seen in a dream.

Do you see how this rewriting of the sentence shows us the way Ms. Porter began with the main idea and then sharpened her description by adding phrases and clauses that supplied more details? In other words, do you see how the phrases numbered (4) give details about the clause numbered (3), how the clause numbered (3) gives details about the clause numbered (2), and how the clause numbered (2) gives details about the main clause (1)?

Apply this way of looking at sentences to some passages from professional writing and from your own writing. Such analyses will probably teach you an important truth: less-experienced writers do not use as many cumulative sentences as professionals, and when they do use them, their sentences usually do not go beyond two or at the most three levels of generality.

Having learned this truth, the next obvious step is practice. That means writing several different kinds of cumulative sentences, following as many patterns as possible—main clause, then adjective phrase, or noun or verb phrase, or any one of several types of clauses. Sometimes too a phrase or a clause might precede the main clause, with one or more clauses then following it. Try first to perfect writing on two levels of generality, then work on three or more. You might ask your instructor for further assistance.

> Practice and thought might gradually forge many an art.
> *Virgil*

One more word about the terminology used in A2–A4. Notice that *all* sentences must fall into one of the first four categories— i.e., simple, compound, complex, or compound-complex. But not all sentences can be categorized as coordinate or subordinate, cumulative or periodic. A simple sentence, for example, might be neither coordinate nor subordinate, neither cumulative nor periodic. These last four terms refer instead to *options* that writers can use to achieve greater variety in their sentences and to better express what they want to say.

A5. Repetition and Emphasis

While needless repetition has no place in good prose (as discussed in Chapter 1), some circumstances invite repetition and make it fruitful. Consider the following paragraph by Loren Eiseley, from *The Immense Journey*. In it he describes a dramatic moment in a forest glade. A group of sparrows has just watched helplessly as a young sparrow was eaten by a raven. Then:

> The sighing died. It was then I saw the judgment. It was the judgment of life against death. I will never see it again so forcefully presented. I will never hear it again in notes so tragically prolonged. For in the midst of protest, they forgot the violence. There, in that clearing, the crystal note of a song sparrow lifted hesitantly in the hush. And finally, after painful fluttering, another took the song, and then another, the song passing from one bird to another, doubtfully at first, as though some evil thing were being slowly forgotten. Till suddenly they took heart and sang from many throats joyously together as birds are known to sing. They sang because life is sweet and sunlight beautiful. They sang under the brooding shadow of the

raven. In simple truth they had forgotten the raven, for they were the singers of life, and not of death.

The number of repetitions here is remarkable. In case you missed some, these are the most obvious ones:

> It was then I saw the judgment. It was the judgment. . . .
> I will never see it again. . . . I will never hear it again. . . .
> so forcefully presented. . . . so tragically prolonged. . . .
> another took the song. . . . and then another. . . .
> they took heart and sang. . . . They sang. . . . They sang. . . .
> the singers of life. . . . and not of death.

Here repetition plays a valuable role. It heightens the drama of what was for Eiseley a very important moment, and it gives special emphasis to this paragraph as the climactic paragraph for a section of his book.

Be alert for ways in which you can use repetition as effectively as Eiseley. Here, for example, are two student sentences that drive home their message through artful repetition:

> Every day my environment grows colder: the weather grows colder, this room grows colder, the people grow colder, I even grow colder towards myself.

> Life allows for countless rich experiences if you are open to them, if you retain your youthful optimism, if you keep a light heart and never forget the potential brilliance of the present moment.

Do you see how these sentences are made more memorable, more insistent because of their repetition? See if there are ways your own sentences can profit from this technique. (At the same time you must bear in mind a corollary: repetition must be used sparingly, lest it call too much attention to itself.)

There are other patterns a good writer uses besides repetition of words or phrases. One pattern is based on the rhythm of our speech. It tries to provide repetition not of words or phrases but of *units of sound*, much like poetry does. Consider this sentence by John Ruskin in which he describes the onset of a rainstorm in an Alpine valley:

> And then you will hear the sudden rush of the awakened wind, and you will see those watchtowers of vapor swept away from their foundations, and waving curtains of opaque rain let down to the

valleys, swinging from the burdened clouds in black bending fringes, or pacing in pale columns along the lake level, grazing its surface into foam as they go.

There is one small use of word repetition here (". . . you will hear. . . , and you will see . . ."), but for the most part this sentence relies for its effectiveness on the rhythm that undergirds it and becomes apparent when you read it aloud. The nearly equal length of each of the separate units making up the sentence (twelve, thirteen, eleven, nine, nine, and eight words, respectively) gives us a sense of the rush of the storm as it sweeps through the valleys in great gusts of wind. This rhythm of sound is even augmented by other devices borrowed from poetry, devices like alliteration (using the same first consonant, as in "pacing . . . pale," "lake level").

Closer to home, here is a sentence in which a student writer describes her Grandpa's singing as she recalled it from her childhood:

> I would sit there listening to Grandma's sobs from the kitchen, and watch the tears of pain flow down Grandpa's cheeks, but his strong voice never faltered and his courage never failed.

Can you feel the rhythm of "his strong voice never faltered and his courage never failed"?

Achieving such rhythm is admittedly difficult, in part because it depends so much on "feel." But it is a goal worth keeping in mind.

A second pattern is more easily accomplished. Quite often in sentences we list items in a series, especially when making use of parallelism or repetition. In these circumstances it is important to arrange the items in a precise order, usually from least important to most important, as in this student-written example:

> My brother is petty, devious, sometimes even cruel.

Here the brother's three vices are arranged in ascending order, from least to most important. If you doubt the need for such a careful arrangement, consider an alternative version of the sentence:

> My brother is devious, cruel, sometimes even petty.

As you can see, the effect of the sentence is destroyed because the emphasis does not fall where it should. When you list items, make sure to order them for proper emphasis.

Speaking of emphasis, remember to put your sentences in the active voice whenever possible. Don't write a sentence like this one:

> The effects of his addiction are described by De Quincey in *The Confessions of an English Opium Eater.   student paper*

Instead write:

> De Quincey describes the effects of his addiction in *The Confessions of an English Opium Eater.*

It is not that the active voice is so good, but rather that the passive voice can dissipate the power of a sentence.

Sometimes, of course, the passive voice is unavoidable. But I had a history teacher in high school who thought that the passive voice was more "refined" than the active. Consequently his lectures to us would contain sentences like, "It will be learned by you for tomorrow what were the causes of the Punic Wars" or "Today the rise of the nation-state will be discussed by me." Take care that such weak, unemphatic sentences are avoided by you.

Part A seems to have been based on a paradox. On the one hand I said that you needed to achieve variety in your sentences, variety both in length and in type. On the other hand I also encouraged you to use certain repeated patterns, in words, rhythms, and word order, to give your prose a better emphasis. Paradoxes, however contradictory they may at first appear, do after all state a truth: in this case, the truth that writing good sentences means using both variety and pattern simultaneously.

This ability to live cheerfully with apparent contradiction is a sign of intellectual maturity. Our example drawn from writing is like the happy tension described by the Zen master Yao-shan. A young monk asked him, "What does one think about while meditating?"

"About nonthinking," Yao-shan replied.

"How does one think about nonthinking?" puzzled the monk.

"Through superthinking."

EXERCISES

1. In the following sentences, tell which words are: a. subjects$_1$,
b. subjects$_2$, c. complete verbs, and d. predicates.

a. A man without mirth is like a wagon without springs; he is
    jolted disagreeably by every pebble in the road.   *Henry Ward
    Beecher*
b. If you pick up a starving dog and make him prosperous, he
    will not bite you. This is the principal difference between a
    dog and a man.   *Mark Twain*
c. Education is what you have left over when you have forgot-
    ten everything you have learned.   *Anonymous*
d. Of his sentences perhaps not more than nine-tenths stand
    straight on their legs; the remainder are in quite angular
    attitudes, buttressed up by props [of parentheses and dash-
    es], and ever with this or the other tagrag hanging from
    them; a few even sprawling helplessly on all sides, quite
    broken-backed and dismembered.   *Thomas Carlyle*
e. Mighty is he who conquers himself.   *Lao Tzu*
f. God the first garden made, and the first city, Cain.   *Abraham
    Cowley*
g. An inhuman moralist I can no more endure than opium that
    has not been boiled.   *Thomas De Quincey*

2. Identify the following student-written sentences as simple,
compound, complex, compound-complex, cumulative, or
periodic. In some instances more than one term will apply.

a. Two ex-convicts brutally slaughtered an innocent family of
    four.
b. I always thought that life was too precious to waste on work.
c. I'm settled into my room now: clothes hung up, refrigerator
    plugged in, plants and posters all in place.
d. Freezing is one of the least-damaging food processing meth-
    ods, and many items could be free of additives if they were
    frozen.
e. I really intend, now that this case is over and my workload
    has lightened, to take my first extended vacation.
f. For four years I had to wear a coat and tie, and if a teacher
    saw me with my coat off he could give me demerits.

g. Their very number makes it difficult to identify potentially dangerous criminals.

h. Each area of the hospital establishes its own visiting hours within the general guidelines.

i. I found out that I was capable, that I had the knowledge and the confidence necessary for this job, despite what my boss thought.

j. Multiple-choice questions usually offer four possible answers.

3. Combine each of the following pairs of (mostly) simple sentences into one complex or compound-complex sentence. In other words, convert one of the sentences into a dependent clause and include it in the other sentence. Emphasize the more important idea and use the appropriate subordinating pronouns or conjunctions.

a. According to the "big bang" theory, the universe was formed by an explosion 10–20 billion years ago. This theory is now accepted by the scientific establishment.

b. Older people need contact with younger people. This is especially true when older people are confined to nursing homes.

c. Soon I was escorted to the back to meet "Mr. Raymond." "Mr. Raymond" was to cut my hair.

d. In South America there are many superstitions similar to those in North America. There are others that are different: spilling wine is good luck, leaving a broom upside-down in a corner will get rid of unwanted guests, rain on a wedding day is good luck.

e. The reason tv viewers get very frustrated watching sports events is not the failure of their favorite team. The reason is that their advice is not being followed by the coaches.

f. The province of Quebec is French-speaking. The province of Quebec is where there is talk of separating from the rest of Canada.

g. The school sent a nasty letter to your parents. This happened when you had "earned" more than twenty demerits.

h. Juan Carlos de Borbón was appointed chief of state by the Spanish dictator Francisco Franco. Juan Carlos is now king of Spain.

4. Study the following paragraph by E. B. White closely. Observe especially its variety in sentence length and in sentence type. Prepare a summary of your observations. The paragraph is from an essay called "A Slight Sound at Evening."

> There is also a woodchuck here, living forty feet away under the wharf. When the wind is right, he can smell my house; and when the wind is contrary, I can smell his. We both use the wharf for sunning, taking turns, each adjusting his schedule to the other's convenience. Thoreau once ate a woodchuck. I think he felt he owed it to his readers, and that it was little enough, considering the indignities they were suffering at his hands and the dressing-down they were taking. (Parts of Walden are pure scold.) Or perhaps he ate the woodchuck because he believed every man should acquire strict business habits, and the woodchuck was destroying his market beans. I do not know. Thoreau had a strong experimental streak in him. It is probably no harder to eat a woodchuck than to construct a sentence that lasts a hundred years. At any rate, Thoreau is the only writer I know who prepared himself for his great ordeal by eating a woodchuck; also the only one who got a hangover from drinking too much water. (He was drunk the whole time, though he seldom touched wine or coffee or tea.)

5. Convert the following clauses into cumulative sentences by adding words, phrases, and dependent clauses. You can use the three sentences on p. 88 as models.

EXAMPLE: the wind blew harder (clause)
             Suddenly the wind blew harder, pushing the tree limbs against the windowpanes, whining through the many cracks that I should have puttied the previous fall. [cumulative sentence—adds phrases and clause]

a. the rain fell heavily
b. it was a typical Saturday night
c. the cigarette burned slowly in the ashtray
d. some tv commercials are really bizarre
e. he looks like a 1930s gangster
f. everybody has a secret ambition

g. movies have offered many unintended lessons
h. she smiled
i. most politicians love the sight of a large crowd
j. the pain was unbearable
k. every family has at least one colorful ancestor

6. The following passages are monotonous, dull. Rewrite them. Use coordination and subordination to show the connections between ideas.

a. My most important vacation memory is of my cousin Bud. Bud was tall, dark-haired. He grabbed me in his huge hands. He lifted me high into the air. He planted a kiss on my cheek. The kiss was itchy. His moustache was prickly. This was at the time we first met. My heart was his from that moment on. In the next few days he took my sister and me shopping. He took us to the movies. He took us to the county fair. My father said I was too young for pierced ears. My mother insisted growing girls had to eat their beets. Bud stuck up for me in those quarrels. That vacation lasted only five days. Bud is the only memory left. The reason is the way he seemed larger than life. I was a highly impressionable ten-year-old.

b. In high school I was a jock. I didn't like the image. I especially didn't like being considered dumb. I tried to fight the image. It was hard. After all I still played football. Events have a way of tripping you up. During one game I was playing offensive guard. This was in my junior year. On a certain play the guard is supposed to "pull." He is supposed to block the defensive tackle on the other side of the ball. Meanwhile the other guard is supposed to block the nose-man. The nose-man is the defensive player opposite the center. I got confused. I pulled to block the tackle. I should have stayed to block the nose-man. The other guard did his job correctly. This of course made him run straight into me. THUNK! Down I went. My teammates were groaning. The coaches were screaming. Two thousand spectators were roaring with laughter. Suppose I wanted to find a good way of showing how stupid jocks were. I could not have found a better way than this.

Practice is the best of all instructors.
Publius

7. Rewrite the following paragraphs in order to give them more variety in sentence structure. Make any other improvements you can.

a. All my life people have called me by some name other than my own. I was called "Pat" by my first grade teacher. She confused me with my sister Pat. I had to endure this mixup all through grammar school and high school. Even at times people I went to school with called me "Pat." I don't see why they would confuse us, because we look nothing alike. Even now in my new job this still happens to me. I have been working at the same place for over eight months. You would think the other employees would know me by now. I am called "Linda," or "Cheryl," but never Nancy. You would think they could remember who I am, because I don't look at all like Linda or Cheryl. I guess I should start wearing a name tag.

b. I am an incurable junk collector. The best example of this is my bedroom. On every available space are statues, bottles, stuffed animals, and assorted knickknacks. Relatives or friends mention something they gave me ten or more years ago. I go into my room and find it, much to their amazement. People ask me if my room gets too crowded or if I lose anything. I say no, it is only the dusting I find difficult.

c. The future of the U.S. economy does not look good. This is because we will probably have both inflation and a slow growth. The reason for this pessimistic view is government regulation. In the last decade we have spent too much money and not saved enough. We have spent a lot of money on government projects and on Arab oil imports. We have not saved enough, so there is not enough money to invest in future projects. The United States needs new policies to correct these ills. Such new policies might include removing limits on the interest that banks can pay on savings accounts. Another policy might be to encourage energy conservation by new taxes.

8. Review the most recent paper you have turned in, as suggested on pp. 76–77. Do you find that your paper reflects the observations on p. 77 about lack of variety in sentence length and sentence type? If so, rewrite one page of the paper, incorporating the suggestions for variety contained in this section.

9. Study the use of repetition in the following paragraph by Joan Didion, from *Slouching Towards Bethlehem*. Prepare a short summary of what you observe.

This is a story about love and death in the golden land, and begins with the country. The San Bernardino Valley lies only an hour east of Los Angeles by the San Bernardino Freeway but is in certain ways an alien place: not the coastal California of the subtropical twilights and the soft westerlies off the Pacific but a harsher California, haunted by the Mojave just beyond the mountains, devastated by the hot dry Santa Ana wind that comes down through the passes at 100 miles an hour and whines through the eucalpytus windbreaks and works on the nerves. October is the bad month for the wind, the month when breathing is difficult and the hills blaze up spontaneously. There has been no rain since April. Every voice seems a scream. It is the season of suicide and divorce and prickly dread, wherever the wind blows.

10. Revise the following sentences for greater emphasis.

a. As the storm grew more violent the wheel was gripped tightly by his sweaty hands.
b. With a fury stemming from both pain and rage, "Damn you!" she screamed.
c. Some messages are being sent by the subconscious to the conscious mind and the subconscious represses other messages.
d. "Say it now!" was the one overriding thought I had in mind.
e. Chuckles, outright laughter, and smiles greeted the opening sentence of his campaign speech.
f. The fish was netted by Dustin, trembling with eagerness, and swung up and into the boat.
g. The differences are many; in some instances they are fundamental.

11. Discuss the use of emphasis in the following passage by L. E. Sissman, from " 'Into the Air, Junior Birdmen!' "

Detroit, summer, 1938. A spun-gold Sunday morning. In my small, north-facing bedroom, I wake slowly to the Sunday sounds.

Big yellow Detroit Street Railway trolleys trundle infrequently by, a high, electric hum above the fierce metallic screech of the wheels upon the rails. A few early cars shift and start off from the Warren Avenue lights. Over on the polyglot East Side, a hundred various Catholic churches, Slavic churches, Scandinavian churches flung up by homesick immigrants begin their solemn monody of calling the faithful—and the habituated—to Mass or service. And then, faint but clear above the choirs of bells, comes the unignorable whine of a single-engined airplane. I slip out of bed, whip on my spectacles, and, after some drawing and quartering of the sky, descry a plane high over the Hotel Palmetto, Residential Rates. It is a Stinson monoplane, and the pilot, perhaps purely for his pleasure, is executing a series of shallow, lazy dives and zooms.

12. Study the following three passages closely. Observe how the authors achieve variety through coordination and subordination, periodic and cumulative sentences, repetition, and emphasis. Write one-paragraph summaries of what you observe about each passage.

a. There is a rumor that the National Winter Garden Burlesque has fallen a victim to the current purity wave and been obliged to abate the Aristophanic license for which it was formerly celebrated. The management of the National Winter Garden (not the Broadway Winter Garden, of course, but the one at Second Avenue and Houston Street) has been kind enough to supply the *New Republic* with a season pass, and, as the result of a recent visit, the writer of these notes is happy to announce that this report is entirely without foundation and to recommend the Minsky Brothers' Follies as still among the most satisfactory shows in town. The great thing about the National Winter Garden is that, though admittedly as vulgar as possible, it has nothing of the peculiar smartness and hardness one is accustomed to elsewhere in New York. It is refreshing because it lies quite outside the mechanical routine of Broadway. Though more ribald, it is more honest and less self-conscious than the ordinary risqué farce and, though crude, on the whole more attractive than most of the hideous comic-supplement humors of uptown revue and vaudeville. Nor is it to be confounded with the uptown burlesque show of the type of the Columbia, which is now as wholesome and as boring as any expensive musical comedy. The National Winter Garden has a tradition and a vein of its own.   *Edmund Wilson, The Shores of Light*

b. There is no suggestion, however, that he draws the gun reluctantly. The Westerner could not fulfill himself if the moment did not finally come when he can shoot his enemy down. But because that moment is so thoroughly the expression of his being, it must be kept pure. He will not violate the accepted forms of combat though by doing so he could save a city. And he can wait. "When you call me that—smile!"—the villain smiles weakly, soon he is laughing with horrible joviality, and the crisis is past. But it is allowed to pass because it must come again: sooner or later Trampas will "make his play," and the Virginian will be ready for him. *Robert Warshow, "The Westerner"*

c. Whenever anything alarming happened to the landward side—or sometimes just because it was getting so hot—she would go back into the water, up to her waist, or even up to her neck. This meant, of course, that she had to walk upright on her two hind legs. It was slow and ungainly, especially at first, but it was absolutely essential if she wanted to keep her head above water. She isn't the only creature who has ever had to learn to do it. Although, as we have seen, she is almost unique in having learned to walk upright all the time, there is another mammal who does it for part of the time, and probably for the same reason. The beaver, whose ancestors also spent a good deal of time in shallow water, whenever she is transporting building materials or carrying her baby around, has the habit of getting up on her hind legs and proceeding by means of a perfectly serviceable bipedal gait.   *Elaine Morgan, The Descent of Woman*

B. CORRECTING SENTENCE PROBLEMS

> Who errs and mends,
> To God himself commends.
> *Cervantes*

Can you recall hearing a young child recite one of his first poems? Usually it goes something like this:

My mom loves tea
My mom loves me
And sometimes she gets a little too picky.

Good poems they are, too—direct, warm, and candid. When we think of them as *poetry,* however, they jar. Like the example above, such poems will have too many syllables in some of the lines, or they will change rhythmic patterns, or the rhymes won't quite rhyme. In short, these poems will strike us as a little "wrong."

So too with sentences. Sometimes, quite unintentionally, when we don't have quite the right arrangement of words in a sentence, it sounds "wrong." The result is confusion for your readers. Remember, they rely solely on the conventions of the sentence to give order to and help them make sense of what they read. When confusion occurs in a paper you write for one of your classes, the paper is likely to come back with a sentence or sentences marked for revision, perhaps by means of symbols like *frag, coh, shift,* and *awk.* This section can help you interpret these symbols. Its purpose is to explain how to find out what is wrong with a sentence and what kind of changes you should make.

B1. Sentence Fragments

The first of these problems is perhaps the most obvious and is certainly one of the most frequent. The reason your problem sentence distracted your reader may be that what you have written is not really a sentence after all. Perhaps instead it is a sentence fragment, often abbreviated by the symbol *Frag.* A sentence fragment, as its name implies, is a part—a fragment—of a full sentence. For example, the subject and/or the verb might be missing, as in this student-written example:

FRAGMENT: What agnosticism means to those who profess it.
REVISION: I wonder what agnosticism means to those who profess it.

Or maybe the form of the verb is not the complete form necessary for a sentence, as in this example from a student paper:

FRAGMENT: Liberalism giving way to conservatism in today's world.
REVISION: Liberalism is giving [gives, will give] way to conservatism in today's world.

In student writing, fragments most commonly occur with sentences beginning with subordinating conjunctions like *since*, *because*, and *although*. You will remember from pp. 80–81 that these conjunctions signal the beginning of a subordinate, i.e., dependent clause, one that cannot stand by itself. We therefore expect that this dependent clause will be accompanied by a complete, *independent* one, since each sentence must have at least one independent clause. If no independent clause is present, the result is a sentence fragment, as in this example from a student paper.

FRAGMENT: Since self-confidence begins with self-respect.
REVISION: Since self-confidence begins with self-respect, we must value our own achievements.

Now I must emphasize to you right away that sentence fragments are not always wrong. Our everyday speech abounds in them: *Ready to go? Sure.* So when you record that speech on paper, in the form of dialogue, naturally you will use fragments often. Fragments are also common in much of modern advertising copy:

Élan. Spirit. Dash. Animation. Characteristic of this Blazer as of all Christian Dior clothing. Styled to project the personality of the individual . . . to make you feel like no one else . . . to underscore your own *élan*.

Furthermore good writers often use fragments to achieve special effects:

Rain all night until dawn. No sleep. Christ, here we go, a nightmare of mud and madness. . . .   *Hunter Thompson*

Finally, we are accustomed to fragments used as transitions: *Now for my last point.* . . .

If fragments are so common, so much a part of what we read every day, and if their use can be perfectly appropriate, you might begin to wonder, "What's the problem?" Perhaps your paper has one or more sentences your instructor has labelled *frag* or *fragment*, and you are not sure why you cannot do once or twice what professional writers do all the time.

The answer is that fragments are exceptions to normal sentence structure. Like all exceptions, they can be used only with good reason. Two good reasons stand out as justifications for fragments. The first is that we expect fragments in certain spe-

cial circumstances like dialogue, transitions, and advertisements. I would be willing to bet that what your instructor circled
on your paper was neither dialogue nor a transitional device nor
advertising copy. The second good reason is the creation of a
special effect, so long as the reader has no trouble filling in the
missing parts of the sentence. By noting the fragment on your
paper, your instructor probably is saying either that he or she
does not see how you have created any special effect or that the
missing parts of your sentence cannot be reconstructed easily.
So, since neither of these two "good reasons" applies to your
sentence, it would be better if you had not made an exception to
the normal pattern.

If you are still in doubt about whether your use of a fragment
was legitimate or not, a good test is to ask yourself this question:
did you know you were using a fragment at the time you were
writing it? If you did, and your use of it was deliberate, maybe
you have a case. But nineteen fragments out of twenty are used
unconsciously. If your problem sentences were written this way,
you probably should read through this section very carefully.

Also there are degrees of permissibility among sentence
fragments. Fragments in recorded dialogue, for example, are
hardly ever wrong. At the other extreme, fragments that result
from using an improper verb form are hardly ever right. Between these extremes are countless fragments, each of which
must be judged on its own merits. Regarding this grey area,
remember that professional writers have made these decisions
hundreds of times. Because of their wide reading and their experience, they can usually make tactful choices. You have less
experience in such matters, and therefore you are better off
playing the percentages. A complete sentence is never wrong; a
fragment might be. If there is any doubt, be safe for now and
avoid the fragment. Then, as you gain more experience in writing, you will find yourself making occasional use of fragments,
but you will do so with the self-assurance born of long practice.

> The privileges of a few do not make common law.
> *St. Jerome*

Let's review again some examples of common sentence fragments. Try to clarify in your own mind what fragments are and

what should be done about them. The first and probably most frequent type of sentence fragment, as I mentioned before, is the dependent clause that stands alone. Here is a passage from a student journal, a sentence followed by a sentence fragment:

> I worry about whether I will get a job. Although I am convinced that new opportunities will open up before the end of spring.

The reason this kind of fragment is encountered so often is that it looks deceptively like a complete sentence. It has a subject ("I") and a complete verb form ("am convinced"), and it is readily understandable to the reader. The only reason it needs to be revised is that it is a dependent clause, since it begins with a subordinating conjunction ("Although . . ."). One good solution is to attach it to—or make it depend upon—the preceding sentence.

> I worry about whether I will get a job, although I am convinced that new opportunities will open up before the end of spring.

Alternatively, the fragment can be expanded into a complete sentence by adding a new independent clause.

> I worry about whether I will get a job. Although I am convinced that new opportunities will open up before the end of spring, I still can't help being anxious about my prospects.

Either way, the dependent clause is now attached to an independent clause and the fragment is eliminated. (The *meaning* of the two revisions of course is different.) For further reference, consult the section of this chapter on subordination, p. 80.

The second type of fragment is similar to the first. It occurs when the writer uses a phrase rather than an independent clause, in other words when he or she omits the subject and/or the predicate, as in this example from a student journal (a sentence plus a fragment):

> In physical appearance I look like many other teenagers. With my eyes brown, my hair black.

This second type of fragment is a little easier to identify than the first because it does not resemble a complete sentence so closely. Here the fragment has no verb and perhaps not even a subject (we are not sure of the function of "eyes" or "hair"). The remedies for this type of fragment are also similar, such as including the phrase in a preceding sentence or attaching it to a newly created subject and verb.

> In physical appearance, with my brown eyes and black hair, I look like many other teenagers.

> In physical appearance I look like many other teenagers. I have brown eyes and black hair.

A third type of fragment results from using an inappropriate verb form, thereby leaving the sentence without a complete predicate. Here is another example of a sentence followed by a fragment, from a newspaper letter.

> Politicians fear newspapers. Knowing the power of the written word.

"Knowing" is inappropriate because verb forms with the *-ing* ending do not constitute complete verbs (see pp. 68–69). In other words, they cannot form predicates on their own. For example, *knew, will know,* and *know* are complete verb forms; in the revision, the complete verb form *know* should be chosen because it is in the present tense and therefore corresponds to the tense of the earlier sentence. Also, the subject ("politicians") should be represented by a pronoun *(they):*

> Politicians fear newspapers. They know the power of the written word.

If this kind of fragment occurs frequently in your writing, and especially if the nature of this type of error is not immediately clear to you, the chances are that the real difficulty is not the fragment, even though your paper might be marked that way. Instead the problem is most likely a weak grasp of verb forms. Verb forms are a very important matter, and I'd suggest you review the section on them in Chapter 6 (pp. 350–354).

A final type of fragment usually results from the writer's momentary confusion, as in this example from a student journal:

> Terry, who claims that he really worries about passing calculus, nevertheless playing bridge in the union rather than getting ready for the midterm.

Here the writer identified his subject ("Terry"), then got going on a perfectly good dependent clause. When the time came to return to the main clause he forgot that he had not yet provided a complete predicate and went on to compose a phrase of the sort described in the preceding paragraph (here "playing bridge in the union"). One way to solve the problem would be to add a complete verb form for the predicate:

> Terry, who claims that he really worries about passing calculus, nevertheless *wastes* several hours each day playing bridge in the union rather than getting ready for the midterm.

Alternatively, you could revise the phrase so that it contains a complete verb and forms an independent clause:

> Terry, who claims that he really worries about passing calculus, nevertheless *plays* bridge in the union rather than getting ready for the midterm.

Haste and inadequate proofreading are normally the cause of the kind of sentence fragment we've been discussing. A simple practical solution is to ignore all dependent clauses and other extraneous elements as you reread each of your sentences; check just the subject-predicate "heart" of the main clause and see if it is capable of standing by itself as a complete sentence. Had the writer of the previous example followed this procedure, he would have seen this: "Terry . . . playing bridge in the union." Immediately the difficulty would have been apparent.

Sentence fragments are very common in student writing. If you need help in this area, be assured you are far from alone. Let me summarize for you a six-stage "cure": 1. reread the preceding paragraphs on fragments; 2. examine the four common types of improper sentence fragments described and make sure you know *why* each example needs to be changed; 3. when you do not understand why a change is necessary, consult the other cross-referenced entries in this handbook that give background information; 4. study the sentence fragments your instructor has identified in your papers, noting which of the four types they seem to resemble; 5. rewrite your own sentence fragments as complete sentences; 6. for further practice, write the exercises given on pp. 123–124. Your prose should be healthy in no time. If your fragments do not fit one of the four types discussed here, or if you are still not sure about some points, ask your instructor for additional suggestions.

B2. Fused Sentences

If your instructor has noted that your paper has a "fused sentence," sometimes abbreviated as *fus* or *f s,* probably you have written a sentence that in its structure looks like this one:

> The lovers will meet in a turret on the ruins of an ancient city the time chosen for the poem is the moment just before they catch sight of each other.   *student paper*

Actually the term "fused sentence" (singular) is misleading, because there are really two sentences here rather than one. After all there are two noun subjects$_1$ ("lovers" and "time"), two verbs ("will meet" and "is"), and the other components that would be necessary for two separate, independent sentences. The problem is that there is no punctuation mark or transition word between them (i.e., between "city" and "the"), as there must be if these are two independent units.

To eliminate a fused sentence, you can use a period and capitalization to preserve the idea of two separate independent sentences:

> The lovers will meet in a turret on the ruins of an ancient city. The time chosen for the poem is the moment just before they catch sight of each other.

A semicolon would keep them as a single sentence and still allow the two units to be separate:

> The lovers will meet in a turret on the ruins of an ancient city; the time chosen for the poem is the moment just before they catch sight of each other.

Still a third possibility is to combine the two units:

> The lovers will meet in the turret on the ruins of an ancient city, the poem beginning just at the moment before they catch sight of each other.

This last alternative, because it involves the creation of a sentence modifier (see p. 343), is not the easiest choice, but under some circumstances it might be the best.

Of course you may understand all of this perfectly well, and the fused sentence on your paper might be the result of simple carelessness. If so, you know the remedy as well as I do. But if you made the mistake in all innocence, and especially if you are not sure even now exactly what is wrong, the problem may be a rather serious one. Perhaps you are not yet familiar with the structure of a complete sentence. Under this circumstance I would urge you to look at pp. 65–70 on sentence structure, pp. 386–389 on punctuating the end of sentences, and pp. 137–141 on transition words.

B3. Shifts

Sentences are expected to have a certain logic to them, to be consistent from one part of the sentence to another. But sometimes that consistency is lacking, because the writer has used one grammatical form in the first part of the sentence and then without good reason has shifted to another grammatical form later in the sentence. We need to examine five kinds of such shifts: shifts of tense, voice, and mood, which have to do with verbs, and shifts of person and number, which have to do with pronouns.

A shift of tense, often abbreviated on papers by *t, tense, tnse,* and *shift,* occurs when your sentence has two or more verb forms that logically ought to be consistent with one another but are not. Consider this example from a student paper:

> We were just coming out of the drugstore when suddenly he is standing there right in front of me, staring at me.

The first verb is "were coming," and it describes a continuing action in the past. The verb of the second clause, "is standing," describes an action that happened at the same time—the "coming" and the "standing" occur simultaneously. Yet the tense of the second clause shifts. Instead of describing a continuing past action, as "were coming" did, it describes a continuing present action, "is standing." So what the sentence needs is to have the unintended shift eliminated by making the tense of the two verbs the same, either both in the past or both in the present:

> We were just coming out of the drugstore when suddenly he was standing there right in front of me, staring at me.

> We are just coming out of the drugstore when suddenly he is standing there right in front of me, staring at me.

Please notice two important cautions about shifts in tense.

1. A simple change in tense is not wrong. Many sentences change tenses quite properly, as in this example:

   > I have known many young people who, particularly in late adolescence, come to a belief in magic, to compensate for their having been deprived of it prematurely in childhood.   *Bruno Bettelheim*

   The difference is that in this case our sense of time has not been violated. The verb of each clause has the tense appropriate to express the time of the action described in the clause.

2. Keeping the tenses the same throughout a sentence does not guarantee the sentence will be consistent. Can you see what is wrong with this example?

   > I was thoroughly exhausted after supper because I worked hard all afternoon.

   "Was" and "worked" are the same tense—and therein lies the problem, because clearly the working had taken place *before* the state of exhaustion, had in fact caused the state of exhaustion. Our revised sentence corrects this unintended shift by putting the second clause further back in time:

   > I was thoroughly exhausted after supper because I had worked hard all afternoon.

So keep aware of the *time logic* of your sentences. Make sure that the tense of any verb is the logical tense for that verb when it is seen in relation to the tense of other verbs. Be especially careful about sentences that shift from the past tense to the present, like our first example above. These are the most frequent sources of confusion. Here is another example to help you clinch your understanding of this point:

> I dropped my quarter into the machine but nothing comes out.

Because these two events happened at the same time, there is no reason to shift from past tense to present. Therefore "comes" should be *came:*

> I dropped my quarter into the machine but nothing came out.

> When it is not necessary to change, it is necessary not to change.
>
> *Lord Falkland*

Shifts in voice or mood occur less frequently. Shifts in voice happen when part of a sentence is in the active voice and part of it is in the passive—when there should be parallel construction:

> Although we formed a committee to study the problem, the observation was made by all of us that such a committee would not provide any easy solutions. *faculty memo*

Technically this sentence is grammatically correct. But there is no good reason for shifting from the active voice ("formed") to the passive ("was made"). Since it is generally better to avoid the passive, as discussed on p. 93, putting the verbs in the active voice would improve the sentence:

> Although we formed a committee to study the problem, we all observed that such a committee would not provide any easy solutions.

A shift in mood arises when a sentence begins in one mood—e.g., declarative (a statement)—and then changes to another—e.g., interrogative (a question). Here is an example from a newspaper letter:

> The Carter Administration intends to discourage gas-guzzlers by taxing them heavily, and what is this going to accomplish?

The first half of this sentence, up to the comma, is declarative: it makes a statement. The second half is interrogative: it asks a question. But changes in mood can occur only between sentences, not within the same sentence. The writer should make these two halves into separate sentences or at the very least replace the comma with a semicolon.

> The Carter Administration intends to discourage gas-guzzlers by taxing them heavily. What is this going to accomplish?

Pronouns can cause aggravation too. (Abbreviations for pronoun errors can include *shift, pro* or *pron, ref, number, person*.) In fact the most frequent shift of all for most writers involves pronouns, and that is the unintended shift in number. In such cases one part of a sentence will refer to a singular person or thing, and a different part of the sentence will refer to the same person or thing in the plural. For example:

> Sometimes a customer will barge right to the front of the line, and then they demand immediate service, as if they had been waiting all day.

"Customer" (singular) is the subject₁, but the pronoun "they" is used to refer to it. Such a shift from one number to the other within the same sentence should be removed, like this:

> Sometimes customers will barge right to the front of the line, and then they demand immediate service, as if they had been waiting for hours.

Alternatively, of course, "customer" could be kept singular and the pronouns could be made singular as well.

Because this kind of shift is so frequent, we should look at another student-written example:

> The adoptee would know not only more about his genealogy but also more about themselves and how they function.

Do you see that the writer of this sentence first considered "adoptee" in the singular ("adoptee," "his") but then shifted the pronoun number to the plural ("themselves," "they")?

By now you can probably guess that a shift in person means an unnecessary change in the person of a pronoun from one part of a sentence to another. For example, this sentence, from a magazine article:

> A good hiker puts in maybe thirty miles a day, and by then you really know the meaning of the word *tired*.

This is a compound sentence. The first independent clause describes hikers in the third person, but the second independent clause, in referring to those same hikers, uses the second-person pronoun *you*. Again either of two revisions is possible, so long as the writer is consistent:

> A good hiker puts in maybe thirty miles a day, and by then he or she really knows the meaning of the word *tired*.

> On a good day's hike you put in maybe thirty miles, and by then you really know the meaning of the word *tired*.

> All good writing is like swimming under water and holding
> your breath.
>
> *F. Scott Fitzgerald*

The important thing to remember about all these kinds of shifts is the ultimate goal: consistency. If you can become aware of the need for this consistency—if you can see, for example, how logic demands that verb tenses be related to one another according to the times when various events have taken place—then you will help the reader by making such distinctions clear. In the meantime, while you are developing this awareness, correct those shifts that instructors or other readers call to your attention.

B4. Mixed Constructions

Shifts are not the only source of illogicality in sentences; sometimes confusion arises when a writer begins a sentence with one kind of construction and then later uses another kind incompatible with the first. The result is called a mixed construction, often abbreviated *mis, mixed,* or *coh[erence]*. An example would be a sentence like the following one from a student paper:

> By the look in his eye and the way he twisted his hands provided
> evidence enough of his guilt.

The problem here is that the sentence opens with a phrase and then proceeds directly to the verb, "provided." Because the phrase is a long one and because it includes a clause within it, the writer forgot that after all it was still just a phrase and that no proper subject$_1$ had yet been stated. The sentence must be revised so that the phrase has a subject$_1$ it can modify; in this case the subject becomes the pronoun "we":

> By the look in his eye and the way he twisted his hands we had
> evidence enough of his guilt.

Perhaps a better alternative is to convert the phrase itself into a proper subject:

> The look in his eye and the way he twisted his hands provided
> evidence enough of his guilt.

Just as a dependent phrase cannot be a subject by itself, neither can a dependent clause:

> Because your vitamin intake decreases makes dieting a danger to your health.   *student paper*

Again the writer could provide a subject[1] that the dependent clause can modify:

> Because your vitamin intake decreases, dieting can be a danger to your health.

Or, the clause can be made into a noun plus a phrase:

> The decrease in your vitamin intake makes dieting a danger to your health.

Forms of the verb *to be* cause their own special set of difficulties. The verb *to be* is a linking verb. Therefore it sets up an equation: the subject is said to be in some way the same as the complement, i.e., the noun or adjective that follows the linking verb. Occasionally the subject is mistakenly linked, not to a complement that can be equivalent to the subject, but rather to an adverb clause. This is particularly true of adverb clauses introduced by *where* or *when*, as in these two student-written examples:

> Revenge is where you make another person suffer for what he has done to you.

> The highest honor this country can bestow is when the president awards the Medal of Freedom.

Such sentences need revision because adverb clauses are usually supposed to modify verbs, and in these cases they do not modify the verb "is" but instead try to serve as complements. So a legitimate complement—a noun or an adjective—must be used in place of the clause:

> Revenge is the act of making another person suffer for what he has done to you.

> The highest honor this country can bestow is the Medal of Freedom awarded by the president.

The necessary equation has now been established: "Revenge" = "act," "honor" = "Medal."

The *is where* and *is when* constructions have a close relative, *the reason is because*, found in sentences like the following:

> The reason many people file their income tax forms too late is because they fail to plan far enough ahead. *newspaper item*

"Reason" needs a genuine complement after the linking verb "is":

> The reason many people file their income tax forms too late is their failure to plan far enough ahead.

"Reason" = "failure" and the equation is restored.

B5. Omitted Words

Sometimes necessary words are left out of a sentence through simple neglect. Perhaps you are writing swiftly and your mind is flying ahead of your fingers, so that you think the word but your pen fails to record it. Or perhaps as you type up the final copy of a handwritten draft you skip past a word in the draft. The result might be a sentence that is clear to the reader even though a word has been omitted:

> The president's economic advisors, no matter what their plans, must face the inevitability congressional revision. *magazine article*

Immediately we recognize that the word *of* has been inadvertently left out of its proper position before "congressional" and must be restored.

In other sentences, however, the omitted word may not be so obvious, and the meaning of the sentence will then be unclear. This, for example:

> Some of the amendment's feel that the prospects for E.R.A. this year are very shaky indeed. *newspaper item*

We know that a plural noun has been left out after "amendment's." But what noun? Perhaps the word is *supporters, defenders,* or *proponents;* then again it might be *opponents* or *enemies.*

The only solution for such mistakes is careful proofreading. But another category of omitted words is even more troublesome and probably would not be eliminated in the proofreading stage. This category usually illustrates Alexander Pope's statement that "a little learning is a dangerous thing." For example, a writer may know that the following sentence is quite proper even when the bracketed words "who have" are removed:

> Volunteers who have given more than five hours of their time or [who have] contributed more than $10 are entitled to go to the annual banquet.   *newsletter*

The reason the second "who have" combination can be dropped is that its presence is understood—in other words, the reader sees the paired verbs "given" and "contributed" and knows that "who have" applies to them both.

Occasionally, however, the tense of these paired verbs might change. When the tense changes, both verbs must be written out in their entirety. Should part of one be omitted, as "who have" was omitted above, the result is a sentence like this one:

> Medicine has and always will attract people concerned just with making money.   *student paper*

The writer of this sentence assumed that, since a form of *attract* is the verb in both cases, one auxiliary can be left out as understood. But it can't, because the change in tense from past ("has") to future ("will") means that the form of the verb *attract* must also change—*has attracted* for the past, *will attract* for the future. The sentence should read like this:

> Medicine has always attracted and will always attract people concerned just with making money.

Prepositions can cause similar difficulties. It is quite all right to eliminate one of two prepositions used with a compound verb or with two adjectives, *if* the preposition would be the same in both cases:

> I am astounded [by] and even outraged by Young's off-handedness.   *tv interview*

Since "by" goes with both adjectives—"astounded by" and "outraged by"—the first "by" is unnecessary. But verbs and adjectives often have specific prepositions associated with them. For example we say we are charmed *by* people, but we can also be interested *in*, attracted *to*, or angry *with* them. If a writer uses two verbs or two adjectives, and if the appropriate prepositions are different in each case, then both prepositions must be written. If one is omitted, the result is this kind of sentence:

> The framers of Proposition 13 are dedicated and working for the overthrow of our entire taxation system. *newspaper letter*

The preposition "for" goes with "working" all right, but not with "dedicated." The preposition *to* must be used with "dedicated," so the sentence should read:

> The framers of Proposition 13 are dedicated to and working for the overthrow of our entire taxation system.

One final type: can you see what has been mistakenly omitted from these two student-written comparisons?

> Tuition here costs no less than any other private university.
>
> American small cars like the Chevette are now as economical if not more economical than the imports.

These comparisons are not as precisely worded as they should be. The first sentence, if taken literally, says that tuition costs less than university, which does not make sense. In the second sentence, "than" goes quite well with "more economical." It cannot also be appropriate for "as economical" *(as economical than?)*. Yet the absence of any other word after "as economical" implies that *than* is understood. When the omitted words are inserted, the comparisons become exact:

> Tuition here costs no less than it does at any other private university.
>
> American small cars like the Chevette are now as economical as, if not more economical than, the imports.

B6. Lack of Parallel Structure

If two or more parts of a sentence have the same function, the structure of these parts should be the same, in other words parallel. Consider this student-written sentence:

> My philosophy is rooted in the idea of equality and realizing that each person has his or her own strengths and weaknesses.

If you examine that sentence carefully you will see that the word "idea" and the word "realizing" serve the same function. Both are objects of "is rooted in": in other words, "is rooted in the idea" and "is rooted in realizing." But "idea" and "realizing" are not parallel in structure, because the former is a noun and the latter is an *-ing* word, or gerund. While each by itself would be a perfectly appropriate form, when they are used jointly they must be parallel. Therefore the sentence needs to be changed. The best choice is to make "realizing" into its noun form *realization*, so that "is rooted in" has two nouns as its objects:

> My philosophy is rooted in the idea of equality and the realization that each person has his or her own strengths and weaknesses.

Another possibility is to use two *-ing* words as the objects and then to make both clauses similar in form:

> My philosophy is rooted in believing that all people are equal and realizing that each person has his or her own strengths and weaknesses.

As you can see, this second possibility, while correct, does not read quite as well.

Be especially careful of the need for parallelism when you use *-ing* words, infinitives (see the glossary for a definition of *infinitive*), and adjectives. The following three sentences illustrate the proper use of parallelism in such cases:

> Older people *walking* city streets or *taking* public transportation are particularly vulnerable to this type of crime.   *newspaper item*
>
> *To* die, *to* sleep—perchance *to* dream.   *William Shakespeare*
>
> Movie stars are no longer always *handsome*, *virile*, and *diffident*.   *magazine article*

Most writers experience their greatest temptation in those sentences like our first example, where the form of any one of the nonparallel parts would be satisfactory if used alone. Here is another example:

> In tennis, I like volleying and to hit the big serve.   *student journal*

Both of the following sentences are acceptable:

> In tennis, I like volleying.
>
> In tennis, I like to hit the big serve.

The trick is in seeing that when they are used together the sentence has parallel construction:

In tennis, I like volleying and hitting the big serve.

In tennis, I like to volley and to hit the big serve.

Two final examples from student papers may clinch the point.

NOT PARALLEL: The advantages of capital punishment are twofold: 1. those who are truly beyond help will not be allowed back out to commit more crimes; 2. so people will think of the consequences before committing a serious crime.

REVISION: The advantages of capital punishment are twofold: 1. those who are truly beyond help will not be allowed back out to commit more crimes; 2. people will think of the consequences before committing a serious crime.

In the revision, the dependent clause "so people will think . . ." is changed to an independent clause, "people will think. . ."; thus both advantages are stated as independent clauses.

NOT PARALLEL: The foreman was curt, irritable, and a man to be feared.

REVISION: The foreman was curt, irritable, and fear-inspiring.

Remember that there is no single "right" way to revise nonparallel sentence structures. In the last example, for instance, you could avoid the awkwardness of creating an adjective out of the phrase "a man to be feared" by making it function differently:

The foreman was curt and irritable, altogether a man to be feared.

The point is simply that like function always requires like structure.

B7. Awkward or Confusing Sentences

This final category of sentence problems is the hardest to define. In B1–B6 we dealt mainly with sentences that might have been understandable to the reader but that contained some errors in structure. In this case we are talking about sentences for which the reader's reaction can be summed up in just one word: *H-u-u-h-h-h?* Your instructor might signal his or her own *h-u-u-h-h-h?* by using symbols like *awk* or *awkward*, *conf*[*using*], *coh*, *illog*, or maybe just a plain question mark.

When the meaning of a sentence is not clear, one of the reasons, as we saw in Chapter 1, might be the choice of words. But sometimes the sentence itself may be at fault. Consider this example from a student's paper:

> Some scientists claim marijuana causes nausea and dizziness, but the user of marijuana comes nowhere near resembling these effects.

At first reading the sentence is illogical. How can a user resemble an effect? After a moment's thought we can see what happened. Two possible ways of expressing her meaning occurred to our writer:

> . . . but the user of marijuana does not experience these effects.

> . . . but the real effects of marijuana come nowhere near resembling the effects described by scientists.

Because the two possibilities probably came to her simultaneously, they were combined into one hybrid sentence. Either of the original possibilities by itself would be fine. But a combination of them confuses us.

A similar confusion can also result from undue haste in determining what structure a sentence should have. Here is one example:

> Another question about the Chappaquiddick party is why the men who were married were their wives not there.

The writer evidently plunged into the sentence without giving sufficient thought to the possible complications. Her ideas are all there, but they need to be sorted out. As it stands now the last clause says literally that the men were their wives, which of course is absurd. A little reordering of the sentence allows the meaning to emerge clearly:

> Another question about the Chappaquiddick party is why the wives of the married men were not there.

A sentence can also be confusing if it is *ambiguous*, having more than one possible meaning. An ambiguous sentence can be understood in at least one other way besides the way the author intends. Consider this example:

> Pound wrote to Eliot many times while he was editor of *Poetry* magazine in Chicago.

It's not clear from this sentence that Pound, not Eliot, was an editor of *Poetry*. Here is another example of ambiguity:

> The essay was described as the best ever written by the English instructor.

Who wrote the essay? The English instructor or a student? Take care not to confuse the reader by sentences like these that have more than one possible interpretation.

A sentence can also be technically correct but so awkwardly constructed that the reader loses his or her bearings. Try to read this monster:

> If three-quarters of the state legislatures (that is, thirty-eight states in total) ratify the E.R.A. within seven years (every proposed constitutional amendment, once approved by Congress, has a time limit of seven years to be ratified by the states—if the legislatures do not approve by then, the amendment becomes extinct), it will become the law of the land.   *student paper*

By the time readers untangle this knot of parentheses, clauses, and commas to arrive at the true subject—the pronoun "it"— they will have long since forgotten what "it" means. The problem here is like one we will see in Chapter 6, where too great a separation between pronoun and antecedent overtaxes readers' memories and confuses them. Here the abundance of intervening phrases and clauses breaks up the continuity of the sentence and strains the reader's patience and concentration. Better to eliminate the awkwardness by separating the material and putting like ideas together:

> Every proposed amendment, once approved by Congress, must be ratified within seven years or it becomes extinct; if three-quarters of the state legislatures—or thirty-eight states in all—ratify the E.R.A. within the time limit, it will become the law of the land.

That sentence is much less troublesome to a reader.

The causes for confusing, illogical, or awkward sentences are many. Sometimes haste (by the author) makes waste (for the

FUNKY WINKERBEAN   by Tom Batiuk

reader). Sometimes writers cannot see how the possible implications of a sentence could puzzle their audience. Sometimes words are left out because the ideas they represent seem clear to the writer, even though they are not necessarily clear to a reader. In short, the hobgoblin is usually a variation on that ancient lament, "But I know what I *mean!*" The reader would then have to reply, "You may know what you mean, but all I have to rely on is what you *say*, and I don't understand what you say."

If your experience is at all like mine, you often are vaguely aware that a sentence you have just written might be confusing or awkward. You have an uneasy feeling that it's "not quite right." Probably you can't say what, if anything, is wrong with it or how it should be reworded, and besides you are already busy on the next sentence. What I do in such cases is simply put a question mark next to the sentence and then keep right on going. The question mark just means the sentence ought to be looked at again. Later, during the revising process, I reexamine these sentences, weighing them more carefully this time. Reading them now, from a fresher and more objective viewpoint, do I see problems with any of them? If so, which ones? In each case, what is the source of the problem, and how can I go about making the meaning clear to my reader?

EXERCISES

1. The following sentences have been written by student writers. Identify the problem in each case and rewrite the sentence to eliminate it.

a. First of all because the researchers into tv violence are biased.

b. Kay likes walking to work rather than to take the car.

c. The sun came out and was beating down on our heads I was the last one to leave the beach.

d. I hated to enlist but nevertheless I knew it will be the best choice for me.

e. Even though, in the past ten years, there have been two federal laws passed that challenge sex-based discrimination on the job.

f. On any typical weeknight you can see people beaten, car accidents, and people murdered all in your own living room.

g. Love is where you give more than you take.

h. Women want equality to lie within the laws of society.

i. And didn't even find out until the next morning.

j. Which is a necessary thing to do if you want to solve our economic difficulties.

k. Mrs. Wilkes has it all: money, looks, being well liked.

l. To ensure a fair distribution of parts throughout the class.

m. People sometimes have been very generous to me, but just because he gives me something I don't have to like him.

n. Going home for Christmas vacation, which I have looked forward to for several weeks.

o. The bus came towards us and stops right next to the curb.

p. By "equal" a woman means in terms of legality.

q. The city has failed to provide the city employee with the basic necessities of life they are searching for.

r. Laetrile was banned because cancer arouses fake hopes and keeps cancer patients from getting treatment.

s. Because you can't promise the customer a good deal and then not deliver the goods.

t. My mother is often puzzled and even angry with me.

u. Debris left by fishermen or teenagers partying on the lake-front, not caring about the litter they caused.

v. However, I seriously doubt it we have lost the control of our human existence to a conglomeration of nuts and bolts.

2. Take the last three papers you have written. Do any of the seven sentence faults listed in Part B occur more than once in those papers? If so, study carefully the relevant section(s) of Part B, and rewrite the faulty sentences.

3. Convert the following student-written sentence fragments into complete sentences. Let your imagination supply any missing information:

a. Each of the children impatiently waiting for their turn to pin the tail on the donkey.

b. Separate experiences, beyond those forced upon them by the fact that the husband goes to his office, while the wife remains home to clean and shop.

c. Because his arrogance will not allow him to admit he is wrong.

d. The game callers shouting tempting statements to their prospective patrons, promising quick and sure rewards.

e. When all of a sudden I heard a voice yell, "Watch out!"

f. Which certainly will not endear her to the voters.

g. We had decided on the Chicken Kiev until the waiter, frowning as if it was somehow our fault, muttering that they were all out of that item.

h. A funny feeling in my throat and I broke out in a cold sweat.

4. Find three or four examples of sentence fragments used by professional writers. What justifications might the writers offer for these fragments?

5. The following sentences can give you explicit practice with shifts and faulty parallelism. Rewrite the sentences.

a. A very good place to change your tire is on a leveled spot and try to avoid sloping areas such as a hill.
b. Different messages pass our conscious mind and work its way into the subconscious.
c. Depressants have some unusual effects on the body such as a lack of interest in the surroundings, inability to move or talk, pulse and respiratory rate slows, depression deepens.
d. We were led out to the back lot and I find myself staring at the shiny, smiling grilles of brand new Granadas.
e. I wear glasses and I choose black frames because it didn't make me look too old.
f. He spent two hours hunting, trapping, and finally he captured the turtle.
g. Mr. Fugueroa gave us confidence and writes words of encouragement on our homework and tests.
h. I could see she was as delighted giving the earrings as I was to receive them.
i. Governments change quite frequently in Italy and it lasts only about six months on the average.

6. The following sentences are for one reason or another confused, illogical, mixed up. Decide—as well as you can—what the author *intended* to say; rewrite the sentence so that it conveys the meaning you have discovered.

a. The two people with vows of love and desire to spend the rest of their lives together making each other happy.
b. The dress will be done to your specifications and a sense of personal achievement when the garment is finished.
c. Studies have shown women who drink like animals.
d. Clocks are currently for the most part universal in appearance.
e. In conclusion, there is not one single word to describe myself.
f. Man repeatedly establishes himself as possessor of integrity and goodness, far outweighing the collective sum of his negative qualities.

g. Natural parents will be allowed to reunite with the adults they gave up as children.
h. The mind is truly a wondrous organ bursting with feelings.
i. The audience senses the shark's attack and it was audible that they were sympathizing with the boy.

> Backward ran sentences until reeled the mind.
> *Wolcott Gibbs*

7. Rewrite the following student paragraphs, correcting whatever sentence faults you encounter, perhaps making use also of the skills you acquired in Part A (subordination, the cumulative sentence, and so on).

a. Sometimes I really get fed up with the way people act. So much hatred. It's really sickening to hate so many things and people. Realizing you have these prejudices too. I feel rotten trying not to act opinionated. But I find it hard not to cut people up, to say what I really think, and letting my true feelings come to the surface.

b. War has an historical base point. The histories of man are filled with stories of fighting between one group and another and it tells of neverending struggle. The Greeks fought, the Romans fought, the English fought, and then there is the war in Vietnam for us. Man endowed his children with tales of combat and gives them weapons of destruction from the time he first walks. Because man does not truly wish peace, despite what he says to the contrary. Warrior classes have always had the greatest respect. This is still true today. Evidence can be found in anything from our habit of electing presidents only from those who have a military background, to on the other hand military prestige associated with "the uniform," and is this sensible? I believe man is not a rational creature. If you haven't guessed.

3

PARAGRAPHS

> A paragraph [should contain] no unnecessary sentences, for the same reason that a drawing should have no unnecessary lines and a machine no unnecessary parts.
>
> *William Strunk*

Like most people I sometimes prefer an older way just because I am more comfortable with it. Why change unless you have to or unless the new way is better? So I was not overly pleased when I heard from the telephone company a few years ago that our phone number was about to change. Well, not really change: it was just going to be called something different. Whereas for the previous nine years we had been KLamath 5-3720, henceforth we were to be known as 555-3720. Seven-digit dialing had arrived.

Given my natural preference for the more comfortable way, I inquired why the telephone company would no longer refer to us as KLamath 5-3720. After all, the fingers went in the same holes on the dial, and I could read the letters *K* and *L* just as well as I could read the number *5*. Furthermore there was a certain poetry in the older way. You could dial countrified, woodsy-sounding exchanges like GReenfield and FOrest and HOlly Oak, or stuffy, snobbish-sounding ones like ANdover, BRiargate, and WEllesley. It brought a smile when you had to call a plumber for the stopped-up sewer and dialed WEllesley 2-8100. Besides, when you were kids you could mystify teachers or other adults by giving your phone number entirely in letters rather than numbers ("my number is DAY-DRAM").

Yes, said the phone company a bit stiffly, there *was* a reason for this change. It seems that company psychologists had determined through testing that the average person can learn seven digits more quickly and more accurately than he or she can learn two letters and five digits. No one knows why this is so, but the fact can be easily demonstrated. Consequently the phone company was going to respect this evidence by converting to seven digits wherever possible, especially since direct dialing for long-distance calls required three or four additional digits. Their motive, I was assured, was the same as the one that prompted the insertion of a dash after the third digit of a number: such a change helps people organize the number in their minds and then remember it.

Of course I still refer to our number as KL 5-3720. But this experience with the phone company points up a very important truth. The human mind in order to digest a large amount of data must break that data into patterns. Otherwise the circuits overload and then work less efficiently or even short out. For example, if you want to memorize a series of eight digits, like 83197245, psychologists can show that the mind will work best when it arranges the numbers into two groups of three followed by one group of two, thus 831-972-45. Other patterns the mind can impose, like grouping by fours (8319-7245) or by twos (83-19-72-45), won't serve as well. But *any* pattern is better than no pattern at all, as would be the case if you tried to memorize all eight at once. Try to memorize a student identification number or a credit card number and you'll see what these psychologists mean.

> They know enough who know how to learn.
> *Henry Adams*

This truth about the mind's need for grouping patterns has an important application to writing. When we break up an essay into paragraphs, sentences, and words, we do so in part to make it easier for our reader to digest what we say. The reader has to grapple with a myriad of impressions as he or she reads, and we increase our chance of communication if we order our writing in such a way that the mind can process it conveniently. After all, we could still write as the scribes did back in the Middle Ages, when parchment was so expensive that often there were no spaces between paragraphs, sentences, or even words. We could still understand what we read:

Wecouldstillunderstandwhatweread,asthisshows.

But the process would be much more painful.

Paragraphs, therefore, like the sentences we considered in the previous chapter, are a way of giving order to what we say. Paragraphs simply work on the next level up: just as words are grouped into sentences, so sentences are grouped into paragraphs. This chapter will discuss ways to improve your use of this important ordering pattern.

When you begin a paragraph, what must you keep in mind? Two things: the paragraph must be *unified*, and the paragraph must be fully *developed*. Weak paragraphs will almost always be characterized by a failure in one or both of these important features. Part A explains paragraph unity; Part B explains paragraph development.

A. PARAGRAPH UNITY

Unity makes strength.
Friedrich von Baden

In Chapter 2 we said that writers did not have to be able to define a sentence, but they must know the function of a sentence and the signs and clues that signal its presence. The same holds true for the paragraph. Dictionary definitions are misleading at best; how can you tell what a "point" is when a paragraph is said to "deal with one point only"? The important test is whether you understand what paragraphs do and can use them effectively.

We have already discussed the function of paragraphs, the way they help us give order to what we write. But "order" is not a very precise description either. How do we know what ordering devices, what patterns to use? How do we know when a new paragraph should begin? If one of your paragraphs has been returned with notations like ¶ *unity*, ¶ *con*[*tinuity*], ¶ *focus*, or *coh*[*erence*], how do you give the paragraph the order it needs?

Again there is a parallel with sentence structure. Just as we intuitively "know" which sentences are grammatical and which not, and have used grammatical sentences ever since early childhood, so too we usually "know" what makes up successfully ordered paragraphs. To prove to yourself that you have this ability, please read the following passage by Ralph Raphael, from his book *Edges*. In its original form the passage consists of two paragraphs, and I would ask you to mark where you think the second paragraph begins:

> The salesmen are all professionals who follow the country fair circuit. The pen vendor, aged forty-three, has been a drummer ever since he was eighteen years old. His sales pitch, repeated verbatim every hour or so, seems to have a will of its own which has little or nothing to do with the stone-faced man who delivers it. It's just a job like any other job, although it demands that he have no home other

than the camper in which he travels. Like the barkers and peddlers of years past, the people of the fair are creatures of the road who remain forever on the outskirts of the communities they serve. But the salesmen are not alone. The "carnies," as the amusement-park folks call themselves, have transformed the country-fair circuit into a way of life. Traveling together in one continuous party, they wear "carny power" insignia on the back of their Levi's jackets and like to hang together when the local toughs start hankering for a fight. They are proud to belong to a select group of "gypsies, tramps, and thieves," self-appointed outcasts from the small-town societies in which they set up shop. Like the salesmen who travel beside them, they live off the suckers . . . who come to the fair to blow a few bucks and catch a passing glimpse of bright lights and fancy things.

Probably you recognized that the second paragraph begins with the sixth sentence, "But the salesmen are not alone." You were not the writer of these paragraphs; nevertheless you knew how they should be organized.

The question is, *how* did you know? What clues, what signals, did you use to arrive at your decision? I would bet that, probably without even realizing it, you used one or more of the following three signals: change of topic, transition word or phrase, or a sense for modern paragraph length.

In Part A we will examine the first two of these three signals in more detail, because they show how you recognize unified paragraphs and, more importantly, they help to explain how you construct them. (The third signal will be analyzed in Part B.) We will also consider in this section other ways to reinforce the order given to a paragraph.

A1. Giving the Paragraph a Clear Focus

While the statement that a paragraph "deals with one point only" is not a very workable one, it touches an important truth. Part of our understanding of what makes a paragraph comes when we realize that a writer is considering a new aspect of a topic. Speaking strictly it would not be right to say that when an author begins a new paragraph he or she "switches topics," because to switch topics completely would be to start a new essay. But we can say that each paragraph should take up a new *aspect* of a topic, or a new subdivision of it, or a new extension of it.

Consider the Raphael passage you just read. It starts with the topic of salesmen at county fairs. The author provides an example, the pen vendor, and devotes four sentences to him and others like him. Then he takes up the subject of the "carnies." Immediately we recognize that a new aspect of his general topic (county fairs) has been introduced. And sure enough the sentences that follow all say something about this new group of people. These sentences form a coherent, distinct unit and therefore can be marked off as a separate paragraph.

So we do have a sense for how new aspects of a topic need to be set off as separate paragraphs, to help the reader organize the material mentally, but how do we distinguish between a new aspect of a topic and a continuation of the topic? The question is one of *focus;* a good analogy would be to think of looking at a subject through a pair of binoculars. When you look through binoculars, you must adjust the focus dial until your subject can be seen clearly. In the process, you dial out all that does not belong to the subject, you zero in on one particular focal point. In writing a paragraph, you do the same thing—you focus on one particular subject and make it clear for the reader.

Here is an example of a paragraph that is "out of focus," that does not concentrate on a single subject:

> It all happened many years ago, when I was starting kindergarten, in fact. I tried a useless "I don't want to go to school." My mother wouldn't co-operate. On arriving, though, it wasn't so bad. I got to know a few kids and everything went smoothly, since they let us out early. The second day is when it happened. Halfway through the day the class was given milk and cookies. The teacher soon noticed that the milk was having its effect on us. The class was formed into two lines, boys and girls. I was told that we were going to the washroom. I protested. . . .

This paper is a simple narrative. As such, we expect each paragraph to focus on the separate events that together make up the story. You probably noticed, however, that while the sixth sentence begins the description of a separate event—the second day at school, the day of the as-yet-unnamed trauma—this separate event is not marked off as a new paragraph. Our sense of paragraph unity is violated. Luckily the remedy is simple. If you catch a problem of this sort when you are proofreading, the insertion of the symbol ¶ will show that you recognize the need for a new paragraph.

A bit more complicated is the case where the writer begins and ends a paragraph with only one subject but allows other subjects to enter part way through. Consider this one:

> Gus, a twenty-eight-year-old hippy, has to be the most egotistical person I have ever had the misfortune of meeting. From the moment he walked in the clinic I could tell he thought himself superior to everyone else. I had gotten this job at the clinic through a friend of my mother's. Although physical therapy was not my intended career, I thought I would get valuable experience in dealing with the public. Anyway, Gus came into the waiting room and introduced himself to the receptionist by telling her what a great lover he was. After boasting about his car and his ability as a skydiver, Gus excused himself to comb his hair and preen before the mirror. Then, as luck would have it, I found he had been assigned to me for his therapy.

Most of this paragraph deals with its subject—detestable Gus. But two sentences, the third and fourth, are devoted to a different matter altogether, i.e., how the author got her job. Yet we can't just begin a new paragraph with the third sentence, because sentences five, six, and seven belong with the first two as part of the introduction to Gus. The only solution is to remove sentences three and four from the paragraph entirely. If the subject of how the author got her job is an important one, it can be treated in a separate paragraph somewhere else in the paper. If the subject has no special value, it should be left out.

Finally we have to face the paragraph that entertains so many topics the focus is lost entirely, leaving only a murky fog:

> Murder is a serious crime. Every day you can look in a paper and read about someone being murdered. I think that the abolition of the death penalty is a major factor in the increase of deaths. A person can now murder someone and be certain he will not be executed. I think that if a person kills someone he deserves to die except in time of war or accidental death. After all the person he murdered didn't want to die. With the re-establishment of the death penalty there would be fewer murders. A person would be less likely to commit murder if he knows he can be executed for his crime. If the death penalty is not re-established there is but one choice: carry a gun. That way if your

life is threatened you get to kill him before he gets to kill you. The law works two ways: if he kills you he goes to jail, and if you kill him you get off on self-defense. There would be less murders if everyone carried a gun. Not many people would try to kill you when they know you carry a gun.

The writer begins the paragraph as if he will focus on a fact: the prevalence of the crime of murder. By the third sentence, however, he is trying to analyze what he believes to be the *cause* of this fact, namely the abolition of the death penalty. By the fifth sentence he is off on still another issue, the *desirability* of the death penalty. Yet in the seventh sentence we are back to the determination of cause and effect—what would be the *effect* of reintroducing the death penalty? Finally the ninth sentence, by urging people to carry guns, hoists the fifth and last flag under which this paragraph is made to sail.

In short, the writer of the preceding paragraph has little sense of what focus means. At least five topics are introduced, each of which deserves one or more paragraphs of its own. The most that can be said of the present paragraph is that it has something to do with murder, guns, and the death penalty. We get a rough idea how the writer feels (very angry). But the haphazard way he spills out his ideas makes it impossible for him to be clear or convincing.

> So quick bright things come to confusion.
> *William Shakespeare*

So it is important to test each of your paragraphs by the question, "Does it have a clear focus?" Unless you can answer yes, the paragraph ought to be rewritten. Sometimes all you need do is split the paragraph, as in our first example. If the paragraph in its original form deals with two topics, one after the other, a simple division at the point where the second topic begins is all that will be required. Sometimes, however, as in the case of the murder-guns-death penalty paragraph, no such easy solution is available. In these cases the best course is to start from the beginning. Take each of the separate topics and make it the focus for a completely new paragraph.

One device that is often helpful in keeping a paragraph focused is the **topic sentence.** Such a sentence often appears first in the paragraph, and it states in a general way the subject the rest of the paragraph will develop.

Some people offer as a rule the idea that "all paragraphs must begin with a topic sentence." Such advice is well intentioned because it is directed to the problem of focus. But the advice can also be misleading because as a statement about *all* writing it is simply not true. Professional writers, for example, use topic sentences in only about 55 percent of their paragraphs and position those sentences in many places besides the first. Often the topic will be implied rather than stated, or else it must be deduced from the other sentences. The important issue is whether the paragraph has a single unified focus, not whether that focus is summed up in an initial topic sentence.

But even though a paragraph need not have a topic sentence, such sentences are often very useful. They enable readers to steer their way more easily by following these signposts the writer has set out. Observe how the italicized topic sentences clarify the focus in each of the following two student-written paragraphs:

> *Another reason we should reject pass-fail grading is that society would no longer be able to determine which students have the ability to go on to medical school, law school, or graduate school.* With the pass-fail system as it is now proposed you could have a potential doctor with an *A* average and a potential doctor with a *D* average, and you would lack any means for telling the difference between them. Thus academically inferior people would become eligible for important positions in our society. I believe that the people who are going to guard my health, take care of my legal matters, and teach my college-age children should be above average in academic ability.

> *The strangest character I ever met was a fellow called Pete Karmanlis.* His old, tattered clothes and drooping moustache gave him the appearance of a hippie right from Haight-Ashbury. His black eyes flashed as he talked, and he accompanied his wild words with even wilder gestures. But this appearance was in sharp contrast to his personality. Peter's father was an old-country Greek and Pete had been brought up as a "gentleman." His manners were excellent, and he delighted in bowing the continental way and kissing my hand ("with your permission, of course").

In the first example, the entire paragraph develops one of the author's reasons for opposing pass-fail grading, and that reason is stated clearly in the opening sentence. In the second example, the remainder of the paragraph (following the topic sentence) tells us more about why Pete Karmanlis was "the strangest character I ever met."

While it is not true that all paragraphs have topic sentences, the statistic just quoted reminds us that 55 percent of all paragraphs *do* have topic sentences. Check your own writing, and if recognizable topic sentences do not occur quite frequently, you are probably neglecting one of the best ways to give your paragraphs the unity readers need.

A2. Using Transitions

You may have identified the beginning point of the second Raphael paragraph (p. 132) by the change to the topic of "carnies." It is also possible that you used the second of our clues: transition words. When you saw the word "But . . ." at the start of the sixth sentence, perhaps you recognized it as a member of that group of words that often marks the beginning of a new topic and therefore a new paragraph. Perhaps you recognized the fact that the entire sixth sentence acts as a transition, a bridge, between the topic of pen vendors and the topic of carnies.

A transition in your life is the passage from one stage to another. Similarly transition words signal a passage from one stage of the discussion of a topic to another stage. At the same time transition words can show the relationship between the first stage and the second.

Transition words do not just tie paragraph to paragraph. They also connect one sentence to another sentence within the same paragraph:

> Murderers usually do not deserve sympathy. *But* the objection to having the state kill them in turn is not sentimental. . . . *Anthony Lewis* [italics added]

And they connect clause to clause within a sentence:

> Thanks to Edith, whose constitutional bewilderment serves as Right Instinct, things eventually calm down on "All in the Family," *but* are rarely resolved or set straight. *Roger Rosenblatt* [italics added]

Transition words are extremely important. They enable you to build bridges from one statement to another, to connect what is to come with what has gone before. Thus you can guide the reader through your subject. In this section we are discussing transition words as they apply to paragraphs, but you should realize that in most cases this material applies equally to transitions between sentences and clauses.

Transition words or phrases show a *relationship*, we said earlier. Sometimes the relationship is one of **contrast,** and it will be shown by words or phrases like these:

however	nevertheless
but	in spite of this
by contrast	on the other hand

Sometimes the relationship is one of **similarity;** the new aspect of the topic is an addition to the other aspects that have already been considered. Words or phrases that show this include:

moreover	second(ly) (or third(ly), etc.)
also	in addition
furthermore	besides
and	next
another	likewise
similarly	in the same way

In narration or description a writer might have occasion to use transition words that establish a **time or place relationship:**

later	farther on
soon	nearby
meanwhile	here
earlier	there

Then too the new paragraph might show the **consequence** of the previous paragraph or else an **example** of it. Words or phrases like the following might be used:

as a result	for example
therefore	as an illustration
consequently	another example
thus	for instance

Finally, the transition words might show a special relationship between the new paragraph and a whole group of paragraphs that have preceded it. The new paragraph might be either a **repetition** or a **summation:**

in other words	in summary
as I have said	in short
to repeat	in brief

> Only connect! That is the whole of the sermon.
> *E. M. Forster*

Most transitions between paragraphs are accomplished by single words, usually conjunctions (like *but, and, therefore*) or stock phrases (like *for example, on the other hand*). These words or phrases appear at or near the beginning of the new paragraph. Sometimes, if one of these common words or phrases does not express the relationship precisely enough, an entire sentence might be used as a transition:

How should we proceed?

The third case is curiously unlike the first two.

Let us move on to the next issue.

The introductory sentence to the "carnies" paragraph could also serve as an example.

This use of complete sentences as transitional devices points up the one important difference between transitions for sentences and transitions for paragraphs. Obviously a sentence could not be a transition for a sentence!

I must emphasize very strongly the importance of transitions for paragraphs. They signal to readers how they should read the upcoming paragraph: what aspect of the topic it will consider, what approach to the topic it will take, how it relates to what has gone before. Readers could perhaps determine these matters for themselves, but the transition words act like rails, keeping them right on course. Readers who have been helped this way will reward you with increased attention to your message.

In this book, for example, I have tried to make frequent use of transition words to ease your way through the text. Just as an arbitrary example, consider the last five paragraphs of section B2 of Chapter 1 (pp. 34–36). All five paragraphs begin with either a transition word ("So . . ."), a transition phrase ("In the meantime. . . ," "Of course . . ."), or a transition sentence ("Why does a reader tune out. . . ?" "This last point . . . cannot be emphasized too strongly."). Even this very paragraph you are now reading uses the transition phrase "for example."

Transition words *within* a paragraph, in other words between sentences and clauses, are also very important as a way of emphasizing the focus of the paragraph. They give readers valuable signposts as they proceed through the paragraph, thus allowing readers to understand the underlying unity of the paragraph. Observe the italicized words and phrases in the following paragraph by F. L. Lucas, from "What Is Style?":

> *Why and how* did I become interested in style? *The main answer,* I suppose, is that I was born that way. *Then* I was, till ten, an only child running loose in a house packed with books, and in a world (thank goodness) still undistracted by radio and television. *So* at three I groaned to my mother, "Oh, I *wish* I could read," and at four I read. *Now* travel among books is the best travel of all, and the easiest, and the cheapest. (*Not* that I belittle ordinary travel—which I regard as one of the three main pleasures in life.) One learns to write by reading good books, as one learns to talk by hearing good talkers. *And* if I have learned anything of writing, it is largely from writers like Montaigne, Dorothy Osborne, Horace Walpole, Johnson, Goldsmith, Montesquieu, Voltaire, Flaubert and Anatole France. *Again,* I was reared on Greek and Latin, and one can learn much from translating Homer or the Greek Anthology, Horace or Tacitus, if one is thrilled by the original, and tries, however vainly, to recapture some of that thrill in English.

Lucas uses transitions to guide us, first posing the topic question ("Why and how. . . ?"), then showing his response ("The main answer . . ."), the origin of that response ("Then. . . ," "So. . . ," "Now . . ."), its limitations ("Not . . ."), and its corollaries ("And. . . ," "Again . . ."). Here a successful writer uses transition words to ease us through his subject and keep his paragraph unified. Take Lucas' paragraph as a model for how you might use transition words yourself.

Much college writing is weakened by its poor or limited use of transition words. Check some of your own recent papers. How often did you begin a paragraph with a transition? When you did, were you using only the most common ones like *but, and,* and *however?* If you find that transition words are scarce and limited to a few choices, you are missing out on one of the easiest ways to guide your reader's attention. Study the list of transitions on the previous pages, and see how they and others like them might be helpful in making your writing clearer to your reader.

A3. Giving the Paragraph a Logical Order

Even if your paragraph has a clear focus and helpful transitions, it can still be weakened by haphazard, illogical organization. Confused or jumbled paragraphs puzzle the reader unnecessarily. This section offers advice on how to make sure that your paragraph is well ordered.

You know from the start what a paragraph is going to do. Perhaps it will tell a story or continue a story already begun. Perhaps it will describe an object or a place. Perhaps it will list something—reasons, or ideas, or a series of items. Your task is to make sure that the order of the sentences in your paragraph is the logical order, given the implied promise you have made to your reader at the start.

Suppose the paragraph will tell or continue a story, for example. Most probably you will need to use **chronological order.** In other words, you will describe the events of the story in the order in which they occurred, from earliest to latest. Here is an example paragraph by Larry McMurtry from his book *The Last Picture Show,* in which he describes part of a basketball game:

> This time it happened to Sonny, and in the very first minutes of play. Leroy Malone managed to trip the gangly Paducah center and while the center was sprawled on the floor Sonny ran right along his back, in pursuit of the ball. Just as he was about to grab it somebody tripped *him* and he hit the wall head first. The next thing he knew he was stretched out beside the bench and one of the freshmen players was squeezing a wet washrag on his forehead. Sonny tried to keep his eyes closed as long as he could—he knew Coach Popper would send him back into the game as soon as he regained consciousness. He feigned deep coma for about five minutes, but unfortunately the

coach was experienced in such matters. He came over and lifted one of Sonny's eyelids and saw that he was awake.

Each event follows the other in chronological order, from Leroy's foul to Coach Popper's lifting the eyelid.

> Beauty from order springs.
> *William King*

Sounds obvious, you say. Of course earlier events go first, later events come after. But you would be surprised how often this simple principle is ignored. Consider this example:

> My habits have not changed when making the transition from high school to college. In my first semester last year I almost set a school record by being late nineteen times for my first-period class. They almost kicked me out. When I came here I told myself I was going to turn over a new leaf. That pledge lasted about three days, and now I am almost always late for political science at 8:30. In high school the cause was usually the fact that I turned off my clock radio and went back to sleep. I wonder if I can cure myself next semester.

If you arranged the events described in this paragraph in their chronological order, obviously the failures so far this semester precede the wish for better luck next semester, and the failures in high school precede the failures so far this semester. The order of the paragraph in its present form is unnecessarily confusing, because the sixth sentence (about the clock radio) is out of its proper position.

Suppose a paragraph describes a place, even a building or a room. Then you need to give it **spatial order,** in other words you describe the space from a single, consistent vantage point, as in this paragraph by Joan Didion, from *Slouching Towards Bethlehem.*

> And then, just past that moment when the desert has become the only reality, Route 15 hits the coast and there is Guaymas, a lunar thrust of volcanic hills and islands with the warm Gulf of California lapping idly all around, lapping even at the cactus, the water glassy as a mirage, the ships in the harbor whistling unsettlingly, moaning, ghost schooners, landlocked, lost. That is Guaymas. As far as the town goes, Graham Greene might have written it: a shadowy square with a filigree pergola for the Sunday band, a racket of birds, a cathedral in bad repair with a robin's-egg-blue tile dome, a turkey

buzzard on the cross. The wharves are piled with bales of Sonoran cotton and mounds of dark copper concentrates; out on the freighters with the Panamanian and Liberian flags the Greek and German boys stand in the hot twilight and stare sullenly at the grotesque and claustrophobic hills, at the still town, a curious limbo at which to call.

Notice how this description of Guaymas begins with the approach from the north on Highway 15, proceeds through the center of town with its square and cathedral, and ends with the wharf and the harbor beyond—exactly the spatial order appropriate for someone whose first encounter with the town is from an automobile.

Again the order of this example paragraph might have seemed easy to arrange. Examine the following description, however. See how it begins with a general view of the Florida Keys, narrows to the white sand beach, then suddenly turns back to the more general view.

Last August we took our yearly vacation at Siesta Key, Florida. This key is located about seventeen miles from the mainland. Its two most impressive features are its warm Gulf breezes and its clear, aqua-colored water. I especially liked one section of beach. The sand was white and warm to the touch. I could skin-dive or snorkel, and when I wasn't busy there were interesting beach people I could talk to. The Florida Keys are also noted for their exciting opportunities for fishermen.

The order of this paragraph lacks the consistency we found in the earlier paragraph on Guaymas, and therefore it confuses and annoys the reader.

When you are planning a descriptive paragraph, the usual order for the paragraph is the order of place. In other words, you might start at one side of an object and work your way to the other side, or you might start at the top and work down, or you might start at the near side and work to the far side (as in Joan Didion's paragraph). Another possibility is to select the most important feature of the person, object, or scene you are describing and then to include the details that help to build that dominant impression.

When your paragraph is to offer a list, a little forethought can pay dividends. If the list is of reasons, for example, the reasons could be arranged in the order of ascending importance, i.e., least to most important. Just as logically the paragraph could begin with the most important and work down to the least important. Either way is possible: the point is that there must be some principle that governs the order of appearance, so the list will not be haphazard. Here is a student-written paragraph that illustrates the benefit of paying careful attention to what we might call **logical or emphatic order:**

> This proposed law [censoring certain movies] is irresponsible. First of all, we already have a rating system which requires theaters to prohibit young people from seeing "X"-rated films, so a new censoring board would only duplicate an existing procedure. If the present procedure isn't always followed, let's just make sure it *is* followed. Secondly, this law would raise an even more important question: will we or will we not observe the Constitution, which guarantees freedom of speech? And the constitutional issue leads me to what I think is the most overriding concern of all, and that is the blindness of the mayor toward the real cause of violence among young people. You can never cure violence by restricting people's rights. Instead you have to recognize that violence comes from poverty, a poor education, a broken home, drugs, alcohol—in other words from the *environment* in which these young people live.

The paragraph develops three reasons and lists them in order of ascending importance. We sense that this writer knew what she was doing, that she was writing in a clear and orderly fashion. This impression helps in a subtle way to make her argument more persuasive.

Mastering the names for these ways of achieving order is not important. Moreover there are other ways besides the ones just mentioned. The vital point is that *some* appropriate order must be evident in your paragraphs if you want them to be readable.

> Order is a lovely thing;
> On disarray it lays its wing,
> Teaching simplicity to sing.
> *Anna Branch*

If your paragraphs have been criticized for lacking order, planning the paragraphs might help. Sometimes the planning can be done in your head; sometimes it is better to plan on paper with a few short notes about how the paragraph will be organized. Consider first the focus your paragraph will have and then decide on the logical order for the kind of paragraph you will write. (Exercises 3, 5, and 9 of this section should be useful if you need experience in planning paragraphs.)

If this kind of foresight is not possible, at least give your paragraphs some *afterthought*. In other words, check each paragraph during the revising process, making sure the paragraph has a clear and logical order. Such an effort will pay great dividends in terms of your reader's attention. It's not so much that a reader will notice how well ordered your paragraphs are. Rather it is a matter of silently preventing the confusion (and exasperation) that a poorly ordered paragraph must cause.

Paragraph unity, we said at the beginning of this chapter, is one of the two essentials. The other is paragraph development, to which we now turn.

EXERCISES

1. Into how many paragraphs would you divide each of the following passages? Where would your divisions occur? Why?

    a. So self-contradictory, indeed, has love become that some of those studying family life have concluded that "love" is simply the name for the way more powerful members of the family control other members. Love, Ronald Laing maintains, is a cover for violence. The same can be said about will. We inherited from our Victorian forefathers the belief that the only real problem in life was to decide rationally *what* to do—and then *will* would stand ready as the "faculty" for making us do it. Now it is no longer a matter of deciding what to do, but of *deciding how to decide. The very basis of will itself is thrown into question.* Rollo May, *Love and Will*

    b. I live on northern Puget Sound, in Washington State, alone. I have a gold cat, who sleeps on my legs, named Small. In the morning I joke to her blank face, Do you remember last night? Do you remember? I throw her out before breakfast, so I can eat. There is a spider, too, in the bathroom, with whom I keep a sort of company.

Her little outfit reminds me of a certain moth I helped to kill. The spider herself is of uncertain lineage, bulbous at the abdomen and drab. Her six-inch mess of a web works, works somehow, works miraculously, to keep her alive and me amazed. The web itself is in a corner behind the toilet, connecting tile wall to tile wall and floor, in a place where there is, I would have thought, scant traffic. Yet under the web are sixteen or so corpses she has tossed to the floor. The corpses appear to be mostly sow bugs, those little armadillo creatures who live to travel flat out in houses, and die round. There is also a new shred of earwig, three old spider skins crinkled and clenched, and two moth bodies, wingless and huge and empty, moth bodies I drop to my knees to see. *Annie Dillard, Holy the Firm*

2. Examine the following student-written paragraph, printed exactly as it was written. Ideally the paragraph ought to be broken into smaller paragraph units: where would you make the divisions and why? Would you have any other suggestions to make to the author of this passage, based on what you have learned in previous chapters?

An egghead is anyone who seems so absorbed in the pursuit of knowledge that she hardly sees the obvious pleasures of life. An egghead would never dream of lazily watching three soap operas in a row on a midsummer afternoon or of getting wasted on a Saturday night, and having to think of an alibi for her parents for staggering in at three in the morning when curfew was at twelve sharp. Instead of living and having fun, an egghead thinks. Starla (not her real name) was one person I knew in high school who fits perfectly into the category of the type of person I have just described. Starla never dated guys, never watched television, never went to dances, and never listened to any together music. Whenever I saw Starla in the halls, her head was bent, her feet shuffled lethargically, and her back twisted into a question mark above the twelve books under her right arm. Her appearance unequivocally suggested lofty contemplation. At noontime, while everyone else gossiped and giggled, Starla sat silently in a corner thumbing through pages of a massive philosophy text. She would always respond to our invitations to come join our conversations with a simple, "No thank you."

3. The phrases and clauses below are all statements about America. If you were to write a clearly focused paragraph on the topic "cultural uniformity in America," which statements would you use and which would you exclude? Using only what you think are the relevant statements, write the paragraph.

a. The system of education, from grade school through college, is similar in every state.
b. McDonalds are everywhere.
c. America is still a haven for immigrants and their diverse cultures.
d. The same television programs are seen in every city in America.
e. The Vietnamese war caused tension and division in America.
f. Regional dialects are disappearing in favor of a standardized American English.

4. Below you will find three student-written paragraphs that are not clearly focused. State the reason(s) for this lack of clear focus and suggest the changes that would be necessary to restore proper focus. Then rewrite the paragraphs.

a. Even though their civil rights are now guaranteed by law, blacks are being exploited in the job market. They are still the last hired and the first fired. Teenage unemployment is higher for blacks than for whites. When employers do hire blacks the reason is often government pressure for "affirmative action," so the employee knows he was hired not because of his ability but because of his skin color. Housing is another problem. Integrated communities are not yet too common; therefore certain areas are still almost exclusively inhabited by blacks or whites. Lending institutions often discriminate against the black home buyer, either by red-lining or by charging higher interest rates on mortgages.

b. What type of person does it take to commit murder? Can a normal person take a life for no apparent reason other than the lust to kill? Such a bizarre act cannot be committed unless the person is mentally deranged. The point is, can we take the lives of such people? This brings up the matter of capital punishment. I feel that a person who kills is not responsible for his acts. Capital punishment is an eye-for-an-eye punishment. The person being punished does not realize what he did. There must be a better solution, a more humane one.

c. [Charmaine's grandmother] would immediately get onto the topic of Dina, her future granddaughter. She lovingly referred to her as the woodpecker who was after her grandson's money. She would relate some of her experiences with the woodpecker. "That city woman stares at me like a woodpecker. I asked her, vat you looking at, do I owe you money or something?" Charmaine's grandmother was sick for a long time, but she refused to see a doctor. She said, "Dat son-of-a- . . . will kill me when I sleep." She thought all doctors were vampires, out to suck both blood and money.

5. Below you will find six topic sentences. Choose any three, and then write well-focused paragraphs using these topic sentences as the starting points.

a. Modern advertising is designed to create needs that do not exist.
b. Somehow examinations always show up more of what I don't know than of what I know.
c. People much prefer gossip to talking about ideas.
d. My most difficult course this semester is. . . .
e. Some people seem to believe that natural resources in this country are unlimited.
f. Everyone has at least one phobia—one irrational fear—like fear of heights or electric appliances or elevators or car-washes.
g. When I was a child, my favorite tv program (book, toy, amusement) was. . . .

> **Whatever you would make habitual, practice it; and if you would not make a thing habitual, do not practice it, but accustom yourself to something else.**
>
> *Epictetus*

6. Here are the beginnings of several paragraphs. Underline the transitional words, phrases, or sentences. What relationship between this new paragraph and the paragraph that went before is being established by each word, phrase, or sentence you have underlined? For example, will this new paragraph contrast with the old one? Add to it? Offer an example of it?

a. Nor is it just a literary gift; it is, I repeat, characteristically human. Almost everything we do. . . .   *Jacob Bronowski*

b. Let us look first at the spurious sexual models conjured up for our anxious society by the sorcerers of the mass media and the advertising guild. Like all pagan deities. . . . *Harvey Cox*

c. Consider our welfare system. Surely unadmitted fear. . . . *George Elliott*

d. In summary, with the onset of the childcentered nuclear family, an institution became necessary. . . . *Shulamith Firestone*

e. There is, for example, the whispering campaign, the circulation of anonymous rumors by men who cannot be compelled to prove what they say. They put the utmost strain on our tolerance. . . . *Walter Lippmann*

f. Let us make an altogether new start here. Let us look at scientific man in his dealings with animals. . . . *Erik Erikson*

g. History also suggests, however, some reasons for the difficulties encountered on the road. In the absence of a paradigm. . . . *Thomas Kuhn*

7. Below you will find five pairs of sentences. In each pair, assume that the first sentence is the concluding sentence of one paragraph and the second sentence is the opening sentence of a new paragraph. Based on the relationship that you see between the two sentences, what seem to you the most appropriate transition words or transition phrases you could use to introduce the second sentence?

a. . . . We were made to feel very much at home.

_____ it came as quite a shock when they told us abruptly the next morning that we would have to leave. . . .

b. . . . So Sunday afternoons are usually pretty quiet in Pine Plains.

_____ , take this last Sunday. . . .

c. . . . So the fourth reason for my not joining was the discriminatory nature of the club's membership.

_____ , I can recapitulate the reasons for my decision in one simple sentence. . . .

d. . . . She danced on and on, oblivious of the noise, the smoke, the smell of cigarettes and beer.

_____ , on the other side of the dance floor, Phil was watching her and doing a slow burn. . . .

e. . . . My inexperience really showed.

_____ there was another factor in my nervousness besides inexperience. . . .

8. What logical ordering pattern is at work in each of the following paragraphs? Explain your answers.

a. But I go back. There are four beliefs that I know more about from having lived with poetry. One is the personal belief, which is a knowledge that you don't want to tell other people about because you cannot prove that you know. You are saying nothing about it but you see. The love belief, just the same, has that same shyness; it knows it cannot tell; only the outcome can tell. And the national belief we enter into socially with each other, all together, party of the first part, party of the second part, we enter into that to bring about the future of the country. We cannot tell some people what it is to believe, partly, because they are too stupid to understand and partly because we are too proudly vague to explain. And anyway it has got to be fulfilled, and we are not talking until we know more, until we have something to show. And then the literary one in every work of art, not of cunning and craft, mind you, but of real art; that believes the thing into existence, saying as you go more than you even hoped you were going to be able to say, and coming with surprise to an end that you foreknew only with some sort of emotion. And then finally the relationship we enter into with God to believe the future in—to believe the hereafter in. *Robert Frost,* "Education by Poetry"

b. Mr. Newton rose early, as usual, just before the sun came up, dressed himself as best he could, and hurried downstairs via the elevator. His white shirt, yellowed by age, pressed nicely, ornamented by a purple and gray striped tie, was tucked neatly into his baggy, gray suit pants. He shifted himself impatiently on the large metallic walker which he used to support his unsteady body. As soon as the elevator door opened he hurried—at a turtle's pace—out of the elevator, getting caught twice in the elevator door, and then headed for the glass door directly ahead. Walking at a pace of one step every fifteen seconds, he finally made it. *student writer*

c. The kitchen held our lives together. My mother worked in it all day long, we ate in it almost all meals except the Passover *seder*, I did my homework and first writing at the kitchen table, and in winter I often had a bed made up for me on three kitchen chairs near the stove. On the wall just over the table hung a long horizontal mirror that sloped to a ship's prow at each end and was lined in cherry wood. It took up the whole wall, and drew every object in the kitchen to itself. . . . A large electric bulb hung down in the center of the kitchen at the end of a chain that had been hooked into the ceiling; the old gas ring and key still jutted out of the wall like antlers. In the corner next to the toilet was the sink at which we washed, and the square tub in which my mother did our clothes. Above it, tacked to the shelf on which were pleasantly ranged square, blue-bordered white sugar and spice jars, hung calendars from the Public National Bank on Pitkin Avenue and the Minsker Progressive Branch of the Workman's Circle; receipts for the payment of insurance premiums and household bills on a spindle: two little boxes engraved with Hebrew letters. One of these was for the poor, the other to buy back the Land of Israel.   *Alfred Kazin, A Walker in the City*

9. Below you will find four lists of items. Choose two of the lists; then include all of the items on each list in paragraphs on the topics indicated. In both cases you will have to decide on a *plan* for the paragraphs. Then depending on your plan—several plans are possible—you will have to rearrange the order of the items on the list so that your paragraph has a coherent order.

a. modern supermarkets

  checkout counters
  frozen food
  meat department
  shopping carts
  produce
  household products
  customer service desk
  dairy case
  canned goods

b. causes of traffic jams

  traffic accidents
  poor weather
  rush hour
  inadequate streets and highways
  special events

c. a sports event

excitement
spectators
teams (competitors)
Coca-cola (popcorn, hot dogs, frozen yogurt)
cheers (boos)
tickets
tension
celebration

d. causes of trend to reject urban living for suburban life

crowded conditions in cities
lack of trees and gardens in cities
pollution problems in cities
high urban crime rates
hectic pace of city life

B. PARAGRAPH DEVELOPMENT

> . . . in nature there is a great, unital, continuing and ever-
> lasting process of development.
>
> *E. H. Haeckel*

When you divided the passage by Ralph Raphael into two paragraphs (p. 131), you might have used still a third clue: your sense for the approximate length of the modern paragraph. This clue is usually the one of which we are least aware. Yet it might be the most important of all.

The reason for the importance of this clue rests in your long experience as a reader. Even if you have never cracked a book that was not assigned in school, you still have read literally thousands of pages of prose. Inevitably you have picked up a sense for the typical length of a paragraph in modern writing. You know—even though you are probably not aware you know—the fact that *on the average* the modern paragraph is between 50 and 150 words long. Of course many paragraphs are shorter and many are longer. But when you read the Raphael passage in its undivided form, you may have sensed that it was longer than usual (it contained 224 words), and you may have begun looking for ways to break it into units more typical in size. Sure enough, the two original paragraphs, with 111 and 113 words respectively, fall within the range we have termed average.

It has not always been thus. If the undivided Raphael passage had been shown to a college student a hundred years ago, he or she probably would have seen nothing amiss. Until our own century the typical paragraph was much longer. Paragraphs of a page or two in length were not uncommon a century ago and earlier. Paragraph size is not an absolute fixed in the mind of God. Just as we might find earlier paragraphs inordinately long, so the Victorian reader would find our shorter units equally strange. (It follows that our shorter paragraphs must be more tightly focused than a Victorian writer would have felt necessary.)

While the trend is now toward shorter paragraphs, we must still recognize that 50–150 words usually means three well-developed sentences *at least*, and probably more. (The Raphael paragraphs are five sentences each.) In fact, my own experience as a teacher tells me that students are more likely to write paragraphs that are too short rather than too long. Just as we saw in Chapter 3 that the typical student sentence might average fifteen words rather than the 20–25 words common among professional writers, so too the typical student paragraph averages only two or three sentences and perhaps some 40 or 50 words. Rare indeed is the paragraph that approaches the 150-word end of the scale. Check a group of your own papers and see if what I have just said holds true for you.

> With sixty staring me in the face, I have developed inflammation of the sentence structure and a definite hardening of the paragraphs.
>
> *James Thurber*

Why are student-written paragraphs shorter than the typical paragraphs of professional writers? Part of the answer may be that without knowing it we are being influenced by the short paragraphs in newspaper and magazine writing. We should not confuse journalistic practice with ordinary paragraphing. Below are two versions of the same article. One is the original newspaper story; the other is the same story paragraphed in the normal way, as if it were an essay.

Two special teams named to speed DC-10 probe
by David Young

Two special teams, one headed by a former Federal Aviation Administration official in Chicago, have been appointed to expedite the agency's investigation of the DC-10 jumbo jet.

The teams will seek the source of the plane's trouble so it can be corrected and the nation's 138 grounded DC-10s can be put back in service.

Langhorne Bond, FAA administrator, ordered the planes grounded last week after American Airlines mechanics found small cracks in pylon structures holding the engines to the wings.

A major crack in the same pylon aft bulkhead was found in the wreckage of the American Airlines DC-10 that crashed May 25 outside O'Hare International Airport, killing 274 persons.

The pylon aft bulkhead is a section of the pylon structure just below one of the points at which it is attached to the wing.

The May 25 crash occurred after the plane's left wing engine and pylon fell off on takeoff.   *Chicago Tribune*, 11 June 1979.

Two special teams, one headed by a former Federal Aviation Administration official in Chicago, have been appointed to expedite the agency's investigation of the DC-10 jumbo jet. The teams will seek the source of the plane's trouble so it can be corrected and the nation's 138 grounded DC-10s can be put back in service.

Langhorne Bond, FAA administrator, ordered the planes grounded last week after American Airlines mechanics found small cracks in pylon structures holding the engines to the wings. A major crack in the same pylon aft bulkhead was found in the wreckage of the American Airlines DC-10 that crashed May 25 outside O'Hare International Airport, killing 274 persons. The pylon aft bulkhead is a section of the pylon structure just below one of the points at which it is attached to the wing. The May 25 crash occurred after the plane's left wing engine and pylon fell off on takeoff.

As you can see, the six paragraphs of the newspaper version would be reduced to two paragraphs in an ordinary essay.

Perhaps, having seen short paragraphs in newspapers or magazines, you have been influenced by these examples. But there is another and even likelier cause for shorter paragraphs: student paragraphs often are not developed enough.

Undeveloped paragraphs are paragraphs that do not elaborate. These paragraphs need additional reasons, comments, examples. If your instructor has called attention to this weakness in your writing, perhaps through such symbols as *dev*[elopment], ¶ *dev,* or *det*[ail], most probably this is what he or she means. And even if your instructor has not remarked on this point—after all, it is a weakness, not an error—chances are you could still profit from the suggestions that follow. Fuller paragraph development can make the difference between a mediocre writer and a really good one. It's that important.

When you begin a paragraph, you make a commitment to the reader. (Often that commitment is implied in the topic sentence.) This commitment is your promise of what the paragraph will be about. Every unified paragraph will have only one such commitment. The good writer, however, knows that he or she must elaborate on that opening promise. Good writers build on the opening statement by offering additional reasons, additional comments, additional examples. Sometimes these additions will be of only one type (e.g., examples); sometimes the paragraph will combine several types.

Usually a writer does not think, "Now I am going to use Method B for the development of good paragraphs." The process is ordinarily not a conscious one. But if you need to develop your paragraphs further, it helps to *make* the process a conscious one. Part B of this chapter offers two practical methods for increasing your awareness of how paragraphs can be developed. These two methods—developing by patterns and developing by coordinate and subordinate structures—are not alternatives. Rather they are two ways of looking at the same process.

B1. Paragraph Patterns

Suppose for a moment you are the author of the following paragraph, copied verbatim from a student paper:

> I enjoy listening to music no matter what I am doing. Music makes me feel relaxed and brightens my mood.

Let's further suppose that this paragraph has been returned to you with a symbol like ¶ *dev* next to it, or perhaps a comment like, "This idea needs more development" or "Don't just generalize, give some examples." What can you do to improve the paragraph?

One possibility is to think about whether you can use one of the traditional paragraph patterns. Many paragraphs—not all, but about half—follow certain familiar patterns, certain familiar methods of naming and then developing a subject. These patterns are not familiar by accident. On the contrary, we know them well because many writers have used them. By acquainting yourself with these patterns and then reviewing them in your mind when you are at a loss for a good means of developing a subject, you may be able to elaborate on your topic more successfully.

This section of the chapter will describe some of the most common paragraph patterns. To learn them, and to see if you can use them (perhaps on a subject such as the "I like music" paragraph), ask yourself the following questions.

First, can you develop your paragraph by means of **example**? This pattern is the most frequently used of all. Paragraphs that use this pattern often begin with a generalization, just like our original paragraph about music. But they are never content to stop there. Instead they go on to illustrate the generalization through one or more detailed examples. Here is a typical example paragraph by M. F. Fasteau from *The Male Machine:*

> What is particularly difficult for men is seeking or accepting help from friends. I, for one, learned early that dependence was unacceptable. When I was eight, I went to a summer camp I disliked. My parents visited me in the middle of the summer and, when it was time for them to leave, I wanted to go with them. They refused, and I yelled and screamed and was miserably unhappy for the rest of the day. That evening an older camper comforted me, sitting by my bed as I cried, patting me on the back soothingly and saying whatever it is that one says at times like that. He was in some way clumsy or funny-looking, and a few days later I joined a group of kids in cruelly making fun of him, an act which upset me, when I thought about it, for years. I can only explain it in terms of my feeling, as early as the age of eight, that by needing and accepting his help and comfort I had compromised myself, and took it out on him.

The generalization—that men find it difficult to accept help from other men—is then illustrated by the author's story of his summer camp experience.

> Example is the school of mankind and they will learn at no other.
>
> *Edmund Burke*

Sometimes the paragraph develops not just one example but several, as in this one written by Arthur Herzog, from *The B.S. Factor:*

> Copy Cant is familiar in advertising (no wonder copywriters are called *copy* writers), but it is more prevalent than is generally realized in fields that take pride in their intellectuality. Consider the title chains of books. Betty Friedan's *The Feminine Mystique* had such a tiny print order and low visibility that *The New York Times Book Review* did not review it. (True, a newspaper strike was in progress, but the *Times* caught up with other books.) "Mystique" became popular and soon mothered a dozen books with "mystique" in their titles: *Jewish, Southern, Masculine,* etc. David Riesman's *The Lonely Crowd* (also neglected by the *Times*), brought out the "crowd" books. Richard Rovere's *The American Establishment* established "establishment" in titles, just as Charles Schulz's *Happiness Is a Warm Puppy* sired a litter of "happiness is" titles.

Four examples show how publishers copy titles from successful books: titles based on *mystique, crowd, establishment,* and *happiness.*

If we return now to the paragraph on music, we can ask if there are any examples that would develop the generalization that music is enjoyable because it relaxes and brightens the mood. Here is a possible revision of the earlier paragraph, one that develops it by an example:

> I enjoy listening to music no matter what I am doing. Music always makes me feel relaxed and brightens my mood. For example, when I am driving to school in the morning I switch on the car radio and tune it to WJJD. Listening to "C&W" music, with its simple ballads of betrayal and lost love, its familiar themes like "goin' back home," its uncomplicated guitar rhythms, all this helps me fight the tension of the expressways. What I see are menacing semis or crazy Volkswagens, what I hear are horns, engines, and screaming brakes, what I smell is diesel exhaust. But my heart and mind are at peace because

the music has carried me away from the city, out to some little cabin in the hills; and as I roar down the Kennedy Expressway I hear myself humming along with John Denver "Take me home, country road."

Here the generalization has been fleshed out by one detailed example.

Alternatively, several examples could be used, each in lesser detail, as Arthur Herzog did in his paragraph on "copy cant." Our paragraph on music might now look like this:

> I enjoy listening to music no matter what I am doing. Music always makes me feel relaxed and brightens my mood. If I'm studying, some light classical music provides a soothing background and still allows me to concentrate. If I'm working around the house, driving the car, or talking with friends, soft rock is what I choose. For parties, however, I like good hard rock—the harder the better—or else disco music. And sometimes, especially when I am driving to school in the morning, I might tune in a "C&W" station just to bring a breath of fresh country air into the smog-laden and noisy atmosphere of the expressways.

Do you see how this paragraph and the one preceding it both use the example pattern, in other words *generalization + illustration(s)?* Without the illustrations the original paragraph is empty, almost trivial. Examine your own writing to see if you can give life to some bare statements by appropriate example.

Could you develop your paragraph by giving a **list of reasons**? This is the second most frequent method of development. Here is an example, by Wendell Berry, from *A Continuous Harmony:*

> Odd as I am sure it will appear to some, I can think of no better form of personal involvement in the cure of the environment than that of gardening. A person who is growing a garden, if he is growing it organically, is improving a piece of the world. He is producing something to eat, which makes him somewhat independent of the grocery business, but he is also enlarging, for himself, the meaning of food and the pleasure of eating. The food he grows will be fresher, more nutritious, less contaminated by poisons and preservatives and dye, than what he can buy at a store. He is reducing the trash problem; a garden is not a disposable container, and it will digest and re-use its own wastes. If he enjoys working in his garden, then he is less dependent on an automobile or a merchant for his pleasure. He is involving himself directly in the work of feeding people.

In the first sentence, Berry states that gardening is an excellent form of ecology. He then lists, in the six sentences that follow, a total of seven reasons the statement is true (the third sentence contains two separate reasons).

If you were to elaborate on the music paragraph by listing reasons, it might look like this:

> I enjoy listening to music no matter what I am doing. One reason is that music entertains me while I'm doing certain routine chores like straightening my room or washing the dishes. Furthermore music seems to relax me, to break the tension of a hard day or an anxious moment. The lyrics of certain songs can also have a special meaning; when Jim Croce says he wants to "put time in a bottle," he echoes what I have often felt myself. A final reason for listening to music is its effect on my mood. When I hear a cut from a good album I am not only entertained, I am actually happier, brighter than I was before.

Four reasons are given for the statement that opens the paragraph.

Another possibility is to develop your paragraph by means of **classification.** Paragraphs that use this pattern develop the topic by breaking it down into its categories or classes. In other words, if you want to say more about Subject X, you might divide Subject X into subtopics; if Subject X is musical instruments, you could discuss wind instruments, stringed instruments, and percussion instruments. Alternatively, using a different principle for the classification, you could divide musical instruments into instruments for orchestra, instruments for popular music, and so on: either way, you now have more to say about the topic, you can develop it further.

For example, when Mortimer Adler wanted to write about book owners, he was able to divide them into three classes:

> There are three kinds of book owners. The first has all the standard sets and best-sellers—unread, untouched. (This deluded individual owns woodpulp and ink, not books.) The second has a great many books—a few of them read through, most of them dipped into, but all of them as clean and shiny as the day they were bought. (This person would probably like to make books his own, but is restrained by a false respect for their physical appearance.) The third has a few books or many—every one of them dog-eared and dilapidated, shaken and loosened by continual use, marked and scribbled in from front to back. (This man owns books.)

We could also revise our paragraph on music by using classification, perhaps like this:

> I enjoy listening to music no matter what I am doing. Music usually has two effects on me. The first is relaxation: no matter how trivial or frustrating the day has been, a favorite record or two on the stereo eases me out of my irritated mood. As my attention gets absorbed in the music I feel soothed, then calmer and more peaceful. The second effect might seem a paradox, but it is equally true: music gives me energy. Especially on a Friday or Saturday night, when I want to party with friends, nothing can give a better emotional high than some good cuts from *Rose Royce* or *Earth, Wind, and Fire.*

This paragraph develops the effects of music on the writer. We can just as easily imagine paragraphs classifying the kinds of music or the causes of musical harmony.

By the way, you may have noticed a strong similarity between this paragraph and the earlier revised paragraph that gave four examples. There is a difference, however. In the most recent paragraph, the intent is to categorize the effects of music. This purpose is fulfilled by listing two and only two effects, a list that presumably exhausts the effects of which the author is aware. In the earlier paragraph, the intent was simply to offer some examples. The paragraph listed four; presumably the list could have been shorter or longer, because it did not propose to be a complete classification.

Ask yourself if you can develop your paragraph by **comparison and contrast.** In such cases a writer explains the topic more fully by showing its similarities to and/or its differences from another member of the same category. Consider as an example the following paragraph, in which the critic Matthew Arnold finds both similarities (comparisons) and differences (contrasts) between the poet Robert Burns and the poet Geoffrey Chaucer. The paragraph is from "A Study in Poetry."

> Yet we may say of [Burns] as of Chaucer, that of life and the world, as they come before him, his view is large, free, shrewd, benignant—truly poetic, therefore; and his manner of rendering what he sees is to match. But we must note, at the same time, his great difference from Chaucer. The freedom of Chaucer is heightened, in Burns, by a fiery, reckless energy; the benignity of Chaucer deepens, in Burns, into an overwhelming sense of the pathos of

things;—of the pathos of human nature, the pathos, also, of non-human nature. Instead of the fluidity of Chaucer's manner, the manner of Burns has spring, bounding swiftness. Burns is by far the greater force, though he has perhaps less charm.

Sometimes writers will restrict themselves to just similarities or just differences. William Murray, for example, having already explained what qualities all surfers share, then devotes a paragraph to showing the differences between one kind of surfer and another:

Most surfers are just nice kids from white middle-class families. They will graduate from college, take jobs, get married and become fathers, and soon they will be surfing once or twice a month, if at all. They will teach their children how to surf, and they will retire gracefully to the outdoor barbecue, the bar and the television set, captured by white collars and brown shoes. But there is another class of surfer that is becoming more and more evident, a hard-core minority of fanatics who are past their teens and for whom life has become an endless summer in search of the perfect wave. It is this dedicated group, for whom surfing is a metaphysic, that dominates the competitive scene, establishes the pecking order on the beach and sets the styles of this new American subculture based almost as much on language and looks as on skill in the water, though the latter is still the basic prerequisite for status.

How might this comparison-contrast pattern apply to our music paragraph? Here is another possible version of it:

I enjoy listening to music no matter what I am doing. Music always makes me feel relaxed and brightens my mood. When music is playing on the radio it has the same effect on me as talking with friends—my attention is diverted from my problems and I feel calmer, more relaxed. Yet music is also different from conversation because it is much more subject to my control. I can hear what I want, when I want. I can change stations, make it louder or softer, even turn it off completely. None of this is possible in conversation unless I want to bring a quick end to some friendships.

Both comparison and contrast appear very clearly in this paragraph.

The last question you might ask is whether you can develop your paragraph by giving a **definition** of its topic. Many terms we use quite commonly have several meanings, and often it is useful to explain precisely which meaning is intended. Definition paragraphs make your meaning clearer. Examine this paragraph by the famous scientist and writer Jacob Bronowski, from *The Reach of Imagination:*

> I am using the word *image* in a wide meaning, which does not restrict it to the mind's eye as a visual organ. An image in my usage is what Charles Peirce called a *sign*, without regard for its sensory quality. Peirce distinguished between different forms of signs, but there is no reason to make his distinction here, for the imagination works equally with them all, and that is why I call them all images.

Bronowski cautions us that he will not employ the word *image* in its narrower sense as something we picture in our mind's eye. He uses definition to show that an *image* for him will be a *sign*, and the meaning of the rest of his essay thus becomes clearer.

> [on being asked to define jazz:] Man, when you got to ask what it is, you'll never know.
>
> *Louis Armstrong*

We return to the music paragraph one last time. To develop the paragraph by means of a definition pattern might be to rewrite it something like this:

> I enjoy listening to music no matter what I am doing. Music for me is any sound that has a rhythm to it. That definition includes of course the more conventional kinds of music, like classical or jazz or rock. But it also includes the swish of cars on the wet street outside my window, or the repetitious thwack of the ping-pong ball coming up from the basement; or even the sound of my own humming. So long as I can feel rhythm I can hear music, and music relaxes me and brightens my mood.

You might not use the word *music* in the same way as the author of that paragraph, but at least you understand what he means.

There are other patterns besides the five familiar ones just described. And these five patterns themselves do not always occur in a "pure" form. Very often a paragraph will contain parts of more than one pattern. You might remember that Jacob Bronowski's definition of image contained a contrast, in this case a contrast between his definition of the word and the definition offered by Charles Peirce. If you are giving reasons or explaining causes, do not hesitate to enrich your paragraph by giving examples or definitions wherever they might be helpful.

Furthermore, to develop a paragraph and to give it order are often one and the same process. If you arrange a list in logical order or tell a story in chronological order, you are also using a pattern of development. The difference between Part A and Part B of this chapter is a matter of emphasis: if you already have enough material and only need to know how to arrange it, Part A is more applicable; if you need more material, Part B should be your concern.

The important point about paragraph development is that it need not be left to chance. There are questions to ask, patterns to use, processes to work out, as this section has shown. What you are looking for are ways to stimulate your imagination, so that it can supply the added information that makes the difference between sketchy paragraphs and thoughtful, penetrating paragraphs.

B2. Coordinate and Subordinate Paragraphs

Earlier we compared sentences and paragraphs to show how similar they are. In this section I want to draw out the comparison a little further. What you know about developing sentences can help you in developing paragraphs.

In Chapter 2 you learned about cumulative sentences, which contain a main (base) clause and then add clauses to provide more detail. Here is a cumulative sentence:

> *Wood ducks were flighting in* to roost on the lake, the drake dandies leading the way, the dying light catching their plumage in a fireburst of color.   *J. D. Scott* [italics added]

The base clause is in italics. The remainder of the sentence consists of phrases and clauses that explain either the base clause or a subsequent clause. In other words, the later phrases and clauses *develop* the subject of the base clause (wood ducks).

Suppose we say that a paragraph is like a sentence. Then what might a **cumulative paragraph** look like?

Cumulative sentences usually begin with the base clause. Cumulative paragraphs usually begin with a sentence we can call the **base sentence.** The remaining sentences of the paragraph then explain or add further details to this base sentence, just as the phrases or clauses do in a cumulative sentence. (You might be tempted to call this first sentence the topic sentence, but since some paragraphs do not really have topic sentences, it is more accurate to stay with the term *base sentence*.)

The best way to see how cumulative paragraphs work is to look at an example. Here is a paragraph written by E. M. Forster from his essay, "What I Believe."

> No, I distrust Great Men. They produce a desert of uniformity around them and often a pool of blood too, and I always feel a little man's pleasure when they come a cropper. Every now and then one reads in the newspapers some such statement as: "The coup d'état appears to have failed, and Admiral Toma's whereabouts is at present unknown." Admiral Toma had probably every qualification for being a Great Man—an iron will, personal magnetism, dash, flair, sexlessness—but fate was against him, so he retires to unknown whereabouts instead of parading history with his peers. He fails with a completeness which no artist and no lover can experience, because with them the process of creation is itself an achievement, whereas with him the only possible achievement is success.

Suppose we separate the paragraph into sentences and then arrange it so that each sentence modifies or adds details to some preceding sentence. That way our paragraph would look like a sentence that has been divided into its clauses and phrases. The Forster paragraph would look like this:

No, I distrust Great Men.

> They produce a desert of uniformity around them and often a pool of blood too, and I always feel a little man's pleasure when they come a cropper.

> > Every now and then one reads in the newspapers some such statement as: "The coup d'état appears to have failed, and Admiral Toma's whereabouts is at present unknown."

> > Admiral Toma had probably every qualification for being a Great Man—an iron will, personal magnetism, dash, flair, sexlessness—but fate was against him, so he retires to unknown whereabouts instead of parading history with his peers.

> > > He fails with a completeness which no artist and no lover can experience, because with them the process of creation is itself an achievement, whereas with him the only possible achievement is success.

The first sentence ("No, I distrust Great Men") is the base sentence. The second sentence explains or modifies the first. The third offers an example of the second, so we mark it as modifying the second, just as we do again when the fourth turns out to be an explanation of the third. The final sentence compares Admiral Toma's failure with the failure of artists or lovers and therefore operates on still a fifth level, as a comment on the fourth sentence.

The value of rewriting the paragraph this way is that we can now see clearly the pattern this paragraph follows. In diagram form here is how it would look:

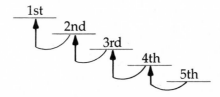

The paragraph develops in an orderly, logical way, as this diagram makes clear. Each sentence grows out of the one preceding it.

Now you can also see better why the first sentence should be called the base sentence rather than the topic sentence. Read the last sentence of the paragraph. Is there any way you could guess that this final sentence is a natural subdivision of the "topic" "I distrust Great Men"? I don't think so. On the contrary, the connection between them becomes clear only when we see how this fifth sentence grows out of the fourth, how the fourth in turn grows out of the third, and so on back to the first. Thus we can say that all the other sentences *depend upon* the first sentence, but they are not necessarily *subdivisions* of it. This dependency we recognize by calling the first sentence the base sentence.

Here is another example, this time a paragraph written by a student about her experience as a volunteer in a retirement home:

> The desolation I found in the Home was almost beyond belief. It was filled with old people crying, pleading for company. Their families, supposedly their "loved ones," brought them to this home to die, rejecting them because they had become useless burdens,

never calling or visiting them. Loneliness can kill—everyone needs someone. When the family you have loved and cared for suddenly turns you away, it is too much to take. The Home, instead of being a happy place for a dignified retirement, was a purgatory where old people suffered and waited to die.

Again we can see how each sentence grows out of the one that precedes it, all the way back to the base sentence at the beginning of the paragraph. Because each sentence depends upon the one before it rather than being a subdivision of the base sentence, the structure of these paragraphs is like the structure of subordinate sentences. Therefore paragraphs like the two we just examined can be called **subordinate paragraphs.**

Not all cumulative paragraphs have a subordinate structure. If we continue the comparison with sentences, another group of paragraphs could be called **coordinate paragraphs,** because like coordinate sentences they consist of two or more separate-but-equal sentences, each of which grows directly out of the base sentence. The following paragraph by Robert Coles from "The Children of Affluence," is an excellent example of a coordinate paragraph. Here it is, arranged to show how each sentence is an independent, equal unit:

It is a complicated world, a world that others watch with envy and with curiosity, with awe, anger, bitterness, resentment.

It is a world, rather often, of action, of talk believed by the talkers to have meaning and importance, of schedules or timetables.

It is a world in motion—yet, at times, one utterly still: a child in a garden, surrounded by the silence acres of lawn or woods can provide.

It is a world of excitement and achievement.

It is an intensely private world that can suddenly become vulnerable to the notice of others.

It is, obviously, a world of money and power—a twentieth-century American version of both.

It is also a world in which children grow up, come to terms with their ample surroundings, take to them gladly, deal with them anxiously, and show themselves boys and girls who have their own special circumstances to master—a particular way of life to understand and become a part of.

By diagram the paragraph might look like this:

```
1st
 ▲      2nd
 |      3rd
 |      4th
 |      5th
 |      6th
 \      7th
```

The first sentence is the base sentence because it limits the paragraph to its subject, the world of the child from a wealthy family. Yet all the other sentences offer separate but equally important details about that world. So all the sentences are parallel to each other—a fact emphasized by their similar opening words.

In the Forster and Coles examples we have seen subordinate and coordinate paragraphs in their "pure" state, which makes it easier to see the patterns they follow. Of course most paragraphs contain some elements from both types and are therefore examples of **mixed paragraphs.** This excerpt from Martin Luther King's letter from the Birmingham jail shows a simple type of mixed paragraph:

> Let us consider a more concrete example of just and unjust laws. An unjust law is a code that a numerical or power majority group compels a minority group to obey but does not make binding on itself. This is *difference* made legal. By the same token, a just law is a code that a majority compels a minority to follow and that it is willing to follow itself. This is *sameness* made legal.

Rewritten to show how it mixes subordinate and coordinate structures, it would look like this:

> Let us consider a more concrete example of just and unjust laws.
>
> > An unjust law is a code that a numerical or power majority group compels a minority group to obey but does not make binding on itself.
> >
> > > This is *difference* made legal.
> >
> > By the same token, a just law is a code that a majority compels a minority to follow and that it is willing to follow itself.
> >
> > > This is *sameness* made legal.

If we diagram the paragraph, this would be its pattern:

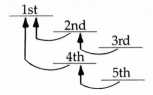

The paragraph is not purely subordinate because sentences two and four clearly have equal status, growing directly out of the base sentence. Neither is it purely coordinate, because sentences three and five do not refer to the base sentence but rather to the sentences that immediately precede them. So we can say the paragraph mixes both subordinate and coordinate patterns.

> Composition is for the most part, an effort of slow diligence and steady perseverance, to which the mind is dragged by necessity or resolution.
>
> *Samuel Johnson*

But you are probably troubled now by a more practical concern. Granted, most paragraphs can be categorized according to one of these three patterns. How can this knowledge help you to be a better writer?

First, an understanding of these three patterns enables you to see the defects of paragraphs that you know are weak but that you don't know how to improve. In the following example a student writer describes the problems some drivers encounter:

> No matter how efficient some people think they are when they drive, their habits irritate others. The driver at the head of a single lane of traffic goes ten miles per hour under the posted limit. Cars back up for blocks behind him. Horns are honking, people are shouting and swearing. Now that person may think he is being properly cautious when in fact he is holding up traffic, which is as annoying as another mistake, never turning down the high beams on the headlights. There are other errors too, like following too close or failing to use the turn signal.

This paragraph came back to the writer with the notation that it "lacks coherence" and "needs development."

At first the writer did not see what these comments meant. Then he decided to arrange the paragraph according to the patterns we have just discussed. When he did, the reasons for these faults became clear. His attempt at an arrangement looked like this:

No matter how efficient. . . .

    The driver at the head of a single lane. . . .

        Cars back up for blocks. . . .

        Horns are honking. . . .

        Now that person may think. . . .

    There are other errors too. . . .

This pattern is unsatisfactory, however. Obviously the second sentence is an example of the bad driving habits the base sentence describes, so we can be comfortable making this sentence as dependent on the base sentence. Sentences three and four also offer no problem—they clearly depend on the second. But how about the fifth sentence, the one beginning "Now that person may think. . ."? We can make it modify the second sentence too, as in the preceding diagram, because it says still more about the slow driver. But to do so we must ignore the second half of it. The second half of the fifth sentence tells about still another bad habit, using high beams, and therefore it belongs in the same position as the second sentence. Our puzzlement is then increased further when we read the last sentence. This final one contains both the third and fourth examples of bad driving habits, yet its position in the diagram as only the second "middle-level" sentence shows that the paragraph in its present form allows for only two such habits.

So one way to see how this paragraph "lacks coherence" is to realize that the paragraph lists four examples of bad driving habits but structurally makes room for only two of them. Giving each of these habits a separate-but-equal sentence of its own would go a long way toward restoring coherence.

This attempt to rearrange the paragraph also shows why it is not adequately developed. Notice that the first bad habit, slow driving, is stated in the second sentence and then developed by three succeeding sentences. Yet the second bad habit, using high beams, gets only a dependent clause tacked on to the fifth

sentence, and the last two habits, tailgating and improper sig-
nalling, must share the final sentence. If all four habits could be
developed in about as much detail as the first one, then the
paragraph would be better proportioned.

Here is how the student writer revised the paragraph in order
to eliminate the weaknesses of the original:

> No matter how efficient some people think they are when they
> drive, their habits irritate others. For example, a driver at the head of
> a single lane of traffic goes ten miles per hour under the posted limit.
> Cars back up for blocks behind him. Horns are honking, people are
> shouting and swearing. Now that person may think he is being
> properly cautious, but in fact he is holding up traffic. A second
> example, equally annoying, is the driver who never dims his head-
> lights. The painful glare of those high beams, especially if they come
> on you from around a curve, can be frightening and dangerous. Then
> of course we can't forget the tailgater. If you cruise an expressway at
> 55, he hangs off your rear bumper like he was slipstreaming you in
> the Atlanta 500. If you encounter him on city streets, he is sure to
> give you a sharp jolt at the stop sign, then blame you for stopping too
> quickly. A close relative of the tailgater is the nonsignaller. This last
> source of irritation has the habit of drifting into the right lane and
> then, without the least hint or warning, swerving across in front of
> you and turning left onto a side street, leaving in his wake a screech
> of brakes and a chorus of angry horns.

If we were to diagram this revised paragraph, it would look like
this:

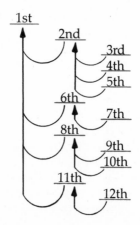

The paragraph now has a coherent structure and a full, proportioned development. Trying to arrange the paragraph according to subordinate, coordinate, or mixed types taught the writer what he had to do to make his paragraph better. The revised version is a good example of a mixed paragraph, with sentences two, six, eight, and eleven depending on the base sentence and the other sentences in turn depending on those four. (The revised version is also, you might notice, a good example of the "development by example" pattern we discussed on pp. 156–157. Looking at paragraphs by patterns or looking at them by types are complementary methods, two different ways of getting to the same goal.)

So if your instructor makes the general comment that your paragraphs lack coherence or lack development, or if he or she makes such comments about particular paragraphs, one way to learn what needs revising is to try the method described in the preceding paragraphs. The patterns that emerge when you try to arrange them this way can help you identify where you went wrong and what you can do to improve.

> But all things are put at the same level by Tao.
> *Chuang Tzu*

The second practical advantage of knowing about these three types of paragraphs is that such knowledge can also help you while you are writing.

Suppose, for example, you are writing a paper about the role of computers in modern universities. Early in the course of writing the paper you find you must say something about the uses to which computers are put. A paragraph on "uses of the computer" begins to take shape in your mind.

Before you put pen to paper, however, think for a moment. Which of the sequences we just discussed seems more applicable here, coordinate or subordinate? Quickly you realize that coordinate is more likely because the paragraph will contain a list, with all the items on the list, i.e., all the uses of the computer, having equal value. Let's assume you can think of three main uses: faculty and student research, academic record-keeping, and administrative services. A rough outline of a coordinate paragraph already begins to emerge:

<u>Uses</u>
  <u>1st: research</u>
  <u>2nd: records</u>
  <u>3rd: services</u>

Such outlines need not be written. Their sole purpose is to remind you of the general form your paragraph will take.

Now you can write the paragraph, fleshing out this initial design. As each of the three uses is taken up, more details, explanations, and examples of each occur to you, and you incorporate them into additional sentences beyond your three basic ones. But these additional sentences will always be dependent upon the three sentences that form the original coordinate sequence. Here is a paragraph that might result from using such a method:

> Despite their cost, computers are essential to a university because they serve three main functions. First, they enable both faculty and students to undertake research that would be impossible otherwise. Students use computers primarily for math courses, but faculty members from all departments and disciplines now find them necessary research tools. Even humanities departments, for example, now use computer-produced word counts to study an author's literary style. The second function of computers is academic bookkeeping, including such tasks as recording grades, issuing transcripts, and tallying class rolls. This work was formerly done by hand, so computers in this case save money and help pay for themselves. Finally, computers are used to keep track of the myriad of items and activities that are part of any large and complex organization. Computers are involved in every kind of administrative service, from printing the payroll checks to taking inventory of the pencils.

The full paragraph would now be diagramed like this:

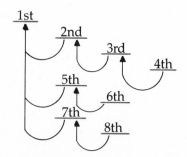

The paragraph is now a mixed sequence, yet this diagram makes clear how the complete paragraph is still related to the original coordinate sequence. The second, fifth, and seventh sentences are coordinate because they each modify the base sentence and they each state one of the three uses.

Coordinate sequences are especially good for paragraphs that give examples, or list, or classify, or in some other way divide the subject into parts. If your paragraph attempts one of those tasks, experiment with a coordinate structure as the clearest way to develop your subject.

Another advantage of the coordinate sequence is that it encourages the writer to use repetition. When we discussed repetition before (Chapter 2), we praised artful repetition within sentences. But repetition can also occur from one sentence to another sentence, so that the entire paragraph can be drawn together by the use of these **repeated phrases.** Consider again the paragraph by Robert Coles, the one in which he describes the world of rich children:

> It is a complicated world, a world that others watch with envy and with curiosity, with awe, anger, bitterness, resentment. It is a world, rather often, of action, of talk believed by the talkers to have meaning and importance, of schedules or timetables. It is a world in motion—yet, at times, one utterly still: a child in a garden, surrounded by the silence acres of lawn or woods can provide. It is a world of excitement and achievement. It is an intensely private world that can suddenly become vulnerable to the notice of others. It is, obviously, a world of money and power—a twentieth-century American version of both. It is also a world in which children grow up, come to terms with their ample surroundings, take to them gladly, deal with them anxiously, and show themselves boys and girls who have their own special circumstances to master—a particular way of life to understand and become a part of.

Every one of the seven sentences in this paragraph contains the phrase "it is a world." Yet so artful is Coles in the way he varies this phrase that we are never conscious of boredom or monotony.

Sometimes in going from one sentence to another writers repeat not phrases but grammatical structures. Repeating grammatical structures can be called **parallelism.** Here a student describes the view from her dorm room window late at night:

> Cars going down the street, turning left into the parking lot. Sidewalks a grey streak, followed by a green patch of grass and then a grey streak of road. Room lights in Stebler Hall going on or off in irregular patterns, but mostly off. A couple passing by on the sidewalk, whispering to each other like people usually do when it's very late. Then all is quiet and I am left alone in the silence and the growing darkness, wondering at the mystery of it.

Each sentence except the last begins with a noun—*cars*, *sidewalks*, *room lights*, *couple*—that will be the focal point of that sentence. The nouns are not repeated, but the form of the sentence is. (You probably noticed, by the way, that these parallel sentences are also sentence fragments. Here the writer uses them deliberately to give the effect of a catalog, in this case a catalog of the objects that attract her attention as she looks out the window.)

> **Writing isn't hard; it's no harder than ditch-digging.**
> *Patrick Dennis*

On the other hand, if your paragraph will narrate a story, explain a process, or define a term, perhaps a subordinate sequence might be better. As an example, suppose we were to rearrange the one-paragraph definition of *image* by Bronowski (p. 162). It forms a perfect subordinate sequence:

> I am using the word *image* in a wide meaning. . . .
>
>   An image in my usage is what Charles Peirce. . . .
>
>   Peirce distinguished between different. . . .

Closer to home, suppose you are about to write a paragraph satirizing the registration process at your college. You realize that the paragraph will take on the form of "do-this-and-then-this-and-then-this," each step growing out of the one that precedes it in the sequence. A rough mental outline of the paragraph will therefore show a subordinate sequence:

With such an outline clear in your mind you are ready to write. The outline reminds you to be very sure that each sentence in your paragraph follows clearly and logically from the one before it. When the paragraph is finished it might look like this:

> The first step in living through the terror of registration is finding the right line—after all, many students have spent two patient hours only to find they were in the line for parking permits. When you have found the right line and earned your way to the front, be prepared for the inevitable response: "Those classes are closed— cantcha read the board?" Well no you can't, as a matter of fact, because the bulletin board is over in the corner, you certainly can't sacrifice your place in line, and you have forgotten your telescope. Discouraged but undaunted, you start all over again and after two more hours you are rewarded with a schedule that specialized in 8:00 A.M. classes and 4:00 P.M. labs. Now you are ready to move on to the bursar's table, to pay for the privilege of taking these early and late classes. From there it is just a mercifully quick stop for an I.D. card and you can be on your way. As you leave, it dawns on you that registration is just like an oversized Monopoly game, except you never get to "go" anywhere and *they* always keep the $200.

Each of the six sentences following the base sentence depends upon the one directly ahead of it. A subordinate sequence is the underlying pattern of the finished paragraph.

We have seen that a writer can use several methods of development in the same paragraph. Similarly, most paragraphs combine both coordinate and subordinate sequences. In fact, it is probably fair to say that *the typical paragraph is a mixed sequence and uses more than one method of development.* We considered each of these patterns separately and in their purest forms, so that we could understand them more easily. Hopefully this better understanding leads to increased awareness, and increased awareness leads to increased use. But most writing combines all of these sequences and methods.

The following paragraph by Susanne Langer, from "The Prince of Creation," illustrates this mixture.

> The answer is, I think, that man's mind is *not* a direct evolution from the beast's mind, but is a unique variant and therefore has had a meteoric and startling career very different from any other animal history. The trait that sets human mentality apart from every other is its preoccupation with symbols, with images and names that *mean*

things, rather than with things themselves. This trait may have been a mere sport of nature once upon a time. Certain creatures do develop tricks and interests that seem biologically unimportant. Pack rats, for instance, and some birds of the crow family take a capricious pleasure in bright objects and carry away such things for which they have, presumably, no earthly use. Perhaps man's tendency to see certain forms as *images*, to hear certain sounds not only as signals but as expressive tones, and to be excited by sunset colors or starlight, was originally just a peculiar sensitivity in a rather highly developed brain. But whatever its cause, the ultimate destiny of this trait was momentous; for all human activity is based on the appreciation and use of symbols.

Two sentences, the second and the last, depend directly on the base sentence and therefore give the paragraph some coordinate structure. At the same time we find the second sentence modified by four sentences that grow out of it and form a subordinate structure. We can also observe several methods of development at work: explanation (second sentence), cause and effect (third), example (fifth), cause and effect again (sixth).

I should conclude this chapter with a word of caution. The importance of full paragraph development does not mean *all* paragraphs must be long ones. Quite the contrary. Sometimes you will find opportunities for the deliberately short paragraph. When you need an attention-getting opening paragraph, when you want your concluding paragraph to offer a "punch line," when you wish to give special emphasis to one or two sentences: on these and other occasions a short paragraph will serve you well. Like the extra-short sentences we discussed in Chapter 2, brief paragraphs are quite acceptable if used deliberately and knowledgeably. But I think you should master the material in this section on paragraph development before you decide whether you are ready to make these exceptions.

Short, underdeveloped paragraphs are the more common weakness in student writing. But sometimes I do encounter seemingly endless paragraphs, perhaps even an entire paper that consists of nothing but one interminable paragraph. Almost always, however, this extra length comes not from a fuller development of the topic, but rather from a failure to see natural divisions in the subject matter; such papers are really several shorter paragraphs that have been lumped together, like a casserole made of leftovers. If you have written paragraphs of this sort, study very carefully the suggestions for paragraph unity offered in Part A of this chapter.

Paragraphs are like sentences, we said—sentences writ large. If we observe them from another direction, however, we could also say that paragraphs are essays writ small. In other words, essays are to paragraphs as paragraphs are to sentences. We turn our attention to the college essay in Chapter 4.

EXERCISES

1. Develop two of the topics in each of the following categories into full paragraphs, using the methods prescribed. Or, you may prefer to choose your own topics.

a. Develop by example, either one detailed example or several undetailed ones:

  dilapidated automobiles
  good teachers
  salesclerks
  cheating
  success

b. Develop by classification:

  bosses
  friends
  rock groups
  cities (or towns)

c. Develop by comparison and/or contrast:

  liking and loving
  cities and towns
  junior colleges and universities
  "pure" science and "applied" science
  movies in theaters and movies on tv

d. Develop by definition:

  success
  tenderness
  hero (or heroine)
  propaganda
  representative government

2. Choose one of the topic sentences below. Write a paragraph using any one of the methods of development listed in Question 1. Then write it again, using a different method of development. Finally, write the paragraph a third time, this time mixing two or more methods of development.

a. My neighborhood differs from any other section of the city.
b. Sexually explicit tv programs are a disgrace to the society that supports them.
c. Modern "conveniences" only make life more complicated.
d. When in trouble, punt.
e. In my high school you could tell the jocks right away.

3. Below you will find three student-written paragraphs that need further development. Rewrite them, choosing any method of development discussed in this chapter.

a. Life runs in cycles. My first day in college reminded me in several ways of my first day in high school.
b. I like the sounds of nature. They keep me alert yet make me feel relaxed and peaceful. I try to hear the sounds of nature whenever I can.
c. Freedom is a precious commodity, but we could lose it. Everybody says they value freedom. But what are they doing to preserve it? Nothing.

4. What methods of development do you see employed in these paragraphs? Study them closely. The first one is by Aldo Leopold from *A Sand County Almanac;* the two under b. are by a student writer.

  a.   The most glamorous hobby I know of today is the revival of falconry. It has a few addicts in America, and perhaps a dozen in England—a minority indeed. For two and a half cents one can buy and shoot a cartridge that will kill the heron whose capture by hawking requires months or years of laborious training of both the hawk and the hawker. The cartridge, as a lethal agent, is a perfect product of industrial chemistry. One can write a formula for its lethal reaction. The hawk, as a lethal agent, is the perfect flower of that still utterly mysterious alchemy—evolution. No living man can, or possibly ever will, understand the instinct of predation that we share with our raptorial servant. No man-made machine can, or ever will, synthesize that perfect coordination of eye, muscle, and pinion as he stoops to his kill. The heron, if bagged, is inedible and hence useless (although the old falconers seem to have eaten him, just as a Boy Scout smokes and eats a flea-bitten summer cottontail that has fallen victim to his sling, club, or bow). Moreover the hawk, at the slightest error in technique of handling, may either "go tame" like *Homo sapiens* or fly away into the blue. All in all, falconry is the perfect hobby.

b.   What happened to the local beauty shops, the ones named "Marge's" or "The Powder Box"? They were simply decorated: two or three chairs in the waiting room with copies of *True Confessions* on a tray table; four sinks, four setting chairs, four hairdryers. The beauticians worked at small counters cluttered with pins, clips, rollers, and hair-spray. Pictures of boyfriends or movie stars lined the mirrors, and the mirrors were set against a background of floral wallpaper and a plain white linoleum floor. These shops weren't much to look at, but the service was good, the girls amiable, and the cost low.

Now these same shops have grown into salons, with Art Deco interiors. Graphic walls, chrome-and-leather chairs, hanging plants, and disco music provide a much less personal atmosphere. After customizing your hair for two hours, the "hair stylist" (now a *he*) will insist you redo your face to go with the cut. Behind him stands an elongated counter with his own private stock of beauty supplies, and when he presents his bill you realize why he never reveals his last name.

5. Review the use of subordinate and coordinate sequences as ways of finding the weaknesses in a paragraph. Apply this method to the following student-written paragraph. When you have determined its weaknesses both in coherence and in development, suggest how the paragraph could be rewritten to eliminate those weaknesses.

War is nothing more than a racket. It creates business and profit for the businessman, opens up jobs for the unemployed, and creates a rise in the economic wealth of a nation. War is the ways and means of bringing one country and another country together to fight for what they believe is right. During wartime a country is as closely knit as it will ever be. There is no more discrimination between race, creed, or color, just an inborn need to put all our forces together and head for victory, which is a word with many meanings. Victory possibly is the ending of a war or the proving of a point. All in all "to the victor belongs the spoils" because he receives power, land, wealth and the loser backtracks to find out where he went wrong. So in conclusion war is just a business to bring wealth and power, nothing more and nothing less.

> If we have a correct theory but merely prate about it, pigeonhole it and do not put it into practice, then that theory, however good, is of no significance.
>
> *Chairman Mao*

6. In the following selection from President John F. Kennedy's inaugural address, identify the parallelism and repetition, both between paragraph and paragraph and between sentence and sentence.

To those old allies whose cultural and spiritual origins we share, we pledge the loyalty of faithful friends. United, there is little we cannot do in a host of new cooperative ventures. Divided, there is little we can do—for we dare not meet a powerful challenge at odds and split asunder.

To those new states whom we welcome to the ranks of the free, we pledge our word that one form of colonial control shall not have passed away merely to be replaced by a far more iron tyranny. We shall not always expect to find them supporting our view. But we shall always hope to find them strongly supporting their own freedom—and to remember that, in the past, those who foolishly sought power by riding the back of the tiger ended up inside.

To those peoples in the huts and villages of half the globe struggling to break the bonds of mass misery, we pledge our best efforts to help them help themselves, for whatever period is required—not because the Communists may be doing it, not because we seek their votes, but because it is right. If a free society cannot help the many who are poor, it cannot save the few who are rich.

To our sister republics south of our border, we offer a special pledge—to convert our good words into good deeds—in a new alliance for progress—to assist free men and free governments in casting off the chains of poverty. But this peaceful revolution of hope cannot become the prey of hostile powers. Let all our neighbors know that we shall join with them to oppose aggression or subversion anywhere in the Americas. And let every other power know that this hemisphere intends to remain the master of its own house.

To that world assembly of sovereign states, the United Nations, our last best hope in an age where the instruments of war have far outpaced the instruments of peace, we renew our pledge of support—to prevent it from becoming merely a forum for invective—to strengthen its shield of the new and the weak—and to enlarge the area in which its writ may run.

Finally, to those nations who would make themselves our adversary, we offer not a pledge but a request: that both sides begin anew the quest for peace, before the dark powers of destruction unleashed by science engulf all humanity in planned or accidental self-destruction.

4

THE COMPLETE
PAPER

When spider webs unite, they can tie up a lion.
Ethiopian proverb

When you learn to drive a car you study dozens of separate skills, from turning the ignition key to applying the brakes. Yet driving a car is not merely the sum of those skills, like adding up shifting + steering + acceleration + braking. Although you learn all of these skills independently, you still must be able to combine them into one overriding skill: the ability to pilot a three-thousand-pound machine even when it is hurtling down an expressway at fifty-five miles per hour. Furthermore, when you are on that expressway and some idiot cuts into your lane right in front of you, there is no time to say to yourself, "Now I must push hard on my brake and then I must check the mirror to see if I can change lanes and then I must steer to the left." People become accident statistics that way. Instead you must be able to use your skills *instinctively* and *simultaneously*.

So too with the complex skill of writing. We have talked about many separate skills in this book. But good writing is not just the sum of those skills, it's not a matter of good words + good sentences + good paragraphs + good punctuation. Instead we need to combine, to integrate those skills. This means helping you use them instinctively and simultaneously, as you confront the challenges every writer must meet in college work.

In short, this is the chapter where we begin to put it all together. Just as there is a time for putting aside the driver training manual and getting behind the wheel, so too there is a time for shifting our focus away from separate writing skills and toward the successful combination of those skills in a good college paper.

The greatest number of papers you will write in college are going to be short ones—let's say five pages or less. That is where we should begin. This chapter divides the process of writing these short papers into four stages: finding a topic (Part A), planning the paper (Part B), writing the paper (Part C), and revising it (Part D).

Of course you should not think of this division into four stages as you would a recipe. Good writers do not say, "I just finished stage three, now it's on to stage four." Writing, I said a

185

moment ago, is a *process*. We study the composing process just as we do any other process: as a series of continuous actions that bring about a certain result. Many of these actions go on simultaneously. Often a writer is planning and writing and revising all at the same time.

Nevertheless we can look at that writing process unfolding through time, as this chapter tries to do. Separating the continuous action into four stages allows us to analyze it clearly and conveniently.

Moreover this chapter can also be valuable if you are using this text as a resource book for particular writing errors and your instructor's comments always seem to be variations on certain familiar themes: "paper needs better organization"; "topic insufficiently developed"; "provide more examples." The comments might not bother you so much except for the fact that they are often accompanied by a grade that shows that the instructor means something important by them. What you need is a more successful strategy for developing the papers you write. Parts B and C of this chapter can offer special help here.

Or suppose your problem is agony of the spirit: a certain stage in the writing process causes you almost unbearable pain. Perhaps it's the stage of deciding what you will write about. Perhaps you have little trouble deciding what to write about, but you can never figure out how to get started, how to get pen moving across paper. What you need is a different way of approaching the task, plus some tips on how others—including professional writers—have met it successfully. Any one of Parts A through D might help, depending on which part seems most directly related to your needs.

A. FINDING A TOPIC

> I am still of the opinion that only two topics can be of the least interest to a serious and studious mood—sex and the dead.
>
> W. B. Yeats

This situation may be familiar:

Scene: a student's room, late at night. *Cast:* only one—the student writer (you?). *Plot:* student is in conflict partly with himself ("Why didn't I start this damn thing sooner?"), mostly with a seemingly intractable paper due the next morning. As the curtain rises on this tearful melodrama, our hero is heard to mutter, "What can I write about? What can I *possibly* write about?"

First principle: you can write well only about what you know. I learned that principle the hard way when I was a freshman in college. One week the instructor asked us to write a short story. I wrote what I thought was an exciting little story. It was all about a circus performer (a knife-thrower, as I recall); it had a spine-tingling climax and it was written in my very best style. But the story came back to me accompanied by one short sentence of dismissal: "You don't know anything about circuses."

The instructor was right. I didn't know anything about circuses and therefore I could not write familiarly about them. Writers must stick to what they know. You can supplement what you know by reading more and learning more, of course. But that's not going to help much at midnight on the night before the paper is due. So the wisest step is to take a short inventory of what you know, thus giving yourself a chance to see what material you could use for the paper.

What *do* you know? First of all, you know yourself—your life history, your fears, your dreams, your successes and failures. If the paper can be autobiographical or descriptive, perhaps you need go no further. Let your mind play freely over your past and your present. Every memory or idea that occurs to you occurs to you for a reason. After all, hundreds of things happen to us every day that we promptly forget and never remember again. Try to unravel the thread and find out *why* some particular memory or idea lingers, because in that reason may lie the secret of how you can make the story appeal to someone else. For example, almost everybody can remember their first day of school, not because each person's first day is so different from anyone else's, but rather because that day is an important rite of passage for all of us.

You also know lots of information about a wide variety of subjects. Jobs, hobbies, friends, interests, books you've read, tv programs you've seen, subjects you've studied in or out of school—you know something about all of these and more. If your paper will explain or describe something, these are the places to search.

And you have opinions too. When you talk to friends, what excites you? What makes you enthusiastic, or irritates you, or arouses your indignation? If your opinions interest a friend in conversation, often they can be made to interest a reader too.

The important issue really is not "What am I going to write about?" Almost anything can make a good topic. During one week in January 1978, for example, the nationally syndicated columnist Bob Greene wrote about the following five topics: 1. a sixty-year-old thief dying of emphysema, 2. advice to the lovelorn from a mailroom employee, 3. a man whose only profession is getting his name in the paper—149 times so far, 4. a go-go girl who strips for Jesus, and 5. a botched kidnapping attempt in a small town. In themselves these certainly are not subjects of world-shattering importance. Yet Greene manages to make us care about them and share his fascination.

The secret therefore is not what to write about—it's saying something interesting about the topic no matter what it is. Consequently, you must be excited about the subject yourself before you can make it interesting to others. Good writers have something they are burning to say. Once you have settled on a subject that is important to you, you are ready to communicate that fascination to others.

> If a man cares enough about tiddledy winks, his book about tiddledy winks will be a great book.
>
> *Matthew Bruccoli*

So just for the moment take *any* area of interest to you. You want to know whether you can find a good paper topic within that area of interest. The key to whether or not a paper will be successful lies in your answers to three important questions:

- Can I narrow this subject area to a manageable size?
- Do I have sufficient information on the subject?
- Can I adapt the subject to my reader?

If the answer to each of these three questions is yes, the subject area will be quite acceptable.

Let's explore how to answer these three questions.

A1. Narrowing the Subject

First you need to know if you can narrow the potential subject. Here is how that process works.

Suppose one area of interest that occurs to you is the job you had last summer. Suppose further that the job was at a fast-food franchise, say a Burger King. You want to know whether these job experiences can provide a paper topic.

For many people the most natural way to look at a subject is the chronological way. In other words, they see an experience just as they would a story, proceeding from beginning to end. Look at your time on the job in this chronological way. If you examine it closely, many small topics might emerge: 1. "how and why I was hired," 2. "my first day on the job," 3. "the up times and down times during the summer," or 4. "when and how I left the job." Doubtless the list could be longer.

But the chronological way is far from the only way to look at an experience. Instead of considering the job according to a time frame, first day to last day, you could analyze a slice of it. For example you could ask yourself some questions about what you saw and did on any *typical* day. Then you might get several quite different topics: 1. "my duties on the job," 2. "rush periods vs. slack periods," 3. "best and worst parts of the job," 4. "the amount of money a franchise makes each day," 5. "people I worked with," 6. "my pay and how I spent it."

If you think about the job still further, you will probably find that you also had opinions about it. Sometimes these opinions were about personal issues, but sometimes they were about larger public ones: 1. "the food we eat at such places is good (bad) and inexpensive (overpriced)"; 2. "Americans spend too much money on convenience foods" (or "convenience foods make possible an easier, better life for all of us").

Please notice two things about this analysis of topics derived from a job experience. First, these topics lend themselves to a wide variety of types of papers. If your instructor requires a personal experience paper, for example, you could use "how I was hired," or "my first day on the job," or "the rush period." If an expository paper is needed, i.e., one that explains some-thing, then "my duties" or "the money a franchise makes" or "types of customers" would be eligible. If the paper should be argumentative, either "the food is good (bad)" or "the value of convenience foods" would do quite well; both of them can be framed as statements about which people can legitimately differ.

These last topics also remind us that a paper topic need not show its origin in your own experiences. You could write about Americans spending too much on convenience foods without ever once mentioning that you had worked at Burger King. Similarly you could write an expository paper on "how people get jobs" without discussing the particular job-hunting experiences that led you to your conclusions.

> Some of my best [ideas] have come to me at the kitchen sink.
>
> *Agatha Christie*

The second thing to notice about this analysis is that so far we have moved down only one level of generalization, from your job in general to particular aspects of that job. Sometimes, however, you will have to move down more than one level. Suppose what had first occurred to you was not "my job at Burger King" but rather "the crazy jobs I've had." Then you would have had to restrict the subject from jobs in general to the Burger King job in particular, then maybe to "the good things about my job," and perhaps finally to a still more specific topic, like "the best thing about my job." We might diagram your thinking like this:

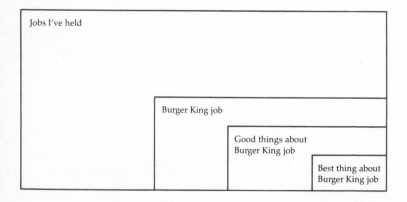

The clue to a good topic is therefore a simple bit of advice: say a lot about a small subject area rather than a little about a large subject area. For nine papers out of ten, this advice is applicable and extremely important. In fact, the principle behind the advice is so important that it could almost be elevated to the status of a rule worth memorizing: *A lot about a little is greater than a little about a lot.*

Why is this so? The reason is the same one that governs the writing of paragraphs—the need for sharp focus. You might recall the analogy of the binoculars in Chapter 3, how we have to adjust the focus knob precisely before we can get a clear view. We said that a paragraph must also have a sharp, precise focus before it can be clear to a reader. The same thing holds true for papers and essays.

Let's change the analogy somewhat. Have you ever had the experience of comparing a beautiful scene and a photograph of that same scene? The photograph will show all the familiar details, but you realize too how much the camera has not captured. Important qualities, like breadth and depth and the sheer splendor of it all, are somehow diminished or lost. The picture is *of* the scene but is *less* than the scene.

Yet at the same time you can look at a close-up picture of a person or of an object like a flower and see things in the photograph that you never observed in "real life." The camera holds up for our attention details we could have seen but didn't. In these cases the picture is *of* the scene and *greater* than the scene.

Writers are like cameras. When they try to offer a huge, panoramic view of a subject, they often fail. The subject is so much more than the few details that can be offered about it that the subject dwarfs the treatment. But when a small part of the subject is examined closely, in great detail, then both the writer and the photographer can do their best work. Their closeups reveal what we might have thought or seen but did not, and we react with both surprise and gratitude.

A2. Assessing Your Information

Suppose now that you have been able to answer yes to the question of whether or not a subject area can be narrowed to a manageable size. The second question asks you to decide if you have sufficient information about the topic.

This question is usually a little easier to answer, because the very process of narrowing the topic also makes you aware of what you know and don't know about it. Most of the time the answer is going to be yes. The fact that you have chosen a topic means that it interests you; interest in turn stems from experience and therefore knowledge. This is especially true if the topic is a narrative or descriptive one. Your own life history affords all the "data" you need for writing the paper. When you have decided on topics like "my first day on the job" or "those frantic rush hours," you know already that your own experiences can give you all the information you need.

> Nothing will sustain you more potently than the power to recognize in your humdrum routine, as perhaps it may be thought, the true poetry of life. . . .
>
> *Sir William Osler*

Sometimes, however, you will decide you don't really have enough information on a particular topic. For example, suppose the topic that occurs to you is "the profits of a Burger King franchise." If you never saw daily tallies of receipts or annual financial statements, you probably do not have enough data to write about this topic. If you saw the receipts for only a few days, that data won't help much unless you know whether the days were good, bad, or average. Furthermore before you start writing you probably ought to know something about operating costs and about the relative size of this franchise compared to others. If there is no way to get the needed information, then you should drop the subject and work on something else.

However, if the information can be found, you needn't abandon the topic. After all, writing about a subject offers an excellent chance to learn something new. Maybe you can get the information easily, perhaps by checking some books or notes that are nearby, perhaps even by making a phone call or two; then the topic might still be a good one. Notice the word *easily*. For a short paper usually you are not expected to go beyond the resources readily available to you.

Another possibility: you know the information exists, but getting it will require extensive work in the library. Such a topic might be perfect for a longer library/research paper. Chapter 5 will discuss this kind of paper in detail.

Perhaps you are not sure at first just how much information about a subject you really do possess. Then you need to ask some questions. Questions can be systematic ways of finding out about a subject. For example, if the possible topic is "a typical Burger King franchise," here are some questions you might ask about it:

- What does a Burger King franchise look like from the outside?
- How is the interior arranged, and why is this arrangement used?
- How many employees does a typical franchise have, and how much are they paid?
- What types of jobs do these employees perform?
- What kinds of foods are served, at what prices?
- What is the quality of the food, and how does it vary?
- What kinds of customers does a typical franchise attract?

By asking questions such as these, you avoid the time-wasting habit of thinking aimlessly about a subject. Instead you have set up a systematic method of inquiry. As a result of applying that method, you will know, first, whether or not you have sufficient information for a paper; and second—presuming the information is enough—you will have pinned down the material that can go into the paper when you write it.

Sometimes you can use questions that help you view a potential subject as a problem. Looking at the subject as a problem enables you to think about it in a systematic way, just as you would any other problem, whether it be fixing your car or mending a broken friendship. When you think about any problem, you go through at least the following four questions:

- Why is this problem really a problem?
- What are the possible solutions to the problem?
- What goals must be met by any possible solution to the problem?
- Given the goals, what is the *best* solution?

Suppose your Burger King experience suggests a topic like "Americans spend too much money on convenience foods." If you view this proposed topic as a problem, your thinking might go like this:

- Why is spending money on convenience foods a problem? (Immediately you would think of several reasons: the amount of money spent each year, the poor nutritional value of many of these foods, the waste of resources that could be devoted to other purposes, the assault on America's taste buds, the decline of cooking skills. . . .)

- What possible solutions are there? (These would range from severe measures like outlawing convenience foods to milder steps such as educating the public, perhaps through the schools.)

- What goals must be met by any possible solution? (Clearly, any solution must be simple, practical, respectful of liberty, and—above all—effective.)

- What is the best solution? (Perhaps you will call for an advertising campaign designed to acquaint the buying public with the nutritional risks they incur and with the enormous amount of money they waste.)

Once more, by using a set of questions, you will have gathered the available material and learned whether or not the material is enough to support a paper.

A3. Adapting to the Reader

And so we come to the third and last question: can you adapt your subject so that it suits your reader? The ability to take into account your audience is a very important writing skill.

Before you know whether the subject can be adapted, you must answer a prior question—who *is* your reader? Sometimes an instructor will provide this information when assigning the paper. "Address this paper to a classmate," he or she may say, or "Write the paper as if your reader is someone who knows nothing about your subject." In these cases you know who your reader is supposed to be. But if you have not been given such instructions, try to visualize a possible reader. Will it be a classmate? Your instructor? A friend? When I say "visualize the reader," I mean just that. Picture him or her in your mind's eye. If your reader is a category of people, like "classmates," take one particular person and let that person stand for all the other members of the category.

Then ask some questions about this reader. How much does he or she probably know already about the proposed topic? In other words, what knowledge can I presume and what must I be sure to explain? What opinions does the reader have that will color his or her response to the topic? Can I assume an interest in the topic, or must I *make* the reader interested?

Going back for a moment to the job at Burger King, some topics derived from that experience are easily adapted to any audience. Whether your reader will be a classmate or the instructor or a friend, you can assume first of all that the reader knows only a few surface details about your job. (Some classmates may have had jobs similar to yours, but the majority have not.) As for the reader's interest, some topics have a ready appeal. We have all eaten enough hamburgers at fast-food franchises to be interested in some "inside information" on how the food is prepared or on how an employee can ever manage to survive the pressures of rush hour.

But other topics have more limited appeal. The economics of a franchise might be an interesting subject for a business course. But it might not do as well in a freshman English course if it will require highly technical explanations. So you might have to rule it out, simply because, while it interests you, it cannot be adapted for your intended audience. (If you *can* adapt it, of course, so much the better.)

Still other topics will interest a reader only if developed in certain ways. A paper on "my first day at the job" is not inherently exciting. To succeed you must *make* it interesting. Perhaps you can do this by showing the funny things that happened, in which case the humor of your paper justifies its claim on your reader's time. Perhaps you will stress the terrors of that first day, and you can involve your reader in your plight by making him or her share your feelings—after all, you can count on your reader having gone through similar days at one time or another.

Just remember the one important question every reader asks: "Why should I read this?" First get an answer. Then keep both the reader and the answer in mind as you write the paper. That's part of the secret of powerful writing.

EXERCISES

1. The list that follows contains experiences almost everybody has had or situations most people have been in. Choose five of them; then, for each one, arrive at four separate topics: one narrative topic (telling a story), one descriptive topic (describing a person, a place, or an object), one expository topic (explaining something), and one argumentative topic (defending a position on an issue about which people can differ).

a. First day in secondary school
b. A job
c. A crowd of which you were a part
d. Travel—short or long trip
e. Separation from a friend
f. Love—familial or otherwise
g. Choosing a college
h. A conflict with authority

2. Narrow each of these topics to a scope suitable for a three-page paper:

a. Recent political scandals
b. The advantages of family life
c. U.S. policy toward China
d. Portrayal of children on tv programs
e. Dating patterns in high school

3. How much information would you need before you could proceed on the following topics? How readily do you think that information can be obtained?

a. The typical pre-med student
b. Advertising revenue for college yearbooks
c. Grade inflation
d. Discrimination against women in the restaurant industry
e. The rise in single-parent families

4. Assume your reader is a classmate. What assumptions would you make about your reader's reaction to the following topics? How much interest is he or she likely to have? How much prior knowledge?

a. Air pollution in your town or city
b. The 1952 presidential election
c. Factors influencing success in college courses
d. The coal strike of 1978
e. Professors' salaries
f. Carburetor malfunctions as a cause of engine stalling

5. Now assume that your reader is the instructor of your course. Using the same topics as in the previous question, what changes in your assumptions are necessary? Are there any topics for which you would not have to change your assumptions?

6. Find a back issue of each of the following magazines: *Cosmopolitan, Reader's Digest, Field & Stream, Jet,* and *The American Scholar.* What assumptions about its readers does each magazine make? How do the advertisements bear out these assumptions?

"Any ideas, Mom? I'm the sole survivor of a nuclear attack, and it's got to be no less than two pages double-space."

Drawing by P. Barlow; © 1963 The New Yorker Magazine, Inc.

B. PLANNING THE PAPER

Let us always devote ourselves first to the steps of preparatory work.

Hu Shih

People have been thinking and talking about how to write for thousands of years. Back in the fourth century B.C. the philosopher Aristotle said that, so far as he could tell, writing consisted of invention (deciding what to say), arrangement (deciding how to organize it), and style (deciding what words would best express it). Observe that of those three segments, two of them take place before the writer ever puts down a single word!

Your success as a writer therefore depends in no small measure on the ability to think through a topic before starting to write. Notice I didn't say think *about* the subject. Anyone can spin wheels for an hour: "Well what should I say . . . nah, that's dumb . . . but maybe I could . . . still and all . . . that's no good either. . . ." Such thinking gets you exactly nowhere. What I am talking about is the ability to think *productively*, so you know where to start. This section offers suggestions on how to make your "thinking time" bear fruit.

Of course, writers use a variety of planning methods. Some writers like to plan everything in great detail ahead of time, then write quickly. Others like to have just a kernel idea to begin with; they do the rest of their thinking as they go along. Some writers use written outlines; others do not. This section will respect such differences in method. But no matter what method you use, *some* foresight, *some* planning is necessary.

In Part A of this chapter we discussed how you can find something to write about. Quite often, however, you will not have that problem, because your instructor will tell you what to write about. Some college writing assignments are very specific, like this one from a political science course:

Write a paper of 2,500 words on the topic of why the term *interest group liberalism* is a better term for the phenomenon we used to call *pluralism*.

Others will simply describe in a more general way the kind of paper you are to write, like this one from an ROTC course:

Write on any aspect of national security that interests you.

And even if the subject has been left completely up to you, and you have found a topic, you still need to know how to proceed with that topic.

In this section we will divide writing assignments into six major categories, requiring different approaches, or strategies. These six categories, divisions of Part B, are each headed by a question about a specific writing assignment; for instance, "Does the assignment ask you to tell about something that happened?" Once you have a yes answer to one of the six questions, you will know which category of writing assignment you are dealing with and you can proceed to the description of that specific category. For each type of assignment there are various examples of topics taken from a variety of courses within the past several years; you can compare your own assignment to these to make sure you have the right category. Whether your instructor has given you a topic or you have chosen one yourself, you can use these six questions to formulate an approach to your assignment.

B1. Does the Assignment Ask You to Tell about Something That Happened?

"Something that happened"—the phrase covers several possibilities. It can mean something that happened to you:

Write a brief autobiography recounting the major steps in your mathematical education. [from a mathematics course]

Tell about an experience that made a deep impression on you. [from a composition course]

Describe a personal experience in which you encountered what you interpreted as prejudice. [from a psychology course]

It can also mean something that happened to people you know and even people you don't know. Most often this last group is made up of people who have participated in important events about which you have learned.

Describe the sequence of actions taken by President Kennedy during the Cuban missile crisis of 1962. [from a history course]

These topics require you to tell a story. For this reason they are often called assignments in *narrative writing*. Please note that here narrative writing does not mean fiction, like novels or short stories. In these cases the stories you are asked to tell are true stories, and you draw them from either your own experience or your knowledge of somebody else's experience.

You know how some people tell a joke well? And how other people always blow the punch line or ruin the joke some other way? Think of someone you know who tells stories very well, and then think of the qualities that make for good storytelling. The good joketeller or storyteller has at least two important gifts: 1. a good memory, especially for significant details, and 2. a sense of timing, building the story up to its dramatic conclusion ("So then the cowboy goes up to his horse the third time and he says. . . ."). These same two gifts, the use of detail and the timing that gives a story its "punch" or its "point," characterize the well-written narrative paper.

First you need **details.** If you are writing about yourself, a big hurdle is recognizing the fact that your experiences *can* be interesting to others, that people *do* want to hear about what has happened to you. But you will hold their attention only if you can re-create your experience for them. You must make them see, feel, and hear what you saw, felt, and heard. It is natural to fear that a detailed account of your experiences will just be "boring." Conquer that fear. Make your story come alive with sharp, vivid, familiar details.

We worry that a detailed story will tire readers. But in fact the easiest way to bore them is to give a very general story covering a lot of territory. That's why those "my summer vacation" papers in high school were so deadly. Instead you need to take a very few incidents in your life and develop them with significant details.

> Life is painting a picture, not doing a sum.
> *Oliver Wendell Holmes*

Here, for example, is the first paragraph of a narrative paper in which the writer tries to cover too much:

It can be quite difficult to pinpoint one event in my life that could honestly be considered an insight. Since there are many events that determine one's moral values, a great many factors must be considered. Growing into an adult is one event. There are many changes you go through in order to reach maturity. Also friends help you develop into a social being and I have been very fortunate in this respect. Another element I can think of is job responsibility. Owning a car, as I have for the last three years, is another event in my life that has been quite important.

The paragraph is deadly dull. It attempts too much, it offers no concrete details, it needs to be trimmed (notice the excess words and the cumbersome passive voice).

Here is the opening of that same narrative paper after the author limited it to a single experience that she wanted to create in detail:

"Miss Tychanski, come up here!" The summons roused me from the fitful doze that usually overcame me during English class. Suddenly I felt the adrenaline flowing, and my face must have turned scarlet. Mrs. Roberts was clearly angry, and as I approached her desk I could see her nostrils flaring, as if she was restraining herself only with great difficulty. I was about to undergo an experience that would drastically change my concept of what it means to be just or fair in this world.

Do you see how the second version absorbs our attention much more readily? It's the details that do it.

Even when the story you are telling is about someone else, perhaps an important historical figure, details still play an important role. First list all the details and incidents you can think of that apply to the story. Then consider the length of the assignment and choose the most significant details and incidents, leaving aside lesser ones you simply can't squeeze in. When you write the story, be as specific as you possibly can.

The ordering of events for a narrative paper is almost always very simple. The order is by *time*—this happened and then this and then this—chronological order. Good transitions between sentences and paragraphs (discussed in Chapter 3) make clear the cause and effect relationship between the events in the story. The reader sees, not just how Event B happens *after* Event A, but rather how Event B happens *because* of Event A.

But even though the order of the paper is determined by the sequence of events, you still need to plan how to tell the story. Planning in this case means keeping in mind the second quality of a good storyteller: **timing.** Remember that a writer must build a story, give it punch even if it lacks a punch line.

To make sure that your story has good timing and builds to a conclusion, start by asking yourself a question: "What is the point of this story? Why am I telling it?"

Sometimes the reason will be obvious. If you tell about an incident that was especially funny or especially exciting or especially dangerous, your reader will know why the story is important. In such cases you simply build the story so that the funniest or most exciting or most dangerous part occurs near the end, at a moment toward which the whole story has progressed.

Many other stories are not inherently funny or dramatic. Instead they are valuable because of what they can teach us about human life. So long as the story has a point, in other words so long as it can have meaning for the reader as well as for you, then it is worth telling. In writing such narratives you need to keep in mind the point of the story. The incidents and details should be selected and described in such a way as to lead the reader toward this central meaning. Yet a caution is necessary: let the events *suggest* the meaning. Don't bludgeon the reader with your "message." If the details of the story can't suggest the meaning by themselves, maybe you need a different story.

In summary, if you tell a story, here are some steps you can follow:

1. List as many details as possible, especially sensory details, the ones that can make the reader relive the experience with you.
2. Tell the story in chronological order, using as many of the details as possible.
3. Arrange the story so that it leads up to a natural conclusion or "point."
4. Let the story suggest its own meaning.

B2. Does the Assignment Ask You to Describe Something?

Many paper topics require you to describe something or someone, as in these two topics from composition courses:

Describe the ugliest or the most beautiful place you have ever seen.

Describe in detail someone you knew at your high school, whether classmate or teacher.

Assignments that require *descriptive writing*, as it is often called, can be found in other types of courses too:

Describe seven pieces of art based on Greek and Roman mythology that can be found in the Art Institute of Chicago. After naming the title and the artist, tell in detail what the piece looks like and what mythological story it represents. [from a mythology course]

Observe a group of people waiting in line; write a two-page summary of what you see. [from a sociology course]

Select a communication event, such as a hospital emergency room or a courtroom trial. Observe the event for a minimum of one hour, and then give a detailed account of what you saw. [from a communications arts course]

Notice that the mere presence of words like *describe* or *description* does not guarantee that the topic calls for descriptive writing. Sometimes these words are used together with other words to mean something else. For example:

Describe an ethnic community's linguistic, cultural, and social contributions to Buffalo, New York. [from a linguistics course]

Here the word *describe* is used as a synonym for *summarize*. If the assignment does not require you to go beyond what you receive from your five senses, if you are free simply to describe what your senses tell you, then the assignment is for descriptive writing. On the other hand, if you must rely on other data, or if you must analyze or interpret, then the assignment may include descriptive writing but belongs also to some other category (most probably extended definition or elaboration on a topic, discussed in section B5 of this chapter).

The first need for a descriptive paper is a **plan.** When you describe something you will provide lots of details about it, and those details must be organized in a sensible way.

Many kinds of plans are possible: you can describe an object, for example, by starting at the left side of it and working toward the right, by working from its top to its bottom, or by starting with its most important feature and then moving to features of lesser importance. The kind of plan is often not as important as the existence of a plan, because without one your details will seem haphazard and confusing.

> By the work one knows the workman.
> *La Fontaine*

Plans for descriptive papers are really the same as plans for descriptive paragraphs. Do you remember the Joan Didion paragraph in Chapter 3, where she drew our attention from the mountains to the seacoast town of Guaymas and then out into the bay, following the route of a traveller along Highway 15? Here is a longer description, also by Joan Didion. Observe how this time the author first views the subject from "higher up," from a greater distance, then comes in close to show us features typical of the landscape and the towns. The passage is taken from *Slouching Towards Bethlehem*.

Let us try out a few irrefutable statements, on subjects not open to interpretation. Although Sacramento is in many ways the least typical of the Valley towns, it *is* a Valley town, and must be viewed in that context. When you say "the Valley" in Los Angeles, most people assume that you mean the San Fernando Valley (some people in fact assume that you mean Warner Brothers), but make no mistake: we are talking not about the valley of the sound stages and the ranchettes but about the real Valley, the Central Valley, the fifty thousand square miles drained by the Sacramento and the San Joaquin Rivers and further irrigated by a complex network of sloughs, cutoffs, ditches, and the Delta-Mendota and Friant-Kern Canals. . . . The Valley road, U.S. 99, three hundred miles from Bakersfield to Sacramento, is a highway so straight that when one flies on the most direct pattern from Los Angeles to Sacramento one never loses sight of U.S. 99. The landscape it runs through never, to the untrained eye, varies. The Valley eye can discern the point where miles of cotton seedlings fade into miles of tomato seedlings, or where the great corporation ranches—Kern County Land, what is left of DiGiorgio—give way to private operations (somewhere on the horizon, if the place is private, one sees a house and a stand of scrub oaks), but such distinctions are in the long view irrelevant. All day long, all that moves is the sun, and the big Rainbird sprinklers.

Every so often along 99 between Bakersfield and Sacramento there is a town: Delano, Tulare, Fresno, Madera, Merced, Modesto, Stockton. Some of these towns are pretty big now, but they are all the same at heart, one- and two- and three-story buildings artlessly arranged, so that what appears to be the good dress shop stands beside a W. T. Grant store, so that the big Bank of America faces a Mexican movie house. *Dos Peliculas, Bingo Bingo Bingo.* Beyond the downtown (pronounced *down*town, with the Okie accent that now pervades Valley speech patterns) lie blocks of old frame houses— paint peeling, sidewalks cracking, their occasional leaded amber windows overlooking a Foster's Freeze or a five-minute car wash or a State Farm Insurance office; beyond those spread the shopping centers and the miles of tract houses, pastel with redwood siding, the unmistakable signs of cheap building already blossoming on those houses which have survived the first rain. To a stranger driving 99 in an air-conditioned car (he would be on business, I suppose, any stranger driving 99, for 99 would never get a tourist to Big Sur or San Simeon, never get him to the California he came to see), these towns must seem so flat, so impoverished, as to drain the imagination. They hint at evenings spent hanging around gas stations, and suicide pacts sealed in drive-ins.

The second key item in a good description is the use of **abundant details.** In the preceding selection, notice how many details are worked into the description. Ms. Didion did not simply tell us there were occasional towns, she named them. She did not simply tell us the Sacramento Valley was flat. Instead she tried to make us *feel* how flat it was: we see the arrow-straight highway, the unvarying landscape, the peeling paint in the impoverished towns.

The Didion passage gives us many carefully chosen details, included because the writer wants to give us a specific impression. Good writers never include details just for their own sake. Often they select ones that will help them create a **dominant impression.** A landscape, a building, a room, even a person, will have one characteristic that is more striking than the others. A writer will fasten on this characteristic as a focusing point for his or her description. Ms. Didion chooses words that give the impression of monotony, both in the landscape and in the people who inhabit it.

By the way, as writers we tend to think first of visual details, or what we have seen. Yet we have five senses, not just one. Are there ways to include in your description what you have *touched, smelled, heard, tasted?* The following sentence by Norman Mailer from *Miami and the Siege of Chicago* includes all five senses.

A great city, a strong city *with faces tough as leather hide and pavement* [touch], it was also a city with faces where the faces took on the broad beastiness of *ears which were dull enough to ignore the bleatings* [sound] of the doomed, *noses battered enough to smell no more the stench* [smell] of every unhappy end, *mouths*—fat mouths or slit mouths— *ready to taste the gravies* [taste] which were the reward of every massacre, and eyes, simple pig eyes, *which could look the pig truth in the face* [sight]. [italics added]

Admittedly that sentence is unusual, but it points up the kind of sensory awareness that makes for good description.

The last important item in a good description is a **fresh choice of words.** Think about these words from the Didion passage: "ranchettes," "sloughs," "seedlings," "scrub oaks," "leaded," "amber," "tract," "blossoming," "drain." Or these from the Mailer sentence: "beastiness," "bleatings," "stench," "slit," "gravies," "massacre." Do you know the meaning of most of these words? Would you have thought of using them in an essay? Most people would answer yes to the first question, but no to the second. In other words, good description requires not so much that you learn new words—although new words can help—as that you use more of the words you already know. (Chapter 1 can offer guidance here.)

B3. Does the Assignment Ask You to Explain the Cause of Something?

Research is usually just another name for exploring *how* and *why* questions. How does monetary policy influence the business cycle? Why do these chemicals react this way? Why does this poem affect us the way it does? Whether carried on in the academic world or in some other community, research is basically an attempt to find out the causes of things.

Therefore it should come as no surprise that many college writing assignments are directed toward finding causes. Some examples:

Write a paper of five to ten pages explaining the reasons for the recent population explosion in non-industrial nations. [from an anthropology course]

The paper is to be an original paper of approximately five pages double-spaced in which you explain the cause of a chemical phenomenon not discussed in class. [from a chemistry class]

Sinclair Lewis says that Babbitt leads a life of "barren heartiness"; write a short (two- to three-page) paper explaining how Lewis could arrive at that judgment of Babbitt. [from a history course]

Cause-and-effect relationships can be very simple: you flip the switch, a light fails to turn on, and you find that the cause of this failure is a burned-out bulb. These relationships can also be very complex. What caused the Vietnamese War? Dozens of possibilities come to mind, such as American anticommunism, Vietnamese nationalism, the 1954 Geneva agreements, Lyndon Johnson's pride, Ho Chi Minh's pride—the list could go on and on, and all the entries on the list could be plausible.

If your assignment is to write a paper involving cause and effect, three steps should be part of your planning. First, determine the **emphasis** of the paper, especially whether the emphasis is on causes or on effects. The three topics mentioned previously, for example, all emphasize finding causes: the cause of the population explosion, of a chemical phenomenon, of a judgment, or point of view. But some topics, particularly in the natural sciences and the social sciences, emphasize effects:

Trace culture's effect on maturation. [from a psychology course]

Lab report: three to five pages, reporting the effects observed from performing the experiment on p. 171. [from a physics course]

The point is that in most cases you will be given causes and asked to find effects, or else you will be given effects and asked to find causes. Be sure to know in which direction you are supposed to move.

Then it's time to do some **listing:** listing the causes or listing the effects, as the case may be. Put down as many as you can think of—prune them later if you must. If you are listing the results from lab or field experiments, be sure you include all the results, not just some of them.

The last step before you write is **evaluation.** If you are writing about causes, examine each possible cause very carefully. Ask some questions. Is the cause very close in time to its effect? If so, is there another cause, still further back in time, that is equally responsible? *More* responsible? (That burned-out bulb is the immediate cause of the light failing to go on. But the causal relationship may not be as simple as it first appears: after all, the bulb burns out after 750 hours of use because the factory built it that way, and the factory in turn built it that way because the American economy depends upon planned deterioration.)

More questions. Is this cause sufficient by itself to explain the effect or is it only one among several others? (Lyndon Johnson's pride might have contributed to our involvement in Vietnam, but it was certainly not the only factor.) Must this cause be present before the effect can take place, or could other causes produce the same result? ("American anticommunism" gives a partial explanation for our presence in Vietnam, but the French too had gotten bogged down in just such a war two decades earlier.)

Answering these questions forces you to be careful and precise in writing about the causes you have listed. And by reversing the direction of the questions you can learn to be just as precise when your task is to write about effects.

> Find out the cause of this effect,
> Or rather say, the cause of this defect,
> For this effect defective comes by cause.
> *William Shakespeare*

Consider the following passage from Alvin Toffler's *Future Shock:*

The culture shock phenomenon accounts for much of the bewilderment, frustration, and disorientation that plagues Americans in their dealings with other societies. It causes a breakdown in communication, a misreading of reality, an inability to cope. Yet culture shock is relatively mild in comparison with the much more serious malady, future shock. Future shock is the dizzying disorientation brought on by the premature arrival of the future. It may well be the most important disease of tomorrow.

Future shock will not be found in *Index Medicus* or in any listing of psychological abnormalities. Yet, unless intelligent steps are taken to combat it, millions of human beings will find themselves increasingly disoriented, progressively incompetent to deal rationally with their environments. The malaise, mass neurosis, irrationality, and free-floating violence already apparent in contemporary life are merely a foretaste of what may lie ahead unless we come to understand and treat this disease.

Future shock is a time phenomenon, a product of the greatly accelerated rate of change in society. It arises from the superimposition of a new culture on an old one. It is culture shock in one's own society. But its impact is far worse. For most Peace Corps men, in fact most travelers, have the comforting knowledge that the culture they left behind will be there to return to. The victim of future shock does not.

Take an individual out of his own culture and set him down suddenly in an environment sharply different from his own, with a different set of cues to react to—different conceptions of time, space, work, love, religion, sex, and everything else—then cut him off from any hope of retreat to a more familiar social landscape, and the dislocation he suffers is doubly severe. Moreover, if this new culture is itself in constant turmoil, and if—worse yet—its values are incessantly changing, the sense of disorientation will be still further intensified. Given few clues as to what kind of behavior is rational under the radically new circumstances, the victim may well become a hazard to himself and others.

Now imagine not merely an individual but an entire society, an entire generation—including its weakest, least intelligent, and most irrational members—suddenly transported into this new world. The result is mass disorientation, future shock on a grand scale.

This is the prospect that man now faces. Change is avalanching upon our heads and most people are grotesquely unprepared to cope ,ith it.

Do you see how Toffler's emphasis is on the *effects* of the two causes he has named (culture shock and future shock)? Do you see the implicit list of these effects? (The list starts with "bewilderment, frustration, and disorientation"; you should have no trouble continuing it from there.) And do you see the careful weighing of relationships in sentences like the third one, which says that future shock is a "much more serious malady" than culture shock?

B4. Does the Assignment Ask You to Compare and/or Contrast?

"Comparisons are odious," complains the old saying. But without them we would be handicapped in making our ideas clear to others. In fact, the ability to see resemblances and differences is so important a sign of intellectual maturity that many college writing assignments require you to make use of it. Here are some examples:

> Compare the concepts of justice in Scott's *Heart of Midlothian* and Dickens' *Bleak House*. [from a literature course]

> Compare the political process of Great Britain with the political process of France. [from a political science course]

> Give your intelligent reaction to one of the books on the following list by comparing it to the book you reported on earlier in the semester. [from a sociology course]

> Compare the Lamarckian and Darwinian theories of evolution. [from a natural science course]

Technically, *to compare and contrast* means *to find similarities and differences*. But in practice, as the four preceding examples show, the word *compare* by itself has come to mean finding both; the word *contrast* by itself means to find differences only.

> No comparison; no judgment.
> *Edmund Burke*

So what makes for a successful comparison? The first step is again a simple **listing.** Put down all the similarities you can detect, then all the differences. (Only the second kind of list is necessary if your task is to contrast.) Be thorough; make the list as complete as possible.

Your next step is to establish a **ranking.** Granted that Item A and Item B can be compared fifteen ways, but which ways are more important and which less? You will fare better if you take the most important points of comparison and describe them in detail. Irrelevant or trivial points only distract the reader and waste the space you could be devoting to more productive discussion. For example, if you are contrasting two-year and four-year colleges, you may want to stress the fact that technical programs such as auto mechanics are often taught at the former but seldom at the latter. On the other hand, the fact that your cousin Alfred liked his two-year college but did not like his four-year college most probably does not merit your reader's attention.

The final step is determining a **pattern.** Suppose your contrast of community colleges and four-year colleges results in a list of four important differences—size, cost, curriculum, and faculty—so you will contrast them using these four criteria. One pattern would involve proceeding first through the two-year colleges and then through the four-year colleges, like this:

Two-year colleges: 1. size
                     2. cost
                     3. curriculum
                     4. faculty

Four-year colleges: 1. size
                     2. cost
                     3. curriculum
                     4. faculty

Alternatively, you could go through each basis of contrast, item by item, looking first at the two-year college and then immediately contrasting it with the four-year college. Your pattern would look like this:

Size: 1. two-year colleges
             2. four-year colleges

Cost: 1. two-year colleges
             2. four-year colleges

Curriculum: 1. two-year colleges
             2. four-year colleges

Faculty: 1. two-year colleges
             2. four-year colleges

Item-by-item patterns like this one usually allow for more specific, more detailed comparisons. Simpler subjects might suit the first pattern more easily, especially since that pattern enables you to avoid the danger of the "ping-pong" effect, one of the risks of an item-by-item pattern. The important point is that you must have a pattern, because it organizes your comparison or contrast and makes it easier for your reader to follow your thinking.

Consider the following paragraphs by Bruce Catton from "Grant and Lee: A Study in Contrasts" as an example of good comparison-contrast writing:

Back of Robert E. Lee was the notion that the old aristocratic concept might somehow survive and be dominant in American life.

Lee was tidewater Virginia, and in his background were family, culture, and tradition . . . the age of chivalry transplanted to a New World which was making its own legends and its own myths. He embodied a way of life that had come down through the age of knighthood and the English country squire. America was a land that was beginning all over again, dedicated to nothing much more complicated than the rather hazy belief that all men had equal rights and should have an equal chance in the world. In such a land Lee stood for the feeling that it was somehow of advantage to human society to have a pronounced inequality in the social structure. There should be a leisure class, backed by ownership of land; in turn, society itself should be keyed to the land as the chief source of wealth and influence. It would bring forth (according to this ideal) a class of men with a strong sense of obligation to the community; men who lived not to gain advantage for themselves, but to meet the solemn obligations which had been laid on them by the very fact that they were privileged. From them the country would get its leadership; to them it could look for the higher values—of thought, of conduct, of personal deportment—to give it strength and virtue.

Lee embodied the noblest elements of this aristocratic ideal. Through him, the landed nobility justified itself. For four years, the Southern states had fought a desperate war to uphold the ideals for which Lee stood. In the end, it almost seemed as if the Confederacy fought for Lee; as if he himself was the Confederacy . . . the best thing that the way of life for which the Confederacy stood could ever have to offer. He had passed into legend before Appomattox. Thousands of tired, underfed, poorly clothed Confederate soldiers, long since past the simple enthusiasm of the early days of the struggle, somehow considered Lee the symbol of everything for which they had been willing to die. But they could not quite put this feeling into words. If the Lost Cause, sanctified by so much heroism and so many deaths, had a living justification, its justification was General Lee.

Grant, the son of a tanner on the Western frontier, was everything Lee was not. He had come up the hard way and embodied nothing in particular except the eternal toughness and sinewy fiber of the men who grew up beyond the mountains. He was one of a body of men who owed reverence and obeisance to no one, who were self-reliant to a fault, who cared hardly anything for the past but who had a sharp eye for the future.

These frontier men were the precise opposites of the tidewater aristocrats. Back of them, in the great surge that had taken people over the Alleghenies and into the opening Western country, there was a deep, implicit dissatisfaction with a past that had settled into grooves. They stood for democracy, not from any reasoned conclusion about the proper ordering of human society, but simply because they had grown up in the middle of democracy and knew how it worked. Their society might have privileges, but they would be privileges each man had won for himself. Forms and patterns meant nothing. No man was born to anything, except perhaps to a chance to show how far he could rise. Life was competition. . . .

So Grant and Lee were in complete contrast, representing two diametrically opposed elements in American life. Grant was the modern man emerging; beyond him, ready to come on the stage, was the great age of steel and machinery, of crowded cities and a restless, burgeoning vitality. Lee might have ridden down from the old age of chivalry, lance in hand, silken banner fluttering over his head. Each man was the perfect champion of his cause, drawing both his strengths and his weaknesses from the people he led.

Yet it was not all contrast, after all. Different as they were—in background, in personality, in underlying aspiration—these two great soldiers had much in common. Under everything else, they were marvelous fighters. Furthermore, their fighting qualities were really very much alike.

Each man had, to begin with, the great virtue of utter tenacity and fidelity. Grant fought his way down the Mississippi Valley in spite of acute personal discouragement and profound military handicaps. Lee hung on in the trenches at Petersburg after hope itself had died. In each man there was an indomitable quality . . . the born fighter's refusal to give up as long as he can still remain on his feet and lift his two fists.

Daring and resourcefulness they had, too; the ability to think faster and move faster than the enemy. These were the qualities which gave Lee the dazzling campaigns of Second Manassas and Chancellorsville and won Vicksburg for Grant.

Do you see the pattern behind this comparison and contrast? Chart it on a piece of paper. If you can see how Catton arranged his discussion, you have before you a good model for writing this kind of essay.

B5. Does the Assignment Require an Extended Definition or Elaboration on a Particular Topic?

The four types of papers explained so far all have certain words or phrases that help you recognize them, such as *tell the story, describe, explain the causes, compare.* But quite often you are not asked to analyze the topic in so specific a way. Instead the topic is simply named, and you are expected to elaborate on it: i.e., to say more about it, to explain it, to analyze it, to develop it. This type of writing assignment is more common than any other.

Some assignments require you to elaborate on the meaning of a particular term. This is called an **extended definition.** Here are some examples:

> Define justice. [from a philosophy course]
>
> Write an extended definition of one of the following: ripoff, X-rated, funky. [from a composition course]
>
> Explain Augustine's concept of God. [from a theology course]

Other assignments ask you to explain the most important ideas in a particular book (the familiar **book report**). Some books on which students have been asked to report recently include the following:

> Germaine Greer's *The Female Eunuch* [from a women's studies course]
>
> Viktor Frankl's *Man's Search for Meaning* [from an anthropology course]
>
> C. Wright Mills' *The Power Elite* [from a political science course]
>
> Michael Arbib's *Computers and the Cybernetic Society* [from a mathematics course]
>
> Fritjof Capra's *The Tao of Physics* [from a physics course]
>
> Vine Deloria Jr.'s *Custer Died for Your Sins* [from a history course]

Most commonly, the topic for the paper is simply stated by itself:

> Courtly love in medieval Spanish literature [from a Spanish course]
>
> Crime and police in U.S. history [from a criminal justice course]
>
> Zen and the art of math learning [from a mathematics course]
>
> The Bakke case and "reverse discrimination" [from a history course]

Principal aims and characteristics of *The Acts of the Apostles* [from a theology course]

Concepts of honor in Renaissance drama [from a literature course]

Brief history of ichthyology [from a biology course]

These last topics, depending on the length required and on their relative difficulty, might also be appropriate for the library research paper (see Chapter 5). For the time being, so long as we assume that any research needed for them is easily accomplished, we can treat them as short papers.

To write papers on these topics, first be sure you can **define terms.** You cannot write about courtly love in medieval Spanish literature until you are fully certain what *courtly love* means. If you are discoursing on crime and police in U.S. history, what do you mean by *police?* (For example, if the National Guard or federal troops are called upon to quell a riot, is such activity an example of policing or not?) An assignment that asks you to relate Zen and math learning obviously means more by *Zen* than simply the doctrines of a particular oriental religion; instead *Zen* should be taken in a wider sense, one that includes a whole complex set of attitudes toward who we are and how we live.

Not every paper will require a definition of terms. An essay on the Bakke reverse-discrimination case, for example, might not need such an exercise. (Then again it might—what exactly is "reverse discrimination" anyway?) And even if you do have to clarify some terms for yourself, you might not have to repeat those definitions explicitly in the paper, especially if you can be confident your reader knows them. But the value of defining terms lies in the added understanding of the subject this process gives to you, the writer. Furthermore you will be clued in to those situations where you must give an explicit definition in the paper itself.

Next comes the stage in which you **gather information.** Most probably, as I said before, this process will not be very lengthy for a short paper. (Book reports are the obvious exception.) While you are brainstorming the topic or looking up information on it, be sure to take notes on what you discover. Jot down any relevant fact, no matter how trivial, because it is much easier to discard material than it is to remember what you have forgotten. If the information gathering gets too lengthy, or if you must use the library or type the paper in a special form, turn to Chapter 5 for further guidance.

Then **select.** Not everything can be dumped into the paper just because you happen to know it. Consider the prescribed size of the paper and adjust your expectations to it. Remember that each page will contain only one or two fully developed paragraphs on the average and that no significant point should get anything less than one paragraph. So if you are writing a four-page paper on the Bakke case and you can expect to make eleven important points, you had better think again. Our rule, you will recall, is that a lot about a little is better than a little about a lot.

Respect for that same rule suggests the fourth step: **amplify.** Now is the time to put to use those paragraph development skills we discussed in Chapter 3. Classify, compare, contrast, define. Above all, illustrate by examples. Never assume that just because your discussion is clear to you, it must therefore be clear to someone else. Be patient, cover the ground thoroughly, in detail, so that your understanding of the topic is conveyed as clearly and directly as possible to your reader. If you cannot make your point clearly, perhaps you do not understand the subject as well as you think you do!

> If you're not able to communicate successfully between yourself and yourself, how are you supposed to make it with the strangers outside?
>
> *Jules Feiffer*

The following very short essay by Bertrand Russell called "What Good Is Philosophy?" shows the virtues we have been discussing:

> If you wish to become a philosopher, you must try, as far as you can, to get rid of beliefs which depend solely upon the place and time of your education, and upon what your parents and schoolmasters told you. No one can do this completely, and no one can be a perfect philosopher, but up to a point we can all achieve it if we wish to.
>
> "But why should we wish to?" you may ask. There are several reasons. One of them is that irrational opinions have a great deal to do with war and other forms of violent strife. The only way in which a society can live for any length of time without violent strife is by establishing social justice, and social justice appears to each man to

be injustice if he is persuaded that he is superior to his neighbors. Justice between classes is difficult where there is a class that believes itself to have a right to more than a proportionate share of power or wealth. Justice between nations is only possible through the power of neutrals, because each nation believes in its own superior excellence. Justice between creeds is even more difficult, since each creed is convinced that it has a monopoly of the truth of the most important of all subjects. It would be increasingly easier than it is to arrange disputes amicably and justly if the philosophic outlook were more wide-spread.

A second reason for wishing to be philosophic is that mistaken beliefs do not, as a rule, enable you to realize good purposes. In the middle ages, when there was an epidemic of plague, people crowded into the churches to pray, thinking that their piety would move God to take pity on them; in fact, the crowds in ill-ventilated buildings provided ideal conditions for the spread of the infection. If your means are to be adequate to your ends, you must have knowledge, not merely superstition or prejudice.

A third reason is that truth is better than falsehood. There is something ignominious in going about sustained by comfortable lies. The deceived husband is traditionally ludicrous, and there is something of the same laughable or pitiable quality about all happiness that depends upon being deceived or deluded.

You can see how Russell has defined a term *(social justice)*, gathered his reasons and selected three of them (one to each paragraph), and then provided examples of each reason (e.g., sectarian strife, the medieval plagues, and deceived husbands).

B6. Does the Assignment Ask You to Defend an Opinion?

You might be surprised to know that on the average almost one-fifth of all your writing assignments in college will require you to defend a belief or conviction. This type of paper is most frequent in upper-division (junior and senior) courses. Sometimes the issue will be defined for you; your task is to choose one side of the issue and defend it:

Are people violent due to nature or nurture? [from an anthropology course]

Can prisons rehabilitate offenders? [from a criminal justice course]

Select an environmental consequence of nuclear generating plants; make a value judgment about this consequence, using any ethical framework you wish, so long as you *defend* your reasons for or against. [from a chemistry course]

Should the Equal Rights Amendment be approved? [from a political science course]

Other assignments will offer more latitude for you as writer, like these two topics from philosophy courses:

Write an essay stating and defending your position on the topic "what it is to be a human being."

Develop and defend your *own* position on any issue you choose (e.g., freedom) by considering reasonable objections to it of the type the authors of this course would make.

Some people make a distinction between **opinion papers,** in which you simply state what you think about a particular issue, and **argumentative papers,** in which you urge your reader to believe something or do something. In both cases, however, you are called upon to explain yourself and therefore you must be clear, logical, and persuasive. The factor that unites all the topics of this category is the freedom given to you to stake out your own position. Presumably the instructors who framed the topics listed previously did not care whether you chose nature or nurture, did not care whether you thought prisons could rehabilitate or not, did not care whether you thought human beings were apes or angels. They would grade you, not on whether you chose the "right" side, but rather on *how well you defended the side you chose*.

So the first thing you must do in writing this kind of paper is to decide what your opinion on the topic is and then **summarize your opinion,** if possible in a single sentence. (In most cases, you will already have an opinion based on your reading for the course or on class discussions; if not, you may need to read more, ask some questions.) In writing opinion papers, it is absolutely essential to clearly express your opinion in a sentence, called a *thesis sentence* (to be discussed further in Part C of this chapter). After all, you cannot defend your thesis until you have stated it clearly and concisely.

Once you have written a possible thesis sentence, in other words a one-sentence summary of your opinions, apply two tests to find out whether it is usable. First test: is the thesis sentence a question? If so, rule it out. No question can be a thesis sentence for an argumentative paper, because a question does not tell us your conclusion. Don't write, "Are people violent by nature or by nurture?" Instead write, "People are violent by nature, not nurture" (or vice versa). Second test: does the thesis sentence offer an opinion that everybody would agree with? If so, again rule it out. Opinion papers thrive on controversy. If no reasonable person could disagree with what you say, then no controversy exists and your paper is an example of one of the five earlier categories. For example, this thesis sentence is unacceptable: "The violence in human nature is a troubling problem." Who could quarrel with that statement? But start naming causes, or start naming solutions, and you will have no difficulty finding a genuine controversy. Just ask yourself if the statement you have chosen to defend is one about which people of sound mind can differ.

Then you need to **define terms.** If you claim that people are violent by nature, what do you mean by *nature?* Do you mean just biological heredity—i.e., the genes received from one's parents? In that case I might be born violent and you might be born peaceable, simply because our parents have given us "bad" genes or "good" genes. Or do you take *nature* in a wider sense to include the biological inheritance we all receive as human beings? In that case you might find some propensity for violence in all of us, perhaps because we are descended from certain aggressive species of primates. The meaning you assign to the term *nature* will clearly affect the conclusions you reach. Furthermore you owe your reader the chance to decide whether he or she agrees with you without any confusion over what a word means.

Next you should decide whether to support your opinion by *inductive* or *deductive reasoning.* Inductive reasoning is the accumulation of examples that, taken together, suggest a conclusion. When you count automobiles on the highway and then conclude that 20 percent of them are of foreign manufacture, you are reasoning inductively—thousands of cars are the examples that allow you to state your conclusion.

Deductive reasoning, by contrast, begins with a principle and then shows conclusions that follow from that principle. When you begin with the principle that frustration leads to aggression, when you further observe that Nation A has been very frustrated recently, and when you then conclude that Nation A is likely to become aggressive, you are reasoning deductively. Sometimes a topic will require you to reason from examples, sometimes it will require you to reason from principles, and sometimes it will require you to reason from both.

If you are going to argue inductively, make sure you have gathered as many facts as you can to support your conclusion. The success of your paper will depend on how persuasive your evidence is. Make sure too that you don't exceed what the evidence will allow. If 51 percent of the people responding to a questionnaire answer a certain question one way, you might safely conclude that a majority of those responding hold a certain opinion. That does not mean that everybody holds it, or even that a "great" majority holds it. It does not even mean that a majority of *all* people agree with the 51 percent of those polled, unless you can show that the population answering the questionnaire is a representative sample of the population at large.

If you are going to argue deductively, make sure that the general principles from which you reason are unassailable. There is little profit in claiming that Nation A is violent because "everybody is violent." Who says your general principle is correct? Instead you must begin with a principle everybody accepts. If your principle is open to question, concentrate first on making the principle itself clear and persuasive, perhaps through inductive reasoning. Then you can proceed to deductive reasoning, in other words to drawing conclusions from the principle, with greater safety and confidence.

Now you are ready to **marshal the reasons for your opinion.** Put them down in order: 1-2-3-4. You may not want to itemize them quite so directly in the essay itself, but at the planning stage you will find it useful to have such a list. The list will help you outline your paper, and it can also show weaknesses in your argument. (If you have only one reason for your opinion, and that reason is itself not very strong or convincing, then maybe you had better give the matter more thought!)

> Thinking is the activity I love best, and writing is simply thinking through my fingers.
>
> *Isaac Asimov*

Finally, take pains to **refute objections to your opinion.** I said earlier that you should be defending an opinion with which people of right mind can differ. Picture those reasonable opponents, in fact make them your intended readers. Show them, very patiently and very respectfully, why you believe your opinion is more valid, or tenable, than theirs. Think of their most likely objections and respond as intelligently as you can to those objections.

This short essay by the conservative economist Milton Friedman, "Prohibition and Drugs," can serve as an example of these five steps:

> "The reign of tears is over. The slums will soon be only a memory. We will turn our prisons into factories and our jails into storehouses and corncribs. Men will walk upright now, women will smile, and the children will laugh. Hell will be forever for rent."
>
> This is how Billy Sunday, the noted evangelist and leading crusader against Demon Rum, greeted the onset of Prohibition in early 1920. We know now how tragically his hopes were doomed. New prisons and jails had to be built to house the criminals spawned by converting the drinking of spirits into a crime against the state. Prohibition undermined respect for the law, corrupted the minions of the law, created a decadent moral climate—but did not stop the consumption of alcohol.
>
> Despite this tragic object lesson, we seem bent on repeating precisely the same mistake in the handling of drugs.
>
> On ethical grounds, do we have the right to use the machinery of government to prevent an individual from becoming an alcoholic or a drug addict? For children, almost everyone would answer at least a qualified yes. But for responsible adults, I, for one, would answer no. Reason with the potential addict, yes. Tell him the consequences, yes. Pray for and with him, yes. But I believe that we have no right to use force, directly or indirectly, to prevent a fellow man from committing suicide, let alone from drinking alcohol or taking drugs.
>
> I readily grant that the ethical issue is difficult and that men of goodwill may well disagree. Fortunately, we need not resolve the ethical issue to agree on policy. *Prohibition is an attempted cure that makes matters worse—for both the addict and the rest of us.* Hence, even if you regard present policy toward drugs as ethically justified, considerations of expediency make that policy most unwise.
>
> *Consider first the addict.* Legalizing drugs might increase the number of addicts, but it is not clear that it would. Forbidden fruit is attractive, particularly to the young. More important, many drug addicts

are deliberately made by pushers, who give likely prospects their first few doses free. It pays the pusher to do so because, once hooked, the addict is a captive customer. If drugs were legally available, any possible profit from such inhumane activity would disappear, since the addict could buy from the cheapest source.

Whatever happens to the number of addicts, the individual addict would clearly be far better off if drugs were legal. Today, drugs are both incredibly expensive and highly uncertain in quality. Addicts are driven to associate with criminals to get the drugs, become criminals themselves to finance the habit, and risk constant danger of death and disease.

Consider next the rest of us. Here the situation is crystal-clear. The harm to us from the addiction of others arises almost wholly from the fact that drugs are illegal. A recent committee of the American Bar Association estimated that addicts commit one-third to one-half of all street crime in the U.S. Legalize drugs, and street crime would drop automatically.

Moreover, addicts and pushers are not the only ones corrupted. Immense sums are at stake. It is inevitable that some relatively low-paid police and other government officials—and some high-paid ones as well—will succumb to the temptation to pick up easy money.

Legalizing drugs would simultaneously reduce the amount of crime and raise the quality of law enforcement. Can you conceive of any other measure that would accomplish so much to promote law and order?

But, you may say, must we accept defeat? Why not simply end the drug traffic? That is where experience under Prohibition is most relevant. We cannot end the drug traffic. We may be able to cut off opium from Turkey—but there are innumerable other places where the opium poppy grows. With French cooperation, we may be able to make Marseilles an unhealthy place to manufacture heroin—but there are innumerable other places where the simple manufacturing operations involved can be carried out. So long as large sums of money are involved—and they are bound to be if drugs are illegal—it is literally hopeless to expect to end the traffic or even reduce seriously its scope.

In drugs, as in other areas, persuasion and example are likely to be far more effective than the use of force to shape others in our image.

Notice how Friedman has taken sides on a controversial issue (the prohibition of drugs), clarified the grounds upon which he will argue (expediency, not ethics), itemized his reasons (effect on us, effect on addict), and refuted his opponents (drug traffic cannot be ended). You may not agree with his conclusion, but you cannot help but admire the persuasiveness of his argument. Similarly, your instructors may not agree with the conclusions you reach, but they will reward papers in which you defend your opinions clearly and intelligently.

One last word about planning your paper. Sometimes an assignment will require a yes answer to more than one of the preceding six questions. For instance, this assignment from a history course combines the opinion paper and elaboration on a topic:

> This essay of three typed pages should show an understanding of the main idea in Segundo's book and should also include your own opinion of this main idea.

This assignment, from a philosophy course, combines the opinion paper, elaboration on a topic (extended definition), and comparison and contrast:

> For the major project you will be required to summarize the theories about free will offered by any two authors we have read; after summarizing them, show the contrast between them and (if you wish) express a judgment about which theory you accept.

Obviously you will need to combine the suggestions made under each relevant heading before you are ready to start the paper. As an example of writing that combines two or more types of approaches, read again the short selection from Alvin Toffler's *Future Shock* (pp. 208–9). The passage is primarily cause-and-effect analysis, but it also includes definition and elaboration.

EXERCISES

1. The following are topics that illustrate each of the six planning methods described in this chapter. Use them as starting points for papers:

a. narration:

Write about an experience that revealed something heretofore unknown about a friend or a member of your family.

Tell about an event whose significance became clear to you only after the event was over.

Write a short essay describing a recent date or some other social engagement.

b. description:

Describe your room in a way that enables us to learn something about who you are.

Write a character sketch of someone you remember from your childhood.

Describe the building that most typifies for you the college you attend.

c. cause and effect:

Why did you decide to attend college?

Why is violence so prevalent in the movies and on tv?

How do you account for the fact that almost half of the American people do not vote in national elections?

d. comparison and contrast:

Compare two sports with which you are familiar.

Contrast two of your college teachers in terms of their teaching styles.

Compare and contrast commuter students and resident students.

e. elaboration:

What does "equality of opportunity" mean?

Explain the biological process called cloning.

Summarize a book you have read recently in your major field and explain its significance for someone who wants to understand that field better.

f. opinion:

Is "reverse discrimination" legitimate?

Should the government exercise stricter control over prime-time television programs and, if so, why?

Is the adulation of sports heroes harmful to children?

2. Examine the last few papers you have written. To which of the six categories does each belong? Can you see any ways in which you could have improved those papers by following the planning methods described in this section? If so, where?

3. Below you will find a variety of types of topics. Decide which of the six methods is best for each. How would you go about planning papers on these topics? (Don't be concerned if you don't have enough information to actually write the paper.)

a. Comment on the statement that "all truth is relative."
b. Should education be directed primarily toward preparing students for a job?
c. Describe an occasion when you made a deep personal commitment to some future goal.
d. The Scopes "monkey" trial.
e. What similarities and differences do you see between the Stalinist purge trials of the 1930s and the American "red scare" of the late 1940s and early 1950s?
f. Define *cybernetics*.
g. Summarize your present political philosophy. What do you think are the causes for your holding that philosophy?
h. England and the rise of industrialism.

C. WRITING THE PAPER

Of all those arts in which the wise excel,
Nature's chief masterpiece is writing well.
John Sheffield, Duke of Buckingham

You may have observed that this chapter is more than half over and we have not gotten to the opening sentence of a paper yet. That's exactly as it should be. Remember, Aristotle said that two-thirds of the writing process goes on in the head before pen touches paper. If you have planned well, the actual writing of the paper will proceed more quickly.

C1. Two Preliminaries: Thesis Sentence and Outline

Before you try to write the first sentence of a paper, take a moment to write a more important sentence: your **thesis.** What is a thesis sentence? It's simply a statement of what the paper is about. In order to tell "what the paper is about," a good thesis sentence does more than just name a topic; it goes on to summarize briefly what you will say about the topic. For example, the first of the two sentences below simply names a topic, while the second offers a real thesis sentence:

This paper is about cybernetics.

This paper describes modern cybernetics and contends that cybernetics, because of the opportunity it offers to free us from mindless routine, is the single most promising development in contemporary American life.

A good thesis sentence is direct, straightforward. It does not ask a question. Instead it answers questions; it tells us the writer's purpose.

I recommend that you write a good thesis sentence, perhaps on a separate index card, before you start any paper that is not narrative or descriptive. The reasons are two very practical ones. First, the thesis sentence reminds you of the task you have undertaken. It stands as a kind of summary statement for all that mental activity described in Parts A and B. Secondly, the thesis sentence can be kept next to you during the writing of the paper. As you finish each paragraph you can ask yourself, "Does this paragraph contribute in some way to the task described in the thesis sentence?" If the answer is no, you have an immediate warning that you are straying from your topic.

Most textbooks about writing tell you that you should always draw up an **outline** before you start to write. The problem with such advice is that many excellent writers have never used an outline in their lives. Alberto Moravia, for example, claims that his novels are "not prepared beforehand in any way." Furthermore those writers who do use outlines rely on them in quite varying degrees. Some create very detailed outlines and adhere to them slavishly. Norman Mailer wrote *The Naked and the Dead* only after compiling a whole file drawer full of notes and a complete "life history" for each projected character. Others jot down just a few key words and don't worry if they change their minds later on. All of these writers order their thoughts clearly. The difference is that for some the process is internal and for others it must be to one degree or another external, in other words, written down.

So what can I tell you about outlines that would be both true and useful? Just this. If no instructor has ever criticized the order of your paper, if instead your papers are complimented for their coherence and their clear structure, then don't concern yourself with outlines. Apparently your internal processes for creating order are sufficient for your purposes. All your reader cares about is the result, not the means for attaining those results.

> Too many writers are premature; they should organize their ideas better before writing a piece. I do tremendous organizational layouts on any pieces before I actually write them; I take notes on matchbook covers, napkins, anything.
>
> *Woody Allen*

But if you are like most of us, you need all the help you can get. Here is where an outline can help. It offers a chance to summarize those plans we discussed in Part B. Once you have defined your tasks, use the outline as a way to list the strategies you will employ. Also the outline can remind you of the main divisions of your topic and can help you distinguish between larger and smaller categories. Of course you should not be a slave to your outline—after all it's *yours*, and you can always change it later if necessary.

In general, the shorter and simpler the paper, the shorter and simpler the outline. For a three-page paper on cybernetics, for example, this might be a sufficient outline:

Thesis: Cybernetics affects every aspect of our lives.

  I. Definition of cybernetics
 II. Applications
     a. At home (examples)
     b. At school (examples)
     c. At work (examples)

But a larger, more complicated paper, especially the kind of paper we will discuss in Chapter 5, needs a different outline. For example, following is the outline I used in writing this chapter. If you look carefully at both the outline and the chapter, you will see that the final product *resembles* the outline but is not identical with it. Outlines are slaves, not masters.

Chapter 4: The Complete Paper

Intro
A. Choosing a topic
    1. Narrowing the topic
    2. Information—is it enough?
    3. Adapting to the reader
B. Planning (the seven approaches to a topic, illustrated by examples of assignments from various courses)
    1. Narrative
    2. Descriptive
    3. Cause and effect
    4. Comparison and contrast
    5. Extended definition or elaboration on a topic
    6. Opinion
    7. Argument
C. Writing (this section illustrated by examples drawn from professional writing)
    1. Opening—stories, surprises, metaphors, quotations, questions, emotions, etc.
    2. Thesis sentences
    3. Outlines
    4. Writing the paper
    5. Endings—avoid repetition
D. Proofing and revising
    1. Rewriting—"speeders" and "bleeders"
    2. Format—type, ms., margin, title, following instructions
    3. Proofreading—symbols, etc.

C2. Getting Started

Do you sometimes find it almost unbearably painful to write the first few words of your paper? Are there times when the blank sheet just stares back at you, defying you to think up a good opening sentence?

If so, you have a case of "writer's block." Some cases are severe, some mild, but all are painful and frustrating. One comforting thought is that you share this malady with almost everyone who has ever tried to write. The novelist William Styron, for example, bemoans "the pain of getting started each day," and concludes: "Let's face it, writing is hell." Other writers report the same frustration. "Each morning I wake up with fear and trembling, knowing the typewriter is waiting for me," says Irwin Shaw. James Jones, the author of *From Here to Eternity,* took a half hour each day just to convince himself he was ready to write. Then, once he was "convinced," he smoked ten more cigarettes, drank a half dozen cups of coffee, and reread yesterday's mail—all this before he put down a single word!

I can't offer you some magic elixir that will make the problem go away—if I could do that, I'd have bottled it and sold it to Styron, Shaw, and Jones. What I can do is suggest remedies that others have tried and found helpful. Experiment with them. If an idea works for you, use it. If it doesn't, discard the idea and try another.

Here, in no particular order, are some possible remedies for "writer's block."

1. Use a cassette recorder. Many people can *say* what they want to put down even though they cannot write it. If you can compose orally, by all means do so, even if it's just the opening paragraph. Perhaps a simple listing of your ideas will be helpful. Then replay the tape and write down what you hear. This transcript will often give you at least a start, a rough draft from which you can begin the actual writing.

2. Skip the opening paragraph. Go directly to the second or some later paragraph, one you can write quickly. Then later on you can return to the opening and by that time the block will be gone.

> The last thing one settles in a book is what one should put first.
>
> *Blaise Pascal*

3. Exercise vigorously for a short period of time. This suggestion may seem frivolous, but it is based on a sound physiological principle: an increase in the oxygen supply to the brain often results in increased efficiency. Anything to break the deadly cycle of "How shall I start? How shall I start?" is bound to be helpful.

4. Try mnemonic devices. In other words, use rituals that free your memory and allow ideas to come forward. No rules govern what makes a good ritual—each writer's rules are individual, usually based on something that happened on a day when he or she was particularly creative. Ernest Hemingway used to sharpen twenty pencils before he began to write (and then composed standing up at a typewriter!). Willa Cather read a passage from her Bible. Thornton Wilder took a brisk walk. It's not *what* you do that is important. The value is in the ritual itself, because it liberates your imagination, it makes you say, "Now I am ready to write."

A final word of advice is to consult the list of ideas for **typical opening paragraphs** that follows. Any one of them might offer a good possibility, and then you're off and writing. The fact of the matter is that some openings are good, some mediocre, and some downright terrible. A weak introduction gives readers a poor disposition before they read what you have to say. Either they will put the paper aside and never finish it at all, or else— perhaps because they are obligated to do so—they will continue reading but without much enthusiasm or goodwill.

Fortunately, good openings for papers often fall into recognizable categories. Here are some categories you might find useful.

1. An anecdote. Open with a very brief story that illustrates or introduces your topic. Usually this story will be drawn from your personal experience or from the experience of someone you know. For example, Martin Luther King opened one chapter of his account of the civil rights struggle in the South with a description of Mrs. Rosa Parks refusing to give up her seat to a white man and thus launching the Montgomery bus boycott. Just be sure the story you tell relates to your subject and that its relevance is clear to your reader.

2. A quotation. A succinct quotation can serve the same purpose as a story. Here is the opening paragraph of an essay by Mayme Logsdon that discusses why one should learn mathematics:

> A pupil of Euclid, when he had learned a proposition, inquired: "What advantage shall I get by learning these things?" Euclid called a slave and said, "Give him sixpence, since he must needs gain by what he learns."

But don't quote the dictionary, even to start a definition paper. Essays that begin, "According to Webster's dictionary . . ." are following a pattern so hackneyed that readers will groan.

3. A question. A good question can hook your reader's interest. Erich Fromm, for example, writes:

> What is the kind of society and the kind of man we might find in the year 2000, provided nuclear war has not destroyed the race before then?

Notice I said a *good* question. Nothing can deter a reader more than a silly or obvious question. "Have you ever wondered why I chose to come to this university?" (No, I haven't.) "Is it easy to become a veterinarian?" (Of course you are going to say it isn't.) Ask genuine questions, ones for which the answer isn't obvious, ones in which your reader might really be interested.

4. An expression of strong emotion. To stir your reader's curiosity, make a strong statement, such as this one by L. E. Sissman:

> I've grown damn sick and tired of having the youth culture, whatever that is, rammed down my throat by members of my own generation.

Don't fake it, however. Be angry only when you really are angry. If you simply playact, the rest of your essay will give you away, and your reader will feel deceived.

5. Figurative language. In Chapter 1 we talked about metaphor and its ability to clarify your meaning. Metaphors can even help clarify the purpose of an entire essay. Ashley Montagu wants to write about the American character, and he begins his essay this way:

> There is an electric spark in the air. Americans may not be consciously aware of it; nevertheless they behave as if they were affected by it: they are jumpy, alert, excited, hopping about all over the place like jack-in-the-boxes.

If you open your essay with figurative language, just be sure your choice is a fresh one. Beware of the cliché or the tired metaphor: "They say you should look before you leap." Use them only if you can give them an unusual twist: "To look before you leap is good advice for most folks, but all it ever teaches me is how far I will fall."

6. A surprise. Mildred Kavanaugh:

> Some feminists shout for equal pay for equal work, others want abortion on demand. All I am asking is that women be treated like men on the obituary page.

A surprising opening signals to readers that your mind is awake and active. They will anticipate hearing what you have to say.

7. An introduction. An introduction to the topic is acceptable so long as it is kept brief and lively:

> The theory of mutation is a concept as exalted as that of time or death.

In that one-sentence paragraph Robert Ardrey names his topic (the theory of mutation), stresses its importance, and shows the approach to it he expects to take.

The danger to avoid is the kind of opening that one writer has called "throat-clearing." In such paragraphs all the author really says is "ahem" once or twice, settling into the topic like an old hound dog flopping down on a favorite rug. Here is an example:

> It is quite difficult to pin-point one event in my lifetime that could honestly be considered a turning point. More than one event has an influence on you. But I will try to describe one important occasion, even though there are many other factors that could be considered.

That paragraph doesn't engage readers, it doesn't carry them forward, it doesn't really *say* anything.

C3. Writing the Paper

I cannot tell you "how to write," a magic formula that will make all the right words tumble out onto your paper. No one can. Writing is still in many ways a mystery, just like all the really important things in life.

But I can give you a few recommendations you should keep in mind as you write. These suggestions do not remove the mystery, but they help confine it.

1. Follow your outline. No outline can be of any service unless it is used. Once you have written a successful outline, which in turn is based on the strategy you have chosen, the direction of your paper should be clear. If the paper will compare and contrast, for example, you will already have decided what similarities and differences to discuss and what emphasis you will give to each point. The paper can now almost write itself.

2. Develop each issue fully. We saw earlier that the secret of a good sentence was development of its core idea and the secret of a good paragraph was development of its topic. This is also true on the level of the complete essay. Your paper will be clear and convincing in proportion to the amount of detail you provide. Only by amplifying each point you make with stories, examples, or explanations can you help your reader come close to your view of the subject. Of course good development doesn't mean being repetitious or wasting words. Instead it means realizing how clear and how detailed you have to be in order to bridge that gap between your understanding of the subject and your reader's. The paragraph development skills of Chapter 3 will help you achieve these goals.

> If you have one strong idea, you can't help . . . repeating it
> and embroidering it. Sometimes I think that authors should
> write one novel and then be put in a gas chamber.
> *J. P. Marquand*

Here is where it may become necessary to change your outline. Sometimes as you begin developing a particular part of the paper, you may discover that a full treatment of this section will carry you much further than you had thought. You realize you have started on a topic worthy of a paper in its own right. Conversely there are times when you begin an issue and then realize you have nothing much to say about it—you can't treat it in detail because you don't *know* any details. In both cases you may have to go back to the outline and do some crossing out or rearranging. Better to eliminate a subtopic rather than leave it undeveloped or allow it disproportionate space.

Similarly, you might find new ideas occurring to you as you write, ideas that had escaped your attention when the outline was drawn up. Jot down those ideas when they come (it's surprisingly easy to forget them). Then see how they can be worked into the outline in a sensible way, so that they will find a place in the completed paper.

3. Use effective transitions. You have both an outline and a thesis statement next to you as you work. But remember that your reader must rely on you for guidance. Transitions between paragraphs make clear your intentions. You and the reader are like two bicyclists, one following the other; transitions are the hand signals by which the leader tells the follower which way he or she proposes to go.

In Chapter 3 we discussed the various kinds of transitions: contrast words, comparison words, time or place words, consequence words, example words, summation words (see pp. 137–141). These same transitions can be used as the mortar that binds together the building blocks of your paragraphs. Here, for example, are the opening words of eight paragraphs that make up one section of Alvin Toffler's book *Future Shock:*

> For most people, the first such juncture. . . .
> In the past, . . .
> A second critical life juncture. . . .
> A third significant turning point. . . .
> Among the more conventional couples of tomorrow. . . .
> This third marriage. . . .
> Not all these marriages will survive until death, however, for the family will still face a fourth crisis point. . . .
> Of course, . . .

Observe how Toffler keeps us right on track with these transitions—we can almost tell how the essay develops just by reading the transitions.

I suggested earlier that you keep the thesis sentence by you as you write. When you begin a new paragraph, ask yourself if you have created a good transition between the previous paragraph and this new one. Then check the transition against the thesis sentence: does the transition suggest how this new paragraph furthers the development of the topic defined by your thesis sentence? If it doesn't, should it?

4. Find a good ending. Your last paragraph should be more than just a quick dash over the same ground. Particularly deadly is the "conclusion" paragraph, like this one:

> In this paper I have explained how the hobbyist can detect and control diseases in his fish. The tropical fish hobbyist will be able to enjoy his pets to a greater extent knowing he is in control of fish disease.

Instead, look for a way to send your reader away still thinking. Rather than "wrapping it all up," let the reader do some of his or her own packaging. Here are some suggestions for possible good endings:

a. Let your final paragraph pick up on a story, a quotation, or a theme used at the beginning of the paper.

b. Propose a question that will prod the reader into thinking further on the subject.

c. Speculate about the future—where might this subject lead us next year? Twenty years from now?

d. Offer a concluding story, or perhaps an appropriate quotation from another writer.

e. Surprise your reader. A good one-sentence paragraph can have special impact if it comes last. When Mary McCarthy closed a review of a book by J. D. Salinger, she posed a series of questions for the author. Then she added one more sentence, the final paragraph; the question it asked showed her true opinion of Salinger:

> Or [did Seymour kill himself] because he had been lying, his author had been lying, and it was all terrible, and he was a fake?

Suddenly, surprisingly, we realize the extent of Ms. McCarthy's contempt for the author she is reviewing.

EXERCISES

1. Consider the following five opening paragraphs. What makes them particularly effective?

a. Does the yeti, or "abominable snowman," really exist? Or is it just a myth without practical foundation? For the last four months our Himalayan mountaineering and scientific expedition has been trying to find out—and now we think we know the answer. *Sir Edmund Hilary*

b. Love! Attar of libido in the air! It is 8:45 A.M. Thursday morning in the IRT subway station at 50th Street and Broadway and already two kids are hung up in a kind of herringbone weave of arms and legs, which proves, one has to admit, that love is not *confined* to Sunday in New York. Still, the odds! All the faces come popping in clots out of the Seventh Avenue local, past the King

Size Ice Cream machine, and the turnstiles start whacking away as if the world were breaking up on the reefs. Four steps past the turnstiles everybody is already backed up haunch to paunch for the climb up the ramp and the stairs to the surface, a great funnel of flesh, wool, felt, leather, rubber and steaming alumicron, with the blood squeezing through everybody's old sclerotic arteries in hopped-up spurts from too much coffee and the effort of surfacing from the subway at the rush hour. Yet there on the landing are a boy and a girl, both about eighteen, in one of those utter, My Sin, backbreaking embraces.   *Tom Wolfe*

c.   In Greenwich Village a dreamy young beggar in a tattered Ivy League summer suit and a buttondown collar with both buttons missing turns on an uptown couple to ask, "Gimme a quarter for a Cadillac, hey?"   *Herbert Gold*

d.   What will it be like to live in a predominantly metric nation?   *Frank Kendig*

e.   November fourteenth has been good for humanity: it has given the world such people as the inventor Robert Fulton in 1765, artist Claude Monet in 1840, Prime Minister Jawaharlal Nehru of India in 1889, and Prince Charles of England in 1948. But its primary significance for me lies in the fact that on this day in 1960 I made my own quiet entrance.   *student paper*

2. Go over some recent papers you have written, checking the introductory paragraphs and the concluding paragraphs. Are there any cases where you fell victim to "throat-clearing" or tired "in conclusion . . ." paragraphs? Do you see any ways in which the suggestions made in Parts C2 and C3 of this chapter would have been helpful?

3. For the papers considered in Exercise 2, did you use an outline? If not, try to outline the papers now, after they are completed. Can you come up with clear, simple outlines? If you cannot, perhaps your papers would have been more coherent had you used outlines.

4. Again looking at those papers—did you have a thesis sentence for each? If so, write them out. If not, see what difference clear thesis sentences might have made.

5. Choose *one* of those recent papers, the one that seems to you most deficient. Revise it, making sure you: 1. develop an outline, 2. write a thesis sentence, 3. offer an effective opening paragraph, 4. develop each subtopic fully, and 5. finish with a lively concluding paragraph. How much of an improvement did these five steps make?

6. Locate two or three magazines aimed at the general public. Which techniques discussed in this chapter were employed in these magazines? How do they engage the reader's attention and make him or her want to read further?

D. REVISING THE PAPER

> The main rule of a writer is never to pity your manuscript. . . . I say that the wastepaper basket is a writer's best friend.
>
> *Isaac Bashevis Singer*

Finally words are down on paper. However, the difference between unsuccessful writers and successful writers is often this: unsuccessful writers think they are now done, while successful writers know they are not.

D1. Rewriting the Paper

Somewhere along the way you were probably advised always to write a first draft and then to rewrite completely. If you are like most people, you agree with this advice in theory, but you hardly ever follow it.

Most people don't rewrite because they lack the time. Like the character in the scenario I described in Part A of this chapter, they finish a paper on the night before it is due. The most they have time for is reading through the paper quickly, trying to spot grammar or spelling errors. This last activity is an important one, but it is *not* rewriting. The proper name for it is proofreading (see D3, later in this chapter).

You may expect me to exhort you to give up your sinful ways and promise to rewrite every paper from now on. Perhaps I will, perhaps I won't. Whether you should always write a second draft depends on the circumstances. It depends in particular on how you write the first draft, on whether you are what I call a "speeder" or a "bleeder."

A speeder is someone who races through the first draft of a paper quickly and easily. He or she doesn't worry about each word, each sentence—the important thing is to get *something* written. This kind of writer works like a sculptor in clay: first you get a large amount of material in front of you, shapeless but pliable; then you form it, going over it carefully and slowly, working and reworking the original lump of clay until it resembles what you first imagined. Speeders know that much of their creative energy will go into the rewriting process, and so they use the quick first draft much as sculptors use that first lump of clay.

Many professional writers work this way. Georges Simenon, the great master of detective novels, finishes his first draft of a book in only a little over a week. Anthony Trollope used to work even faster: five thousand words a day, week after week, pen dashing across paper. If your habits of composition indicate that you are a speeder, you must then allot a significant amount of time for rewriting. Second and maybe third drafts are essential parts of how you write, and if you do not include them your writing will suffer. Anita Loos, for example, claims she rewrites every piece about twenty times.

What does it mean to write a second draft? Usually it means *writing the paper again*, from start to finish. You change, add, subtract, and reorder at every step of the way. If a writer simply goes back over a first draft, crossing out a few words here and inserting a few there, the improvement will be very slight. Instead you need to invest just as much energy in the second draft as you did in the quickly written first draft. Simenon, for example, sets aside one day of rewriting for every two days spent in the first writing.

Then come the bleeders. These are writers who sweat blood as they compose, writers for whom every word is an agony, "every sentence a victory." William Styron, who you may recall said that "writing is hell," finishes only two or three handwritten sheets each day. Joseph Conrad worked even more slowly —perhaps one typewritten page a day.

If you are a bleeder, you rewrite too, but you do it in your head rather than on paper. Consequently the first draft that emerges may be much closer to the final product than it is for a speeder, because like Styron you have a "need to perfect each paragraph—each sentence even—" as you go along. You still need to revise, to check language and organization. But you can probably work directly with the first draft rather than completely rewriting the paper.

No special advantages go with being either a speeder or a bleeder. Both have to rewrite, both have to invest time in thinking about alternative ways of communicating with their readers, both have to proofread their final copy. Poor writers are the ones who speed but don't rewrite, or who speed when they should bleed.

> Ther nys no werkman, whatsoevere he be,
> That may bothe werke wel and hastily.
> *Geoffrey Chaucer*

Revising is not something you do once, after everything else is complete. Instead it is a constant, on-going process. Even if you are a speeder, the very act of rejecting one word and choosing another as you write means that you are revising while you write. Every writer revises at every stage. The only difference is whether his or her composition habits require a second full draft before going on to the finished paper.

If revision is a constant process, of what does that process consist? Clearly, revising means engaging in at least the following five activities: 1. crossing out words, 2. adding words, 3. substituting one word or group of words for another word or group of words, 4. changing the order of words, and 5. combining groups of words.

Perhaps you can see the revision process most clearly through an example. Here is a paragraph that appears later on in this book, p. 317:

> The truth is, most people have only the vaguest idea of the meaning of grammar, and they usually associate it with making mistakes when speaking. Here are some other misconceptions: 1. most errors in writing are grammatical errors; 2. grammar is necessary to speak and write well; 3. only a few select people (English teachers?) have

ever mastered grammar. The surprising truth is that: 1. most "errors"
are in semantics or usage, not in grammar; 2. many people have
become excellent writers without ever undertaking any formal study
of grammar; 3. everybody—including you—knows a great deal
about English grammar and has known it since learning to speak.

Now here is the original draft of that paragraph, plus revisions:

> The truth is, most people have only the
> vaguest idea of ~~what grammar is~~ the meaning of
> grammar, and they usually associate it with
> making mistakes when speaking. Here are some
> other misconceptions ~~about grammar~~: 2. grammar
> is necessary to speak well and write well;
> 1. most errors in writing are grammatical
> errors; 3. only a few select people (English
> teachers?) have ever mastered grammar.
>
> The *surprising* truth is that: 1. many people
> have ~~written quite well~~ become excellent writers
> without *ever* undertaking any formal study of grammar;
> 2. most "errors" are in semantics or usage, not
> grammar; 3. everybody--including you--knows a
> great deal about English grammar, and ~~you have~~
> *has known it* ~~been aware of this~~ since learning to speak.

If you examine the changes between the first draft and the
final version of the paragraph, you will find examples of each of
the five kinds of revision mentioned above. In particular you can
note: 1. words crossed out ("about grammar," in the second
sentence); 2. words added ("surprising" and "ever" in the
third sentence); 3. words substituted for others ("become
excellent writers" replaces "written quite well," "the meaning of

grammar" replaces "what grammar is"); 4. changes in word order ("most errors in writing . . ." is put ahead of "grammar is necessary. . . ," and as a consequence items one and two below must be reversed also); 5. groups of words are combined ("knows a great deal about English grammar" and the separate clause "you have been aware of this since learning to speak" are now combined into "knows a great deal about English grammar and has known it since learning to speak"). My purpose in making these changes was to give the passage a clearer order and a better wording. In *none* of these changes was I "correcting an error." Instead I was simply trying to improve my writing by making it clearer to you, the reader. This improving process is what we mean when we talk about revision.

Of course revision can operate on a level higher than the paragraph. Sometimes you will find it necessary to remove a whole section of your paper, or else you might find yourself writing two new paragraphs to be inserted at a place that requires more development. But whatever the size of your changes, you will discover that they will usually be one of the five types we just discussed.

D2. *Preparing the Final Manuscript*

When you put your paper in its final form, you need to observe certain conventions about how it should appear.

First, **type the paper** if you possibly can. I can think of at least four reasons for this recommendation. The first two benefit you directly; the second two benefit your reader:

1. Typing eliminates any negative reaction a reader might have to your handwriting.
2. Mechanical errors (such as spelling and punctuation) are easier to spot in cold, impersonal type.
3. Typed papers can be read more easily, thus allowing the instructor to concentrate more on your message than on your medium (i.e., script).
4. Typing eliminates confusion (is that squiggle an *o* or an *a*?).

And of course all four reasons ultimately work to your advantage, because the gratitude of an instructor cannot do you any harm. Statistical studies have shown that a typed paper has a better chance of getting a high grade than the same paper untyped. Most instructors—including yours, I am sure—take great precautions to avoid misjudging a paper because of poor handwriting. But why take a chance?

> It was very pleasant for me to get a letter from you the other day. Perhaps I should have found it pleasanter if I had been able to decipher it. I don't think that I mastered anything beyond the date (which I knew) and the signature (which I guessed at). . . . Other letters are read and thrown away and forgotten, but yours are kept forever—unread.
>
> *T. B. Aldrich to E. S. Morse*

When you type, use unlined, white, 8½-by-11-inch paper. Onionskin makes for hard reading. Use a ribbon that is reasonably fresh and make corrections properly, whether through erasure (erasable bond can help), correction fluid, or correction strips. Double-space, type on one side only, and leave inch-and-a-half margins on all four sides. Number each page except the first, usually in the upper right-hand corner. Generally a short paper will not be the kind that requires footnotes, but if your paper does require them, follow the methods described in the next chapter.

If you must handwrite the final copy, do everything in your power to make the writing legible. Use standard, white, 8½-by-11-inch, lined paper. Remember that handwritten pages often contain only about half as many words as typed pages. So if your assignment is supposed to be two or three typed pages in length, a handwritten paper of two pages might be woefully inadequate, especially if your handwriting is large and sprawling.

Give your paper a title. Center the title on the top of the first page, leaving some space before your name appears and then some more space before you begin the first paragraph. Alternatively the title and your name can appear on a separate title page as described on p. 268 and illustrated on p. 280.

What kind of a title? It's best if you can find one that is short, informative, and humorous or provocative. Some examples are:

"Brave Words for a Startling Occasion" (Ralph Ellison)
"Howtoism" (Dwight Macdonald)
"On the Importance of Being Free" (Walter Lippmann)
"First Aid for a Bus Rat" (student)
"My Emancipation Proclamation" (student)

Finally, respect your instructor's requirements. He or she may specify certain ways for your paper to be written. You might be asked to include certain information along with the title, like the course and section number or the date or the instructor's name. You might be asked to staple or not to staple, to fold or not to fold, to have a title page or not to have a title page. Usually there are reasons for these requirements. Simple prudence would suggest that you respect your instructor's wishes in these matters.

D3. Proofreading the Paper

Now you are ready to give the paper a last proofreading before you turn it in. This is not the time for major changes—they will have been made at the rewriting stage. If a major change suddenly becomes necessary, you ought to retype that section of the paper. Instead this is the time for catching things like spelling, punctuation, or typographical errors.

Use standard correction devices. For example, to correct a misspelled word, draw a line through the word and write in the correct word above:

        . . . noting this example and ~~takeing~~ *taking* care not to . . .

To add a missing word, insert a caret (∧) at the proper place and write the word directly above it:

                                not
        This plan, while ∧ typical, is nevertheless . . .

The same holds true for a missing letter within a word:

                like th ∧ s.
                        i

Two transposed letters can be reversed and thus put right by a curved line(∿):

> Without knowing h̶t̶e̶ name it is impossible . . .

And letters accidentally separated can be joined by two arcs:

> No one dou͡bts their sincerity . . .

To show that a new paragraph should begin even though you failed to indent, put the symbol ¶ immediately before the first word of the sentence that should begin the paragraph:

> . . . large and sprawling. ⌐Give your paper . . .

Conversely, the symbol *no* ¶ tells the reader to ignore a paragraph indention you have made and to read the passage as a single paragraph:

> Use standard correction devices.
>
> *no* ¶ For example, to correct a misspelled word,
>
> draw . . .

Many writers find it difficult to proofread their own work. A student when shown a paper containing several obvious mistakes will often say, quite sincerely, "But I *did* proofread that paper." When we know what we intended to write, it is often difficult to look objectively at what we did in fact write. A hint: try proofreading your papers backwards, last word to first. That method won't turn up missing words or mistakes in sentence or paragraph structure. But it will help you find misspellings and typographical errors, because it divorces your words from their meaning and lets you see them in perfect isolation.

> Editing is the most companionable form of education.
> *Edward Weeks*

In summary this chapter has tried to offer you a plan for writing a good short paper. Short papers represent perhaps 60 percent of your written work in college. But the other 40 percent is important too, and forms the subject of the next chapter.

EXERCISES

1. Here is a short list of successful essay titles. Why do you think they appeal to readers?

"Is There Any Knowledge That a Man *Must* Have?" (Wayne C. Booth)
"Through the Dark, Glassily" (Richard Gambino)
"The Perils of Obedience" (Stanley Milgram)
"Springtime Reality: Exams 5, Me 0" (student)
"A Few Words about Breasts" (Nora Ephron)
"What You See Is the Real You" (Willard Gaylin)
"Bamboozle Me Not at Wounded Knee" (Terri Schultz)

2. The following passage from a student paper is in severe need of proofreading. Restore it to its proper form.

When I was little I used to wait everyday at the front window
with my nose pressed up agianst the glass. My grandma told me
thats' why I have a pug nose now, but you know how Gradmas are.
You're probaby wondering the reason for my stunting the growth
of my nose by keeping a virgil at the window. Actually it was
a man; at age five the only other man in my life besides my
father. My Gradma called him Paddy. my mother called Dad, and
to me he was Grandda. Every evening when I heard Grandma setting the table I would be at me station, waiti ng for a figure
far in the distance to come limping towards home. He would
come belowing in the door just as I hit the peak of my excit-
ment and gather me into his arms like a sheperd would gather the
smallest of his sheep. Inevitably a voice arose from the
kitchen: "Paddy, if you get that child all exdited she wont be
able to eat her dinner. Then Grandda would straigten up and we
both would go overto the piano bench for our evening ritual.

5

THE LONG PAPER
AND
ESSAY EXAMS

That's the name of the [writing] game—words, patience, and revision.

Irving Wallace

Almost half of your college writing assignments remain to be discussed in this text. This other half, which includes the long paper and essay questions, causes a disproportionate share of student illness. Sometimes the illness is real; sometimes it is what we can charitably call psychosomatic. ("Well, see, I couldn't get this paper in on time because I've been real sick, see, and could I have an extension until Monday?") In either case the ailment is usually curable. This chapter tries to offer some effective home remedies.

A. THE LONG PAPER

In your work and in your research there must always be passion.

Ivan Petrovich Pavlov

This section might have been called "The Research Paper." But I chose the present title because it emphasizes how research papers differ from short papers only in their greater length. When you think of the research paper you might also think of footnotes, bibliographies, and other requirements you have heard about. But these other matters, while they are customarily taught in connection with longer papers, can be used on short papers too. The only true difference, I repeat, is length.

Length itself, however, deters many students. "How can I ever fill up ten pages? God knows I have a hard enough time writing two." This is a natural anxiety, but one that can be reduced.

A1. Before You Start

You begin just where you might expect—with the fact that you must **choose a topic.** Your first step ought to be to ask a question of your instructor (unless his or her assignment sheet answers the question for you). The question is simple but crucial: should the paper be a research paper or a library paper?

These two kinds of papers are similar in many ways. Both are long, both involve footnotes and a bibliography, both require extensive use of the library, and both follow the same format for the final manuscript. The only difference is that a genuine research paper must either report something new or stake out a new or controversial position on familiar material. A library paper has no such restriction.

To make this difference clearer, think for a moment about the kinds of work people do that we label *research*. Sometimes they come up with new findings, new physical or chemical laws, new explanations. The biochemist who explains the properties of a new organic compound, the political scientist who collects and analyzes data on a local election, the literary scholar who publishes a hitherto unknown manuscript are all engaged in the kind of research that reports something new. Sometimes, on the other hand, researchers cover well-trodden ground but do so in a fresh, original way. They believe they can offer a new interpretation of an old subject, or they believe that the commonly held opinion on a certain subject is wrong. The biochemist who suggests a new hypothesis about the origin of life, the political scientist who claims we have misjudged the appeal of a certain candidate, the literary scholar who contends we have misinterpreted *Hamlet* are all engaged in research too, the kind that takes a new or controversial position on familiar material.

Many long papers written by students, however, do not contain either of these types of research. Instead they summarize a body of material. Their purpose is to draw a large amount of information from a wide variety of sources, then to condense the information and give a clear, coherent account of it. Such papers do not intend to offer discoveries or to argue cases. Because they are longer and require extensive work in the library, a more accurate term for them is *library paper* rather than *research paper*, although the latter term is sometimes used.

The majority of longer college writing assignments are for library papers rather than research papers. Here, for example, is a list of suggested term-paper topics from a European history course:

"The Social Protest of Honoré Daumier"
"The Opium War of 1841"
"The Assassination of Archduke Franz Ferdinand"
"The 'War Guilt' Clause of the Versailles Treaty"
"Mussolini's March on Rome"
"Auschwitz"
"The Berlin Blockade"
"The Marshall Plan"

None of these (and the original list is much longer) calls for the student to unearth new information or to argue a new interpretation. He or she is expected rather to offer a summary of what is already known.

Nevertheless a considerable number of college instructors do insist on research papers in the restricted sense of that term. A nursing student was asked by her instructor to write a ten-page paper developing either side of the question "Food Additives —Helpful or Harmful?" A student in a political science course was required to analyze a book in the light of these two questions:

- Do you find this critique of America persuasive?
- What do you think will happen in the next twenty years or so that is related to this criticism?

A history professor prefaces his list of topics with these words:

> *Remember that you are writing an argument.* History is the discipline that develops and revises explanations for groups of events in the past. Take a clearcut position on an issue and sustain it throughout your essay, although you should make the other positions clear as well. Never lose track of the position you are defending.

All of these are examples of research papers, sometimes referred to collectively as "critical" papers.

Find out right away if your paper is to be a library paper or a research paper. The answer will have a significant effect both on the topic you choose and on the treatment you give to the topic.

If your assignment is to write a library paper, you simply need a body of material you can summarize. Sometimes a list of possible topics will be given in class. If not, you can arrive at a satisfactory topic by the same process I described in Part A of the previous chapter: surveying what you know and what interests you, narrowing the subject area, weighing your information, and adapting the subject to the reader. Answering a series of questions about a possible topic or approaching the possible topic as if it were problematic and in need of solution might also help.

In a long paper you need not restrict the topic quite as much as you do for a shorter paper. Now you have room to give a larger topic the detail it requires. Whereas "The Versailles Treaty" is too general for a three-page paper, you might be able to give it an adequate treatment in eleven pages. (But "World War I" is still out.) Nor do you have to be content with a topic for which you already have all the information you need. The instructor who assigns a library paper gives you the opportunity—in fact *wants* you—to expand the range of what you know.

If your assignment is to write a research paper, the process works a little differently. First ask yourself if there is something new on which you can report. Don't automatically assume the answer is no. Many valuable topics lie waiting to be explored, topics that can be researched easily and that will be interesting to others. An example might be student attitudes toward a particular problem: think what you can accomplish with a tape recorder or a notepad and a few hours of conversation with your friends. Or consider topics about which you happen to have special expertise. One student worked in the office of a car dealer. With proper permission she used the records at her disposal and wrote a very good paper for a business course on the profit margins and pricing policies of a typical suburban dealership. Researching a new subject might not be as difficult as you think, provided of course that the structure of your course allows for such experimentation.

Nevertheless your research paper will probably exemplify the other type, the kind that argues a position on familiar material. You can follow the same methods for selecting a topic as you would for a library paper, i.e., the methods described in Chapter 4. But you must take the additional precaution of making sure you have an arguable thesis. An arguable thesis, remember, is one that offers a position with which reasonable people can differ. Often you will not be able to write a thesis statement until after you have worked in the library for a while. The girl who wrote on food additives, for example, did not know whether she thought they were harmful or not until after she had evaluated the conflicting testimony. But at the very least you should choose a topic that lends itself to opposing views, and you should realize that at some point you will have to stake out your territory and defend it.

Once you have found your topic (or your instructor has "found" it for you), the next step is to **plan the paper.** Again the composing process is similar to the one described in Chapter 4. Ask the six questions to determine whether the paper will be a narrative, descriptive, cause and effect, comparison and contrast, extended definition, or an opinion paper. Then develop a strategy based on the kind of paper you are writing.

Because the material for a longer paper can be unwieldy, outlines are often very useful. Naturally the outline for a longer paper will be more complicated than for a shorter one. Start with a **preliminary outline,** because you don't yet know much about your subject. Later you will revise it and add to it as your reading and library work progresses; soon you will be filling in details and rearranging the order of your subtopics. For now you can be satisfied with a rough idea of where you are going and approximately how you might get there. A preliminary outline on food additives, for example, might look like this:

    I. The question (thesis made clear)
   II. Definitions (of additives, for instance)
  III. Size of the problem
  IV. Benefits of additives (list)
   V. Risks (list)
  VI. Solution?

That outline does not tell you much, but it points the paper in the right direction. After your library work is complete you can then draw up the final outline (see p. 228). The final outline is your plan for organizing the complete manuscript. But before we talk about the complete manuscript, we should look at those library activities you need to have finished.

One added note: library papers and research papers differ in both topic and approach, but they do not differ in their procedures for gathering and then presenting information. From now on, I will use the term *long paper,* because what I say applies equally to the library paper and the research paper.

A2. Finding Sources

The easiest way to show how a long paper gets written is to follow a typical paper from its beginning to its completion.

Suppose you have been narrowing your topic by using the suggestions offered in the previous section. One of your interests, let us further suppose, is capital punishment. The publicity given to this issue in recent years has made you conscious of the moral implications of the death penalty, and you want to weigh those issues carefully and arrive at a logical and defensible judgment about them. You have been told to write a research paper, so you know that eventually your paper ought to take a firm position on the issue. Tentatively you are prepared to argue that capital punishment is wrong. But you also know that you should explore both sides of the question before you commit yourself.

Just to remind yourself of what comes next, you might draw up a very sketchy outline of the topic as you first see it. Like this:

   I. Statement of thesis (for or against)
  II. Brief history of capital punishment in U.S.
 III. Present relevance—Supreme Court decision, Gilmore case, etc.
  IV. Reasons to support thesis
   V. Answers to opponents' objections

That is about all you can say right now. This simple outline merely reminds you of what you must do. In fact, it does not even say which side of the case you plan to take—the outline will serve equally well for a defense of capital punishment or an attack on it. Before you can be more specific, however, you will have to learn more about the issue. And that means going to the library to draw up a list of sources.

> Libraries have been very deeply established in the ethic of America. They go right along with the flag.
>
> *Clara Stanton Jones*

First stop is the card catalog. You know that books can be looked up under subject headings as well as under author or title, so you head for the *D*'s to check on "Death penalty." You figure the card catalog will show you all the books on that topic your library holds.

Nothing. A big zero.

Next step is the reference section, where you find or ask for one of the most valuable but least known works: *The Library of Congress Subject Headings*. These two volumes list every imaginable subject heading and then show under what other subject the entry might be classified. In other words, you look up "Death penalty" and it says "See Capital punishment." Therefore libraries that use the Library of Congress cataloging system will list all of their holdings on this topic under the subject heading "Capital punishment." (Some libraries use the older Dewey decimal system, which arranges the call numbers differently—see your librarian for details if you have to make the adjustment.)

Back you go to the card catalog, this time to the *C*'s. Success! You find several books under the heading "Capital punishment." Here is the card for one of them, reproduced exactly as I found it in the library of my own university.

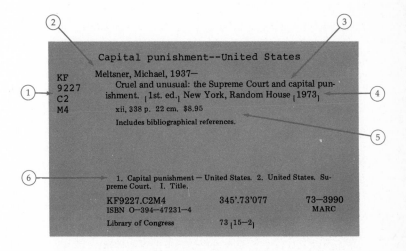

The numbers surrounding this sample card point to the places on the card where you will find, in order:

1. Call number. This number tells you where to find the book in your library. The number here is from the Library of Congress classification system; if your library uses the Dewey decimal system, the number will be somewhat different.

2. Author. Michael Meltsner, who was born in 1937, is the author. If he were an editor or translator, his name would be followed by *ed.* or *trans.*

3. Title. The full title is *Cruel and Unusual: the Supreme Court and Capital Punishment,* although the last six words could be called the subtitle.

4. Publication facts. In this case, you learn that the book was published in New York City by Random House in the year 1973 and that this is the first edition of the book. Subsequent editions, if any, would have a separate entry.

5. Book size. The Meltsner book has 12 (xii) pages of prefatory material and 338 pages of text; its original cost was $8.95. The size (22 centimeters) tells you the book is not just a small pamphlet. Moreover you discover that the book contains a bibliography, in other words a list of sources; this list might prove useful.

6. Subject headings. This section of the card tells you that this same book is listed under both the subject "Capital punishment—United States" (in fact, you will note at the top of the page that this card itself is the subject card for that heading), and the subject "United States. Supreme Court." Cards will also be found under the title and the author.

You begin a list of books on the topic of capital punishment. The Meltsner book goes on it, let us assume, and any other books found under this subject heading. Your list might resemble this one:

Bedau, H.A., *The Death Penalty in America* (HV 8551 M2)
Black, Charles, *Capital Punishment* (HV 8698 B47 1974)
Gowers, Sir Ernest, *A Life for a Life?* (HV 8694 G6 1956)
Meltsner, Michael, *Cruel and Unusual* (KF 9227 C2 M4)
Sellin, Johan T., *Capital Punishment* (HV 8694 S4)

Some of the books in the card catalog you have ruled out, perhaps because they are printed in a language you don't read (like Karl von Amira's *Die germanischen Todesstrafen*), perhaps because they seem out of date (like L. T. Beman's *Selected Articles on Capital Punishment*, published in 1925). So far you are content with just putting down the author, a short version of the title, and the call number. Later on, if you decide to actually use the book, you will need more information.

Now you have the beginnings of a source list for your topic. Books are not the only possibilities, however. Articles in magazines and journals may also be important, yet they will not be listed separately in the card catalog. How to find them? The next step is to return to the reference department and consult the periodical indexes.

> Knowledge is of two kinds. We know a subject ourselves, or we know where we can find information on it.
>
> *Samuel Johnson*

For popular magazines, use the *Reader's Guide to Periodical Literature*. Of course this guide cannot include every magazine, but it does offer a generous sampling of articles from popular magazines like *Psychology Today, Harper's, Newsweek, Time,* and others. Consulting the volume covering the year from March 1976 to February 1977, and looking under "Capital punishment," you find no less than twenty-five entries. Here is one of them.

Problem of Capital Punishment. H. A. Bedau.
 bibl il Cur Hist 71: 14–18 + Jl '76.

Translated, that entry means that an article with the title "The Problem of Capital Punishment," written by H. A. Bedau, appeared in the magazine *Current History.* The article was illustrated, contained a bibliography, and was published in the July 1976 issue. The July 1976 issue in turn was part of volume 71, and the article in question began on pages 14–18 and was then continued (+) later on in the same issue. A list of abbreviations at the beginning of the *Reader's Guide* can help you do this translating.

So you add the Bedau article and any other article that seems important to the list of sources you have been compiling. Again a short form will do:

Bedau, "Cap. Pun.," *Current History,* 71, p. 14+
Gaddis, "Death as Cover-up?" *Nation,* 222, p. 37+

Go back for the last ten or a dozen years, until you have what you feel is a full and representative list. You must be selective—otherwise, on a subject the size of this one, you will soon drown.

The *Reader's Guide* covers the popular press. But you want to know what other experts think, too. What about the scholarly journals not included in the guide?

Your first resource is the *Social Sciences Index*. This series does for scholarly articles what the *Reader's Guide* does for more general articles. The original title for the bibliography was the *International Index*, in 1965 it was renamed the *Social Sciences and Humanities Index*, and then in 1974 it was split into a separate *Social Sciences Index* and a companion *Humanities Index*. Since capital punishment is more closely allied to the social sciences than to the humanities, begin with the *Social Sciences Index* for the most recent years, then work your way back through the joint volumes for the years before 1974. As before you will probably have to limit yourself to perhaps the last decade.

Again you check under the heading "Capital punishment," and again you are rewarded with several entries. For example, the volume covering the year from April 1976 to March 1977 lists eight articles: three from *The Economist*, one each from *The American Journal of Economics and Sociology*, *The American Journal of Orthopsychiatry*, *Freedomway*, *Criminology*, and *Crime and Delinquency*. You add the ones that sound most promising to your source list.

Back to the card catalog, this time to check your list of articles against the journal holdings of your library. If your library does receive the magazine or journal, note the locations of the journal or ask where it is kept. If your library does not receive a particular scholarly journal, cross that article off your list. (For example, of the six journals listed in the previous paragraph, my university library subscribes to only four.)

If your library does not receive a certain popular magazine, however, don't be hasty in crossing off the article. Many college or university libraries will not purchase a magazine like *Psychology Today*, but your local city or county library may very well have it, since their clientele is different. Check the local library, perhaps by phone, and find out what they hold. While you are at it, especially if you make a personal visit, don't forget to see what *books* the local library might have that your college library does not.

Two other short steps will complete your search. The reference departments of libraries contain a vast assortment of more specialized bibliographies and reference works. These books might contain valuable leads, so ask your librarian which ones might be the most helpful. Then check on newspapers. Most college libraries carry the *New York Times*, and perhaps other papers as well, on microfilm. Use the *New York Times Index* to locate entries. That way you would not miss the article about the Gallup poll on capital punishment that appeared in the *Times* on April 29, 1976, which might give you an idea of how the daily press has covered this subject.

Now your initial list is complete, so it is time to invade the stacks in search of the books and journals. Don't worry if your list seems long. You won't find everything—books can be misplaced, lost, stolen, at the bindery, or in the hands of another borrower. Furthermore some of the books and articles that you do find will seem, on closer inspection, peripheral to your interests. Use a book's table of contents or the abstract of an article as a way of helping you decide how useful it will be.

Remember too that this is only a starting list. As you read further you will probably meet several references to still other books and articles on your topic, and you will find yourself making one or more trips back to the library to supplement your initial collection.

Still, the first list has given you a body of material to work with. What do you do with it?

A3. Taking Notes

Putting together your preliminary list of sources should take you only a few hours. The next step, taking notes on the material, requires much more time, anywhere from one to four weeks if it is done properly. So begin your project early enough to allow enough time for all the stages. Anything less than a month for a paper of ten pages or more is probably too little time, unless the course you are taking is a highly condensed one. Starting early also gives you the added advantage of being able to ask the library to recall potentially useful books that have been borrowed by someone else.

> Plan ahead: it wasn't raining when Noah built the ark.
>
> *poster*

Most people prefer to take notes on index cards because the cards can be arranged in whatever order is required by the final outline. Let's assume you are using index cards. You will need to keep two types of cards: regular note cards and bibliography cards.

Bibliography cards. Make a separate entry for each book or article you read. Include on the card the author(s) and a full description. For a book the description includes title, publisher, place and date of publication, and (where it applies) the edition and the number of volumes. A bibliography card for the Meltsner book described previously might look like this:

The value of including the call number is that it enables you to find the book again quickly should you have a sudden need for it after you have returned it.

For an article, the description includes the article's title, the name of the journal or magazine, the volume number, the date, and the inclusive pages on which the article can be found. Like this:

ıformation you know you encountered but did

A4. Writing the Paper

 checked the books and articles you felt you
other words the ones that sounded (from the
cription) like they dealt with your topic directly,
ave compiled what seems to you like more than
ds, you can begin to write.

your rough outline into a *final outline*. Now
much more about the subject, you can commit
sis and give a detailed and explicit summary of
cture. Here is an example:

Outline

l punishment should be abolished and never

d
States
nial Times and Nineteenth century
ntieth century
r abolition
d against a class (i.e., poor, blacks, etc.)
from hysteria
n witch trials
o-Vanzetti case
nbergs
es
bergh case
othy Evans case
ers insane
titutional
th Amendment
decision
decision—Nixon Court

enalty deters (but no—see statistics)
enalty removes offenders permanently—Barzun (but

 (plea for action)

Notice that the author's last name appears first in the upper
lefthand corner. This makes for easy alphabetizing when you
type up the final bibliography.

You draw up only one bibliography card for each book or
article you use. No matter how few or how many note cards you
collect from that source, there is still only one bibliography card.

Note cards. These are the cards on which you jot down everything that might prove useful when you write the paper. You can
include in your notes several kinds of information:

1. statements of fact

2. summaries of important statements by the author whose work you are reading

> ### S. Court decisions
>
> Meltzner believes Nixon chose Justices Powell & Rehnquist in part because they could be counted on to support the death penalty
>
> Meltzner, pp. 258-265

3. direct quotations of statements that seem especially important

> ### arguments against
>
> "Legislators will draft mandatory death statutes to net the Charles Mansons and Richard Specks of the future, but no set of rules will avoid catching men whose deeds are far less reprehensible, or whose character arouses sympathy."
>
> Meltzner, p. 312

4. ideas of your own
   will promptly for
   down

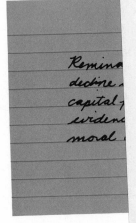

> Remina
> decline
> capital
> evidenc
> moral

Notice that whenever
heading in the upper
Court decision; argumen
preliminary outline an
later, when it is time to
are plainly marked, so
between what was quo

When you encount
graphs and tables, co
braries have one, and f
minutes. Be sure to wr
of your photocopy.

Knowing what kind
solve the dozens of littl
read—questions like, '
this statement?" Only
In the meantime the s
that *might* help. Nothin
ity of your final paper t
out of too much materi

needing some in
not record.

When you have
should read, in
title or other des
and when you h
enough note car

First, convert
that you know
yourself to a the
the paper's struc

Thesis: Capita
reinstated.
  I. History
     A. Englan
     B. United
        1. Colo
        2. Twer
 II. Reasons fo
     A. Directe
     B. Results
        1. Sale
        2. Sacc
        3. Rose
     C. Mistake
        1. Linc
        2. Timo
     D. Murder
     E. Uncons
        1. Eigh
        2. 1972
        3. 1976
III. Refutation
     A. Death
     B. Death
        does it?)
 IV. Conclusion

Such an outline helps give order to what otherwise might be a large, unmanageable subject.

Now you can arrange your note cards in the approximate order you will use them, in other words in the order suggested by your outline. The subtopic headings in the upper right-hand corner should help: for example, put all the cards on "history" together and all the cards on "reasons against—S. Court decision" together, and so on. You will have a few cards that fit into more than one subtopic and a few that fit into none. Don't worry—just keep them where you can consult them quickly when the opportunity arises.

You are ready to start the first draft. The composing process here is no different from the one described in Chapter 4: find a good opening, state a clear thesis, develop each part fully, make careful transitions, frame a pointed conclusion. Just be sure to note which sentence or which paragraph will need a footnote (more on this later).

The only additional suggestion I would make is to be sure that your writing style is relatively formal. That does not mean to use flat committee prose—good writing is lively writing. It simply means you make only a very limited use of contractions, colloquialisms, the pronoun *I*, and other signs of informality. Try to write as clearly and forcefully as possible. Show that you care, that you have something you really want to say.

As you write, you may find yourself using a source that seems untrustworthy or that contains statements that conflict with statements from other sources. Whom should you believe? Which statements will you adopt and which will you reject? You need to be able to *evaluate your sources.*

Sometimes you can evaluate sources on the basis of external evidence. If the conflict is over certain facts, and if one source is more recent than the others and reports studies that make earlier studies outdated, then you will prefer the more recent source. If the conflict is over facts and one source is more complete and authoritative than another (e.g., *Webster's Third International Dictionary* versus the cheap paperback dictionary cited in Chapter 1), choose the more reputable source. If the conflict is over opinions and one opinion comes from the *National Enquirer* tabloid and the other comes from the *Washington Post,* you might be inclined to give the latter at least the initial preference. If the conflict is over opinions and one writer is an expert in the subject and the other clearly is not, you might want to give more weight to the expert's testimony. (Notice I say *might*—experts can be wrong.)

External evidence is not always enough, however. A book or article may offer an opinion and you simply are not sure whether you can rely on the opinion or not. Suppose, for example, that in your investigation of capital punishment you came across the book *Capital Punishment: The Inevitability of Caprice and Mistake* by someone named Charles L. Black, Jr. The very title makes clear Black's position on the death penalty. Furthermore he seems to make some potent arguments against it. But you want to know whether you can trust Black and his conclusions. Since you are not an expert yourself (although you are fast becoming one), you would like to know what the experts said about Black's argument.

Your first resource is the *Book Review Digest* in the reference department of your library. Since Black's book appeared in 1974, you try the 1975 volume, and you are rewarded by a list of no less than six reviews, in *America, Choice, Library Journal, National Review, New York Times Book Review,* and *The New Yorker.* Four of these reviews are summarized and excerpted for you. The

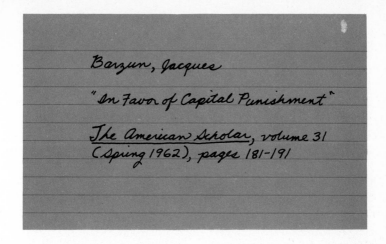

Notice that the author's last name appears first in the upper lefthand corner. This makes for easy alphabetizing when you type up the final bibliography.

You draw up only one bibliography card for each book or article you use. No matter how few or how many note cards you collect from that source, there is still only one bibliography card.

Note cards. These are the cards on which you jot down everything that might prove useful when you write the paper. You can include in your notes several kinds of information:

1. statements of fact

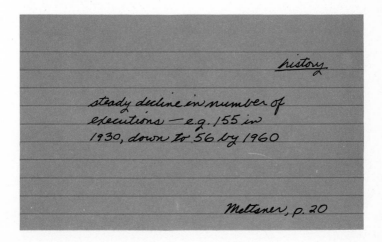

2. summaries of important statements by the author whose work you are reading

> S. Court decisions
>
> Meltsner believes Nixon chose Justices Powell & Rehnquist in part because they could be counted on to support the death penalty
>
> Meltsner, pp. 258-265

3. direct quotations of statements that seem especially important

> arguments against
>
> "Legislators will draft mandatory death statutes to net the Charles Mansons and Richard Specks of the future, but no set of rules will avoid catching men whose deeds are far less reprehensible, or whose character arouses sympathy."
>
> Meltsner, p. 312

4. ideas of your own that occur to you as you read and that you will promptly forget (believe me!) if you don't write them down

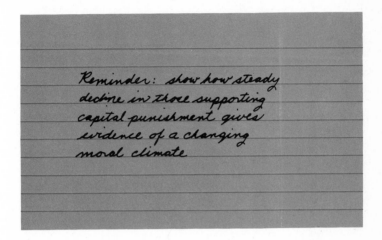

Reminder: show how steady decline in those supporting capital punishment gives evidence of a changing moral climate

Notice that whenever possible these cards have a little subtopic heading in the upper right-hand corner (e.g., *history; S[upreme] Court decision; arguments against*). This heading is keyed to the preliminary outline and makes it easier to group the note cards later, when it is time to write. Notice also that direct quotations are plainly marked, so you will experience no confusion later on between what was quoted and what was only summarized.

When you encounter long quotations or material such as graphs and tables, consider the use of a photocopier. Most libraries have one, and for a nickel or a dime you can save several minutes. Be sure to write down the original source on the back of your photocopy.

Knowing what kinds of things go onto note cards does not solve the dozens of little practical questions that come up as you read—questions like, "Will I ever have any use for this fact or this statement?" Only more experience can give you real help. In the meantime the safest practice is to write down anything that *might* help. Nothing gives you more confidence in the quality of your final paper than the opportunity to pick only the best out of too much material, and nothing is more frustrating than

needing some information you know you encountered but did
not record.

A4. Writing the Paper

When you have checked the books and articles you felt you
should read, in other words the ones that sounded (from the
title or other description) like they dealt with your topic directly,
and when you have compiled what seems to you like more than
enough note cards, you can begin to write.

First, convert your rough outline into a *final outline*. Now
that you know much more about the subject, you can commit
yourself to a thesis and give a detailed and explicit summary of
the paper's structure. Here is an example:

Outline

Thesis: Capital punishment should be abolished and never
reinstated.
  I. History
      A. England
      B. United States
          1. Colonial Times and Nineteenth century
          2. Twentieth century
  II. Reasons for abolition
      A. Directed against a class (i.e., poor, blacks, etc.)
      B. Results from hysteria
          1. Salem witch trials
          2. Sacco-Vanzetti case
          3. Rosenbergs
      C. Mistakes
          1. Lindbergh case
          2. Timothy Evans case
      D. Murderers insane
      E. Unconstitutional
          1. Eighth Amendment
          2. 1972 decision
          3. 1976 decision—Nixon Court
  III. Refutation
      A. Death penalty deters (but no—see statistics)
      B. Death penalty removes offenders permanently—Barzun (but
         does it?)
  IV. Conclusion (plea for action)

Such an outline helps give order to what otherwise might be a large, unmanageable subject.

Now you can arrange your note cards in the approximate order you will use them, in other words in the order suggested by your outline. The subtopic headings in the upper right-hand corner should help: for example, put all the cards on "history" together and all the cards on "reasons against—S. Court decision" together, and so on. You will have a few cards that fit into more than one subtopic and a few that fit into none. Don't worry—just keep them where you can consult them quickly when the opportunity arises.

You are ready to start the first draft. The composing process here is no different from the one described in Chapter 4: find a good opening, state a clear thesis, develop each part fully, make careful transitions, frame a pointed conclusion. Just be sure to note which sentence or which paragraph will need a footnote (more on this later).

The only additional suggestion I would make is to be sure that your writing style is relatively formal. That does not mean to use flat committee prose—good writing is lively writing. It simply means you make only a very limited use of contractions, colloquialisms, the pronoun *I*, and other signs of informality. Try to write as clearly and forcefully as possible. Show that you care, that you have something you really want to say.

As you write, you may find yourself using a source that seems untrustworthy or that contains statements that conflict with statements from other sources. Whom should you believe? Which statements will you adopt and which will you reject? You need to be able to *evaluate your sources*.

Sometimes you can evaluate sources on the basis of external evidence. If the conflict is over certain facts, and if one source is more recent than the others and reports studies that make earlier studies outdated, then you will prefer the more recent source. If the conflict is over facts and one source is more complete and authoritative than another (e.g., *Webster's Third International Dictionary* versus the cheap paperback dictionary cited in Chapter 1), choose the more reputable source. If the conflict is over opinions and one opinion comes from the *National Enquirer* tabloid and the other comes from the *Washington Post*, you might be inclined to give the latter at least the initial preference. If the conflict is over opinions and one writer is an expert in the subject and the other clearly is not, you might want to give more weight to the expert's testimony. (Notice I say *might*—experts can be wrong.)

External evidence is not always enough, however. A book or article may offer an opinion and you simply are not sure whether you can rely on the opinion or not. Suppose, for example, that in your investigation of capital punishment you came across the book *Capital Punishment: The Inevitability of Caprice and Mistake* by someone named Charles L. Black, Jr. The very title makes clear Black's position on the death penalty. Furthermore he seems to make some potent arguments against it. But you want to know whether you can trust Black and his conclusions. Since you are not an expert yourself (although you are fast becoming one), you would like to know what the experts said about Black's argument.

Your first resource is the *Book Review Digest* in the reference department of your library. Since Black's book appeared in 1974, you try the 1975 volume, and you are rewarded by a list of no less than six reviews, in *America, Choice, Library Journal, National Review, New York Times Book Review,* and *The New Yorker.* Four of these reviews are summarized and excerpted for you. The summaries tell you that Charles L. Black, Jr. happens to be Luce Professor of Jurisprudence at Yale University and the nation's foremost authority on constitutional law. Furthermore the excerpts are without exception highly complimentary to his book, calling it "persuasive" and a "most concise, complete, and satisfying treatment." Evidently this is a book to be reckoned with, at least insofar as it discusses constitutional law.

Perhaps these capsule reviews satisfy you. If not, you can always read the complete reviews in the original journals. Furthermore you have the opportunity of going on to a second resource, the reviews from scholarly journals indexed in the *Social Sciences Index*.

As for evaluating articles, your chief reliance must be on the source, i.e., the journal or magazine itself. Does it have a known bias? If so, does that bias seem to affect the statements you are considering? If your subject is the death penalty, for example, you might not be surprised to find that the conservative *National Review* is for capital punishment and the liberal *New Republic* is against it.

Now, while you are writing, is the time to keep in mind the distinction between research papers and library papers we made earlier. If your paper is supposed to be a genuine research paper, are you offering new information or—the more likely possibility—are you developing a clear proposition about your subject? Make sure that you have formed a thesis, that you have stated it directly within the first couple of paragraphs, and that you are now organizing your paper around the defense of it. If your paper is a library paper and you do not have to defend a proposition, at least be sure your paper has a purpose and that this purpose is readily apparent to every reader. Consider also whether your paper would be a better one with a controversial thesis, even though one is not required. A paper that simply outlines the capital punishment controversy might be acceptable. But wouldn't you rather read an essay that took one side and gave a lively and vigorous defense of it?

You may find yourself rewriting more of the long paper than you did the shorter ones. The larger the paper, the more unwieldy it becomes. Besides, you are still acquiring new information even as you write, and this information must find a place. Don't worry if the completed draft departs from the final outline—remember that outlines are servants, not masters.

> It is a bad plan which admits of no modification.
> *Publius Syrus*

For most people, the completed first draft is handwritten, unless you can "think" with a typewriter. (After twenty years of typing I still can't.) Now, after revising the draft, you are ready to type the final version. Even if you are not going to type, you still need to prepare a new clean manuscript. Whether typed or handwritten, the final version is going to include both footnotes and a bibliography.

A5. *Typing the Paper: Footnotes and Bibliography*

Type in accordance with the instructions for manuscript form on pp. 242–243. Put your last name and the page number in the upper right-hand corner of each page, because the pages might get separated in your instructor's briefcase and you want to be sure the paper can be identified and reassembled. Include a separate title page, with the title centered on it, and your name, the date, and the course number in the lower right-hand corner.

That brings us to *footnotes*. Number the footnotes consecutively throughout the text. At each place in the paper where you use material that must be footnoted, insert the footnote number at the end of the material, typing it somewhat above the regular line, like this:

```
    . . . cost perhaps $2 billion for 1979 alone.[15]
```

The footnote itself will appear either at the bottom of the page or else in a separate section at the end of the text, just before the bibliography. Use whichever location your instructor prefers. If he or she expresses no preference, you will find it easier to type them all together at the end, because it is hard to know exactly how much room to leave at the bottom of each page when the number and size of the footnotes vary. When notes appear at the end, by the way, they are more accurately termed *endnotes* or just *notes*.

For the rest of this chapter we'll assume the notes can be gathered at the end of the paper. However, if you must put them at the bottom, interrupt your text at a place where you still have room to type the notes for that page. Then type a short horizontal line to separate the text from the footnotes and type the footnotes in the form shown on pp. 272–275.

What must be footnoted? Some categories are clear. Pertinent facts, statistics, and tables need footnotes. So do stories, explanations, or other remarks of your own that cannot be fitted into the text but that you think are important. A third group is made up of all direct quotations.

There is a fourth category. Its boundaries are less clearly defined, and perhaps for this reason it causes students and teachers more confusion than all the others combined. I refer, as perhaps you have guessed, to the summary and/or paraphrase.

The general principle can be stated easily. Whenever your paper summarizes, restates, or makes use of the opinions or interpretations of someone else, you must use a footnote. Not to do so is a breach of honesty, since the ideas are not your own and should not be offered as if they were. Furthermore the footnote helps your reader retrace the steps you have taken to arrive at your conclusion.

The principle is clear, but the application of it is more difficult. The delicacy comes in deciding what makes a legitimate summary or paraphrase. Here, for example, is a paragraph from the Charles Black book discussed earlier.

> I think the answer has to be that, after all possible inquiry, including the probing of all possible methods of inquiry, we do not know, and for systematic and easily visible reasons cannot know, what the truth about this "deterrent" effect may be. We know that, on raw data, there has been somewhat more homicide in capital punishment states than in non-capital punishment states. But we cannot draw any valid conclusions from this, for factors other than the punishment system may easily explain the difference. The general problem that blocks knowledge here is that no adequately controlled experiment or observation is possible or (so far as we can see) ever will be possible. We have to use uncontrolled data from society itself, outside any laboratory.

A legitimate summary of that passage, condensing the passage to a single sentence and offering a footnote reference, would be:

Charles Black, on the other hand, contends that we will never know for sure whether capital punishment is an effective deterrent to crime. [7]

Here is a legitimate paraphrase of the passage. Paraphases restate the meaning of a passage, giving more details and coming closer to the original wording than a summary does. This paraphrase is proper because it offers a footnote and avoids using Black's words:

Charles Black contends that we do not know and will never know whether capital punishment can effectively deter people from crime. Current data is inconclusive, he says, because it may well be contaminated by other factors. Furthermore it is impossible to draw up a satisfactory experiment when you cannot use a control group. [7]

However, this paraphrase is not legitimate:

We do not know and will never know whether capital punishment can effectively deter people from crime. Current data is inconclusive, because it may well be contaminated by other factors. Furthermore it is impossible to draw up a satisfactory experiment when you cannot use a control group.

The words may not be Black's, but the *ideas* are clearly his. Yet the author never acknowledges this debt by means of a footnote. Paraphrases are very useful to a writer because they condense a large body of material that would otherwise have to be given in direct quotation. Their usefulness, however, does not cancel the debt to the original author. Document just as fully when you borrow ideas as when you borrow words.

This paraphrase pays the debt of a footnote. But it too is illegitimate, this time for a different reason:

The answer has to be that, after all possible inquiry, including the probing of all possible methods of inquiry, we do not know, and for obvious reasons cannot know, the truth about this "deterrent" effect. We have data showing there has been somewhat more homicide in capital punishment states than in non-capital punishment states. But we cannot draw valid conclusions from this, because other factors might explain the difference. The problem is that no adequately controlled experiment is possible or ever will be possible. [7]

This passage, because it lacks quotation marks, pretends to be a paraphrase. But in reality it is a direct quotation, with only a few words changed or left out. The reader deserves to be told that the passage contains Black's *words* as well as his ideas.

The only exception—and here is where the lines begin to blur—is an idea in the public domain. Not all ideas in a book or an article are unique to the author. Suppose, for example, you had not heard of the 1972 Supreme Court decision on capital punishment before you started your paper. After all, you might have been in grade school then, or perhaps you were living in another country. Now you find several authors mentioning that decision and saying that it caused intense public controversy. You want to say the same thing in the first paragraph of your paper. There is no need to footnote this statement just because you had not heard of it before you began your research. The idea is a common one, obvious, widely shared, and easily proved; therefore you can restate it without acknowledgment. Of course if you use somebody else's *words,* either directly or in close paraphrase, then you must cite their work. Otherwise, so long as the idea is put in your words, a footnote is unnecessary.

Let me give you another example. Almost every freshman writing handbook like this one has a chapter on the research paper. And almost every chapter on the research paper has a few paragraphs on paraphrasing. The ideas I have been developing in the last few paragraphs are not presented for the first time here. But neither are they presented for the first time in other handbooks. I do not need to put a footnote here referring to all those other handbooks just because they have sections comparable to the one you are now reading. These rules about paraphrases are in the public domain, and so long as I offer them to you in my own words I am being honest with you.

What happens when you cannot decide if an idea is in the public domain or not? When in doubt, footnote. It won't hurt and it might help.

How to footnote? That depends on whether the work is a book or an article. It also depends on which style manual you are asked to use. This chapter is based on the *MLA Handbook for Writers of Research Papers, Theses, and Dissertations,* which is the most common style manual for humanities and business courses. Papers for courses in the natural or social sciences may need alternative methods—see A7 for a discussion of the biggest differences.

For books and pamphlets, the first time you refer to a work you must include its author, title, publisher, place and date of publication, and the page number of the material you are using. Type and punctuate the information like this:

```
7
 Charles L. Black, Jr., Capital Punishment:   The Inevi-

tability of Caprice and Mistake (New York:   W. W. Norton, 1974),

p. 25.
```

Notice that this footnote contains the following items, in order: 1. author's name in normal word order, followed by a comma; 2. the full title, underlined to indicate italics; 3. a set of parentheses followed by a comma—within the parentheses one finds the city of publication, a colon, the publisher, a comma, and the year of publication; 4. the *p.* abbreviation for *page (pp.* for *pages)* and then the page number, followed by a period.

Any later references to the same book require only author and page number, plus a shortened title if you use more than one work by the same author:

```
14
  Black, pp.   71-73.
15
  Bedau, Death Penalty, p. xi.
```

However, some books offer special difficulties. Here are the most common problems and how to solve them:

1. The book has more than one author.

```
22
  N. K. Teeters and J. Hedblom, Hang by the Neck (Spring-

field, Ill.:   Charles C. Thomas, 1966), p. 43.
```

Note that *Springfield* is followed by the abbreviation of its state, Illinois, for clarification—unlike such cities as Chicago, Boston, New York, or London, it is not obvious what state (or foreign country) it is in.

2. The book is an anthology, a collection, and therefore has an editor rather than an author.

   [23]Hugo Adam Bedau, ed., preface and introduction to The Death Penalty in America: An Anthology (Garden City, N.Y.: Doubleday, 1964), p. 6.

   Bedau's remarks are found in the introductory material to the book, as cited here; if you cite one of the articles included in this anthology, see footnote 17 on p. 275.

3. The book is a translation.

   [26]Fyodor Dostoyevsky, Crime and Punishment, trans. David Magarshack (Baltimore: Penguin Books, 1951), p. 216.

4. The book has more than one volume.

   [31]Luke O. Pike, A History of Crime in England (London: Hodder and Stoughton, 1876), II, 489.

   The roman numeral *II* indicates the second volume of this two-volume work; when the volume is specified, the *p.* before the page number is omitted.

5. The book has more than one edition.

   [34]E. Roy Calvert, Capital Punishment in the Twentieth Century, 5th ed. (New York: Harcourt, 1936), p. 111.

6. The note refers to an encyclopedia entry.

   [37]A. E. Woods, "Capital Punishment," World Book Encyclopedia, 1958, III, 1224–1225.

   The author of the entry has his initials printed at the end of it, and you can then discover his name by resorting to the list of

contributors in the first volume; the year—*1958*—specifies
the edition you used, the roman numeral III gives the volume
number, and the page numbers—as before—need not be
preceded by *pp*.

7. The work was written by one author and then edited by
   another.

    [44]Clarence Darrow, <u>Attorney for the Damned</u>, ed. Arthur

Weinberg (New York: Simon & Schuster, 1957), p. 93.

If you encounter a special problem not covered by these seven
examples, check a style manual in the library or ask your instructor for advice.

> In front of excellence the immortal gods have put sweat,
> and long and steep is the way to it, and rough at first. But
> when you come to the top, then it is easy.
>
> *Hesiod*

Articles are treated a little differently. The first reference includes author, title of the article, name of the journal, volume
number, date, and page reference. Arrange and punctuate it like
this:

    [5]Jacques Barzun, "In Favor of Capital Punishment," <u>The</u>

<u>American Scholar</u>, 31 (1962), 185.

The author's name is given in the normal word order, the article's title is capitalized and put within quotation marks, the
journal's title is underlined (italicized), the volume number—
31—is followed by the year (1962) within parentheses, and the
page number is not preceded by *p*. Later references to the same
article require just the author's last name and the page number,
this time with a *p*. or *pp*.:

    [12]Barzun, pp. 187–189.

Once more I should point to a couple of exceptions and ways to solve them.

1. The essay or article is part of an anthology rather than in a journal.

[17]Victor Evjen, "Let's Abolish Capital Punishment," in *Capital Punishment*, ed. James McCafferty (New York: Lieber-Atherton, 1974), p. 221.

2. The article is anonymous, from a popular magazine.

[16]"Closing Death Row," *Time*, 100 (10 July 1972), 37.

3. The note refers to a book review, with the reviewer's name first.

[18]J. J. Paris, rev. of *Capital Punishment: The Inevitability of Caprice and Mistake*, by Charles L. Black, Jr., *America*, 132 (8 March 1975), 175.

4. The note refers to a newspaper article. (If the newspaper article has a by-line, put the author's name before the title.)

[19]"Gallup Poll Shows 65% Favor Death Penalty," *New York Times*, 29 April 1976, p. 40, col. 8.

These four examples can serve as models for treating the most common exceptions.

This whole array of customs and exceptions can be confusing, I know. Perhaps I can best simplify it by reducing these customs to a formula, a formula not unlike the ones you might have met in high school chemistry or biology. All you need do is plug in the proper data, and the formula guarantees an acceptable footnote. First, the formula for the first reference to the usual single-author, single-volume book:

> author's name (first name first) + comma + title (underlined) + opening parenthesis + city of publication + colon + publisher + comma + year of publication + closing parenthesis + comma + *p.* or *pp.* + page number(s) + period

The formula for a first reference to a standard journal article is this:

> author's name (first name first) + comma + opening quotes + article's title + comma + closing quotes + journal's title (underlined) + comma + volume number + opening parenthesis + date of issue + closing parenthesis + comma + page number(s) + period

The formula for later references both to books and articles is simply this:

> author's last name + comma + *p.* or *pp.* + page number(s) + period

These three formulas will cover perhaps 90 percent of the footnotes in the usual long paper.

One final comment about footnotes. If you have mentioned the name of the author or the title of the article in the text of your paper, you need not repeat that information in the footnote itself. For example, if in your paper you say, "Jacques Barzun makes an eloquent plea for the death penalty in his article 'In Favor of Capital Punishment,' " then the footnote needs only the journal title and the information that follows it. Avoid needless repetition in footnotes as much as you would anywhere else.

The bibliography. After you have typed out your note page(s), it is time for the *bibliography*. First determine if the bibliography should include only the works cited in your notes or if it should list all the sources you looked at, whether or not you cited them (your instructor may give you instructions about this). Then label the bibliography clearly: "Bibliography of

Works Cited" or "Bibliography of Works Consulted." (There are other kinds of bibliographies too, such as annotated or selective bibliographies, but they need not concern us here.)

Bibliographies are arranged in alphabetical order by author, so the author's last name goes first this time. Enter books and pamphlets this way:

Black, Charles L., Jr. <u>Capital</u> Punishment: The Inevitability

of <u>Caprice</u> and <u>Mistake</u>. New York: W. W. Norton, 1974.

Comparing this entry to the footnote for the same book on p. 272, you will note that the punctuation and indention are different and the page reference has been eliminated.

The seven exceptions described on pp. 272–274 would appear in a bibliography this way:

1. The book has more than one author.

Teeters, N. K., and J. Hedblom. <u>Hang by the Neck</u>. Springfield,

Ill.: Charles C. Thomas, 1966.

2. The book is an anthology with an editor rather than an author.

Bedau, Hugo Adam, ed. <u>The Death Penalty in America</u>; An

<u>Anthology</u>. Garden City, N. Y.: Doubleday, 1964.

3. The book is a translation; both author and translator are named.

Dostoyevsky, Fyodor. <u>Crime and Punishment</u>. Trans. David

Magarshack. Baltimore: Penguin Books, 1951.

4. The book has more than one volume.

Pike, Luke O. <u>A History of Crime in England</u>. 2 vols. London:

Hodder and Stoughton, 1876.

5. The book has more than one edition.

```
Calvert, E. Roy.  Capital Punishment in the Twentieth Century.
     5th ed. New York:  Harcourt, 1936.
```

6. The work was written by one author and then edited by another.

```
Darrow, Clarence.  Attorney for the Damned.  Ed. Arthur
     Weinberg.  New York:  Simon & Schuster, 1957.
```

7. The reference is to an encyclopedia entry.

```
Woods, A. E.  "Capital Punishment."  World Book Encyclopedia
     (1958), III, 1224-1225.
```

Sometimes articles are listed separately in a bibliography. But for the average paper this separation is unnecessary—combine books and articles, again following the alphabetical order of author ' last names. The bibliographical form for the standard article is like this:

```
Barzun, Jacques.  "In Favor of Capital Punishment."  The
     American Scholar, 31 (1962), 181-191.
```

This time you note the inclusive pages; in other words, the Barzun article began on page 181 and ended on page 191. No *p.* or *pp.* is used.

The four exceptions explained on p. 275 could appear in a bibliography in these forms:

1. The essay is part of an anthology.

```
Evjen, Victor.  "Let's Abolish Capital Punishment."  In
     Capital Punishment.  Ed. James McCafferty.  New York:
     Lieber-Atherton, 1974.
```

2. The article is anonymous and appeared in a popular magazine; it is alphabetized by the first word of the title.

```
"Closing Death Row."  Time, 100 (10 July 1972), 37.
```

3. The note refers to a book review.

```
Paris, J. J.  Rev. of Capital Punishment:  The Inevitability

    of Caprice and Mistake, by Charles L. Black, Jr.

    America, 132 (8 March 1975), 175.
```

4. The note refers to a newspaper article; it is alphabetized by title.

```
"Gallup Poll Shows 65% Favor Death Penalty."  New York Times,

    29 April 1976, p. 40, col. 8.
```

Proofreading. At last you have finished typing. Now you are ready for the final step before handing in your paper: proofreading. In this case proofreading means just that—proofreading, not rewriting. All major rewriting should have been done before you began typing. Proofread with special care if someone else typed the paper for you—remember that you bear full responsibility for whatever appears with your name on it.

Is the paper in order? *C'est fini!*

A6. A Sample Paper

It helps to have a concrete model from which you can work. Here is a research paper that illustrates the steps described in A4 and A5. The paper has an arguable proposition, and it builds upon the outline drawn up on p. 264. Some comments in the margins call your attention to features worth noting.

> Example is always more efficacious than precept.
> *Samuel Johnson*

THE DEATH PENALTY: title, all caps,

RETRIBUTION OR REVENGE?   centered on page

James O'Leary   name

English 201   course

5 May 1978   date

about 2″ head margin on first page only

THE DEATH PENALTY: title repeated, centered

RETRIToriBUTION OR REVENGE?

quadruple space

Debate over capital punishment is not new--we Americans have argued about it ever since colonial times. Furthermore the dispute has often been very emotional, because most people rely on "gut feelings" that tell them either that capital punishment is good and necessary or else that capital punishment is simply another form of murder. The recent controversy in our state legislature over whether and how to restore the death penalty makes it impossible for us to ignore the issue any longer. Concerned citizens must commit themselves. After studying this issue as thoroughly and dispassionately as possible, I am ready to contend that capital punishment should never be reinstituted in our state.

clear statement of arguable thesis

Capital punishment has a long but not very honorable history. American practice grew out of our English heritage. The English at one time had as many as 240 capital crimes, some of them as minor as stealing a piece of bread or a length of rope. These laws were enforced vigorously. During the reign of Henry VIII, for example, about 72,000 people were hung and many others beheaded. Children as young as eight years old were executed. The form of execution was often brutal and bloody, like the practice of removing a convicted traitor's entrails while he was still alive and then later displaying both his head and his entrails in a public place. Huge crowds gathered in a festive atmosphere to witness these gory events.[1]

1″ margin

1″ margin

footnote, number slightly raised

Because the early colonists were often fleeing the tyranny of the English government, they at first dealt with capital crimes much more leniently. This was especially true of the Quaker-influenced colonies. South Jersey, for

1″ margin

name and page number
begins here

O'Leary   page 2

example, had no executions at all during the first forty-five years of its

existence. But other colonies more closely resembled the mother country.

North Carolina was willing to make such crimes as bigamy and forgery capital

offenses.[2]

During the twentieth century the death penalty has experienced a slow

statistic, needs foot-note

but steady decline. Several hundred people were executed each year at the

turn of the century. By 1930 the number had dwindled to 155, and by 1960 it

was down to 56.[3] When the Supreme Court declared all previous capital statutes

well-known fact, needs no foot-note

to be unconstitutional in 1972, it seemed to many that we had regained the

vision of the early Quaker colonists and that the death penalty had itself died.

Not so. The Court had merely ruled that all existing statutes were dis-

criminatory, but it left room for legislatures to redraw the statutes so that

they met the new guidelines specified by the Court. Many states hastened to

comply. In 1976 the Court affirmed its earlier decision by approving some of

another well-known fact

the new laws, and in 1977 Gary Gilmore became the first person to be executed

author's late addition to final manu-script

one of

under them. Because so many states are grappling with the issue, including

our own state, we must examine the relevant facts. Should this state or any

state pass laws reinstating the death penalty, it would have to ignore five

very important facts about capital punishment. These facts also constitute

my reasons for opposing the death penalty.

Fact number one: the death penalty discriminates against the poor and

against minority groups, especially blacks. In the United States, if you have

money and connections you will not get the death penalty. The rich can afford

to hire lawyers who will provide thorough pretrial investigation, skilled repre-

sentation in court, and--should the verdict still be "guilty"--effective peti-

tions for a reduced sentence or a new trial. The poor must rely on overworked public defenders. Since blacks make up a disproportionate share of the poor

use of statistics as support
in this country, they suffer doubly. Statistics illustrate this pattern of discrimination: of the 210 persons awaiting death on December 31, 1960, 110 of them--over half--were black.[4] The testimony of Warden Lewis E. Lawes of Sing Sing is even more forceful: "In the twelve years of my wardenship I

short direct quota- tion
have escorted 150 men and one woman to the death chamber and the electric chair. . . . In one respect they were all alike. All were poor, and most of them were friendless."[5]

A second fact: imposition of the death penalty often results from public hysteria. American history affords numerous examples of groups of people dying because of a public clamoring for action against some real or imagined menace. During the Salem witchcraft trials of 1692, over twenty people were executed on the testimony of excited adolescent girls. The "red scare" that followed the First World War led directly to the Sacco-Vanzetti case, in which two

familiar history, no footnotes
Italian immigrants were electrocuted, not because their guilt had been proved beyond a reasonable doubt, but because local officials (including their judge) feared their political views and wanted to make an example of them. A similar fear of communism during the McCarthy era led to the execution of Julius and Ethel Rosenberg, whose petty espionage would probably rate a ten-year jail sentence today. In all of these instances the social climate made it all but impossible for judges and juries to arrive at a fair and impartial verdict. Yet people paid with their lives for this irrationality, because the system of capital punishment makes no room for later changes of mind in a less heated atmosphere.

Thirdly, innocent people are sometimes executed. While such mistakes may not be too frequent, they do happen, and even one such mistake would be too many.

development by a single example — this paragraph summarizes four paragraphs in the original source

The most airtight case is not immune to error. In 1949 a man named Timothy Evans was accused of the murder of his wife and child in London, and he confessed to the crime. Later he rescinded his confession and said a man named Christie had killed them. Christie, a former policeman, denied it, and testified for the prosecution. Evans was convicted and hung. Three years later the authorities discovered that Christie had killed Mrs. Evans, the child, and several prostitutes.[6]

In our own country the most famous case of mistaken identity is probably that of Bruno Hauptmann, executed for the Lindbergh kidnap-murder. Recent evidence makes it much more likely that Hauptmann was as innocent as he insisted he was. A special irony of the case is that while Hauptmann was pleading his innocence, no less than 205 people were willing to confess their guilt![7] This fact, plus the fact that over a quarter of all "positive identifications" made in line-ups are mistakes,[8] should remind us of how shaky even the most "reliable" testimony can be.

These 205 would-be confessors surely had twisted, perverted minds. Yet they point up still another fact about murderers, the only class of criminals who are now executed: all murderers are psychologically sick, even if only temporarily. The Charles Mansons, Richard Specks, and Sirhan Sirhans of this world are alive today only because of the 1972 Supreme Court decision. But now that the immediate passions have cooled, can we seriously argue that these men were sane when they committed their crimes? No one believes they should be let free to kill again. But neither do we believe that they were normal, rational people who could appreciate the enormity of their crimes.

Finally, these first four sets of facts lead me inevitably to another: the fact that capital punishment as presently used is unconstitutional.

author's correction of error caught in proofreading O'Leary page 5

The primary reason for judging c*a*pital punishment unconstitutional is that
it violates the Eighth Amendment, the one that bars any "cruel or unusual"
punishment. The death penalty violates both standards. It is cruel because
it inflicts a very painful death—many who have witnessed electrocutions, for
example, speak about the smell of burning flesh afterwards. It is also cruel
because it results in great psychological pain, as in the case of someone like
Caryl Chessman, who spent twelve years on death row before the postponements
were exhausted and he went to the gas chamber.

The death penalty is "unusual" in the most literal sense of that term.
It does not happen often, and it does not happen at all to those who are rich
and white. Even of those indicted for first-degree murder, only about 1 percent would actually be executed.[9] Any punishment applied so infrequently and
so randomly can have only a small impact on the mind of a potential criminal,
yet it will have terrible consequences for those unfortunate few who become
its victims. Warden Lawes again: "Capital punishment has never been and can
never be anything but an uncertainty."[10]

Furthermore any law, it if is to be constitutional and worthy of our
respect, must be applied without regard to race, color, creed, or wealth. Yet
we have seen how the death penalty discriminates. The "unfortunate few" always
turn out to be poor and often black. Of those executed for rape in the years
1930 to 1965, a staggering 92 percent were black, and all but ten of these
executions took place in Southern states.[11] Yet blacks are but the latest
victims. Before them the Irish, the Germans, the Italians, and other immigrant
groups suffered disproportionately because they were then poor and politically
feeble.

Obviously it can be said that the Supreme Court has declared capital

O'Leary page 6

punishment to be constitutional. The 1976 decision, however, should not be

viewed as a legal decision so much as a political one. Michael Meltsner, an

authority on the Court's debate over this issue, proves rather conclusively

that President Nixon made his choices for the Supreme Court partly on the

basis of the candidate's support for the death penalty. Justices Powell and

Rehnquist in particular were picked for this reason.[12] Furthermore, Charles

L. Black, Jr., Luce Professor of Jurisprudence at Yale University and the

nation's foremost authority on constitutional law, argues that the death

penalty violates not only the Eighth but also the Fourteenth Amendment:

". . . there is not enough 'due process of _law_' in our system to make it an

acceptable instrument for the 'deprivation of life.'"[13]

these sentences summarize 8 pages in the original

lead-in identifies this authority

Many arguments have been made in favor of capital punishment. Some of

them are frivolous or even bloodthirsty. But others have been offered by

serious, reflective people. I would like to examine these arguments more

closely, in order to show why I think they are inadequate.

author is being fair to opponents

The first argument offered by supporters of capital punishment is that

the threat of death deters crime. They claim that if the death penalty were

eliminated entirely the murder rate would soar because people would not be

afraid to kill. Special attention is paid to the murderer sentenced to life

imprisonment: what sanction is left that can frighten him, except death?

Evelle Younger, a former California Attorney General, sums up this school of

thought with a flat claim: "The importance of the death penalty for murder

lies in the fact that it has proved to be a deterrent."[14]

But Mr. Younger offers no proof for his claim. The reason is simple--he

hasn't got any. In fact, the few statistics available suggest the opposite

conclusion. For example, a comparison of the murder rates in a state before

and after the abolition of capital punishment shows that such states have
experienced no appreciable rise in homicides. Professor Thorsten Sellin has
been a tireless investigator of this subject, and he offers numerous examples.
Colorado averaged 15.4 convictions per year for murder before it abolished
the death penalty, 18 per year after abolition, and then 19 per year when the
death penalty was restored. When Delaware dropped the death penalty in 1959
the murder rate actually shrank, from an average of 22.3 per year before
abolition to 14.3 per year after.[15] Another study by Professor Sellin compares
states with the death penalty and states without. "The conclusion is inevitable that the presence of the death penalty—in law or practice—does not
influence homicide death rates."[16] Capital punishment, he says elsewhere,
"has failed as a deterrent."[17]

**develop-
ment by
numerous
examples**

  Still, many will dispute these facts. Reason, they say, tells us clearly
that at least <u>some</u> criminals, no matter how few, will stop short of murder if
they believe they might die for it. Otherwise why would criminals fight so
hard to avoid the death penalty? If even one life is saved because of this
fear, capital punishment has served its purpose.

  One cannot argue with such reasoning, because it rests so much on guesses
about how the criminal mind works. Deterrence can probably never be proven or
disproven fully. The wisest words are Charles Black's:

triple space

    I think the answer has to be that, after all possible inquiry,
    including the probing of all possible methods of inquiry, we do not
    know, and for systematic and easily visible reasons cannot know,
    what the truth about this "deterrent" effect may be. We know that,
    on raw data, there has been somewhat more homicide in capital punish-
    ment states than in non-capital punishment states. But we cannot

**direct quota-
tions of more
than four lines
are indented
like this**

ellipses to show words left out   O'Leary   page 8

draw any valid conclusions from this. . . . The general problem

that blocks knowledge here is that no adequately controlled exper-

iment or observation is possible or (so far as we can see) ever

will be possible. We have to use uncontrolled data from society

itself, outside any laboratory.[18]

triple space

A second popular argument is that capital punishment is the one sure way

to prevent a murderer from killing again. Put the criminal in jail, so the

argument goes, and he will only serve a few years before being paroled and

set free to murder someone else. Specific cases of repeat offenders are often

mentioned. Execution represents a "final solution" for convicted murderers.

Again Thorsten Sellin has statistics that rebut this argument. Murderers

are the group of criminals least likely to repeat their crime. The state of

Ohio, for example, paroled 273 first-degree murderers between 1945 and 1965.

Not a single one of them was ever convicted of that crime again. The state of

New York released some 514 murderers during the same period. Only one committed

another murder, and that crime occured when he killed two drinking companions

in a brawl.[19]

One final argument remains to be treated, perhaps the most sophisticated

argument of all. The death penalty is necessary, some proponents say, because

it satisfies a very legitimate need for retribution. Society has been wounded

by the murder, and only by repaying the crime with death can society express

its horror and insist on the fundamental value of human life. Perhaps the

most articulate defender of this position is Jacques Barzun, whose essay in

The American Scholar entitled "In Favor of Capital Punishment" offers the

opinion that anyone who has a true respect for the sanctity of human life must

support the death penalty.[20]

pronoun I is used very sparingly; style of essay is formal

O'Leary   page 9

I do not understand how we can show our value for life by taking away life. What we are really asking for is not justice but revenge. Revenge may be a very powerful motive, but it is not a very trustworthy one--in fact the Bible says that the Lord intends to keep that power to Himself rather than entrust it to humans. We can demonstrate more respect for life by refusing the opportunity for revenge. The advancement of any civilization can be measured by its respect for life. If the state takes away life, this cheapens life and gives some legitimacy to murder. ("It's not _what_ you do, it's why you are doing it.") Former Attorney General Ramsey Clark puts it best:

triple space

no paragraph indentation (long quote, but not a separate paragraph in the original)

There is no justification for the death penalty. It cheapens life. Its injustices and inhumanities raise basic questions about our institutions and purpose as a people. Why must we kill? What do we fear? What do we accomplish besides our own embitterment? Why cannot we revere life and in so doing create in the hearts of our people a love for mankind that will finally still violence?[21]

triple space

last paragraph ties in with first page

The next few years will be crucial ones for determining the fate of the death penalty. Public support for the death penalty, which had been shrinking for several decades, now seems to be on the rise again. According to a recent Gallup poll, fully two-thirds of the American people support capital punishment.[22] Almost every state legislature is preparing new laws for capital crimes,

argument ends with call to action

if they have not already done so. At a time like this, when we seem to be resurrecting the tradition of the Salem witch trials rather than the tradition of the Quaker colonists, anyone who feels as I do--that the death penalty should be abolished--has a special obligation to make himself heard.

2″ head margin on first page only

O'Leary   page 10

number
raised
and
indented

NOTES
quadruple space

¹ Elinor L. Horwitz, Capital Punishment U.S.A. (Philadelphia: ←── standard book citation
Lippincott, 1973), pp. 21-31.

Bedau ──→ ² Hugo A. Bedau, ed., The Death Penalty in America: An Anthology
is the
editor
(not
author)
but the
fact
cited is
from
Bedau's
intro-
duction
(Garden City, N. Y.: Doubleday, 1964), p. 6.

³ Michael Meltsner, Cruel and Unusual: The Supreme Court and Capital
Punishment (New York: Random House, 1973), p. 20.

⁴ Sara Ehrmann, "For Whom the Chair Waits," Federal Probation   standard article citation
Quarterly, 26 (1962), 19.

⁵ Quoted by Victor Evjen, "Let's Abolish Capital Punishment," in ←── essay by one author appearing in a book edited by another
Capital Punishment, ed. James McCafferty. (New York: Lieber-Atherton,
1974), p. 221.

⁶ Horwitz, pp. 170-171.
⁷ Ehrmann, p. 21.   } second references
⁸ Horwitz, p. 168.

⁹ Giles Playfair and Derrick Sington, The Offenders: The Case Against
Legal Vengeance (New York: Simon & Schuster, 1957), p. 264.

author's ──→ ¹⁰ Life and Death in Sing Sing (Garden City, N. Y.: Doubleday, 1928),
name
given in
the text
itself
p. 157.

¹¹ Thorsten Sellin, ed., Capital Punishment (New York: Harper and Row,   Sellin is editor, but the statistics are his
1967), p. 34.

¹² Meltsner, pp. 258-265.

¹³ Charles L. Black, Jr., Capital Punishment: The Inevitability of
Caprice and Mistake (New York: W. W. Norton, 1974), p. 94.

O'Leary   page 11

14 "Capital Punishment: A Sharp Medicine Reconsidered," <u>American</u> <u>Bar</u>
<u>Association</u> <u>Journal</u>, 42 (1956), 196.

15 Sellin, p. 123.

some → 16 Sellin, p. 138. One possible explanation, of course, is that murder ⌐
people   is almost always done on impulse, and therefore could not be deterred by ── author adds
would   punishment.   ── comment of
use   his own
Ibid   17 Sellin, "Death and Imprisonment as Deterrents to Murder," in Bedau,
here,   ed., <u>The</u> <u>Death</u> <u>Penalty</u> <u>in</u> <u>America</u>, p. 284.   shortened
meaning   ↑   title
the same 18 Black, p. 25.
as the
preced- 19 Sellin, pp. 185-186.   author, title, and journal omitted
ing note 20 31 (1962), 181-191. ◄────── (given in text itself)

21 "To Abolish the Death Penalty," in McCafferty, ed., <u>Capital</u> <u>Punish</u>-
<u>ment</u>, p. 180.

22 "Gallup Poll Shows 65% Favor Death Penalty," <u>New</u> <u>York</u> <u>Times</u>, 29 April
1976, p. 40, col. 8.   standard newspaper citation

2″ head margin on first page only

bibliography clearly labeled — not a list of all
the works consulted, but only of those used in notes

LIST OF WORKS CITED

quadruple space

← typical
article
entry; note
inclusive
pages

Barzun, Jacques. "In Favor of Capital Punishment." The American Scholar,

indent
second
lines
5 spaces

    31 (1962), 181-191.

Bedau, Hugo A., ed. The Death Penalty in America: An Anthology. Garden

    City, N. Y.: Doubleday, 1964.

← typical
book
entry

Black, Charles L., Jr. Capital Punishment: The Inevitability of Caprice

    and Mistake. New York: W. W. Norton, 1974.

Clark, Ramsey. "To Abolish Capital Punishment." In Capital Punishment. Ed.

    James McCafferty. New York: Lieber-Atherton, 1974.

Ehrmann, Sara. "For Whom the Chair Waits." Federal Probation Quarterly, 26

    (1962), 14-25.

Evjen, Victor. "Let's Abolish Capital Punishment." In Capital Punishment.

    Ed. James McCafferty. New York: Lieber-Atherton, 1974.

"Gallup Poll Shows 65% Favor Death Penalty." New York Times, 29 April 1976, ← anonymous
news-
paper
article,
alphabe-
tized by
title

    p. 40, col. 8.

Horwitz, Elinor L. Capital Punishment U.S.A. Philadelphia: Lippincott, 1973.

Lawes, Lewis E. Life and Death in Sing Sing. Garden City, N. Y.: Doubleday,

    1928.

Meltsner, Michael. Cruel and Unusual: The Supreme Court and Capital Punish-

two
authors;
only
first has
last
name
preced-
ing first
name

    ment. New York: Random House, 1973.

Playfair, Giles, and Derrick Sington. The Offenders: The Case Against Legal

    Vengeance. New York: Simon & Schuster, 1957.

Sellin, Thorsten, ed. Capital Punishment. New York: Harper and Row, 1967.

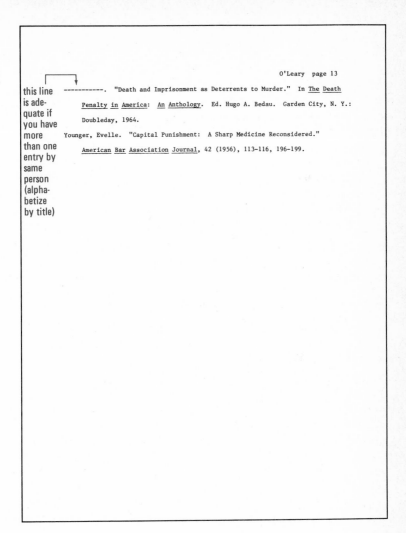

O'Leary   page 13

this line ----------. "Death and Imprisonment as Deterrents to Murder." In The Death
is ade-
quate if   Penalty in America: An Anthology. Ed. Hugo A. Bedau. Garden City, N. Y.:
you have
more   Doubleday, 1964.
than one   Younger, Evelle. "Capital Punishment: A Sharp Medicine Reconsidered."
entry by
same   American Bar Association Journal, 42 (1956), 113-116, 196-199.
person
(alpha-
betize
by title)

A7. Scientific Papers

The method of compiling notes and bibliography described in the previous three sections is the most common one, as noted before. It will serve you well in composition courses, business, history, literature, and philosophy courses—in fact, in almost any course except those in the social and natural sciences. Since it is quite likely you will be writing papers for courses in these two areas, you should know how their practices differ.

The main difference is in footnoting. The social and natural sciences commonly use no footnotes or endnotes. Instead a writer refers to his or her sources by a short coded expression within the text itself. This coded expression tells the reader which item in the bibliography is the source for the material the writer is using.

For example, suppose in the course of a paper you have occasion to cite the following article in support of your case:

Harrison White, "Cause and Effect in Social Mobility Tables,"

<u>Behavioral</u> <u>Science</u>, 8 (1963), 14-27. [MLA form]

In scientific writing there would be two common ways to refer to this article. One way uses a coded expression that includes the author's name and the year of publication; the other uses a code number.

In the **author and year system,** you insert within parentheses the last name of the author you are citing and the year his or her study was published. This information comes at the appropriate place in the text itself and allows the reader to turn immediately to the reference list at the end of the paper. (Scientific papers use the word *References* in place of the word *Bibliography*.) By finding the author in this alphabetical list and then locating the particular study the author published during the year in question, the reader can find the source.

For our White example, suppose this is the sentence in your text that you must support by a reference:

This conclusion is further supported by a study undertaken by

Harrison White.

Normally all you need do to complete the reference is include the year of publication within parentheses:

```
This conclusion is further supported by a study undertaken by

Harrison White (1963).
```

However, if the sentence in the text does not provide the author's name, then the author's last name must also be included within the parentheses:

```
An earlier study (White, 1963) also supports the conclusion I

have been advancing.
```

If you must include a specific page number, as in the case of a direct quotation, add a comma and the page number:

```
This conclusion has been termed "most convincing" by Harrison

White (1963, 22).
```

If there is more than one author, give the last names of both:

```
Recent experiments (Hannan and Freeman, 1977) confirm this point.
```

More than one investigation by the same author or authors would be listed chronologically:

```
Cantril (1941, 1965) is the only expert who seems to disagree.
```

If more than one investigator arrived at the same conclusion, list all of them, in alphabetical order and separated by semicolons:

```
Other researchers (Ryder, 1965; White, 1963) share this concern.
```

Your reader, should he or she wish to check your sources, would now turn to the list of references at the end of your paper. That alphabetical list would include every source to which you gave an author-and-year citation in the text. A list based on the works mentioned above might look like this:

Cantril, H.   1941.   The Psychology of Social Movements.   New
     York: Wiley.

——————.   1965.   The Pattern of Human Concern.   New Brunswick,
     N. J.:   Rutgers University Press.

Hannan, M., and Freeman, J.   1977.   "The Population Ecology of
     Organizations."   American Journal of Sociology 82 (March):
     929–964.

Ryder, N.   1965.   "The Cohort as a Concept in the Study of Social
     Change."   American Sociological Review 30 (December):   843–61.

White, H.   1963.   "Cause and Effect in Social Mobility Tables."
     Behavioral Science 8 (January):   14–27.

The reader finds his or her source by locating the author's name. Whenever necessary, as in the case of the Cantril reference, the year will differentiate one work from another. If more than one work was published by an author in the same year, the works will still appear chronologically in the references (a March article, for example, before an August one); the textual citation will add small letters (White 1963a; White 1963b).

If you examine the list of references above, you will notice some differences between the format of these entries and the format you learned earlier. The principal differences can be summed up as follows:

1. Initials are often given instead of authors' first names.
2. The year of publication and a period follows immediately after the author's name.
3. Journal names are not followed by a comma.
4. Volume numbers for journals are followed by the month, within parentheses, and a colon.

This format is not the only format used in scientific papers. Sometimes article titles are not put in quotation marks, for example, or journal names are not italicized. But the reference list above would be acceptable for the great majority of scientific papers.

The **number system** is a different way of providing the coded expression within the text. The reference list at the end is exactly the same, but each item on the list is numbered. Then, in the text itself, all you need do is put in parentheses the number of the reference item you wish to cite.

Using the earlier examples, you would first number every item in the list of references. The two Cantril books become numbers one and two, followed by the articles of Hannan and Freeman (3), Ryder (4), and White (5). Then in your text you simply refer to these books and articles by number:

```
These conclusions are supported by Ryder (4) and also by

Cantril (1), (2).
```

Note how a separate set of parentheses is required for each of the two Cantril books. If the author's name is not mentioned in the text, it is sometimes included inside the parentheses:

```
We now know (White, 5) the cause of this reaction.
```

If you must cite a particular page number, include it also within the parentheses:

```
But Hannan and Freeman disagree, claiming the earlier study

"stretches the available evidence" (3, p. 931) and cannot be

relied upon.
```

No matter which you use, the author-and-year system or the number system, you may find that your instructor requires certain specific ways of preparing tables, graphs, and other data. He or she might also recommend ways to divide your material, such as *cover page* + *abstract* (a one-paragraph summary) + *text* (including introduction, method, results, conclusion, discussion) + *references* + *tables*. Obviously you should conform to these suggestions, too.

Scientific writing may differ in its format from writing submitted to teachers in other disciplines. But scientific writing has just as much need for clarity, just as much need for thoroughness, just as much need for persuasiveness, as any other kind of writing. The skills we have been describing in this chapter and the preceding ones will be important to you in every kind of writing you undertake.

> In science the credit goes to the man who convinces the world, not to the man to whom the idea first occurs.
>
> *Sir Francis Darwin*

EXERCISES

1. Put the following information into proper footnote form:

a. a book written by Sidney Coulling entitled *Matthew Arnold's Controversies* and published by the Ohio University Press, located in Athens, Ohio; the book was published in 1974 and you wish to cite from page 81.

b. William Kane's article "Toward a New Aesthetic" appeared in the second volume of the *Tufts Review,* spring 1970 issue; you cite from page 22 of an article that occupied pages 21 through 27 of that issue.

c. Katherine Ann Porter's short story "The Circus" was reprinted in an anthology edited by Edward M. White and entitled *The Pop Culture Tradition;* this anthology was put out by W. W. Norton of New York in 1972; Ms. Porter's story occupies pages 118 to 123, and you quote a section on page 120.

d. on August 7, 1890, the *New York Times* carried an account of the first electrocution under the headlines "Far Worse Than Hanging"; this item appeared on page 1, columns 5 and 6.

2. Take the four footnotes produced by the previous question and make them into a short bibliography.

3. Study carefully the long paragraph beginning, "To make this difference clearer . . ." on p. 250. Then prepare: 1. a one or two-sentence summary of the paragraph; 2. a legitimate paraphrase of sentences four, five, and six; 3. a direct quotation of sentence five. Include appropriate footnotes.

4. If you can, study very closely a long paper you turned in recently. What type of paper was it supposed to be—a library paper or a genuine research paper? Did you outline it? Did you have a complete file of both bibliography and note cards? Does the first paragraph state the paper's thesis clearly? Is the paper well organized and fully developed? Are the footnotes and bibliography in proper form? If the answer to any of these questions is no, check the relevant sections of this chapter for guidance on how you might have improved it.

5. Locate one or two of the following books in the card catalog of your college or university library. Reproduce the information about the book given on the card and interpret it as shown on pp. 255–256.

> Roger Sale's *On Writing*
> Sigmund Freud's *Civilization and Its Discontents*
> Peter Berger's *The Sacred Canopy*
> Marshall McLuhan's *Understanding Media*
> Charles Darwin's *On the Origin of Species*
> William Shirer's *The Rise and Fall of the Third Reich*

6. Compile a short preliminary list of sources for one of the following topics:

> Self-censorship in the movie industry
> Government aid for private schools
> How language is acquired by young children
> The U-2 incident of 1960
> H. D. Thoreau's theory of civil disobedience

B. ESSAY QUESTIONS

> In examinations, fools ask questions that the wise cannot answer.
>
> *Oscar Wilde*

Recent research shows that essay questions form part of over half of the examinations given in a typical college or university. Even in business courses or in natural science courses such as biology or chemistry, about one quarter of all exams include essay questions. For the social sciences and humanities the percentages, as you might expect, are much higher. If you are tempted to doubt these figures, perhaps because so far your courses have not relied heavily on such questions, your doubt may stem from still another fact: the frequency of essay questions is at its *lowest* in the freshman year but increases steadily as a student progresses to higher-level courses.

Knowing how to write a good response to an essay question will be vital to your academic success. Fortunately the ways to write good essays can be demonstrated. This section describes a proven method for writing successful essay answers.

B1. A Sample Question

Despite what some students believe, there are measurable differences between good essay answers and poor ones. Instructors do not just grade whimsically, awarding an *A* here and a *D* there as their fancy dictates. The differences between a good essay and a poor essay will be clear to anyone who compares them.

To discover how true this is, read the following two essays, printed here exactly as they were written. Both students have studied for the exam, but one has a successful strategy and the other does not. Observe the differences:

The Question

Summarize the qualities of the Byronic hero. Show how they are manifested in "Lara," "Childe Harold's Pilgrimage," and "Manfred." [30 minutes—from a literature course]

Response 1

The Byronic hero is an archetypal hero of Byron himself. He has more emotions, more capabilities, can suffer better. Basically, his philosophy is "Anything you can do I can do better." In "Lara" Byron mentions that he does in his life, what others fail or don't want to do. (I had a quote memorized from this poem, but I'll be damned I forget it!) In "Childe Harold's Pilgrimage" Byron's hero shows his egocentricism. (There's probably no word like this, but I'll make it up; just like Poe and tin-tin-nabulation.) Byron compares himself with Hamlet, Napoleon, and finally the ultimate Christ. In this poem he says that everyone and their deeds are done in vain. But not Byron. "But I live, and live not in vain." "Manfred" denys everything. He believes we make our own heaven and hell. Manfred tells the abbot, "'Tis not so difficult to die" and he will "die, as I lived, alone." Byron considers himself the perfect hero because man, in general, is corrupting the earth and himself. "I love not Man the less, but Nature more."

Response 2

The Byronic hero is often noble in birth, sensual, intense, strong, alienated from the everyday world, seemingly cool (but actually tender of heart), reflective, restless, idealized, physically handsome, and often cynical or melancholy. "Lara" offers an excellent portrait of all these qualities, for as Count Lara is described we can visual the smile on his lip that is nevertheless cold and removed, and we are told in great detail about his alienation. Looking down from a mountain-top, figuratively, he senses the envy and imperception of those below him. Though he must walk among the "common" people, he will never feel a part of them. Also, poor Count Lara is doomed to a life of difficult love affairs because he has been born so physically attractive. Finally, despite his somewhat concealed contempt (combined with, paradoxically, a true love of humanity) he charismatically draws the attention of all those who meet him.

The restless image of the Byronic hero is what is first illustrated in *Childe Harold's Pilgrimage*. Byron describes his self-imposed exile from England to Italy. He has cynically cast England and its current ethical system from his mind and heart. In Italy he seeks a more enlightened people—although, typical of the Byronic hero, he has a cynical attitude toward people in general. Byron does not spare himself any criticism of wasted passions or misdirected energy, however. He equates himself with Napoleon, for both burned their energy (fire) too quickly for their own good. Byron admits to many sensual experiences, and though he speaks negatively of them, he still cannot ignore the attraction of love—even though true love is extremely hard to find. In this poem Byron again refers to the doom he was slated for because of his physical attractiveness. He certainly expressed great moodiness in the poem, also, and a great deal of reflection on everything from his own personal failures to the tragic defeat of Napoleon at Waterloo.

In "Manfred," Byron portrays a sensitive, reflective man who is prepared to accept all the consequences of his life. He has lived the life of the Byronic hero and through to his end he is skeptical (cynical) of the worth of a religious man such as the abbot. Manfred believes he is his own salvation or damnation. He feels alienated from the world and desires only extinction. Because he has had a tragic love affair, we can also assume he was physically beautiful and sensual.

Now ignore for a moment the fact that you did not take the course on which this question was based. I wager that the clear superiority of the second response compared to the first is still quite apparent to you. Without knowing a thing about English Romantic poetry, you could tell that the second essay deserves a better grade. Why is this so?

Let's begin with what the two responses have in common. Both take into account the task the question imposes. Both refer, quite properly, to all three poems, and both give considerable evidence of careful reading and diligent study. Furthermore both observe similar traits in the Byronic hero—for example, his cynicism and his large capabilities, especially for suffering. Both even mention similar details: Childe Harold's comparison of himself with Napoleon, Manfred's acceptance of the fate he has brought upon himself.

In these respects the first essay is successful. This answer has its virtues and we should not neglect them. (Note, for example, that the first response mentions some details that the second does not.) But our recognition of the virtues makes us doubly aware of the severe faults that weaken the answer.

The very first sentence gets the author off on the wrong track. The Byronic hero is said to be an archetype of Byron himself. But where does the question ask the author to talk about the relationship of the poet to his creations? Granted, much can be said about the relationship between Byron and the heroes he describes in his poetry—but say it somewhere else, not here. The author, once in pursuit on this false scent, follows it relentlessly throughout the rest of the essay. Thus fully half of the response is given over to a discussion that is not false, just irrelevant.

This irrelevance is certainly not intended by the writer. But quite soon we encounter other irrelevancies the author ought to have controlled: his quotations. Evidently the writer had taken the trouble to memorize these lines, and by God they were going to be fitted in somehow—otherwise how would the instructor be impressed? Yet these quotations, while accurate, have in most cases nothing to do with the traits of the Byronic hero. So considerable space (and time) is wasted.

In literature quotation is good only when the writer whom I follow goes my way, and, being better mounted than I, gives me a [ride].

Ralph Waldo Emerson

Then too we notice how the essay lacks a coherent structure. It consists of one paragraph only, a shapeless blob sorely in need of discipline. We feel that the author quickly started his pen on that first sentence and never looked back. This lack both of foresight and hindsight is reflected too in the errors that disfigure the essay: "egocentricism" for *egocentrism*, "denys" for *denies*, the missing punctuation before "Christ."

The second essay, by contrast, has a very clear structure. Thirty minutes results in three well-developed paragraphs, one on each poem. The greater length of the essay comes from its greater use of detail in each sentence. (It might surprise you to know, for example, that the second essay has only four more sentences than the first, i.e., twenty vs. sixteen.) This greater amount of detail allows the author to say more: to list a dozen qualities rather than a half-dozen, to offer more precise statements about the poems themselves.

Moreover the writer of the second essay sticks more firmly to the task. From the very first sentence, which gets right down to the business of listing qualities, we know that the author has the job in hand and intends to get on with it. Every sentence after the first relates directly to the topic. Yet the paragraphs each have their own point, their own contribution to make: the Childe Harold paragraph, for example, discusses the restlessness of the Byronic hero, a quality that does not apply so strongly to Count Lara.

The second response has its faults: it is occasionally repetitious, it has a weak ending, the word "visual" should be *visualize*. But even more clear is its merit, its evident superiority, over the first response.

I am convinced that many (most?) students who fare badly on essay examinations have studied just as much as the students who do well. Their problem is not a lack of preparation; rather they are victims of two weaknesses, the wrong *kind* of preparation and no workable strategy for writing the answers. These weaknesses can be cured, as the next sections will show.

B2. Before the Test

As you prepare for a test that will include essay questions, keep in mind the *goals* of such tests. Remember, instructors can grade a multiple-choice test easily: all they need do is see which box has been checked, and often a machine will even do the scoring for them. So if an instructor has chosen to read the answers to essay questions, most probably the reason is that he or she can accomplish certain important goals much better with such questions. These goals might include testing the following:

1. the ability to distinguish between what is important and what is not so important and to detect general trends

2. the ability to relate, to make comparisons (for instance, of one historical period to another or of one literary work to another)

3. the ability to apply the material learned in one course to other fields, to solve other kinds of problems in a fresh, original way

4. the ability to grasp methodology, to understand how a particular discipline works

As you can see, most instructors use essay questions because they want to know more than whether you have read the textbook and attended the lectures, important as those two activities are. They want to know if you *understood* what you read and heard and if you can *use* it.

Now keep your instructor's goals in mind as you prepare for the exam, because they affect how you prepare. Specifically, they suggest that it will not be enough to simply reread the text and the lecture notes. Good preparation will require in addition the following steps.

1. Be sure you see the larger patterns in the material you study. Memorize facts, yes. But also know which facts are the most important ones and which facts can be related to which other facts—in short, be able to distinguish and relate. Then think of these facts as part of the subject you are studying. For example, if your assignment was to read William Styron's *The Confessions of Nat Turner*, how you review the novel for a test depends on the course for which it was assigned. If the course is U.S. history, you might concentrate on what the novel tells us about a crucial period in the American South before the Civil

War. If the course is sociology, you might take special note of what the novel says about slavery as a social institution. If the course is literature, you might study the development of the plot or of the character Nat Turner.

   2. **Pose sample questions to yourself.** Because this advice is not uncommon, you may be tempted to dismiss it ("I've tried that and I've never yet guessed correctly which questions will be on the test"). Such a reaction, while quite understandable, misses the point of the exercise. Of course it is unlikely you will guess what questions will be asked. The value of posing questions is that it accustoms you to "handling" your material. The more you work with it, the more confident you become of your ability to respond to questions on it. This reduces the danger of panic, and your chances of success increase proportionately. The purpose is similar to the one that motivates lifeboat drills on a cruise ship: while in theory everybody might know what to do in an emergency, in times of danger it's better to have had a rehearsal.

   3. **Review the verbs commonly used in essay tests.** An essay question imposes some task on you. The nature of the task will usually be defined most clearly by the verbs your instructor chooses. Different verbs mean different tasks. No matter how much you have studied, failure to keep to the required task will cost you heavily. Yet failures of this sort are very common. They account for a high percentage of those cases where a student prepares very diligently, only to be frustrated and bewildered by a low grade. Those are the moments when life seems terribly unfair.

   Here are the verbs most commonly used in essay questions, together with a description of the tasks they imply. For each I have included an example or two, drawn from actual essay tests given within the last three years in a variety of courses and departments.

   1. **To analyze** is to examine something very closely and critically; it also might mean to break something down into its parts. Example:

   Characters in plays usually face moral and emotional crises; analyze these "crisis points" in two characters from two plays we have discussed. [30 minutes—from a German literature course]

2. **To compare** is to find similarities (and sometimes to find differences too); to *contrast* is to find differences only. Examples:

Compare and contrast the religion of the Vedas with the religious development of the Upanishads. [20 minutes—from a comparative religion course]

Contrast the basic assumptions, general methodology, and technique of descriptive linguistics with those of anthropological linguistics. [30 minutes—from a linguistics course]

3. **To define** is to state precisely the meaning of a word or a concept. Examples:

Define what Webster means by *authority*. [20 minutes—from a sociology course]

What is photosynthesis? [10 minutes—from a biology course]

> "Where *I* use a word," Humpty Dumpty said, in rather a scornful tone, "it means just what I choose it to mean—neither more nor less."
>
> "The question is," said Alice, "whether you *can* make words mean so many different things."
>
> *Lewis Carroll*

4. **To describe** is to summarize, outline, or in some other way to give a brief "picture" of the subject. Examples:

Describe George Kennan's interpretation of America's role in international history. [25 minutes—from a political science course]

Describe the chemical interactions between light and dark reactions of photosynthesis. [20 minutes—from a biology course]

5. **To discuss** can mean to describe or identify. Example:

Discuss three categories of arms control progress. [30 minutes—from an ROTC course]

It can also mean to react in some way, for example to a quotation:

Discuss this statement: "Renaissance writers made distinctive contributions to a modern understanding of history and the writing of history." [45 minutes—from a history course]

6. **To enumerate** is to list, in 1-2-3 fashion, providing a brief description of each item on the list. Example:

Enumerate the major postwar American strategic doctrines. [30 minutes—from an ROTC course]

7. **To evaluate** is to find both the good and bad points of a particular subject. Examples:

Choose one of the many theories about the origin of agriculture and then evaluate it. [20 minutes—from a botany course]

Evaluate the theories of the neoclassical sociologists (Simon, et al.) about formal organizations. [35 minutes—from a sociology course]

8. **To explain** is to make something plain and understandable, usually by giving details about it. Examples:

Explain the motivation theory that helps us understand the behavior of Mr. B. in *Wheels*. [15 minutes—from a business course]

What place did the Enlightenment give to religion? Explain your answer fully. [30 minutes—from a history course]

9. **To identify** is to name and usually to describe briefly. Example:

Identify the two sets of leaders in each House of Congress. [20 minutes—from a political science course]

10. **To outline or summarize** is to condense a large body of material, selecting only the most important parts of it. Example:

Summarize the contributions of John Dewey to American primary education. [18 minutes—from an education course]

11. **To relate** is to show the connection(s) between one thing and another. Example:

Relate Keats's theory of negative capability to his own poetry. [50 minutes—from a literature course]

12. **To trace** is to show the progress of a subject through time. Example:

Trace the influence of Sir Joshua Reynolds on early nineteenth-century British painting. [25 minutes—from a fine arts course]

Other verbs can appear too, verbs like *assess, defend, develop, expand, show.*

The important thing is to learn to recognize all the verbs and to know what they ask you to do. Remember too that unless you do this ahead of time, the knowledge will be of little use.

B3. Writing the Examination

Let's assume now that you have undertaken the three-step preparation described in the previous section. Good preparation is very helpful. But it will bear fruit only if you combine it with an effective strategy for answering the question you are asked. This strategy consists of four steps:

1. Categorize the question.
2. Develop an appropriate method of answering the question.
3. Write out the answer clearly, sticking to the topic.
4. Reread the essay.

Step 1. Categorize the question. With a little experience you will find that you can very quickly assign a question to one of the following three categories. (Again, examples are included from real courses.)

Long identifications. Basically, these questions are just longer versions of the short-answer identifications you have known since grade school. They do not call for any creativity. The instructor is simply testing your knowledge; there is clearly a "right" answer, and if you have studied you are probably home free. Such questions are often introduced by *who, what, where,* or *when. Define, identify,* or *summarize* can also fit into this category. Examples:

What is a denomination? [5 minutes—from a comparative religion course]

Define the term *segmentation.* [10 minutes—from a biology course]

Specified relationships. Here too the instructor has in mind what will constitute a good or "right" answer. But in addition to asking you to reproduce certain facts, he or she also expects you to relate these facts to other facts in specific ways.

In short, you have to be able to *assimilate* and *distinguish* information.

Questions that ask you to *compare* or *contrast* often belong in this category. So do questions requiring you to *evaluate, assess, relate, explain, defend,* or *trace*—or questions that begin with *why* or *how.* Examples:

Why would semantics be considered central to any theory of linguistics? [20 minutes—from an anthropology course]

Contrast the post-World-War-II military alliances with the pre-war variety. [25 minutes—from a history course]

Open-ended questions. Only in this last category do we find questions for which the instructor has no preconceived ideas about what makes a good answer. Instead he or she gives you considerable freedom. The intent is not to invite you to shovel a certain objectionable material. Nor are you required to echo the instructor's own opinions. Rather he or she will be concentrating on *how* you answer. A good essay will reveal knowledge of the subject, but more importantly it will show that it was written by an intelligent and thoughtful person.

Questions in this third category can also be identified by key words: *discuss, suppose, argue for or against.* Here is an example, taken from an astronomy course:

Imagine that you are a taxpayer in Florence during the year after Galileo published the *Starry Messenger.* Galileo has applied to the government for financial support to further his investigations. Would you urge the government to give him a grant? Why or why not? [30 minutes]

Clearly the instructor will allow you to choose either alternative. The success of your answer will depend partly on your knowledge of Galileo and his times. But it will also depend on your ability to "think out loud" about Galileo's relationship to the political, religious, and economic currents of his day. Here is another example, this time from a literature course:

Devise an alternative ending for two plays we have read. What would be the consequences of your ending for the theme, character development, and structure of the play? Would your ending succeed? Why or why not? [45 minutes]

Again the quality of the answer will depend as much on its *how* as on its *what*.

The importance of categorizing a question should be coming into focus. Immediately you know how much freedom you have in shaping your answer. For the first category, none; for the second, no freedom either, but the answer requires a more complicated mental process; for the third, true freedom, but still more emphasis on your creative powers. Furthermore, since these categories are arranged here in order of increasing difficulty, you can usually expect the time to be allotted proportionately—less time for questions in the first category, more time for the second, still more for the third.

> All excellent things are difficult.
> *Spinoza*

With practice you can categorize essay questions in a matter of seconds. By so doing you guarantee a safe start.

Step 2. Develop an appropriate method of answering the question. This means knowing the key verbs defined in Part B2 of this chapter and being able to recognize what tasks each implies. Once you know the tasks you can quickly calculate a rough mental outline of your answer. Recall, for example, the question from an anthropology course: "Contrast the basic assumptions, general methodology, and technique of descriptive linguistics with those of anthropological linguistics." Immediately you know to stress only the differences and to divide the answer into three parts. So the answer can be sketched like this:

Assumptions, descriptive vs. anthropological
Methodology, descriptive vs. anthropological
Technique, descriptive vs. anthropological

That outline for answering the question will most likely bring success.

Sometimes more than one task is involved. A political science instructor asked this question: "Define *federalism*, distinguish it from *unitary government*, and give an example of each system within the United States." A good answer must combine three skills; it might look like this in outline:

Definition of federalism
Differences from unitary government:
1.
2.
3.
Example of federalism
Example of unitary government

While you develop an appropriate method, keep in mind also the amount of time you can devote to a question. Your answer should always be as detailed as possible given the time available. Don't overestimate what you can accomplish. On the average, a student can expect to write only about one well-developed paragraph (five or six sentences) for every ten minutes of work. So for a half-hour question expect to complete only three full paragraphs, four at the most.

Step 3. Write out the answer, clearly and concisely. This stage occupies the most time—perhaps four-fifths of the total. But if you have given sufficient attention to the first two stages (and if you have studied!), the response should come quickly and easily.

Some tips may be helpful. Don't waste valuable time in your opening paragraph on a restatement of the question. Your instructor knows what he or she asked. Instead get directly into the topic. If you have the leisure to develop an opening paragraph, use it to summarize the approach you will take to the question.

Try to make your answer simple and clear. If you are going to enumerate four reasons and you have thirty minutes, give one paragraph to each reason. Be as direct as you can, especially through the use of transitions: "The second reason is. . . ," "The third reason is. . . ."

Remember to stick to the topic. Essay questions are not opportunities for you to spill out everything you know about the subject. Limit yourself to what is called for; otherwise you waste time. Suppose, for example, you are taking a literature course and the exam question asks you to analyze the attitude of a certain character toward his son. Your first reaction is joyous—

you have read the novel, you know the character. But remember, you must *analyze*, that is, break into parts, examine, explain; and you must analyze only the *attitude* toward the *son*. Don't tell everything you know about the father and everything you know about the son, just to prove to your instructor that you have read the book. Most assuredly don't get off into issues like plot, setting, interpretation, the author's life, whether or not you liked the novel. If you do, your answer can contain many good facts and still be quite unsuccessful.

Step 4. Reread the essay. Save a couple of minutes at the end for going back over what you have written, asking yourself questions like these:

- Did I answer all parts of the question?
- Are the facts I used *relevant* ones?
- Did I develop each subtopic sufficiently?
- Did I use enough transitions so my reader can find his or her way through the essay?
- Are there any glaring mechanical errors?

Some deficiencies can be repaired rather quickly at real benefit to you. Others, like a neglected subtopic, might not be fully repairable in two minutes, but at least you have time for one or two hurried sentences that might limit the damage.

You have probably never seen the essay question analyzed in such detail before. But think of its importance. Psychologists know that students' test-taking skills have an important bearing on whether or not they succeed on tests, regardless of how much they have studied. Despite this fact, most students have spent very little time practicing for essay tests. Since these tests will form a large part both of your writing activity and of your final grades, you would do well to study Part B carefully.

> It takes little talent to see clearly what lies under one's nose, and a good deal of it to know in which direction to point that organ.
>
> *W. H. Auden*

EXERCISES

1. Here are a few essay questions given in recent exams. Of course you are not expected to know the material that would permit you to answer them. But assign them to a *category* and determine which *strategy* would be the most appropriate for someone who has to answer them.

a. In the years after the Civil War the Great Plains underwent vast and rapid change. How do you explain what happened? [30 minutes—from a history course]

b. What are the major strengths and weaknesses in Lavoisier and LaPlace's argument that respiration and combustion are perfectly similar? [15 minutes—from a natural science course]

c. ". . . but what a man is worth is never known until the hour of danger." Comment on this statement in light of the literature we have read this quarter. [50 minutes—from a literature course]

d. Compare and contrast the cultural climate of the Eastern and Western states. [30 minutes—from an anthropology course]

e. Should nine old men decide what law is in the United States? [20 minutes—from a political science course]

f. According to Robert Browning, what qualities must a poet have if he or she is to be successful? Use Browning's own poems as the basis for your answer. [20 minutes—from a literature course]

2. Review three or four recent examinations you have taken that involved essay questions. To which category did each question belong? What was the appropriate strategy? Did you use it? Outline a good answer for those questions that you did not answer as well as you would have liked.

3. Explain in a few words what these terms require you to do.

a. enumerate
b. summarize
c. analyze
d. trace

e. evaluate
f. define
g. relate

4. Think ahead about exams coming up in courses you are taking now. For each course, ask the following questions: What seem to be the main *goals* of the course? The major *trends?* What category of questions am I likely to get on the exam? What sample questions can I think of, and how should they be answered? What kind of reading must I do to be prepared?

6

THE ENGLISH LANGUAGE: GRAMMAR

> What shall I say to the young on such a morning?
> Mind is the one salvation?—also grammar?
> *W. D. Snodgrass*

One of the minor plagues of my life is the ritual question, "What do *you* do?" I have learned over the years that if I say I'm an English professor, I had better wince, because immediately my questioner will step back in mock horror and proclaim, "An English teacher! I'd better watch my grammar!" Yet what they then proceed to "watch" is not grammar at all, but rather the kinds of words they use.

I have a similar experience when I ask freshmen what they expect from a composition course. The usual answer is "grammar and stuff like that." But if I ask what *grammar* is, I am told it is "rules about what words to use" or that it "tells what words mean." Nope, I reply. *Usage* is the description of standard and nonstandard uses of words. *Semantics* is the study of what words mean. Then what could *grammar* possibly be? Puzzled frowns.

The truth is, most people have only the vaguest idea of the meaning of grammar, and they usually associate it with making mistakes when speaking. Here are some other misconceptions: 1. most errors in writing are grammatical errors; 2. grammar is necessary to speak and write well; 3. only a few select people (English teachers?) have ever mastered grammar. The surprising truth is that: 1. most "errors" are in semantics or usage, not in grammar; 2. many people have become excellent writers without ever undertaking any formal study of grammar; 3. everybody—including you—knows a great deal about English grammar and has known it since learning to speak.

You doubt this last truth? Then consider this sentence: *Sam has new five quarters.* Immediately you recognize that this isn't good English, that it should be *Sam has five new quarters.* If asked why the first version was wrong, you might or might not be able to give the technical explanation (i.e., that English word order requires adjectives of number to precede adjectives of quality). The fact is you intuitively know what to do here, and you've probably known this grammatical truth (because that's what it is) ever since you were a small child. Everybody who speaks English knows English grammar; otherwise what they speak would not be English! The only difference is that some people can be explicit about their grammar and some cannot. Speaking is just like walking: all of us know how to do both, but only a few—grammarians in one case, physiologists in the other—can tell us what we are doing.

Let's examine this idea of grammar more closely. Part A of this chapter will discuss grammatical fact and theory and their respective uses. Then, in Parts B, C, and D, we will see how grammar can be applied to your writing. You may be surprised at how few writing problems turn out to be grammar problems, and you may be equally surprised to see how easily these writing problems can be remedied. The exercises at the end of each part will help you strengthen your knowledge of the grammar of standard written English (or what some people call "edited American English").

A. WHAT IS GRAMMAR?

> Grammar, which knows how to control even kings . . .
> *Molière*

Grammar is just another name for an explanation of how a language works. For example, in the French language you form a negative by putting *ne* before the verb and *pas* after it: *Je ne parle pas anglais*. "I do not speak English." This is a grammatical fact. Similarly in English we form negatives by adding an auxiliary verb plus *not* ("I *do not* speak French"); this is a grammatical fact about the English language.

Please notice my use of the term *grammatical fact*, rather than the more common term *grammatical rule*. We often speak of grammar as if it were a set of rules. This is unfortunate, because it suggests that somebody "out there" makes up regulations the rest of us have to follow. *Rule* implies power, authority, control. Those who make rules can also change them. If the state says you cannot exceed 50 m.p.h. on a certain highway, it is perfectly free to lower that limit to 45. But languages do not operate like highway rules. What some people call rules are really just statements of fact, explanations of how language works. I cannot change these facts, nor can you or anybody else.

To go back to our recent example, suppose I am convinced that *not speak* ought to be an acceptable present-tense form in English, without an auxiliary: *I not speak English.* The word *not* already conveys negation; the auxiliary verb *do* is unnecessary and should be eliminated. This makes perfect sense, but I can't do it. The reason is that the English language—English grammar—does not work that way. It is a *fact* that to form negatives you must add *not* and use an auxiliary verb like *do. I not speak English* is simpler and more sensible, but it's not grammatical.

A1. Grammatical Facts versus Grammatical Theories

So grammar on a simple level is a set of facts about a language. These facts of course do not exist in isolation. They are related to each other in various ways, and some people study these relationships in order to form more comprehensive explanations about how the language as a whole works. It is easy enough to say that we form negatives by adding *not* plus an auxiliary, but it is much harder to explain how we form verbs in the English language or how we construct sentences. A brief discussion of grammatical theory can help prepare us to return to the simpler, more practical level of grammatical facts.

A2. Grammatical Theories

Experts in the English language differ in their explanations of how the language works. Grammarians have been trying to explain the English language for over two centuries. Some approaches have been discarded because they were poor explanations, in other words because they did not give a complete enough or accurate enough account of the facts as we know them. At the present time three theories are the most important.

The first and oldest theory is called **traditional grammar.** It has its origins back in the eighteenth century, when the first attempts were made to provide a systematic description of English. Like all good scholars, these earlier grammarians looked first at the other grammars available to them as models. Full explanations of a language—complete grammars, in other words—had already been developed for Latin, which was the principal language of the educated classes in Europe for academic, ecclesiastical, or scientific writing. Latin grammars were based on such things as inflections and parts of speech. When these scholars looked at English, they saw many similar forms. If there were nouns or prepositions in Latin, for example, there seemed to be nouns and prepositions in English too. So naturally the first English grammars were based fairly closely on Latin grammars, and they were successful because they gave satisfactory explanations of many of the important features of our language.

Traditional grammar, as this grammar based on Latin models is now called, was the predominant grammatical theory until the first part of this century. In many ways it is still the most important. I was raised on the eight parts of speech, on infinitives, subjunctives, appositives, and all the other terms that derive from this approach. Maybe you were taught that way too. When people say that schools ought to get back to teaching "good grammar," what they usually mean is the traditional grammar that has been part of our education for so long.

> Ignorant people think it's the noise which fighting cats make that is so aggravating, but it ain't so; it's the sickening grammar they use.
>
> *Mark Twain*

But like many theories, traditional grammar had its difficulties. For example, according to traditional grammar a *verb* was a word that expressed action. But how much action is expressed in *were?* And what more active a word could we want than a noun like *explosion?* Furthermore, traditional grammarians, when confronted with a problem, tended to make subtle distinctions just like the subtle distinctions of Latin. These distinctions, such as when to use *shall* and when to use *will*, were often based more on what the grammarian thought *ought* to be the case than on what people actually were saying. The result was that grammarians strayed from the task of collecting facts, and they began to get their reputation as makers of "a bunch of rules."

In the earlier part of this century, a new school of grammarians decided we should not concern ourselves with what *ought* to be, but with the language as it is actually used. These scholars, who developed what came to be called **structural grammar,** concentrated more on spoken English than on written English. Because English has a more rigid word order than Latin, they identified parts of speech by their form and their position in a sentence. For example, the word *trains* can be either a plural noun *(two trains)* or a present-tense verb *(he trains dogs)*. We determine which of these two possibilities is the intended one by seeing its position in a sentence. If it occupies the initial position, for example, where we usually expect to find the subject, we read it as a subject noun: *Trains pass by here every hour.* If it occupies the position usually filled by verbs, we adjust our interpretation: *He trains seeing-eye dogs.*

Structural grammarians, content with describing what people said, were not so often tempted to invent "rules." Also structural grammar provided satisfactory explanations of problems that traditional grammar could not solve, such as defining a verb. Verbs were no longer "action words"; they were words that could fill certain positions in a sentence.

But structural grammar had its own weaknesses. For example, the concentration on form and position resulted in grammar divorced from meaning. Suppose you had a sentence like this: *High depths act inertly.* According to the rules of form and position, the sentence is fine. It just happens to be perfect nonsense. How can we explain that anyone who speaks English knows such a sentence is just "not English"?

The third and most recent theory of grammar responds to this dilemma. **Transformational-generative grammar,** as it is called, begins with the ability that we all possess to invent sentences that are both complete and meaningful. It deals with function (what a word does) as well as form, and it claims to see two layers in our sentences: the surface layer, which consists of what is actually said or written, and the deep structure, which consists of the "kernel sentences" out of which the surface structure was built. Thus a sentence like *I know she's ready* contains two kernel sentences: *I know (something)* and *she is ready.* Intuitively a speaker of English can "transform" these two kernels into the surface structure. Transformational-generative grammarians want to identify as many of these intuitive transformations as possible, in order to explain our ability to create an infinite variety of sentences that are always grammatical and meaningful.

But even this newest kind of grammar has its difficulties.

Some are on the practical level, such as the fact that learning it requires a difficult new vocabulary. Some are theoretical, such as the problems transformationalists encounter when they try to bridge the gap between syntax (the arrangement of words) and semantics (the meaning of words). Maybe in the future we will have a new and better grammar that will remedy these defects too.

So no grammatical theory is completely satisfactory. All of them have something important to say about how our language is used. The question in your mind probably is a practical one: what is the value of these theories for a person who wants to learn to write better?

> I pass with relief from the tossing sea of Cause and Theory to the firm ground of Result and Fact.
>
> *Sir Winston Churchill*

A3. The Uses of Grammar

You do not need to know theoretical grammar to write well. Millions of people have become skillful writers without ever hearing of kernel sentences or deep structure. But it is useful to know that these theoretical explanations exist, because then you know the origin of those language facts mentioned earlier. They do not come from this text or your instructor or any law-giver. They come instead from descriptions of the English language as it is actually spoken and written. To say that something is "grammatical" or "ungrammatical" is really just the same as saying that it "is English" or "is not English."

While you don't need to know theories, you do need to know basic language facts. As we noted a few pages ago, you have known most of them ever since you were a preschooler. If you read and write extensively, maybe you already know intuitively all of the facts a good writer must know. But if you are like most students, you may not be sure about a few simple but important facts. This is especially true of facts that are more applicable to written English than to spoken English.

Why are the facts of written English a special problem? There are two reasons. The first is that writers have to be more precise, because they do not have the same resources available to them when they write as they do when they talk. No gestures, no voice inflections, no chance for answers to the ritual questions: "Y'know?" "Okay?" "Get me?" To compensate for this lack of feedback, writers want to be as clear as possible, and that means certain grammatical facts that can be ignored easily in speech cannot be ignored in writing. For example, we will be discussing pronoun reference in the next section. In conversation, pronoun reference causes no difficulty; we can augment our pronouns by such gestures as pointing or nodding the head, and if the person or thing to which the pronoun refers is still not clear, someone can stop us and ask who or what we mean. But in writing we have to make sure the pronoun reference is explicit.

The second reason is that written English links all those people who use the language. The dialect of a Scotsman, for example, might be almost unintelligible to you, just as your dialect might puzzle him. But if both of you *write* what you want to express, these barriers disappear and you share common ground. Because written English must cross all differences in nationality, region, class, and culture, it has certain requirements that all who write the language have agreed to observe. Therefore the written language is somewhat more formal— when we write we are more conscious, for example, of matters like verb endings. The care we take in observing these conventions is the small price we pay for the great privilege the written language gives us: the privilege of telling others, some of whom are quite different from us, what we know and what we feel.

> [Writing is] the great bond that holds society together, and the common conduit, whereby the improvements of knowledge are conveyed from one man and one generation to another.
>
> *John Locke*

Your grammatical problems may stem in large part from the fact that you know the spoken language quite well but have less experience with writing. The facts that are essential to both speaking and writing almost everybody knows. The facts that apply more to writing than to speaking are another matter. The purpose of this chapter, therefore, is to acquaint you with those facts most often unfamiliar to student writers. Knowing them and seeing how they apply to your writing is probably all you need to do to eliminate "bad grammar" as a cause of ineffectiveness in your writing.

The lesser-known facts about written English can be drawn from surprisingly few areas, mainly pronouns, modifiers, and verbs. The remaining parts of the chapter take up each of these three in turn. Please recognize that these issues are vital to your success as a writer. If what you write is ungrammatical, I think you can guess what kind of a response you are all too likely to get from many readers. Whether your reader is a teacher or a friend or a supervisor, the best reaction you can expect is puzzlement, and more often than not the reaction will be irritation and perhaps outright rejection ("Why can't this person use good English?").

Now that might seem unfair. You will perhaps wonder why the reader didn't care more about what you were saying than how you were saying it ("It's clear what I *mean*, isn't it?"). Fair or not, however, such criticisms will be made, and your writing won't communicate as well as it should, it won't accomplish what you want it to accomplish. Consequently, if you wish to be an effective writer, there is no alternative but to take command of the material covered in the rest of this chapter.

You can use the remainder of this chapter in one of two ways. If you prefer, you can go over recent papers you have written to identify the grammatical problems you have encountered. (Remember to note only *grammatical* problems—punctuation errors, for example, are considered in another chapter.) Then locate and study carefully the sections in this chapter that analyze your particular problems. The list of common abbreviations for correction symbols given on the inside back cover of this book may give you some idea of where to find the discussion you are looking for; if that fails, try the index.

The second way to approach the rest of this chapter—and this might be the better method if grammar is a frequent or severe problem for you—is to proceed directly through the rest of the chapter all the way to the end. That way you have an overview of the principal facts, some of which may seem new and may need to be studied a second time.

EXERCISES

1. The claim has been made in this chapter that you already know a great deal about English grammar, even if you cannot be explicit about grammatical terms. Examine the following three groups of sentences. State in your own words the most important similarities and/or differences among the various sentences that make up each group.

a. My uncle writes quite often in haste.
   Quite often my uncle writes in haste.
   My uncle writes in haste quite often.
   Quite my uncle in haste writes often.
b. The policeman begged the demonstrators to remove the sign.
   The policeman ordered the demonstrators to remove the sign.
   The policeman promised the demonstrators to remove the sign.
c. The Pittsburgh Steelers defeated the Dallas Cowboys in the Super Bowl.
   The Dallas Cowboys were defeated by the Pittsburgh Steelers in the Super Bowl.
   The ones that the Pittsburgh Steelers defeated in the Super Bowl were the Dallas Cowboys.

2. What are the differences in meaning of the following terms: *usage, grammar, semantics?*

3. Ask a random sampling of people—including people older and younger than yourself—what they understand by the word *grammar.* Are there any similarities in their responses? Do their replies exhibit any confusion about the meaning of the term?

4. Prepare a short paper describing your own training in grammar. In the paper be sure to include answers to the following questions.

a. In what grades was grammar taught in a formal way?
b. What, specifically, were you taught in the way of grammar?

c. Of the three kinds of grammar described in this chapter (traditional, structural, transformational-generative), which kind(s) formed the basis for your instruction?
d. What attitude toward grammar did your teachers convey?
e. What attitude toward grammar did you yourself have?
f. What were the reasons for this attitude?

5. Check a recent group of papers you have written. Ignore all the corrections on your papers that have to do with punctuation; likewise, all the errors in word choice, in spelling, in paragraph structure, in content. Of the remainder, how many are errors in grammar? Of these, how many have to do more with the written than the spoken language (i.e., errors in verbs, in pronouns, or in modifiers)? Do the results of your investigation bear out the claims made in the third paragraph on p. 317?

B. FACTS ABOUT PRONOUNS

Who would succeed in the world should be wise in the use of his pronouns. Utter the You twenty times, where you once utter the I.

J. M. Hay

Words that can be used in place of a noun or noun phrase are called *pronouns*. Like nouns they can change to show case (*who* subject, *whom* object, *whose* possessive) and to distinguish between singular and plural (*I* versus *we, mine* versus *ours*). They can also show gender (*he, she, it*) and person (*I, you, she*). In general pronouns can perform the same functions as nouns.

What makes pronouns different is that they have no meaning of their own. A rose is a rose is a rose, as Gertrude Stein once remarked—but what is a *which*? Pronouns can't make sense until we take into account the persons or objects to which they refer, in other words until we take into account what is called their *antecedents*. This sentence, for example:

The guard inspected my purse thoroughly, although he seemed embarrassed about the whole matter.

The pronoun "he" in this sentence means very little by itself, but in context we know that it quite clearly refers to the antecedent noun "guard."

This section will discuss the most important facts about pronoun forms and about the relationships between pronouns and their antecedents.

B1. Pronoun Forms

We noted that pronouns can change form when they change in case, number, gender, or person. People make very few errors in number, person, or gender (when is the last time you wrote *It are going to bed*?). So our consideration of pronoun forms really gets down to matters of case.

When we discuss the relationship of a noun, pronoun, or adjective to other words in a sentence, we are discussing case. Concretely this means answering questions like, "Is the word a subject? A direct object? An indirect object?" Case is usually determined in English by sentence position. In a sentence like *The bus is coming*, for example, we say the noun *bus* is the subject because it occupies the subject position. Problems of pronoun case are often abbreviated by *case, ca,* or simply *pron (pronoun).*

Let's begin with the subjective case, in other words with subject pronouns. Eight pronouns can fill the subject position in a sentence:

Subject Pronouns

PERSON	SINGULAR	PLURAL
1	I	we
2	you	you
3	he, she, it	they

She and I are going.

We will be back in a half hour.

Who or *whoever* used as subjects are also in the subjective case:

Who is going?

Whoever he is, he must love books.

Goethe was the author who most influenced Thomas Mann.

Ordinarily you won't have too much trouble here, so long as the sentence is short or relatively simple. The tricky parts come when sentences get more complex or when our common speech patterns differ from those required in formal writing.

The first pitfall to negotiate occurs when you have two subjects used with only one verb, i.e., the so-called compound subject. Do you see any problem in this sentence, for example?

> The opposing center and him fell on the loose ball at the same time.   *student paper*

In this instance "him" is not the preferred pronoun form. It may have sounded correct to the writer, but the difficulty becomes clearer when the other half of the compound subject (i.e., "center") is left out:

> Him fell on the loose ball at the same time.

Clearly undesirable, right? Immediately you know to use the subject form *he* rather than the object form *him*. If you have a compound subject, always apply this same test (leaving out the other half of the compound subject) and you will know whether or not you have the best pronoun. If the pronoun acts as a subject, it must be in the subject form.

Similarly people often write *us* in a subject place rather than *we*, when the pronoun is used right alongside a subject noun.

> Us Tareyton smokers would rather fight than switch.   *advertisement*

"Smokers," the noun used in conjunction with the pronoun, acts here as a subject. Therefore in formal writing we would need the subject pronoun *we: We Tareyton smokers*. . . . Again apply the simple test of leaving out the other part of the subject, in this sentence "smokers." You would not say, *Us would rather fight than switch*. So the test gives you a clear indication of which pronoun form is the necessary one.

Pronouns can also directly follow the verb *to be*. When they do, they must be in the subject form. This sentence is therefore correct:

> Her friends suspect it is she who spreads the rumors.   *student paper*

She is the proper pronoun here because it is in the subject form, as it must be when serving as a complement to the linking verb *is.* But you may have been tempted to use *her.* If so, the reason is a very natural one: in speech we quite often use the object form of the pronoun after the verb *to be,* just as we would if the verb were not *to be.* If someone comes home and a spouse calls out, *Is that you?* only a prig would answer, *It is I.* We would all say, *It's me.* But in writing, at least in formal writing, use the subject pronoun forms in cases like these.

Now let's consider the objective case, which like the subjective case has eight forms:

Object Pronouns

PERSON	SINGULAR	PLURAL
1	me	us
2	you	you
3	him, her, it	them

> Are the children coming with us or going with them?
>
> The assistant gave it to me.

Whom is also in the objective case (it functions as an object).

> With whom do you wish to speak?
>
> Whom did they call first?

Pronouns in the objective case can function in three main ways:

1. as direct objects

> Whom is the clerk helping?
>
> Did Tom invite you to the party yet?

2. as indirect objects

> Teresa told us the secret.
>
> The boss promised them a raise.

3. as objects of prepositions

> Is the secretary talking to him or to her?
>
> With whom are the Nelsons staying?

In speaking, many people use *who* as an object instead of *whom,* especially in questions: *Who is the clerk helping? Who are the Nel-*

sons staying with? The reason for this is that we are used to having a subject near the beginning of a sentence, so we use the subjective case *who*. (Questions reverse the normal word order, so in these cases the objects begin the sentences, not the subjects). In formal writing, however, *whom* should be used as an object form.

Bernstein on Words

By Theodore M. Bernstein

More about "whom." In "A Family Affair," the last Nero Wolfe novel, writes Eleanor Sullivan of Ellery Queen's Mystery Magazine, a character says, "Whom did you hear says what?" Archie Goodwin then comments, "I have tried to talk him out of that 'whom.' Only highbrows and grandstanders and school-teachers say 'whom,' and he knows it. It's the mule in him." Once again we are tempted to ask, can it be that whom's doom is really approaching? *Evening Journal* of Wilmington, Del., 25 August 1976, p.12.

Who deems whom *doomed?*

Note also two facts that correspond to points made earlier. Remember we said that if a pronoun was used immediately before a noun subject, it had to be in the subject form ("We smokers"). By the same token, if a pronoun is used immediately before a noun object, it must be in its object form:

Schools must give us taxpayers our money's worth. *newspaper letter*

Here, "taxpayers" is an indirect object. Also when a sentence has compound objects and one object is a pronoun, the pronoun must be in the objective form.

My numerous childhood illnesses brought my mother and me closer together. *Vladimir Nabokov*

Here again you could apply the simple test of removing the other object ("my mother") and seeing what is left. You would not write, *my illnesses brought I*, so *me* has to be the proper pronoun form.

The third case to be considered is the possessive. Let's consider both possessive pronouns and possessive adjectives here:

Possessive Pronouns

PERSON	SINGULAR	PLURAL
1	mine	ours
2	yours	yours
3	his, hers, its	theirs

Possessive Adjectives

PERSON	SINGULAR	PLURAL
1	my	our
2	your	your
3	his, her, its	their

Whose is also in the possessive case:

Whose is this?

Pablo Neruda was the poet whose work won him a Nobel Prize in 1971.

In general, you probably don't have trouble with these possessive forms. In the phrase *my coat*, you know that *my* modifies coat and serves as an adjective just like *old* or *big* or *white*. And if someone says, *Whose is this?* referring to your coat, there is no problem choosing the right possessive pronoun for the answer! But there is one case where possessive adjectives are sometimes forgotten and that is before a word with an -*ing* ending:

I was nervous about his driving the car.

We were happy about their moving to a new house.

Note that the possessive adjectives *his* and *their* are used, not the object forms *him* or *them*.

I should close this section on pronoun case forms by pointing out three more little grammatical facts. The first is that *them* should not be used instead of the demonstrative adjectives *these* or *those*: *Please hand me those keys on the table* (not *them keys*). Second, reflexive pronouns (those with the *-self* ending) are not used as subjects or objects in writing, even though—again— they may be used that way in speech: *Andre got some tuition refund forms at the bursar's office for Brenda and me* (not *myself*). Finally, when the words *than* and *as* appear in a sentence with a comparative adjective or adverb, some detective work may be required on your part before you know what pronoun form is needed to go with them. Here are two examples:

That's the only exam where he did as well as I.

Coffee affects you more than me.

In the first example, the subject form "I" is used, because "I" is the subject of the clause *I did* (where *did* is understood). In the second example, the object form "me" is used, because "me" is the object of the clause *it affects me* (where *it affects* is understood). These little sticklers don't occur very often, but when they do, you will know what pronoun form to use if you can figure out what words are understood and therefore omitted.

> Grammar is to speech what salt is to food.
> *Rabbi Ben Ezra*

B2. Pronoun Agreement

Pronouns get their name from the fact that in most instances they take the place of nouns. By doing so they perform a useful function. If we did not have them we would have to use the noun itself, again and again. Our prose might look like this:

Lenny grabbed the garbage bag, but Lenny saw the garbage bag was leaking, so Lenny shoved the garbage bag inside a second bag.

How much better it is to use pronouns:

Lenny grabbed the garbage bag, but he saw it was leaking so he shoved it inside a second bag.

While pronouns enable us to make a sentence more concise, we cannot lose sight of the fact that each pronoun is replacing a word; this word, the antecedent, appears elsewhere, usually in the same sentence. While it usually precedes a pronoun, the antecedent can sometimes follow a pronoun within a sentence:

Although I don't have *it* now, I can get *the money* to you tomorrow.

And sometimes the antecedent is found in a preceding sentence:

Jack handed me *the tickets.* I put *them* on top of the dresser.

Because of this relationship between a pronoun and its antecedent, the pronoun must agree with the antecedent in number. In other words the pronoun is singular if the antecedent is singular, plural if the antecedent is plural. (Pronouns also agree in gender and person, but native speakers hardly ever make mistakes in those areas.) Agreement in number is usually a simple matter:

W. B. Yeats puts it more graphically when *he* lumps together in one potpourri theologians, scientists, lawyers, and mathematicians. *Matthew Fox* [italics added]

But in a few instances agreement is not so simple. If in one of your papers a pronoun or possessive adjective is circled and the abbreviation *agr* is written next to it, probably you have encountered one of these problem cases. For example, take the situation where the antecedent is *each, either, neither,* or an indefinite pronoun like *everyone* or *somebody.*

Each team member must clean out his locker before May 31st.   *sign in gym*

Somebody had left her sweater in my room.   *student paper*

Formal writing requires singular possessive adjectives for these antecedents, as in the sentences above. In everyday conversation, however, most Americans are very likely to use the plural possessive adjectives in such cases—*their locker, their sweater.* Therefore when we write we have to resist a strong temptation to use those plural forms.

These last two example sentences bring to mind an important issue related to this topic: the use of the generic *he.* The two preceding example sentences are acceptable as is, because in the first *his* refers to people who both writer and reader knew were male, and in the second *her* refers to a person who both writer and reader knew was female. But what possessive adjective should be used in this sentence?

Each laboratory worker must show ____ security pass before entering.

Their would be inappropriate, because the antecedent is clearly singular. Yet the only third-person singular possessives are *his, her,* and *its.* Which do we choose, if any?

The traditional solution has been the so-called generic *he,* where *he* and its derivatives *(his, him, himself)* can refer to any group made up of both males and females. In other words, the *he* pronoun serves two functions: in some circumstances it refers to one or more antecedents who are clearly male and in other circumstances it refers to human beings in general, male or female. In the preceding example, the traditional solution would be to use the possessive adjective *his:*

Each laboratory worker must show his security pass before entering.

Many people in recent years have objected to the use of *he* to refer to all human beings. They believe the pronoun is so firmly linked in our minds with the male sex that it can never be free of sexual bias. We may *say* that the pronoun refers to both males and females, these people contend, but subconsciously—or even consciously—we *think* male. Consequently, supporters of this position would write our example sentence in one of three ways:

Each laboratory worker must show *his or her* security pass before entering. [adds feminine possessive adjective]

Each laboratory worker must show a security pass before entering. [cuts possessive adjective entirely]

Laboratory *workers* must show *their* security passes before entering. [converts subject to plural]

Those who support the traditional practice deny that use of the generic *he* is sexist. They say that the context tells the reader whether the pronoun is masculine or generic. The issue is still debated warmly and has not been settled.

You can usually avoid offending either party to the controversy by cutting pronouns or possessive adjectives or by casting sentences into the plural, as in the second and third of the preceding revisions. A few thorny sentences will remain, sentences where no alternative to a singular pronoun is really satisfactory. This is especially true when the reference continues several times over a long passage. In these cases, the generic *he* may be unavoidable. (See the entry for **Gender,** p. 428.)

There are two other circumstances where agreement in number is not so easily determined. The first of these circumstances is when the possessive adjective has two or more antecedents. Believe it or not, the English language then allows for four possibilities:

1. If the antecedents are joined by *and,* always use a plural possessive adjective:

   Mr. and Mrs. Smith both needed their car.

2. If the antecedents are joined by *or* or *nor,* and the antecedents are both plural, use a plural possessive adjective:

   Neither guns nor tanks have established their value in this conflict.

3. With *or,* if the antecedents are both singular, use a singular possessive adjective:

   Either Phil or Ted will pick us up in his car.

4. Again with *or,* if one antecedent is singular and the other plural, the possessive pronoun or adjective agrees in number with the antecedent closer to it in the sentence:

   Either Karen or her sisters will come to get my sweater, so please leave it out where they can see it. [*they* because plural *sisters* is closer to the pronoun than singular *Karen*]

The other circumstance that might puzzle you occurs when the antecedent is a **collective noun,** like *crowd, family, team,* or even the word *collection* itself. Sometimes collective nouns are used in the singular, sometimes in the plural. To determine whether you want a singular or plural possessive adjective, decide whether the antecedent will be considered as a single unit or as a collection of separately acting individuals. If the former, make both the verb and the possessive adjective singular:

The team is ready for its biggest game of the year.

Here the team acts as a unit. If the individuals that make up the unit act separately, make both the verb and the possessive adjective plural:

> The team opened their lockers.

Here the team acts as a collection of individuals; *its locker* would indicate that the team shared one big locker. This matter is subtle, but sometimes your easiest clue is to decide which verb form seems "natural" (i.e., singular or plural) and then to coordinate the possessive adjective or pronoun with it.

B3. Pronoun Reference

Let's assume now that your pronoun has the right case form according to its function, and the right number form according to its antecedent. There is one further issue to consider: will your reader have any difficulty in knowing what the antecedent is? Every pronoun needs a clear antecedent, a **pronoun reference.** If it does not have one, the sentence should be revised to eliminate any possible confusion for the reader. (Common abbreviations for problems with pronoun reference include: *ref, pro ref,* and *amb ref.*)

The first type of problem is what can be called **ambiguous reference.** *Ambiguous* means capable of being understood in more than one way; ambiguous reference means that there is more than one possible antecedent to the pronoun. Consider this example:

> Norm agreed with Greg that he ought to run for Student Senate. *student paper*

Does the pronoun "he" refer to Norm or to Greg? In other words, does Norm agree that he himself ought to run, or does he agree that Greg should? Either is possible—it's ambiguous—although only one meaning is intended. Here is another example:

> On Saturday I polished my car and straightened up my room; it still needs a lot more work. *student journal*

Which needs more work—the car or the room? To eliminate ambiguous references, the cure is usually simple enough: cut out the pronoun and repeat the intended antecedent.

Norm agreed with Greg that Greg ought to run for Student Senate.

On Saturday I polished my car and straightened up my room; the room still needs a lot more work.

The cure is certainly easy. The difficult part is knowing when the pronoun is ambiguous. After all, *you* know the intended antecedent, so you have no reason to pause over the sentence as you proofread your paper. Furthermore there are many cases where the pronoun is technically ambiguous but where no confusion results:

Nancy stroked the cat's fur. She wished the heat was not quite so oppressive.

In theory "she" could refer to the cat or to Nancy. But the intention is so clearly to refer to Nancy that the sentence needs no revision.

So the only helpful procedure is to read your own writing insofar as possible with the eyes of a stranger. Don't ask yourself if your writing is clear to *you;* instead ask if it will be clear to someone else. Look at your use of pronouns in that way and maybe the problem pronouns will be easier to identify. Above all watch for sentences that mention two items or two people of the same sex and then follow them with a singular pronoun, as in

"I don't want to be a wet blanket, Charlie,
but you were positive that there was gold in them thar hills."

Drawing by Kraus; © 1964 The New Yorker Magazine, Inc.

the Norm/Greg example preceding. That's the most frequent source of ambiguity.

> If things were to be done twice, all men be wise.
> *proverb*

A second kind of problem occurs when a pronoun by its position seems to refer to one antecedent but actually refers to another. Thus:

> The canoe tipped sideways, throwing Pam and me into the water. She sure was hard to handle, especially in the rapids. *student paper*

The position of the pronoun "she" would at first lead you to think that it referred to Pam, its nearest possible antecedent. But then the remainder of that second sentence makes it obvious that the antecedent is the canoe. This problem is not really the same as ambiguous reference, because we eventually determine which antecedent is intended. But we do experience a momentary and rather amusing confusion!

Here is another example from student writing:

> Keats was attacked by the reviewers, so much so that Shelley even thought his death might have been caused by those attacks.

At first glance, "his" might seem to point to "Shelley" as the antecedent. But then we realize that "Keats" is necessarily the choice, especially since it would be awfully difficult for Shelley to talk about the attacks if he himself were dead. So the sentence needs to be revised:

> Keats was attacked by the reviewers, so much so that Shelley even thought Keats' death might have been caused by those attacks.

Again, the cure is to read your writing with the eyes of a stranger, insofar as possible.

A third type of problem is a close relative of the second. If the antecedent and its pronoun get separated by too many other words, readers may forget what the antecedent was by the time they get to the pronoun. And if they forget the antecedent they have to stop and go back to determine it, which causes a temporary delay in reading. Here is an example of the problem, called **remote reference.**

At last I finished stuffing the envelopes. Slowly I cleared off the desk, recapped my pen, and shoved the wastebasket out of sight; then I pulled on my jacket and went to put them in the mail.

Of course "them" must have "envelopes" as its antecedent—there is no other logical possibility. The difficulty is that the antecedent is so remote from the pronoun. It is better in this case to clarify the passage by repeating the antecedent: ". . . went to put *the envelopes* in the mail."

The fourth and last type of problem is **vague reference,** which can happen when a writer uses *it, which, this,* or *that* to refer to a whole idea rather than to a single noun. Sometimes using pronouns in this way causes no difficulty; this sentence, for instance, reads clearly:

We spent the whole week loafing on the beach, which gave us a good tan if nothing else.   *student journal*

We readily understand that "which" refers to the whole activity described in the independent clause. But there are other occasions when the reference is not quite so clear:

The governor's budget proposes heavy cuts in welfare and mental health along with a big increase in highway construction. This is folly, unless he wants to commit political suicide.   *newspaper letter*

"This" might refer to the increase for highways, or perhaps to the proposed cuts, or maybe to the entire budget. The antecedent for "this" is so vague that the pronoun carries no clear meaning of its own. Better to revise it:

The governor's budget proposes heavy cuts in welfare and mental health along with a big increase in highway construction. This entire proposal is folly, unless he wants to commit political suicide.

See to it that whenever possible the pronouns *it, which, this,* and *that* have concrete, nameable antecedents. Make a special effort to avoid the vague, indefinite uses of *it:*

POOR: It says in the paper that more snow is coming.

REVISION: The paper says more snow is coming.

(Of course you will not be able to avoid fixed idioms with the pronoun, as in the phrase "It's snowing.")

EXERCISES

1. Choose the appropriate word to complete each of the following sentences. Explain your choice.

a. Either the dean or the president will sidetrack the proposal, although each will do it for (their/his) own separate motives.
b. (Who/Whom) did you give my glasses to? [formal writing]
c. The American family needs to have (its/their) values examined.
d. Why do most elementary school systems neglect (us/we) overachievers?
e. (Who/Whom) is calling, please?
f. I bought two Dr. Peppers for my sister and (me/myself).
g. The sheriff and his deputies each had (his/their) own role to play in the archetypal plots of the old Grade B westerns.
h. Sandy and (she/her) think only about grades, never about their social lives.
i. I swear my roommate thinks she needs twice as much sleep as (I/me).
j. Crowds take on a character of (their/its) own, some becoming docile, some turning mean or perhaps even violent.

2. Some of the following student-written sentences have a problem in pronoun usage; some do not. If the sentence is correct as is, put a checkmark next to it. If the sentence needs to be changed, make the necessary alterations.

a. Us kids always stuck together whenever the adults pushed us.
b. The sage realizes the young poet's need for his wisdom.
c. He may look overweight, but let me assure you he is twice as fast a runner as me.
d. I put the books on the table, then turned on the stereo, poured myself a Pepsi, adjusted the intensor lamp, changed my shirt, and read the mail; finally I faced the fact that I was going to have to study them.
e. I bought myself a new pair of jeans, just to make myself feel better.
f. Every day my mother straightens up the living room and then washes dishes, but it soon needs doing all over again.

g. Him and the insurance agent went to the garage to check on the damage estimates.
h. The prosecutor and my lawyer agreed that he should have investigated the case more thoroughly.
i. It said on this sheet what we were supposed to do.
j. Probably I would not have gained this knowledge about myself for many more years.
k. One learns their hidden traits when they enter into close personal relationships.
l. The teacher accused me of deception, hypocrisy, manipulation—how could I defend myself against it?
m. We contestants grew restless, waiting for the starter to finish his endless list of rules.

> God does not much mind bad grammar, but He does not take any particular pleasure in it.
>
> *Erasmus*

3. The controversy about whether *he* can refer to all people or just males has been widely debated. Write a short summary of your position on the controversy. In preparing the summary, include some or all of the following activities:

a. Determine the policy in effect for your local newspaper.
b. Check the section on pronouns in a composition handbook published at least fifteen years ago (your library will probably have some older editions) and see what advice it gives.
c. Jot down what you can remember about what you were taught in grade school and high school on this issue.
d. Determine what seems to be the policy in use for this textbook.
e. Read two or three of the many articles published on this topic (your reference librarian can help you locate them).
f. Decide what policy you will follow and why you will follow it.

4. Rewrite the following student paragraph so that each pronoun is the correct one and has a clearly defined antecedent with which it agrees. Also make sure the paragraph has a consistent point of view—e.g., don't let it switch from second per-

son *(you)* to third person *(they)* and then back to second person
without good reason.

> I looked forward to Mondays and Thursdays. It was at these times
> that I would work as a page in the House of Representatives. Your
> expectations about this job are usually shot down the first day you
> work. The number of representatives there are relatively few—I
> could usually count them on my fingers. I would sit back and look at
> the high walls of the House chamber and what a grand sight it was;
> they were loaded with tradition and beauty. The chamber itself is
> characteristic of the serious business conducted within its walls. The
> walnut rostrum is directly in front of an American flag hung verti-
> cally and they have wreaths hanging from the rostrum that tell you
> about union, justice, tolerance, and liberty. Us pages could gaze at
> this splendor all morning long, because they usually gave us almost
> nothing to do. Sometimes we would fetch them coffee, or you might
> have to go out and buy somebody their morning paper if he had
> forgotten to pick up one earlier. It was never anything important, like
> take this to the speaker and see how I should vote. It was mostly a
> matter of us sitting around and them paying us for it.

C. FACTS ABOUT MODIFIERS

> Comment is free, but facts are sacred.
> *Manchester Guardian*

Imagine a world of nothing but subject, verb, and complement.
Our prose would look like this:

> I took a bus. The bus was late. I arrived late. Class had begun. I was
> embarrassed.

In short, we would be writing like third graders.

Much of the difference between how a third grader writes and
how you write lies in your much greater experience at using
modifiers. Given similar data, you might have written the small
paragraph above somewhat like this:

> I took a bus, which was my first mistake. As usual the bus was late,
> very late. Consequently I arrived after class had begun, and I had to
> suffer the acute embarrassment of seeing the teacher glare icily at me
> as I took my seat.

Part of the greater maturity evident in this paragraph comes from such factors as increased sentence length and the use of pronouns. But the most important factor is the use of modifiers such as these: "which was my first mistake" (sentence modifier); "very" and "icily" (adverbs); "after class had begun" (adverb clause); "acute" (adjective).

Because modifiers are so important a part of your style, of anybody's style, you need to make sure you use them as effectively as possible. To do that, you should first be aware of the forms modifiers can take.

The most familiar modifier is the **adjective.** Adjectives usually modify nouns: *green blouse.* Sometimes they follow linking verbs like *is: the sky is **dark.*** They have comparative and superlative forms: ***little, littler, littlest.*** Furthermore a group of words—a phrase, a clause—can act as an adjective: *the hunter **in the red jacket.*** Other parts of speech can become adjectivals, in other words, can fill an adjective position; *the **brick** wall* (noun used as adjective).

Adverbs are the second major category of modifiers. They usually modify verbs *(she smiles **easily)***, adjectives *(**barely** warm soup)*, or other adverbs *(**very** quickly)*. They often have the characteristic *-ly* ending. Adverbs are like adjectives in that they can be compared *(more **easily,** most **easily)***. Their position can be occupied by adverbials *(she goes **today**—noun used as adverb)* or by adverbial phrases or clauses *(she laughs **when she shouldn't)***.

A third important kind of modifier, the **sentence modifier,** is a word, phrase, or clause that modifies, not a noun or a verb, but rather the whole sentence to which it is attached. Let's look at the example seen earlier:

I took the bus, which was my first mistake.

The clause "which was my first mistake" modifies neither "bus" nor "took." Instead it can be understood properly only if it is seen to qualify the entire main clause, i.e., "I took a bus." Therefore the "which . . ." clause is said to be a sentence modifier. Here are two other examples:

In the café, he tells me the story of his life.   *Albert Camus*

Miraculously, no one was hurt.   *newspaper item*

In these two examples, the prepositional phrase "In the café . . ." and the adverb "Miraculously . . ." modify the sentences in which they are found.

So modifiers come in three major forms: adjectives (including adjectivals and adjectival phrases and clauses), adverbs (including adverbials and adverbial phrases and clauses), and sentence modifiers. Now what you need to know are the principal pitfalls writers must avoid if they are going to use these modifiers effectively.

C1. Forms of Modifiers

First pitfall: the sentence *seems* to invite an adverb but in fact requires an adjective. Like this one from a student journal:

> I felt bad when the exam was over—so much endurance had brought such little joy.

The sentence is correct, but you can hardly be blamed if you thought that the adjective "bad" should have been replaced by the adverb *badly*. After all we are used to adverbs in that position, immediately following a verb. The reason we use the adjective rather than the adverb is that the verb *feel* is one of a small group of verbs that act like the verb *to be*. The complement of a form of the verb *to be* is an adjective: *The building is tall*. So too with this small group of verbs that can act like *to be;* they can also take an adjective.

> The basement smells musty.
>
> The wind became violent.
>
> That reply sounds childish.

These verbs are often called **linking verbs** because they do just that—they link subject and complement. The most frequently used linking verbs are *be, become, seem, appear,* and some verbs associated with the senses—*feel, look, smell, sound, taste*.

Perhaps the simplest way to understand how linking verbs work is to imagine them being replaced by the most common linking verb, *to be*. Immediately you would recognize that an adjectival form has to be used. Replace *The wind became violent* with *The wind was violent*. (You would not say, *The wind was violently*.) In the preceding examples, the adjectives that follow the linking verbs clearly modify the subjects of the sentences ("musty basement," "violent wind," "childish reply").

Note that when verbs like *feel, look, sound,* and other linking verbs are not used to link subject and complement (like the verb *to be*), but either have or can have an object, they are modified by adverbs, not adjectives:

With adjective (linking verb)	With adverb (nonlinking verb)
The music sounded beautiful to me.	He sounded the alarm frantically.
Don't you feel good?	I felt for the door cautiously in the darkness.
He looked happy and relaxed.	He looked skeptically at the salesclerk.

Just as adverbs are sometimes used mistakenly in place of adjectives, adjectives are sometimes used mistakenly in place of adverbs. Do you see any problems in this sentence?

Larry speaks real slow, as if each word required a great effort.

In speech the sentence might be quite acceptable. But in writing two problems arise. The first is that "real" is being used as an intensifying adverb, in other words, as a synonym for *very*. When the word is an adverb, it must have its adverbial form, *really*. The second problem is that "slow" also occupies an adverbial position, because it modifies the verb "speaks." You might lose sight of that fact because adverbs usually follow immediately after the verbs they qualify. But in this case "slow" has been bumped over one place by the intensifier *really*. So long as the word functions as an adverb, it needs an adverbial form; thus *slowly* is the right word. A rewritten version of the sentence would look like this:

Larry speaks really slowly, as if each word required a great effort.

(In the rewritten example, *very* would sound better than *really*.)

Remember too that adjectives and adverbs have comparative and superlative forms:

positive	comparative	superlative
hot	hotter	hottest
good (adjective), well (adverb)	better	best
late	later	latest
typical	more typical	most typical
quickly	more quickly	most quickly

In formal writing the comparative forms should be used when two items or qualities are being compared, as in this example from a student paper:

> Of the two Woody Allen movies I have seen so far, *Bananas* is clearly the better one.

Better should be used rather than the superlative *best*. However, use the superlative forms for three or more items:

> To affect the quality of the day, that is the highest of arts.   *Henry David Thoreau*

C2. Position of Modifiers

Problems with modifiers can also arise when a modifier is out of position, although it may be in the proper form. A **misplaced modifier**—abbreviation *mis mod, m m,* or *mis pt*—results in confusion for the reader.

My favorite example of a misplaced modifier comes from a headline in our student newspaper a while back:

> Laura Allende Speaks of Terror and Repression at Loyola

Now of course what the author of that headline meant was that Ms. Allende, daughter of the late president of Chile, had spoken about terror and repression in her own country after the overthrow of her father's government. But the position of the adverbial phrase "at Loyola" makes it seem as if the terror and repression were much closer at hand, and the result is unintended laughter. To eliminate this confusion, the phrase should be moved back to its proper adverbial position right after the verb "speaks":

> Laura Allende Speaks at Loyola of Terror and Repression [in Chile]

For another example of a misplaced modifier, consider this sentence from a student's paper:

> The computer is also used to recall master lists of all a company might own for inventory purposes.

The position of the phrase "for inventory purposes" confuses the reader. Does the author mean that the computer recalls lists of all that the company owns, or merely lists of all that the company owns for inventory purposes? Obviously she means the former, and our confusion is only temporary. But still that temporary confusion would not have happened if the phrase had been placed immediately after the word "used":

> The computer is also used for inventory purposes to recall master lists of all a company might own.

Here is one more example of a misplaced modifier, in this case just a simple adverb:

> I am more and more convinced that I ought not become a doctor lately.   *student journal*

The placement of "lately" at the end of the sentence confuses us, because we wonder how a future event (becoming a doctor) can be said to have taken place "lately." Of course what has been taking place lately is the self-convincing. So when the adverb is put closer to the verb it modifies, the confusion disappears:

> I am more and more convinced lately that I ought not become a doctor.

> Words differently arranged have a different meaning, and meanings differently arranged have different effects.
>
> *Blaise Pascal*

Sometimes the misplaced modifier cannot be corrected simply by putting it in a different position in the sentence. In these cases the modifier will be found to have no word or group of words that it modifies, and so while it "makes sense," grammatically speaking it is dangling there by itself, with no direct connection to the rest of the sentence. The result is what is called a **dangling modifier.** (Common abbreviations: *d m, dng, dgl, dangl mod, dangl part*[iciple]; occasionally *coh*[erence]. Here is an example from a student paper.

> Lacking enough money, the Florida trip was a disaster.

"Lacking enough money" seems to modify the subject noun "trip." But it can't—how would a trip lack money? Instead the phrase modifies the unnamed person who took the Florida trip. To correct the sentence, we could name the person who took the trip and make that person the subject of the sentence:

Lacking enough money, I felt that the Florida trip was a disaster.

There are other ways of adjusting the sentence to eliminate the dangling modifier and still retain the same meaning, such as converting the modifier into a clause:

Because I lacked enough money, the Florida trip was a disaster for me.

You won't have too much difficulty finding a good solution. The trick is in recognizing danglers in the first place. Your best bet for catching most of them is to doublecheck yourself any time you open a sentence with a phrase, making sure the phrase modifies the subject if it is acting as an adjective. If necessary, change the sentence until it hangs together the way it should.

By the way, dangling modifiers occur most frequently at the beginning of a sentence, but that is not the only place you encounter them. Do you know what is wrong with this example and how to revise it?

The house lights were turned down, waiting for the actors to appear on the bare stage.

An expectant audience, yes—but expectant *house lights?*

EXERCISES

1. In the following sentences, choose the appropriate adjective or adverb. Assume the writing is formal.

a. It is (real / really) fun to read letters from friends when you are away at school.
b. Stand (close / closely) to your partner.
c. We can (sure / surely) do better than you predict.
d. The chorus welcomes anyone who can sing (well / good) enough to pass a simple audition.
e. The guitarist played as (loud / loudly) as he could, to hide the fact that he was the (weaker / weakest) of the three musicians.

f. To most drinkers bourbon tastes (smoother / more smoothly) than scotch.

g. When you look at both the Hancock Building and the Sears Tower from a distance, the latter is clearly the (more / most) impressive.

h. When she gets those migraines she feels (miserable / miserably).

i. We would then sneak into our parents' room as (quiet / quietly) as possible.

j. The doctor felt the wound (careful / carefully), probing for splinters of glass.

2. Write four sentences that show the pattern of subject + linking verb + adjective-as-complement. Use each of the following four adjectives as your complements.

jaunty	scarlet
heavier	most pungent

3. Revise the faulty modifiers in these student-written sentences. Be sure you know *why* the modifiers need to be revised or repositioned.

a. Violent shows should be put on tv late at night; this would reduce the chances of children viewing them substantially.

b. She talked real fast and I had a hard time following her.

c. Hearing about the detour, the expressway seemed a much better choice.

d. The back bedroom is the warmest of the two.

e. There has been an increase in the controversy about the development of nuclear energy over the years.

f. Being a devoted baseball fan, the designated-hitter rule seems a travesty.

g. I look back on the day and see it completely different.

h. The conductor spends a lot of time talking about his grandchildren on our train.

i. The golfer shouted "Fore!" as loud as he could, and we ducked real quick.

j. After checking several sources, this paper will conclude that test-tube conceptions are not morally wrong.

4. Compose complete sentences using the following openers. Be sure the opening modifiers are directly tied to the subject.

a. Having explained the reasons for their decision. . . .
b. To avoid failing the course. . . .
c. When feeling boisterous. . . .
d. By determining the wind direction. . . .
e. Grabbing a fresh pencil. . . .
f. Fueled by at least six beers. . . .

D. FACTS ABOUT VERBS

Verbs, like pronouns, cause a disproportionately large share of the problems writers can encounter. If verbs are troublesome for you, most likely the difficulty will be either verb form *(v, vb, tense, tnse, t)* or verb agreement *(agr, v, vb)*. We should begin with form.

> Form is power.
> *Thomas Hobbes*

D1. Verb Form

You know that most verbs have quite regular forms: a present-tense base (the same as the infinitive), a past tense (base + -ed), and a past participle (base + -ed, used with an auxiliary such as a form of *to have* in the perfect, or compound, tenses). Here are some examples:

base	past tense	past participle
join	joined	(have) joined
spill	spilled	(have) spilled
slap	slapped	(have) slapped

In the last example, incidentally, the consonant *p* is doubled in the past and past participle to preserve the vowel sound of the base; what would *slaped* sound like? The verb endings themselves are unchanged.

While regular verbs predominate in our language, there are also hundreds of irregular verbs, and these include some of the most important ones. "Irregular" means just that—irregular and therefore unpredictable. Some of them are irregular in both the past tense and past participle although those two forms are still identical: *cling, clung, (have) clung; grind, ground, (have) ground.* Others are different in all three parts: *be, was, (have) been; know, knew, (have) known; write, wrote, (have) written.* Just to be contrary, there are still others that are *alike* in all three forms: *bet, bet, (have) bet; hurt, hurt, (have) hurt.* Trickiest of all are those with alternate forms: *drink, drank, (have) drunk* (or, informally, *have drank*); *leap, leaped* or *leapt, (have) leaped* or *(have) leapt; stink, stank* or *stunk, (have) stunk.*

Nevertheless you know from experience how to use most irregular verbs. Perhaps the easiest way to resolve doubts you might have is to consult this list of the most "mischievous" ones:

base	past tense	past participle
arise	arose	arisen
bear	bore	borne, *or* born
beat	beat	beaten
bid *(ask, entreat)*	bade	bidden
bind	bound	bound
blow	blew	blown
break	broke	broken
burst	burst	burst
choose	chose	chosen
creep	crept	crept
deal	dealt	dealt
dive	dived, dove	dived
eat	ate	eaten
flee	fled	fled
forbid	forbad, forbade	forbidden
freeze	froze	frozen
hang *(suspend)*	hung	hung
hang *(execute by hanging)*	hanged	hanged
lay *(place, set down)*	laid	laid
lead	led	led
lend	lent	lent
lie *(recline)*	lay	lain
mean	meant	meant
prove	proved	proved *or* proven
ride	rode	ridden

base	past	past participle
ring	rang	rung
rise	rose	risen
seek	sought	sought
send	sent	sent
set	set	set
shake	shook	shaken
shine	shone *or* shined	shone *or* shined
shrink	shrank *or* shrunk	shrunk
sing	sang *or* sung	sung
sink	sank *or* sunk	sunk
sleep	slept	slept
spin	spun	spun
spit	spat	spat
spring	sprang	sprung
steal	stole	stolen
swear	swore	sworn
swing	swung	swung
tear	tore	torn
thrive	thrived *or* throve	thrived *or* thriven
wear	wore	worn
weave	wove	woven
weep	wept	wept
wring	wrung	wrung

Many mistakes that people make with irregular verbs come from trying to make them regular. Perhaps this takes the form of assuming the past and past participle forms are alike when they aren't: *We begun studying last night* (instead of *We began studying last night*). Or maybe it takes the form of assuming the verb isn't irregular and therefore adding the regular *-ed* ending to the base: *The old man spitted into the gutter* (instead of *The old man spat into the gutter*).

Another set of difficulties occurs when writers use forms that are familiar in spoken English but not in standard written English. The solution, of course, is not necessarily to change the way you speak, but rather to learn the forms you will need to use when you write.

Sometimes people write what they *think* they hear; familiar examples are *could of* instead of *could have* or *would of* instead of *would have.* In student papers I often encounter sentences like this one:

> There was no way I could of satisfied my father's demands.

The writer has heard a contraction of *could* and *have, could've;* when pronounced, it sounds just like *could of,* and so the latter is substituted. A similar example is *could care less:*

> He could care less what anyone else thinks of his funny clothes.

The phrase is really *couldn't care less,* as becomes clear when you think about its meaning. But in speech the *couldn't* is often slurred over so quickly that the *-n't* ending gets lost, and then it ends up getting lost on paper too.

Other problems of this sort arise when a student's spoken dialect has verb forms that are not found in standard written English. If you are a black American, for example, sentences like the following might be familiar:

> He see me going.
>
> He coming now.
>
> We be leaving now.
>
> She done been annoying me.

These verb forms are customary in many people's speech. They are not wrong English—they are used in quite regular ways, and in speech they communicate just as well as other forms. But in writing it is better to use the forms of standard written English. Briefly, here are some facts about standard written English that every writer should know.

1. A form of the verb *to be* must be used in each of the following situations:
   a. when it is the only verb in the sentence;

      > She is a smart girl. [Not *She a smart girl.*]
      >
      > They are noisy. [Not *They noisy.*]

   b. when it is used with a verb with an *-ing* ending, either past or present.

      > He is working. [Not *He working.*]

   Note that *be* plus a past participle, e.g., *he be working,* is a form that is not used in standard written English.

2. When *been* is used with a past participle, it is preceded by a form of the verb *to have*.

   She has been sleeping. [Not *She been sleeping* or *She done been sleeping.*]

3. If the past-tense or past-participle ending is *-ed*, it is always added to the written form of the verb, whether or not it is pronounced.

   We defeat*ed* their debate team yesterday. [Not *We defeat their debate team yesterday.*]

   He had shin*ed* his shoes before he left for ROTC drill. [Not *He had shine his shoes before he left for ROTC drill.*]

So far the verbs we have been discussing were in the indicative mood, but there is another mood called the **subjunctive.** One main use of the subjunctive is to express something hypothetical or contrary to fact; for instance, the subjunctive is used after *as if:*

   He spends money as if he had a fortune.

   She talks as if she were a real expert.

Compare the factual statements: *He has a fortune. She is a real expert.* Here are other examples where the subjunctive is used to express something that is hypothetical:

   If I were stranded on a desert island, I'd like to be with you.

   Imagine that Shakespeare were alive today—how would he write?

The subjunctive is also used to express a wish:

   I wish we were coming with you.

   I wish I were thin.

Finally, it is used to express something necessary or mandatory:

   It is essential that he be there by noon.

   I insist that they be given fair treatment.

   The teacher asked that he pay attention and do his homework.

Notice that the difference between the subjunctive and indicative forms is that in the third-person singular present tense the form is like the *I* form *(that he pay, that he study, that he do),* except the verb *to be,* where *be* is used for all persons *(that I, you, he be).* In the past tense, *were* is used for all persons of the verb *to be* in the subjunctive *(if I / you / he were).*

D2. Subject-Verb Agreement

For there be women, fair as she,
Whose verbs and nouns do more agree.
Bret Harte

To discuss subject-verb agreement, there is really only one fact to announce: verbs must agree with their subjects in number—singular verb for a singular subject, plural verb for a plural subject. Sounds simple, but it's not—otherwise there would not be a section of this chapter devoted to the topic! You know that singular subjects take singular verb forms: *The lectern needs a microphone.* And plural subjects take plural verb forms: *The tables need candles.* The difficulties occur in situations where it is not immediately apparent whether the subject should be considered singular or plural.

We can begin with subjects that are always considered singular and therefore take a singular verb.

1. Collective nouns like *faculty, staff, team, family, group,* and *collection,* even though they comprise more than one member, are considered a single entity.

   The graduate faculty is so designated because its members are capable of directing research. [Not *are so designated.*]

   Recall, however, that there is an occasional exception to this—see pp. 335–336.

2. Nouns of time, money, weight, and measurement may sometimes be plural in form but always take singular verbs.

   Ten ounces is all I can spare you.

   Forty cents is now a common price for a cup of coffee.

3. Indefinite pronouns like *anybody, everybody, one, each, either,* and *neither* all take singular verbs.

   Each of us hopes to win.

   Neither deserves to be fired.

   But note that *any* and *none* can be used with either a singular or plural verb.

A second category includes subjects that can take either singular or plural verbs, depending on the circumstances.

1. Compound subjects joined by *or, nor, but also, but not* have a verb form that depends upon whether the part of the compound subject closest to the verb is itself singular or plural. If the part of the subject closest to the verb is singular, use a singular verb.

   Not only the referees but also the timekeeper was confused.

   Here the singular noun "timekeeper" is closer to the verb than the plural "referees," so the verb is singular.
       If the part of the subject closest to the verb is plural, use a plural verb.

   Either Ray or his parents own the car.

   Here the plural "parents" is closer than singular "Ray," so the verb is plural.

2. When relative pronouns are used as subjects, the verb form depends on the antecedent. If the antecedent of the relative pronoun is singular, the verb is singular.

   He is the only rock star who turns me off.

   The antecedent of "who" is the singular "star," so the verb is singular, "turns."
       If the antecedent is plural, the verb is plural.

   Those tirades of hers, which seem to be getting more frequent, really worry me.

   The antecedent of "which" is the plural "tirades," so the verb is plural, "seem."

Finally we can note some special situations in which it is easy to make mistakes.

1. When a subject is separated from its verb by a clause, and when the last word of the clause is a noun different in number from the subject, confusion can result. Here is an example from a student exam:

   The present system of elections have other flaws besides voter apathy.

The mistake was in seeing plural "elections" as the subject and then using the plural verb "have." But if you disregard the phrase "of elections" and harken back to the real subject, "system," the necessity of using the form *has* becomes clear:

The present system of elections has other flaws besides voter apathy.

2. Not all subject nouns ending in -*s* are plural.

Statistics is my favorite subject.

3. Compound subjects joined by *and* must always have plural verb forms.

The blue jay and the starling drive away other birds.

You might be tempted to look only at the part of the subject closest to the verb, i.e., the singular "starling," and to make the verb singular. But the complete subject is the compound subject "blue jay" + "starling"—therefore more than one and a plural verb.   When the word order is inverted, and a

4. When the word order is inverted, and a complement different in number from the subject comes before the verb, it is easy to make the mistake of having the verb agree with its preceding complement rather than with the subject that follows.

Awaiting the victor are two small trophies.

The example is correct because "trophies," not "victor," is the subject—the usual word order has simply been reversed. A similar case arises when a sentence begins with *there:*

There are no longer any silent men in the world today.   *Max Picard*

"There" is a space-filler; "men" is the real subject and must have a plural verb. *There is* would be acceptable only if the subject was singular.

Of course, the facts just discussed—facts about pronouns, modifiers, and verbs—are not all the facts about English grammar. You already know most of the other facts; otherwise you wouldn't be able to communicate in English at all. This chapter includes only those facts that apprentice writers often do not know, especially the ones that apply to writing but not always to speech.

Please be aware too that it is not always possible to make clear distinctions between problems of grammar and other types of writing problems. For example, our discussion of verb forms in conversation versus verb forms in writing might be considered usage rather than grammar. By the same token the section on "shifts" in Chapter 2 might well be included as part of grammar. Just remember that labels are not nearly as important as facts. This book is trying to give you the facts you need to be a more informed writer.

EXERCISES

1. Choose the correct verb form in the following sentences.

a. Three wrecked cars and a dilapidated van (crowds / crowd) their driveway.

a. The reward for our labors (were / was) strawberries and ice cream.

c. Arrowheads (lay / laid) buried in the soil for those adventurous enough to dig for them.

d. My new tee shirt has (shrunk / shrunken) since it was washed.

e. Thirty pounds of lime (was / were) never enough to cover the lawn.

f. He (dealed / dealt) the cards quickly, almost impatiently.

g. The coaching staff (hope / hopes) to recruit at least two high-scoring guards to replace this year's graduating seniors.

h. Everybody in the back rows (hears / hear) only an occasional sentence or two of the lecture.

i. The frozen water had (burst / bursted) the pipes.

j. Either two hours of painting or one hour of chorus (satisfy / satisfies) the fine arts requirement.

2. Revise any of the following student-written sentences that are incorrect.

a. Three hours are all the time I need to rebuild a carburetor.

b. She lended me her comb in the restroom.

c. Most puzzling to Inspector Clouseau is three small clues that he stumbles upon during his investigation.

d. The baby be sleeping now and I can write this paper.

e. A widespread incidence of rashes were reported to the health department.

f. The bull sprung from behind the tree and charged us.

g. The most unfair of all these regulations are the one dealing with child-support payments.

h. When he let out our secret I could of killed him, because we might be suspended or even expelled.

i. Logistics are the biggest problem when you plan a graduation party.

j. I had always shrank from such a responsibility, but now I had no choice.

k. There was speculation that the government might try to clamp down on campaign activities.

l. Acknowledging that the lot of today's women are different, we still find many cases of discrimination in employment.

m. The economy should rebound sharply during the next six months.

n. She staying after class today to talk with the instructor.

o. The complications that result here is that the same bullet could not have hit Kennedy and Governor Connally too.

p. Last night I was once again lead into temptation and bought a six-pack.

q. The only time E.R.A. can enter the private lives of a man and wife are in cases concerning alimony.

r. I replied very firmly that I could care less.

3. Locate a fairly long passage from a magazine or a book. Study the verbs. Note especially the following:

a. verbs in the passive voice (if any)

b. shifts in voice, tense, mood (if any)—see Chapter 2

c. frequency of forms of the verbs *to have* and *to be*

Then study the verbs in three pages of your own writing according to the same three criteria. Do you see any differences in your use of verbs?

4. Write two or three paragraphs describing your movement from one place to another, e.g., from one part of the campus to another, from home to school or work, from city to country. Put all the verbs in the present tense.

Then rewrite the same description, changing all the verbs to the past tense. Do you see any differences in *effect* resulting from this change? What would happen if you rewrote many of the sentences in the passive voice?

7

THE CONVENTIONS

Convention is the ruler of all.
Pindar

On his television show "The Honeymooners," Jackie Gleason played an Archie Bunker-type bus driver named Ralph Kramden. At least once in each episode Ralph would glare at his wife and then snarl, "You're a real sweetheart, Alice." She would growl back and the fight would be on.

That sentence became a trademark for the show. "You're a real sweetheart, Alice." But suppose we encountered the sentence all by itself, in written form. Read out of context, the sentence could be the tenderest, most loving sentiment. No written version would convey Ralph's exasperated, sarcastic tone of voice. For that tone we must rely on additional words, as we have done in these first two paragraphs with words like "snarl," "exasperated," and "sarcastic."

So the written language can never fully represent the spoken language. Even when the words are the same, many important parts of speech like pitch, tone, and accent must be sacrificed. This is the price we pay for that great advantage of writing we spoke about earlier, the ability it gives us to address others without limitations of space or time.

Although writing can never duplicate speech, writers are not by any means helpless. Many devices narrow the separation. For example, the use of italics allows a writer to emphasize one word at the expense of another. Contrast these two sentences:

Who *do* you think I am?

Who do you think I *am*?

The first suggests surprise—apparently you have mistaken me for someone else; who am I really? The second suggests outrage—how dare you address me this way, don't you realize how important I am? Italics let the writer distinguish these tones by showing which words to stress.

Another example of a device that makes writing closer to speech is the comma. When we talk we often use short pauses accompanied by a slight change in inflection. These pauses enable us to catch our breath, but more importantly they tell listeners how to group the words they are hearing so they can understand us better. In writing, commas represent those pauses. Sometimes, as in a very long sentence, they just let us catch our breath:

> What we believe of man affects the behavior of men, for it determines what each expects of the other.   *Leon Eisenberg*

Sometimes they group words in ways that are vital to the meaning of the sentence:

> If you don't know how to cook, all the food in the refrigerator is of no use at all.   *student paper*

Examine the last sentence more closely. Picture it without the comma, in fact the way it was written originally by its author:

> If you don't know how to cook all the food in the refrigerator is of no use at all.

Do you see how the sentence is very confusing without the comma? You would read it as telling about cooking "all the food in the refrigerator," and only a puzzled rereading enables you to sort out the true meaning. This example should eliminate once and for all the idea that commas and other forms of punctuation are not important. However unintentional his mistake may have been, the author of that sentence misled his reader by omitting the comma.

So punctuation marks like commas and periods help readers by showing natural pauses and by clarifying meaning. Sometimes, too, they allow the writer to make distinctions that cannot be made in speech—the distinction, for example, between plural nouns *(cats)* and singular or plural possessive nouns *(cat's, cats')*. Punctuation marks and italics can be grouped together as examples of what we call *conventions,* the subject of this chapter.

Conventions are quite simply customs. In other words they are agreed-upon ways of doing things, and they succeed precisely because everybody agrees they mean one certain thing and not another. For example, in our country the custom is to greet a friend with a handshake. But in Eastern Europe you must greet a friend with nothing less than the traditional hug that the Russians call the *obyátiye.* Neither the handshake nor the *obyátiye* is "better"; both are simply the custom for their own part of the world.

In language the conventions are just as arbitrary—and just as necessary. For example, there is no special reason why sentences have to end with a dot we call a period. Instead we could use an *x* or maybe a slash or any one of a hundred other marks. All of these other marks are just as logical or illogical as the dot. But the English language among others has the custom or the convention of the period dot, and we must accept this custom if we wish to be understood.

First this chapter takes up those conventions that consist of marks within or near words that help us organize those words and see their relationship to other words. In short, Part A discusses punctuation. In the second part of the chapter we examine alternative ways of representing words, alternatives like italics, abbreviation, and capitalization.

A note on how to use the chapter. The early sections of each part, such as A1–A3 and B1, discuss conventions that often allow a writer some freedom and flexibility. Unlike question marks, for example, which are always used in certain prescribed ways, these devices—commas, semicolons, dashes, italics—can sometimes be an opportunity for choice and therefore a part of your style. Even if your writing is generally free of punctuation errors, you should find this material helpful in making you a more sophisticated and versatile writer.

The conventions that do not allow much flexibility are treated in the remainder of the chapter. A4–A7 and B2–B3 are designed to help you with specific problems. Probably you will want to use them when you are in doubt about how to punctuate a particular passage or when an instructor calls your attention to a particular error in one of your papers.

A. PUNCTUATION

The difficulty in life is the choice.
George Moore

Punctuation is perhaps the most common category of errors in student writing. Usually such errors are signaled by red circles and by symbols like *punc, pn* or *p,* or perhaps by silent correction of the offending mark. Often these corrections are met with a helpless shrug—after all, what is a comma here or there anyway? Such a reaction is natural although shortsighted. As we saw a page or two ago, proper punctuation is sometimes vital to the clarity of a sentence, because without it writers risk being misunderstood. They also court the irritation of their readers, because many people equate correctness in punctuation with maturity in writing style.

Yet in many situations the presence or absence of a certain punctuation mark *is* a matter of free choice. In these cases (and these cases only), if you shrug your shoulders when someone recommends a change, your reaction might be a proper one. This section tries to show you the difference; in other words, it explains which punctuation customs are never broken, which ones are sometimes broken, and which ones are simply matters of taste. Learning to punctuate effectively is not hard—it just requires a little patience and attention to detail.

Furthermore if you can understand *why* these conventions exist in the form they do, you will find it much easier to observe them. Most punctuation is based on common sense, not mystery. This section stresses the common-sense basis for punctuation customs, and it combines this emphasis with discussions of how and why writers are sometimes led astray. With this information, punctuation ought not be a mystery to you.

A1. Commas

In the introduction to this chapter I pointed out how commas are used for clarity and for reflecting natural speech rhythm. Both of these reasons are important. Sometimes the presence of a comma is justified by one, sometimes by the other, sometimes by both. Neither reason alone is sufficient to explain all commas. In the following sentence, for example, the natural pace of speech would not allow for much of a pause, yet the commas are necessary:

December 7, 1941, is the date of the attack on Pearl Harbor.

The commas allow the reader to see the relationships within the series of numbers. In other sentences commas are not needed for clarity, but they do give the reader a helpful pause:

We allow time for talking about general writing problems or about selections from a reader, but the focus is always on the student's evolving essay. *journal article*

So both principles are necessary: we insert commas to make sentences clearer and/or to show the pauses of speech. Much of the time these principles coincide. A bit later on I will show you some cases where they conflict or where they give no sure guidance. First, however, we should consider the places where everyone agrees that commas are necessary.

Perhaps the most familiar use of the comma is to **separate items in a series,** if the series consists of three or more things. These items can be nouns, adjectives, or adverbs:

Joyce comes closest, but the strongest influences are out of the past—the Bible**,** Marlowe**,** Blake**,** Shakespeare. *William Styron*

Symbols**,** myths**,** and legends are just as important to us as they are to primitive man. *journal article*

Such an ill-considered**,** hasty**,** and dispiriting view of life must cause her immense misery. *student paper*

He talks quickly**,** confidently**,** eagerly. *student paper*

The items in the series need not be single words. We punctuate phrases and clauses the same way so long as they form a series:

The alley was littered with boxes of garbage**,** plastic bags of leaves**,** and a scattering of abandoned toys. *student paper*

Why do you always demand to know what I am doing**,** where I am going**,** or how I will get there? *letter*

He was entirely rid of his nervous misgivings**,** of his forced aggressiveness**,** of the imperative desire to show himself different from his surroundings. *Willa Cather*

The only exception occurs when the items themselves have much internal punctuation and semicolons are therefore required (see pp. 381–382).

One caution: the most common mistake students make when they punctuate items in a series is to put an extra comma after the last item in the series:

Nixon, Humphrey, and Wallace, were the presidential candidates in the 1968 election.

This writer was accustomed to following each item in a series with a comma, so he extended the principle to the last item too and put a comma after "Wallace." Such a mistake is understandable because it is based on a valuable principle. But the last item should always run directly into the words that follow, and therefore the comma after "Wallace" must be eliminated.

A second required use of the comma is to **mark off free modifiers.** A free modifier (also called a nonrestrictive modifier) is like the short clause "who owned a harness repair shop" in the following sentence:

> When she was twenty-two years old her father, who owned a harness repair shop, died suddenly.   *Sherwood Anderson*

Such modifiers can be cut from the sentence without affecting the meaning of the words they modify. In this case, the meaning of "father" would not change even if the modifying clause were left out. Bound (or restrictive) modifiers, on the other hand, directly affect the meaning of the words they modify:

> The people who had been waiting stood up with their mouths open.   *Frank O'Connor*

The clause "who had been waiting" explains *which* "people"; in other words, it is tied, or "bound," to "people." If the clause were to be left out, the meaning of the sentence would be markedly different:

> The people, who had been waiting, stood up with their mouths open.

The principle here is simple: free modifiers are separated from the rest of the sentence by commas; bound modifiers are not. Free modifiers can include words, phrases, and clauses:

> My father, angry, shouted into the phone.   *student paper*   [words]
>
> Here and there a piece of timber, stuck upright, resembled a post.   *Joseph Conrad*   [phrase]
>
> What if his search, which had been so thorough and so painstaking, was now about to pay off?   *student paper*   [clause]

Free modifiers are set apart by commas preceding them and commas following them, unless of course the modifier comes at the end of the sentence:

The man gave a kind of twisted grin, showing where the teeth had been knocked out above the new scar.   *Robert Penn Warren*

Bound modifiers on the other hand are not marked off by commas:

The waves which come at high tide are even more formidable.   *student paper*

And saddest of all is the tarnish that has appeared on the American sense of history.   *Jan Morris*

The two clauses "which come at high tide" and "that has appeared on the American sense of history" both modify nouns. Because they are bound to "waves" and "tarnish," because they explain which "waves" and which "tarnish" are meant, no commas are possible.

The reason for making a distinction between free and bound modifiers becomes clear if you compare the following two versions of the same sentence:

The newspaper, which came late Friday afternoon, had a small death notice on the obituary page.

The newspaper which came late Friday afternoon had a small death notice on the obituary page.

The first sentence marks off the clause by commas and therefore makes it a free modifier. The second sentence, however, uses the clause to specify *which* newspaper—the one that came late Friday afternoon, not some other one. The clause is now bound— bound, in this case, to "newspaper." Do you see the difference in meaning between the two sentences? Do you also see that this difference is conveyed by the presence or absence of the commas? And if you read the two sentences aloud, can you "hear" the commas in the version with the free modifier?

This distinction is not an easy one. Student writers sometimes err by putting in commas where they should not:

Two policemen came to our school and the one, who did most of the talking, asked for permission to interview me.

The writer clearly wanted the clause "who did most of the talking" to distinguish one policeman from the other—the one who talked more rather than the one who talked less. But the com-

mas set off the clause as a free modifier, so the policeman remains unspecified.

Similarly, commas are often left out at times when their presence is essential, as in this example:

> We sent a petition to the provost who could not ignore it.   *student
> newspaper*

Of course this writer was thinking of only one provost—*the*
provost—when she phrased the sentence. But the absence of a
comma after "provost" makes the clause that follows a bound
clause, as if it were singling out this provost from all other
provosts (the one "who could not ignore it," versus the ones,
presumably, who could). That is not what the author means. So
the comma is necessary in order to make the final clause a free
modifier and eliminate the misreading.

Another convention about the comma is that it can **set off
direct quotations.** If a quotation opens a sentence, put a comma
at the end of it, just before the quotation marks:

> "I want to write a letter to Mom**,**" Chris says.   *Robert Pirsig*

But the comma is omitted if the quotation ends with a question
mark or exclamation mark:

> "Can you imagine anything more absurd?" she cried to a friend.
> *E. M. Forster*

If the quotation ends the sentence, put a comma after the
word that precedes it:

> Then he looked at me and said**,** "I don't want to start trou-
> ble."   *Philip Roth*

Again there is one exception. When the quotation and the words
ahead of it must go together to make a complete sentence, the
comma is left out:

> Culler tells with an abundance of fresh documentation the story "of
> Newman's education, of his work as the educator of others, and of
> his educational thinking as expressed in the *Idea of a Univer-
> sity.*"   *Martin Svaglic*

If only Arthur had not put in that fatal comma. . . .

Here no comma precedes the quotation, because it is not an independent statement. Instead the quotation completes the sentence begun with the words before it.

Finally, if the quotation is interrupted by other words, two commas are needed. One follows the first part of the quotation, just before the quotation marks; the other follows the inserted words:

> "Well, bright boy," Max said, looking into the mirror, "why don't you say something?" *Ernest Hemingway*

Note that "why" is not capitalized in the example above. The reason is that the second part of the quotation simply continues the sentence begun in the first part.

Another required use of the comma is to **organize dates, addresses, and numbers.** These customs are probably quite familiar to you. Earlier we saw how a comma helps the reader distinguish the year from the date of the month: "December 7, 1941, is the date. . . ." In addresses commas usually separate the street from the city, the city from the state, and the state from the remainder of the sentence:

> Send 25¢ and one boxtop to 330 West Fortieth Street, New York, New York, and be sure to include a return envelope. *advertisement*

We group numbers into convenient three-digit units by commas:

> The population of Chattanooga is 179,082. *brochure*

> An operating budget of $58,786,225 is projected for fiscal 1979. *business report*

Commas are also used to **set off informal letter salutations**, as to friends and relatives:

> Dear Ned,   Dear Grandma,

And, finally, commas can **separate abbreviations following a proper noun from the noun itself**:

> Xerox, Inc., recently announced the acquisition of a new subsidiary. *newspaper item*

> Rita Bilodeau, Ph.D., has resigned from her post as director of student services. *newsletter*

We have been discussing uses of the comma that are standard, cases where everyone would agree that commas are necessary for clarity. It should be pointed out here that a comma should be used in any case where a sentence might not be clear without it; look, for example, at this defense of conservatism by the poet Alexander Pope:

Whatever is, is right.

Without the comma, the sentence might be puzzling. Here are other examples:

CONFUSING: Then I was really worried for Debra rarely stayed at the library beyond 10:30.   *student paper*

REVISION: Then I was really worried, for Debra rarely stayed at the library beyond 10:30.

CONFUSING: If I am allowed to predict the future of commodity brokering looks bright.   *pamphlet*

REVISION: If I am allowed to predict, the future of commodity brokering looks bright.

The reader is tempted to understand the original sentences as saying the writer was "worried for Debra" or was going to "predict the future." In both examples a comma prevents such a misreading.

In some cases, though, commas are not obligatory— sometimes they are a matter of choice. Let's move on to these other cases.

Commas can **mark off an introductory word, phrase, or clause**. Here are several examples from professional writing:

Nevertheless, it's delightful to be back.   *Anthony Burgess*

Of earthly possessions, Isadora had little enough to leave.   *Janet Flanner*

As I look back upon my own conception of Esau, he is not nearly as clear and definite a personality as Jacob.   *W. E. B. DuBois*

However, if these introductory words or word groups are short enough, some writers prefer not to separate them from the rest of the sentence by a comma. These examples are also drawn from professional writing:

> Happily we discover that sermons which seriously try to interpret that supreme event possess a moving power out of proportion to the wisdom of their content.   *William Sloane Coffin*

> A few days later a hunting party of Cheyennes sighted a column of bluecoats camped for the night in the valley of the Rosebud.   *Dee Brown*

> If this punishment is right the criminals must have a lot of property.   *Clarence Darrow*

Note how commas are not used after the opening words, phrases, and clauses; there is no comma after "Happily . . . ," "A few days later . . . ," or "If this punishment is right. . . ." When you are in doubt about whether to use a comma, the best bet is to let your ear be the guide. Read aloud the sentence in question. Do you "hear" a comma, in other words do you hear a slight pause between the introductory words and the remainder of the sentence? If so, insert the comma; if not, leave it out. Before leaving the comma out, however, make sure the sentence will not be confusing without it. Remember the example quoted earlier:

> If you don't know how to cook all the food in the refrigerator is of no use at all.

The introductory clause has only seven words, but a comma after "cook" is necessary to prevent misunderstanding.

Another use of the comma is quite analogous: to **separate parenthetical expressions**. Normally if a group of related words has been taken from its customary position in the word order of a sentence and put into another position, that new position is signaled by commas before and after:

> The nineteenth century was**,** for the intellectuals of Western Europe**,** a comfortable period exuding confidence and optimism.   *E. H. Carr*

The phrase "for the intellectuals of Western Europe" appears between the verb "was" and its complement "a period"—hardly the usual place. Ordinarily the phrase would appear at the beginning, as an introductory phrase, and the verb and complement would be joined ("was a period"). Because of this "displacement" the phrase is set off by commas. Similarly the phrase "like you" in the following sentence would normally come at the end, after "spirit":

> Remember, he is not**,** like you**,** a pure spirit.   *C. S. Lewis*

The earlier position requires a pair of commas. Parenthetical expressions are those that do not have a necessary part in the structure of the sentence—they could be put within parentheses and the sentence would still be complete and understandable. They resemble free modifiers, except unlike modifiers they are not tied to specific words in the sentence. Such parenthetical expressions are also set off by commas before and after:

> Many laughed then**,** as we may be tempted to do**,** at all those absolute physicians of the soul. . . .   *George Santayana*

> That method**,** I think**,** is a recipe for disaster on a scale unimaginable only a decade ago.   *political pamphlet*

The clauses "as we may be tempted to do" and "I think" are parenthetical, hence the commas.

Sometimes, however, parenthetical expressions are short enough to allow the author to omit the commas:

> I liked playing football and I knew that by this time I'd have trouble finding another school that would take me.   *Don DeLillo*

The phrase "by this time" is not isolated by commas, most probably because the author realized that commas would slow down the reader too much.

How do you know when parenthetical expressions are short enough so the commas can be eliminated? Again the answer is "by ear." If you sense a pause when you read a sentence aloud, put in a comma; if not, leave it out. (Once again you should make sure that leaving out the commas will not make the sentence confusing.)

Whatever your choice, however, be consistent. Parenthetical expressions within a sentence are either set off by *two* commas or by *none*. The author of the following sentence felt the tension between two or none, but she resolved it in the wrong way by using only one:

> Society for Blake, has stifled man's spirit and actions.

The author needs to add a comma before "for" or remove the one after "Blake."

Another important but variable use of the comma is to **separate the independent clauses of a compound sentence.** Remember that compound sentences have two main clauses, each of which could stand by itself as a sentence. When two main clauses are joined into one sentence by a conjunction like *and,* *but,* or *yet,* a comma before the conjunction helps the reader keep the clauses distinct:

> He did not interfere with the stars, and he did not win over all the greenhorns. *Robert Darnton*

> Half a man's life is devoted to what he calls improvements, yet the original had some quality which is lost in the process. *E. B. White*

Simple enough so far. The variation in punctuation again comes with variation in length. If the independent clauses are reasonably short, the comma can be left out:

> Seventh graders were not tested but the sixth and eighth graders were. *school newsletter*

At the other extreme, two unusually long independent clauses are often separated by a semicolon rather than a comma, simply because the reader welcomes the "heavier" pause that the semicolon provides:

> Form for the poet is the bit and the bridle without which (unless you are an acrobat) you cannot ride your horse; but for the writer of prose it is the chassis without which your car does not exist. *W. Somerset Maugham*

This recommendation of the semicolon becomes almost a requirement if the independent clauses are themselves punctuated by several other commas:

> After all, we are only bound to play our own parts, and do our own share of the lifting; and as in no case that share can be great, so in all cases it is called for, it is necessary. *William Morris*

The semicolon after "lifting" allows the reader to separate the two parts of the compound sentence, because it contrasts with the two commas that precede it and the two that follow.

Please note that the comma appears when the independent clauses are joined by a conjunction. If there is no conjunction, a semicolon must be used instead:

> Bull in pure form is rare; there is usually some contamination by data. *William G. Perry*

Alternatively, of course, the two clauses could be converted into separate sentences:

> Bull in pure form is rare. There is usually some contamination by data.

Often student writers are unaware of this important difference, and the result is a **comma splice**—in other words, two independent clauses are "spliced" by a comma even though no conjunction introduces the second clause. These are examples from student papers:

> Beyond the forests are steep cliffs, at the bottom of the cliffs are huge, moss-covered boulders.

> The key to understanding this concept lies in the word *myth*, it carries an elusive meaning.

> The street was typical of the neighborhood, it was deserted by day but vibrant and pulsing at night, especially Saturday night.

In each case the first independent clause is not followed by a conjunction (i.e., no conjunction after "cliffs," "*myth*," and "neighborhood," respectively). Therefore the comma is not the best form of punctuation. Such comma splices, also called run-on sentences, can be eliminated in a number of ways:

1. Add a conjunction.

> Beyond the forests are steep cliffs, **and** at the bottom of the cliffs are huge, moss-covered boulders.

2. Use a semicolon.

> The key to understanding this concept lies in the word *myth*; it carries an elusive meaning.

3. Divide the material into separate sentences.

> The street was typical of the neighborhood. It was deserted by day but vibrant and pulsing at night, especially Saturday night.

Once more, however, I should note an exception. The tendency in modern prose is to let very short independent clauses be joined by a comma even if no conjunction is present:

> She wants to be a part of all this, she wants to do this thing.
> *Tom Wolfe*

> The bell rang, I started for the door.   *student paper*

> . . . I had a delightful day. In the morning I worked on a
> line in my latest play, and I ended up putting in a comma.
> Then I had lunch, and in the afternoon I thought about that
> line some more. I finished by taking the comma out.
>   *attributed to Oscar Wilde*

Probably by now you are accustomed to my saying there are
"variations" and "exceptions." You realize that some conventions for the comma are inviolable rules, some depend on circumstances, and some depend on taste. Let's study a sentence
that shows examples of each:

> Of course, it doesn't, and nobody really expects it to, but even so I
> hardly supposed that Hitting Away would gallop off with the Withers
> Stakes, as he did at Aqueduct last Saturday.   *New Yorker*

The sentence as punctuated by its author contains four commas.
One comma, the last one, is required by the *rule* that all free
modifiers must be marked off this way. Another comma, the
third one, is required by *circumstance:* it precedes a conjunction
("but") that joins two independent clauses, and these clauses
are long enough to make the comma indispensable. The two
earlier commas, however, are present because of the author's
taste. The first of them marks off an introductory phrase ("Of
course . . .), but the phrase is short enough so that the comma
could be left out. The second comma is like the third in the way
it precedes a conjunction ("and") joining two independent
clauses, but the two clauses are so brief that punctuation might
not be necessary. Note also that the author chose *not* to insert
commas around the phrase "even so," although technically he
or she could have.

In short, there are no less than *eight* ways to punctuate this
sentence, each of them equally "correct"! Besides the original,
here are the seven legitimate alternatives:

(1) Of course, it doesn't, and nobody really expects it to, but, even
    so, I hardly supposed that Hitting Away would gallop off with
    the Withers Stakes, as he did at Aqueduct last Saturday.

(2) Of course it doesn't, and nobody really expects it to, but even so I
    hardly supposed that Hitting Away would gallop off with the
    Withers Stakes, as he did at Aqueduct last Saturday.

(3) Of course, it doesn't and nobody really expects it to, but even so I hardly supposed that Hitting Away would gallop off with the Withers Stakes, as he did at Aqueduct last Saturday.

(4) Of course it doesn't and nobody really expects it to, but even so I hardly supposed that Hitting Away would gallop off with the Withers Stakes, as he did at Aqueduct last Saturday.

(5) Of course it doesn't, and nobody really expects it to, but, even so, I hardly supposed that Hitting Away would gallop off with the Withers Stakes, as he did at Aqueduct last Saturday.

(6) Of course, it doesn't and nobody really expects it to, but, even so, I hardly supposed that Hitting Away would gallop off with the Withers Stakes, as he did at Aqueduct last Saturday.

(7) Of course it doesn't and nobody really expects it to, but, even so, I hardly supposed that Hitting Away would gallop off with the Withers Stakes, as he did at Aqueduct last Saturday.

Which ones do I prefer? Possibly the second or the fourth. Your taste, however, might differ from mine, just as the author's did.

Right now you might be tempted to shrug your shoulders and wonder how you could ever understand the use of commas. Furthermore you may be wondering if the comma errors marked on your papers by your instructor are really errors at all. Since the use of commas is often a matter of taste, why should his or her taste supplant yours?

Let's address the second issue first. True, some occasions for using the comma are matters of taste. But most are not. The majority of commas are determined by rules or by circumstances rather than by taste, as a careful reading of almost any prose passage will show. So the chances are very good that the problem noted by your instructor is a situation where the presence or absence of a comma is not a matter of free choice at all. And even if your problem *is* one of those cases where taste comes into play, remember that taste is partly a product of experience. Since your instructor's experience is greater than yours, weigh his or her suggestion carefully, although the final decision rests with you.

As to the first issue, whether or not the proper use of commas can ever be learned, don't be discouraged. It's all much simpler than it seems. In fact the material here probably can be summed up in two suggestions that cover almost every circumstance:

1. Make sure you know the situations where commas are always required (items in a series, free modifiers, direct quotations, dates, addresses, numbers, abbreviations following names).

2. For cases where circumstance or taste governs the comma, your ear can be your guide. Even in those circumstances where a comma is absolutely necessary, such as with long introductory phrases, long parenthetical expressions, or long independent clauses joined by a conjunction, you will almost invariably hear a slight pause when you read the sentence aloud. That pause is your clue to put in the comma, just as it is a clue in matters of taste as well.

A2. Semicolons and Colons

While semicolons and colons are similar in name and appearance, they serve quite different purposes, as this section will show.

We have already anticipated most of the uses of the **semicolon** when we discussed commas. Recall that a semicolon can **separate two independent clauses when they are not joined by a conjunction:**

> She stood in a frozen attitude; her breath was released in a sigh.   *Tennessee Williams*

Even if a conjunction is present, however, you might still want to use a semicolon to join especially long independent clauses. For example:

> It was truly a beautiful thought to have assumed Bartleby's departure; but, after all, that assumption was simply my own and none of Bartleby's.   *Herman Melville*

Despite the fact that the second independent clause began with the conjunction "but," Melville preceded it by a semicolon because both clauses are fairly long. Note that this was a matter of choice—Melville would not have been "wrong" had he decided to use a comma, although the semicolon is perhaps a wiser choice because it creates a more definite separation of the clauses.

[A] semicolon in its right place is a thing of beauty. . . .
C. Colwell and J. Knox

Also, semicolons are necessary to **mark off long items in a series, especially when those items have internal punctuation.** The reasoning here is simple. The length of these items makes it desirable to give readers a greater "catch-your-breath" pause between each item. Furthermore, if the items in the series have commas within them, these commas could not be distinguished easily from the commas that would separate the items themselves. Semicolons can solve both problems:

> It was supposed and taught that there had been, quite concretely, a creation of the world in seven days by a god known only to the Jews; that somewhere on this broad new earth there had been a Garden of Eden containing a serpent that could talk; that the first woman, Eve, was formed from the first man's rib, and that the wicked serpent told her of the marvelous properties of the fruits of a certain tree of which God had forbidden the couple to eat; and that, as a consequence of their having eaten of that fruit, there followed a "Fall" of all mankind, death came into the world, and the couple was driven forth from the garden. *Joseph Campbell, Myths to Live By*

The most common misuse of the semicolon is putting it between clauses when one of the two clauses is not fully independent. *When a semicolon joins two clauses, both clauses should be capable of being complete sentences.* If a fragment appears in either position, some other kind of punctuation is needed. Here are two examples from student papers, both of which are incorrect:

> Since the sterno cans seemed to be unobtainable; the gang set out to find another method of keeping warm.

> After that, I understood better why Chris was my parents' favorite; his vulnerability.

In the first example, the words to the left of the semicolon form a dependent clause (note how they begin with the subordinating conjunction "since . . ."). They do not form a complete sentence. A comma must replace the semicolon, allowing the dependent clause to link up with the independent clause ("the gang . . ."). In the second example, the writer probably mistook a semicolon for a colon. "His vulnerability" is not a sentence; it acts as an appositive and should therefore be set off by a colon, as we'll see shortly in the discussion of the colon.

In the preceding paragraph I offer rather conservative advice. Some modern writers are abandoning this insistence on no fragments either side of the semicolon, especially when the fragment contains an understood subject and verb. Hunter Thompson, for example:

> Worse, I needed two sets; one for myself and another for Ralph Steadman, the English illustrator who was coming from London to do some Derby drawings.

Although the words to the right of the semicolon do not form a complete sentence, Thompson trusts us to understand "I needed" as the implied subject and verb: "[I needed] one for myself and one for Ralph Steadman. . . ." However, since many readers do not approve of using semicolons this way, I'd advise you to avoid this use of them.

As for **colons,** we just noted their principal use: to **mark off appositive explanations and constructions.** (The preceding sentence is our first example!) An appositive adds to or explains a word or word group that precedes it. You can understand this easier by looking at an example:

> The ego develops canny mechanisms for dealing with the threat of id impulses: denial, projection, and the rest.   *Jerome Bruner*

Here "denial, projection, and the rest" is an appositive construction that explains the noun "impulses." The student sentence from the previous page would, if punctuated correctly, offer another example of an appositive:

> After that, I understood better why Chris was my parents' favorite: his vulnerability.

(When an appositive appears earlier in a sentence, it is usually marked off by commas as a free modifier: *The reason Chris was my parents' favorite, his vulnerability, suddenly dawned on me.*)

Colons can precede any explanation or elaboration of what was said in the first part of a sentence:

> Now, it is clear that the decline of a language must ultimately have political and economic causes: it is not due simply to the bad influences of this or that individual writer.   *George Orwell*

Often the explanation takes the form of a list or a series:

> In the manifest story the events happen in space and time: first, going into the ship's belly; then, falling asleep; then, being thrown into the ocean; then, being swallowed by the fish.   *Erich Fromm*

Notice, by the way, that because his list of events is a long one and because each item has a comma within it, Fromm chooses to separate the items by semicolons rather than commas.

The other important use of the colon is to **precede a direct quotation:**

> This inspired her to say: "But I've made a start; I've been pulling out things of value or things I want."   *Elizabeth Bowen*

> He eyed me, then snarled: "You don't look so smart after all!"   *student paper*

In sentences like these the colon is an alternative to a comma (see pp. 370–372). If the opening clause is a standard one, like *he said* or *she asked*, most writers will stick with the comma. When the opening clause is more unusual, as in the two examples above, some writers now prefer the colon, although of course the comma is still acceptable.

Colons also help to **organize numbers, Bible citations, book titles, and formal letter salutations:**

> 9: 35 P.M.
>
> Deuteronomy 2: 14–15
>
> James A. Ogilvy's *Many Dimensional Man: Decentralizing Self, Society, and the Sacred*
>
> Dear Ms. Connell:

A3. Hyphens and Dashes

Like colons and semicolons, the hyphen (-) and dash (—) are similar in appearance. But the functions of the two are quite different.

Hyphens are a form of internal punctuation; in other words, they occur *within* a word, like apostrophes do, and therefore might even be considered an aspect of spelling. Hyphens **join the separate parts of compound words.** These compound words include:

1. compound nouns, where two or more words are linked to
   form one noun

   mop‑up   speed‑reading
   city‑state   weigh‑in
   self‑interest   clerk‑typist
   get‑together

2. compound adjectives, where two or more words join to work
   as an adjective

   a top‑to‑bottom appraisal   cradle‑to‑grave security
   death‑dealing   slap‑happy
   problem‑solving techniques   up‑to‑date technology

3. and compound numbers

   forty‑eight   seventy‑seventh   nine‑tenths

The difficult question for most writers is whether to hyphenate certain word groups. Compound numbers offer no
problem—they are always hyphenated. Compound nouns are a
little harder. Sometimes they have hyphens (for example,
mop-up or *city-state*); sometimes they don't (for example, *card
catalog*). What principle can explain why *crossbeam* is one word,
cross-examination is a hyphenated compound, and *cross section* is
two separate words? Your dictionary is the best help: look up the
word in question and hyphenate or not as the dictionary shows.
If the compound does not appear in the dictionary, keep the two
words separate (i.e., don't use the hyphen to make a compound).

> The hyphen is being done away with—indefensibly,
> ruthlessly . . . (and) if the hyphen goes, so does the very
> conception of the structure of English.
>
> *Charlton Ogburn*

Compound adjectives are the most troublesome of all. Sometimes your dictionary can help. If the word isn't listed there,
your safest bet is writing the word as a hyphenated compound.
In such circumstances writing the unified word is probably
wrong, because all single words should appear in the dictionary
and this one doesn't. The other alternative, preserving the separate words, is usually—although not always—a more awkward

choice. So the percentages favor the hyphenated compound form. Notice that in many cases words that are hyphenated as compound adjectives are not hyphenated when used as nouns. Compare:

> a cause-and-effect relationship
> the cause and effect of rising prices
>
> hand-to-mouth existence
> living from hand to mouth

Another use of hyphens is to **mark off prefixes in certain words.** Some prefixes are always separated from the base word by a hyphen:

> ex-president   all-American   self-determination

Most, however, are separated only under special circumstances:

1. when the base word is capitalized

   > pro-Castro   non-Asian   ultra-Marxist

2. when the hyphen distinguishes between two words that are written alike but mean quite different things

   > to re-cover (furniture) vs. to recover (from an illness)
   >
   > a co-op (store) vs. a coop (for chickens)

3. in some cases when the last letter of the prefix and the first letter of the base word are the same.

   > anti-intellectual   semi-independent   non-network

Hyphens are also used to **divide a word into syllables.** Sometimes we must hyphenate a word because only part of it can appear at the end of one typed line and the remainder of the word must appear at the start of the next line. In such cases the word should be divided whenever the syllables divide (a dictionary can help if the syllable division is not obvious to you). For example, the word *indulgent* can be hyphenated two ways: *in-/dulgent* or *indul-/gent*. I should offer two cautions, however. Don't hyphenate short words—my seventh-grade teacher said "words of six letters or less." And don't separate compound words anywhere else but at the hyphens they already have (i.e., *mother-/in-law* or *mother-in-/law* but not *mo-/ther-in-law*).

Dashes are often used as an alternative to some other form of punctuation. In fact, no less than five other punctuation marks can be replaced by a dash:

> Hands shaking, dying for a cigarette, he found the pants—a size small but still a fit.   *Richard Goldstein* [alternative to comma]

> During the dinner party, Dick, who consulted a map, announced that Sweetwater was a hundred or more miles west of the route he was driving—the route that would take him across New Mexico and Arizona to Nevada—to Las Vegas.   *Truman Capote* [alternative to parentheses]

> It had been a long few days and I had scrutinized too many details of four vicious killings and something in my mind flailed out now— Jesus Simpson, murderer, cold-blooded killer, compassionate, sensitive, sentimental.   *Joe Eszterhas* [alternative to colon]

> Friday the long awaited happened—M's battalion killed somebody, at last.   *John Sack* [alternative to semicolon]

> His name was Mayhew, it was written out in enormous red letters across the front of his helmet: MAYHEW—You'd better believe it!   *Michael Herr* [alternative to period]

When do you use a dash instead of one of these other punctuation marks? There are no set rules. Sometimes you will want to use a dash for the sake of variety. Sometimes a dash helps because you have already used its alternative (for example, parentheses) earlier in the sentence and can't use it again—like in *this* sentence! And sometimes a writer relies on dashes just because he or she likes them. Norman Mailer, for example, can't get through a paragraph without several dashes, often as many as ten or twelve.

One suggestion I would make is to avoid an excessive number of dashes, because they might give a breathless sort of tone to your writing. This suggestion applies with special force to the more formal writing situations, like research papers, business letters, speeches, or resumés.

A4. Periods and Other End Punctuation

A **period** is the written representation of the falling inflection we hear at the end of every declarative sentence. Ordinarily you are never puzzled about using periods to **end sentences or legitimate sentence fragments:**

I'd like to hear more about Eckankar.

Me, too.

However you should note one unusual case. Sometimes a writer wishes to make a request, but for the sake of politeness he or she poses the request as a question. In such cases the word order is the same as the word order for a question, but no "answer" is expected. Here is an example:

> Would you please send me a copy of your recent article on nutrition. *letter*

A period is the best end punctuation for this polite request, despite the "would-you-send" word order.

The period, by the way, has other uses besides ending sentences. It can **separate numbers written as decimals**:

> 7.286 $4.59   9.6%   12.36 oz.

It can **end abbreviations**:

> Mr.   Ms.   Mrs.   Ph.D.   N.Y.   ibid.   A.M.

A series of three periods form what is called an **ellipsis,** which has a number of uses. One is to **show that words have been deleted from a quotation**:

> Starting as an apprentice, Leyland . . . was able to take over the company by the age of thirty.   *book preface*

Usually an ellipsis appears within a quoted sentence, as in the example above. Sometimes, however, the words to be left out occur at the end of the quoted sentence. Then the ellipsis follows the period that signals the end of the sentence, so the result is *four* spaced dots, three for the ellipsis and one for the period:

> Special procedures govern registration for these classes. . . .
> *college form*

Also the ellipsis can show that a thought has been interrupted or broken off:

> Maybe I should . . . and yet, the more I think of it, I'm convinced I shouldn't.   *letter*

Two other marks besides periods can punctuate the end of a sentence. The first is the **exclamation point,** which gives special

emphasis to a sentence. Here is a brief passage by the writer
Thomas Merton:

> Sermon to the birds: "Esteemed friends, birds of noble lineage, I
> have no message to you except this: be what you are: be *birds.* Thus
> you will be your own sermon to yourselves!"
> Reply: "Even this is one sermon too many!"

Merton's passage illustrates another fact about exclamation
points—they are more common in dialogue than in other forms
of writing.

Modern prose style is very sparing in its use of exclamatory
sentences. If a writer uses such sentences too often, the reader
may become annoyed because he or she thinks the writer is
relying too much on an artificial way of getting attention. This is
the kind of writing I mean:

> The old drunk was just one of my experiences! Since I travel on the
> bus quite frequently, I get to see some pretty weird people some-
> times! I am just grateful there are plenty of sane people left!

The student who wrote this paragraph wanted these concluding
sentences of her paper to be lively and dramatic. Unfortunately
she did not choose the most effective means. Exclamation marks
galvanize the reader like a mild electric shock. If you administer
these shocks too often, the reader gets accustomed to them and
finally sees them only as an annoyance.

Too many exclamation marks might even make your writing
read like Queen Victoria's letters, such as this one to her daughter:

> My poor, dear darling child!
> How dreadfully vexed, worried, and fidgety I am at this untoward
> sprain I can't tell you! How could you do it? I am sure you had too
> high-heeled boots! I am haunted with your lying in a stuffy room in
> that dreadful old Schloss—without fresh air and alas! naturally
> without exercise and am beside myself. Only do take care and let
> some fresh air into your room and do get yourself carried out at least
> to get air!

That kind of fervor overstays its welcome.

The other alternative end punctuation is the **question mark.**
Its most common use, of course, is for the direct question:

Yet what do we live for, except to live**?** *D. H. Lawrence*

How are we to bring order into this multitudinous chaos and so get the deepest and widest pleasure from what we read**?** *Virginia Woolf*

Questions are known by their inverted word order. In other words, a direct question like *Will you go tonight?* has a word order different from the normal declarative sentence, which would read *You will go tonight.* (Indirect questions are treated differently—for example, *He asked if you are going tonight.*)

Sometimes a question is included as part of a regular declarative sentence:

And then—are you following me**?**—the two long pieces should be cut at least one inch shorter. *student paper*

"Should I water the geraniums**?**" she asked. *student paper*

Note that no comma follows the question mark in this example. Less frequently the question mark is used in a series:

How many of them do you want to sell**?** And for how much**?** *pamphlet*

Sometimes too it appears within parentheses, expressing the writer's doubt about a preceding fact:

Wordsworth was about thirty years old (**?**) when he and Coleridge published *Lyrical Ballads.* *examination answer*

A5. Quotation Marks

Quotation marks have a number of uses; one is to **set off a direct quotation**. Nearly everyone is aware of this use of double quotation marks:

As John Anderson says, **"**The psychic income of the job is far less than it once was.**"** *Sanford Ungar*

Student writers are more often confused by other issues, such as: Where do quotation marks go in relation to other punctuation marks? Which quoted passages begin with capital letters and which do not?

The most frequent question is whether quotation marks come before or after the comma or period. The answer is *after:*

> "If he gets his way," Spence declared, "we will have a new super-national community dominated by the multinational corporation." *Jeremiah Novak*

The closing quotation marks follow both the comma after "way" and the period after "corporation."

Colons and semicolons are different—the quotation marks come *before* them:

> Indeed, I am a compulsive reader, a "print nut"; if there is nothing around to read, I will study the labels on ketchup bottles. *S. M. Miller*

Exclamation and question marks depend on circumstance. If the quoted passage itself is a question or exclamation, the quotation marks come *after:*

> "There is a young man waiting for me?" he asked at the reception desk. *Mary Manning*

Suppose, however, the quoted passage is not itself an exclamation or question, but the entire sentence, which includes a quotation, does offer an exclamation or question. Then the quotation marks will appear *before* the end punctuation:

> How stupid I was to keep insisting on "my rights"! *student paper*

As for capital letters, the custom is simple. Begin all quotations that are complete sentences with one capital, just as you would any other sentence:

> "My boy," I say, "you and your friends are very shrewd." *Page Stegner*

The complete quoted sentence begins with "My boy," so "My" is capitalized. "You" is not capitalized, even though it is the first word of the second part of the quotation, because it is not the first word of the full quoted sentence.

Quoted phrases or clauses do not begin with capitals and are worked in as part of the sentence in which they appear:

> He spoke with gusto of a "strong, independent, aggressive" presidency—but for what? *Christopher Lydon*

If a quotation includes within it still another quotation, this second quotation is defined by single quotation marks:

> "I told [my mother] that I wrote *Monkey Business* and she ignored me. 'Marvelous remarks,' she said. 'How does [Groucho] think them up?' " *S. J. Perelman*

The single quotation marks are always inside the double ones.

All quotation marks, whether single or double, come in pairs. Occasionally a writer forgets to put in the concluding set, thereby puzzling his or her reader, as in this example from a student paper:

> My father always says, "Get a good education. He never went beyond the seventh grade, so he has a great reverence for schooling.

Because the writer neglected the closing quotation marks after "education," we at first think the second sentence is part of what the father "always says." Then, part way through, we realize this sentence is *about* the father and could not be spoken *by* him, so we backtrack and start the sentence again. This inconvenience would have been avoided had the writer checked her use of quotation marks during proofreading.

The only time quotation marks are not used in pairs is when a quoted passage is more than one paragraph long. In these cases each new paragraph opens with quotation marks, to show that the quotation continues, but no closing quotation marks appear until the very end, lest it seem as if the quotation were ending sooner than it really does:

> " . . . We went back to the hulk and reshipped our cargo.
> "Then, on a fine moonlight night, all the rats left the ship.
> "We had been infested with them. . . . " *Joseph Conrad*

There are no closing quotation marks after "cargo" or "ship" because the quotation continues in the next paragraph.

Quotation marks can also **designate certain titles.** Titles of short stories, magazine articles, songs, poems, essays, and shows are among those eligible:

> D. H. Lawrence's story "Market Day"
> Joan Didion's article "Why I Write"
> the hymn "Rock of Ages"
> T. S. Eliot's poem "The Wasteland"
> the tv show "Laverne and Shirley"

A writer can use quotation marks to **show that a word is being used in a special way.** In the following sentence, for example, the author intends the word "wonders" to be taken ironically rather than literally:

> Now people go there for the "wonders" and the wild mountain scenery.   *Anthony Brandt*

Slang words especially are often treated this way. But with slang, student writers are more likely to use quotation marks too often rather than too seldom. If you have good reason to use slang, don't apologize for it by unnecessary quotation marks. Apologize in this way only when you want to express disapproval of the words themselves. Compare these two student-written sentences:

WEAK: We had just started to put up the tent when the most "godawful" storm arose.

GOOD: I was amused by his complaint about how "heavy" the information was I had given him.

In the first, the author obviously intends "godawful" as the adjective that best describes the power of the storm. Consequently he would have been better off if he had either left out the apologetic quotation marks or chosen a different adjective. In the second sentence, by contrast, the author apparently does not approve of the word "heavy" as a synonym for *important*, and by the quotation marks she disassociates herself from what she considers weak slang.

A6. Apostrophes

Apostrophes, like hyphens, are examples of punctuation within a word. Probably no single mark is omitted more often than the poor apostrophe, especially when it is used with nouns to **show possession**. In most cases the apostrophe goes before a final *s:*

> the tenant's lease   the children's clothes   somebody's book
> Gail's purse   Denver's bus station

If the noun already ends with *s* (like most plurals), the apostrophe follows the *s:*

> old wives' tales   plumbers' rates   Delores' watch
> the hostess' dress

The purpose of the apostrophe in these cases is simple. It helps the reader distinguish between regular plurals (e.g., *two cars*), singular possessives *(the car's muffler)*, and plural possessives *(the cars' mufflers)*. Granted, we cannot "hear" the difference in these sentences if they are read aloud. But a simple apostrophe offers the reader a very real convenience.

Apostrophes are also familiar in contractions and other places where they help to **show that a letter or letters have been omitted**. For example, this sentence spoken by Huck Finn:

> Jim said the moon could *'a'* *laid* them; well, that looked kind of reasonable, so I didn't say nothing against it. . . . *Mark Twain*

"How many apostrophes in 'fo'c's'le'?"

Drawing by Dove; © 1935, 1963 The New Yorker Magazine, Inc.

The apostrophe in "didn't" shows where the *o* has been left out of *did not*. We use many contractions like this in writing, such as *I'll, I'm, can't, shouldn't, we'd, don't,* and *it's.* The apostrophes in Huck's "could 'a' laid them" are different. This is not a standard contraction. Rather it shows that certain letters are not heard in speech. The full sentence would read *could have laid them,* but Twain uses one apostrophe to replace the *h* and another to replace the *ve* in order to show us that in Huck's dialect these letters would not be pronounced.

Note also the use of the apostrophe to **form the plurals of certain letters, abbreviations, and words**:

the three R's   two *not*'s   ABC's   Ph.D.'s

A7. Parentheses, Brackets, the Slash

Parentheses are used to **enclose explanations or other incidental material.** The important criterion for deciding whether or not a group of words can be put within parentheses is this: can you leave the group of words out of the sentence and still have a complete sentence? If you can, parentheses might be appropriate, because the words are incidental—or "parenthetical"—to the sentence. If you cannot leave them out, avoid the parentheses. Here are some examples:

Columbia has just reissued some of the famous recordings (Album C-29; 8 ten-inch sides, $2.50).   *Otis Ferguson*

The trouble with *mother* and *father* of course is that they suggest authority (as well as love), and thus strike an undemocratic note in the family.   *Morton J. Cronin*

Every living thing (and perhaps many a dead one as well) pays heed to that call.   *Aldo Leopold*

The three main hypotheses regarding the first question are that the mark stands for (1) Advertising, (2) Advantage, and (3) Adventitious.   *Jacques Barzun*

Everything within the parentheses in these examples could be left out and the sentence would still be complete structurally. Note, by the way, that no other punctuation ever precedes an opening parenthesis, and that punctuation following a closing parenthesis (like the comma in the second example) goes outside the parenthesis. Of course the words within the parentheses can have their own internal punctuation, as in the first example. This internal punctuation can even include a period if the parenthetical remark is a full sentence:

> I can only assume that where R.S.V. differs in meaning from K.J.V., the translation has improved. **(**Considering the immense advances in archeology, philology, and other sciences since 1611, this is a reasonable assumption.**)** I am also willing. . . . *Dwight Macdonald*

An important fact about parentheses is that often they are a *choice*. The example sentence by Aldo Leopold, for instance, could also have been written with the parentheses left out or with the parentheses replaced by commas or dashes:

> Every living thing and perhaps many a dead one as well pays heed to that call.

> Every living thing, and perhaps many a dead one as well, pays heed to that call.

> Every living thing—and perhaps many a dead one as well—pays heed to that call.

If you read the four alternatives carefully, you will see that the difference is in the stress given to the phrase "and perhaps many a dead one as well." No punctuation gives the phrase least stress—the phrase becomes fully subordinated to the rest of the sentence. Parentheses give slightly greater stress but still subordinate it. Commas provide still more emphasis, and dashes the most. The ability to choose well among these alternative forms of punctuation is a valuable skill that enables a writer to fine-tune the reader's image of what is being said.

Because their shapes and functions are similar, parentheses are sometimes confused with **brackets.** Just remember that brackets are squared rather than curved—i.e., [ ] rather than ( )—and that brackets are used to set off comments or explanations by the author within passages he or she is quoting. These explanations include filling in words that were absent or represented by pronouns in the original, but which the reader now needs in order to understand the passage out of context:

> "[Darwin] laughed much at this, and came back to it over and over again." *Theodore Baird, quoting Carlyle*

> "With few exceptions, this [i.e., ne'er-do-wells becoming pioneers] seems to be the case in the settlement of all new countries." *student paper, quoting Eric Hoffer*

Both the name "Darwin" and the phrase "i.e., ne'er-do-wells becoming pioneers" were not written by the authors of the quoted passages, Carlyle and Hoffer. Instead they were inserted by the writers quoting the passages, to help us understand them. Because neither was written by the original author they must be put within brackets.

The **slash** is found in short poetry quotations, to **show the division between the lines of a poem.** Here is part of a poem by Dante G. Rossetti, "The Sea Limits"; the slashes show where each new line begins: "Consider the sea's listless chime: / Time's self it is made audible— / The murmur of the earth's own shell."

Occasionally a slash will **join alternative words and indicate that they are options:**

We are pulled out of the space/time continuum.   *student paper*

The traditional he/she/it singular pronouns are no longer sufficient for our language.   *newspaper article*

In the first example, and perhaps the second, hyphens would have been acceptable.

Punctuation marks make up the largest category of conventions in the English language. But there are other conventions too, as we shall see in the next section.

EXERCISES

1. The following sentences illustrate a variety of examples of punctuation. Some of the sentences are punctuated correctly and ought not to be punctuated any other way. Mark these sentences with the letter *C* (correct as is). Some are punctuated in an acceptable way, but other punctuation would also be acceptable. Mark these sentences with the letter *V* (variable), and be prepared to explain the acceptable alternative(s) and your preference. Some are punctuated incorrectly. Mark these with an *I* (incorrect), making sure you know why the sentence needs revision and what the correct punctuation would be. All of the sentences are from student papers.

a. There are three types of students in colleges today; the bookworm, the party-goer, and the jock.

b. He feels he is losing power in the world, the power to succeed and to prove to himself that he still has this power, he beats his wife.

c. Is it true that you come into this world alone and that you die alone?

d. I should mention one more anxiety that all college students male or female experience during their college years.

e. To change a tire you need; a spare tire, a jack and a lug wrench.

f. Finally I want to talk about whether capital punishment reduces crime.

g. Who could convict a man like Flynt of obscenity when he claims to be a close friend of the president of the United States sister; and a deeply religious man at that?

h. Amateurs who have never played the game suddenly become experts.

i. Then it happens the first fight, the undying love these two people vowed for one another changes.

j. Open marriage presents a new and flexible concept allowing each partner to draw upon his or her own special qualities.

k. She has some special interests like making clothes which are very plain and simple looking but neat; cooking for she loves to eat, and just having a good time.

l. A team of misfits challenging the softball champions of Park Ridge should not expect to win, but we did.

m. Would you please be seated.

n. The lotus shaped stage opened and Mick Jagger came strutting up to the microphone.

o. A topic sentence is often quite terse because it will be amplified by the paragraph that follows.

p. An up-set win over the Fortyniners gives them a good chance for the division championship.

q. The world has waited eighteen years to hear of me: I'm afraid it will have to wait eighteen more.

r. After Mr. James was finished with my hair I was taken to the henna department and introduced to Mr. Phillip.

To err is human, but when the eraser wears out the pencil, you're overdoing it.

J. Jenkins

2. The following passages have no punctuation whatsoever. Punctuate them as well as you can. In situations where you have a choice, be ready to explain the decisions you make.

a. I noticed the other salespeople staring and grinning at us and then I felt the color rising to my cheeks

b. That year 1910 was an important one in Mexico the Mexican revolution began

c. The worlds highest capital La Paz Bolivia is at an altitude of 11900 feet

d. Depressants have unusual effects on the body a lack of interest in one's surroundings an inability to move or talk slowing of the pulse and or a deepening depression sometimes accompanied by a deadening of all sensations

e. The doctor i e the one in the green coat entered my room and looked gravely at the information on my chart why was he frowning so much

f. In many less developed countries a strong system of kinship or friendship such as compadrazgo in Spanish America serves as insurance does in richer nations the system provides for help in times of trouble

g. What will tuition be next year he asked

h. Mt Washington 6288 feet tall is the highest peak in New Hampshire

i. What an exciting finish

j. Anyone and I mean anyone who criticizes Steve criticizes me

k. One Renaissance bishop claimed that the world was created at 900 am on the morning of October 23 4004 BC

l. During Easter vacation I spent endless hours applying for any type of job clerk typist waitress secretary you name it

m. Did you know that Tarot cards precursors of modern cards have four suits swords cups coins and clubs These four suits of the Tarot deck represented the four social classes of medieval society swords for nobility cups for the clergy coins for the tradespeople and clubs for the peasants

n. In some islands of Micronesia huge stone coins as big as

twelve feet in diameter are used as currency theres not much problem with theft even though the money lies around in the streets

o. I don't believe we will run out of petroleum in thirty years as some scientists have predicted how about you

p. The Tsar Czar spelling confusion still puzzles me

3. Commas and semicolons cause the major share of any doubts about punctuation, so this exercise gives special attention to them. In the following sentences: 1. delete any commas or semicolons that should not be present, 2. circle any commas or semicolons that could be left out at the writer's discretion, 3. change commas to semicolons or vice versa whenever such a change is required—especially in comma splices, 4. insert any needed punctuation.

a. Underneath the windows were bushes, most of the bushes were gardenias with large white flowers.

b. It is a stately clock ticking away the time hour after hour.

c. All of a sudden, the organ began *Pomp and Circumstance* and I was on my way marching with the music through a large crowded auditorium.

d. The morning was grey and chilling cold, everyone seemed warm though, because almost everyone on the bus was asleep.

e. I got out of bed and headed for the kitchen; but after looking at the clock I decided I ought to start for school right away.

f. The sound that occurs when the firecracker goes off, depends on where you are standing; how far from the explosion.

g. My brother is taller, skinnier, and darker-skinned, than I am.

h. The streets are no longer lined with trees but, the neighborhood still has a homey feel to it.

i. When I looked up, I saw several members of the other team watching our warmup, an audience like that only made us feel more pressure.

j. Little did I know, that within a period of three months I would change my mind.

k. Some of Browning's best known poems include "The Bishop Orders His Tomb," which describes the reflections of a corrupt Renaissance prelate, "Fra Lippo Lippi," which tells about an earthy monk, a man given more to sensuality than to sacrifice, despite his religious vocation, and "Love Among the Ruins," a love poem set in modern times.

l. Everyone, who thought Carter was wrong about the Canal Treaty, should have written his senator immediately.

m. His loud, abrasive, voice rang in my ears.

n. Now, as adults, they demand behavior of their children, that often exceeds both the child's mental and physical capabilities.

4. Punctuate the following passages by adding quotation marks:

a. Don't you dare go was exactly what he said to me observed Philip.

b. Probably everybody is familiar with the poem Stopping by Woods on a Snowy Evening.

c. Aren't you afraid your parakeet will fly away? I asked. I don't care, Helen said. I wish he would. He really is a pain. The parakeet came up close to her ear and gave her a loud kiss. Get away from me, you stupid bird!

   Face it, I said. He loves you. You'll just have to bear it. Secretly I was laughing to myself.

   Did Janice tell you what Sammy did the other day? I said no. Well, she licked her lips, Janice was sitting at the kitchen table. . . .

d. If I hear More Than a Woman one more time I think I'll destroy his stereo piece by piece.

e. Have you read Borges' story The Yellow Rose? he asked me.

5. Write sentences that would be examples of the following:

a. a polite request

b. a direct quotation containing within it another direct quotation

c. an indirect question
d. items in a series, the items being long and having internal punctuation
e. a quoted sentence with words omitted at the end
f. a sentence with a parenthetical expression
g. a question that interrupts a regular sentence
h. a quotation introduced by a colon
i. a quotation with a pronoun that must be explained by words in brackets
j. an exclamation
k. a sentence with a parenthetical expression set off by dashes
l. a quotation with words omitted part way through
m. a direct question

6. Insert hyphens or apostrophes in the following words or phrases wherever they are needed. Unite parts of words that are separated unnecessarily. If you are in doubt, let your dictionary help.

child rearing
its [contraction of it is]
re enforce
semi autonomous
its [possessive pronoun]
two H s
couldnt
post doctoral
great great grand mother
follow up
quarter back

there s
three quarters Chinese
up to date plan
far reaching
five Cs
Philips [possessive of Philip]
anti intellectual
anti American
six tenths
she s [contraction of she is]
self esteem

The governor of Colorado has signed a bill renaming his state's El Paso Community College "Pikes Peak Community College." At least one Colorado legislator, Rep. Joel Hefley, had argued hard for an apostrophe in the new name— "Pike's Peak," he thought it should be—but he lost.

newspaper item

7. The dash is much undervalued as a punctuation mark in most student writing. Find two or three articles or stories in a popular magazine. How often do you encounter dashes? What other punctuation marks could be used instead? Does the frequency of dashes vary from one writer to another?

8. Examine the ways—both conventional and unconventional—that Tom Wolfe uses punctuation in the following passage. What punctuation marks does he use? In which places do you find him exercising a *choice*, i.e., where could a different kind of punctuation be used? What reasons do you think Wolfe had for making the choices he in fact made?

> The Novel seemed like one of the last of those superstrokes, like finding gold or striking oil, through which an American could, overnight, in a flash, utterly transform his destiny. There were plenty of examples to feed the fantasy. In the 1930s all the novelists had seemed to be people who came blazing up into stardom from out of total obscurity. That seemed to be the nature of the beast. The biographical notes on the dust jackets of the novels were terrific. The author, you would be assured, was previously employed as a hod carrier (Steinbeck), a truck dispatcher (Cain), a bellboy (Wright), a Western Union boy (Saroyan), a dishwasher in a Greek restaurant in New York (Faulkner), a truck driver, logger, berry picker, spindle cleaner, crop duster pilot . . . There was no end to it . . . Some novelists had whole strings of these credentials . . . That way you knew you were getting the real goods . . .
>
> By the 1950s The Novel had become a nationwide tournament. There was a magical assumption that the end of World War II in 1945 was the dawn of a new golden age of the American Novel, like the Hemingway-Dos Passos-Fitzgerald era after World War I. There was even a kind of Olympian club where the new golden boys met face-to-face every Sunday afternoon in New York, namely, the White Horse Tavern on Hudson Street . . . Ah! There's Jones! There's Mailer! There's Styron! There's Baldwin! There's Willingham! In the flesh—right here in this room! The scene was strictly for novelists, people who were writing novels, and people who were paying court to The Novel. There was no room for a journalist unless he was there in the role of would-be novelist or simple courtier of the great. There was no such thing as a *literary* journalist working for popular magazines or newspapers. If a journalist aspired to literary status—then he had better have the sense and the courage to quit the popular press and try to get into the big league.

B. OTHER CONVENTIONS

Like—but oh how different!
Wordsworth

Writers are not limited to putting down a word in one way and one way only. Under some circumstances they can represent it several different ways: they can italicize it, capitalize it, or abbreviate it. This section explores these three alternatives, which are also examples of customs or conventions in our language.

B1. Italics

In print we recognize italics by their slanted type: *like this.* Handwritten or typewritten manuscripts represent them by underlining, <u>like</u> this.

Most of the time italics appear because custom requires them. For example they help to **designate titles of books, plays, long poems, movies, paintings, and magazines, and are used for names of ships or planes:**

Atlantic Monthly (magazine)   *Paradise Lost* (long poem)
Othello (play)   *High Noon* (movie)
Bread for the World (book)   *Titanic* (ship)
Mona Lisa (painting)   *Los Angeles Times* (newspaper)

In the following sentence observe how the two magazine titles and the book title are italicized, but the title of the essay, which was not published as a separate book, remains in quotation marks:

He combined the gist of the *Nation* piece with his earlier *Partisan Review* attack on V. L. Parrington, and he used the new version, called "Reality in America," as the lead essay in his influential book *The Liberal Imagination* (1950). *Leo Marx*

Italics also **identify words from foreign languages.** These include phrases or single words used as part of a sentence:

esprit de corps (French)   *ruah* (Hebrew)
Weltanschauung (German)   *arrivederci* (Italian)
de jure (Latin)   *shinyo* (Japanese)

With him it was the *offensive à outrance*—the headlong attack. *John Fowles*

Longer, self-sufficient passages from another language can be treated the same way:

> *Philosophieren*, says Novalis, *ist dephlegmatisieren, vivificieren.*   *Walter Pater*

Words or phrases that originated in another language but that have been fully adopted in English—words like *fiancée* (from French), *prima donna* (from Italian), or *status quo* (from Latin)— are not put in italics. Your dictionary can help in doubtful cases. (Then why, you might ask, were those words italicized in *this* paragraph? Read on.)

Italics can **set off words used as examples:**

> If in addition to the analysis of metaphor a glossary is compiled of key words, such as *law, facts, nature, species, variety, variation,* . . . , it will appear that Darwin's verbal universe is expressed and his language system complete.   *Theodore Baird*

The most frequent use of italics is one that is a matter of choice. Writers can employ italics to **give special emphasis.** Sometimes the emphasis falls upon a single word:

> At least the *idea* of education which Adams, solitary and recusant, imposed upon himself was an exemplary idea.   *Louis Kronenberger*

Sometimes it falls upon a whole group of words:

> The best claim we can make for the higher education . . . is, then, exactly what I said: it should enable us to *know a good man when we see him.*   *William James*

And sometimes it falls upon a key sentence. Italics therefore single out that sentence from the surrounding ones, perhaps because it offers a summary or a conclusion:

> Few of us take the pains to study the origin of our cherished convictions; indeed, we have a natural repugnance to so doing. We like to continue to believe what we have been accustomed to accept as true, and the resentment aroused when doubt is cast upon any of our assumptions leads us to seek every manner of excuse for clinging to them. *The result is that most of our so-called reasoning consists in finding arguments for going on believing as we already do.*   *James H. Robinson*

By all means use italics for emphasis—otherwise you deprive yourself of a valuable way to direct your reader's attention.

Student writers too often neglect the opportunities that italics, like dashes, can provide. My only caution is the same caution that applies to other means of emphasis, like exclamation marks or one-sentence paragraphs: be sparing, don't overuse. If italics appear too frequently their effect is lessened, in the same way good food is enhanced by the delicate use of seasoning but destroyed by recklessness. Again be warned by an example from Queen Victoria:

> My dearest Uncle, . . . The *peace negotiations* occupy every one; *if* Russia is *sincere*, they will end most probably in peace; but *if* she is *not*, the war will be *carried* on with *renewed vigour*. The recollection of last year makes one *very distrustful*.
>
> England's policy throughout has been the *same, singularly unselfish*, and *solely* actuated by the *desire* of *seeing Europe saved* from the *arrogant* and *dangerous pretensions* of that *barbarous power* Russia—and of having *such safeguards* established for the *future*, which may ensure us against a *repetition* of similar *untoward events*.
>
> I repeat now, what we have said from the beginning, and what I have *repeated* a *hundred times*, if *Prussia* and *Austria* had held *strong* and *decided* language to *Russia in '53*, we should *never* have had *this war!*

I dare say the poor uncle must have been thoroughly exhausted by the time he finished that letter. So much excitement could kill a man.

B2. Capitalization

The history of capitalization in the English language is a story of steady decline. There was a time when writers capitalized almost every noun, as well as many other words which they thought deserved special emphasis:

> I HAVE only one thing more to say on the Occasion of the Union Act; which is, that the Author of the *Crisis* may be fairly proved from his own Citations to be guilty of High Treason.   *Jonathan Swift*

But the trend toward diminishing the use of capitals has been a consistent one. It reaches its extreme nowadays in certain greeting cards:

> happy birthday! i finally figured out a way to cure my inferiority complex! i'm going to stop comparing myself to you!

Of course the customs most of us follow are neither as insistent about preserving capitals as Jonathan Swift nor as liberal about dispensing with them as certain greeting card companies. You probably know the obvious places where we all capitalize: **the first person singular pronoun (I), people's names, and the first word of a sentence or legitimate fragment.** These usually offer no difficulty. Moreover we saw how to capitalize direct quotations earlier in this chapter.

Instead most problems with capitalization occur in one specific area: names other than people's names. Which names are capitalized and which are not? It depends on how specific the name is. In general, the more specific the name (in other words the closer it comes to identifying one particular person, place, or thing), the more likely it is to be capitalized.

Here are some concrete situations where writers are often in doubt about whether to capitalize. If the word names **a specific day, month, event, or period,** do capitalize it:

Tuesday	the Battle of Gettysburg
the Protestant Reformation	August

If it names a less clearly defined time, such as a season, do not:

summer	the old days
the medieval period	autumn

If the word names **a specific institution,** do capitalize it:

U.S. Department of Labor	Archmere Academy
University of Oregon	Newberry Library

If it names a general category of institutions, do not:

libraries	graduate schools
recreation departments	city hospitals

If the word names **a specific college course,** do capitalize it:

Sociology 101	Advanced Organic Chemistry
French 2	Studies in Victorian Literature

If the word names a general subject area, do not:

chemistry	a psychology course
the mathematics exam	composition

> If you would not be forgotten, as soon as you are dead and rotten, either write things worth reading, or do things worth writing.
>
> *Ben Franklin*

If the word names **a specific geographical place,** do capitalize it:

Fifth Avenue	a Westerner
North Dakota	Southern hospitality

If it just names a general direction, do not:

eastern journey	to travel west
to go north on a certain road	to take the third street

If the word names **a specific group or party,** do capitalize it:

the Democratic candidate	the Romantic poets
the Orthodox Church	the Socialist Party

If it names a general concept, do not:

all democratic governments	a romantic mood
orthodox (i.e., conventional) ideas	socialist goals

If the word names **a title that refers to a specific person or is part of a person's name,** do capitalize it:

President Lincoln	Emperor Hirohito
Grandma	Professor Somerville

If the word names a category of people, do not:

several presidents	the emperor of Japan
my grandmothers	a professor's obligations

One temptation to which some writers fall victim is the urge to give words special emphasis through capitalization. Consider this sentence, for example:

How dare these hypocrites violate the Supreme Law of the Land?

Now the author of that sentence was quite indignant and wanted to show how presumptuous her opponents were. Therefore she tried to give a Supreme Court decision a certain extra dignity by calling it the "Supreme Law of the Land," all in capitals. But no specific law, institution, or concept bears that title, and so she needs to find a different way of giving voice to her wrath. (*Supreme Court*, of course, would have capitals because it *is* an institution.)

We use capitals in two other places that sometimes cause difficulty. One is the matter of **sacred names.** Most such names, whether they refer to persons or to texts, are capitalized:

the Holy Spirit	the Torah
the Koran	the Buddha
the Bible	the New Testament

Note that the sacred books are not italicized. A word like *Bible*, for example, is not treated as if it were simply a book title.

The other place we should think about capitals is in **titles of works,** where every word is capitalized except conjunctions, articles, and prepositions. Capitalize even these if they are the first or last word in either a title or subtitle:

The Magus (book)

I Am a Camera (play)

U.S. News and World Report (magazine)

Aristotle Contemplating the Bust of Homer (painting)

"The Loneliness of Being Black" (essay)

B3. Abbreviations

An abbreviation is just a different way of writing a word. *Dr.* is shorter than *Doctor*, but a reader will "say" them both the same way. Theoretically we could abbreviate almost every longer word in the language. Having two systems for representing words would be too confusing, however, so we abbreviate only in a few common, agreed-upon places.

The most familiar abbreviations are **courtesy titles and degrees:**

Dr. Catherine Sikorski	Mrs. George Holmberg
Mr. James Winston, Jr.	Michael Cipolla, Ph.D.

Courtesy titles are not abbreviated, however, when they do not precede a person's name:

The senator is seriously mistaken.

Have you called a doctor?

A few other **expressions that derive from foreign languages** are always abbreviated; most are pronounced as abbreviations:

A.M.	etc.	P.S.
P.M.	B.C.	e.g.
i.e.	A.D.	Ibid.

Sometimes a set of initials is so familiar that the organization or object it represents is known more by the initials than by the full name. These **well-known initials** become the common abbreviation, usually written without the period punctuation:

CBS (network)	NATO (military alliance)
ROTC	FM (radio)
FBI	DNA (deoxyribonucleic acid)

The most common mistake student writers make in their compositions or papers is to abbreviate place names, days of the week, or units of measurements, like the following (which should not be abbreviated):

Fifth Avenue	minute
Great Britain	ounces
Mount Everest	pounds
Saturday, December 2	inches

Of course abbreviations for such things might be quite proper in letters, newspaper articles, or recipe books, where space is at a premium. But in most college writing the custom is to spell them out.

This chapter has been concerned with certain customs a writer is expected to know and observe. There is another set of customs every writer should know: customs about how to use certain words. These conventions are taken up in the glossary of usage, which, along with a glossary of grammatical terms, follows the conclusion of this book—a conclusion you have now reached.

EXERCISES

1. Practice the use of italics to give emphasis by writing a half-dozen sentences in which you stress certain key words or phrases by means of italics. Then go back through two of your recent papers and see if there are places where you could have used italics to your advantage. Compare these papers with some articles from a popular magazine; does the magazine use italics more often, and if so, how and where?

2. In the following passages, capitalize and italicize according to the principles explained in this section:

a. virginia woolf's father was the philosopher and critic sir leslie stephen, the editor of cornhill magazine. in 1904 she and her brothers and sisters moved from hyde park gate to 46 gordon square in bloomsbury. by 1912 virginia had married one of her brother thoby's friends, leonard woolf, and she soon published her first novel, the voyage out.

b. some of the material developed by the nebraska curriculum development center is available under the title the rhetoric of short units of composition.

c. when he returned to the united states from europe, baldwin lived in greenwich village in new york city. his first book after his return was the collection of essays entitled nobody knows my name, which was quickly followed by the novel another country. two plays also appeared: blues for mister charlie, produced by the actor's studio, and the amen corner, which played on broadway. his early essay "notes of a native son" continues to be widely anthologized because of what it says about black-white relationships, although baldwin insisted that he did not want to be known "merely as a negro writer."

3. Locate a popular news magazine like *Time* or *Newsweek*. Read through a few of the articles, circling every abbreviation you can find. What seems to be the policy of this magazine regarding abbreviations? Then take a somewhat different kind of magazine—say *The Atlantic*, *Harper's*, or the *New Yorker*. Does the policy here seem to be different? If so, can you guess at a reason that might account for the difference?

> Whatever you would make habitual, practice it; and if you would not make a thing habitual, do not practice it.
>
> *Epictetus*

Glossary of Usage

This glossary deals with usage, in other words the ways in which the English language is used by those educated people who speak and write it. The glossary of usage includes distinctions between words frequently confused, like *farther* and *further* or *lie, lay,* and *lain.* The entries are arranged in alphabetical order.

Accept / except

To **accept** something means to *receive* it:

If you can accept our invitation, please reply by February 15th.   *advertising brochure*

To **except** means to *leave (something) out, exclude:*

Congress agreed to except small businesses from these provisions.
newspaper item

Except as a preposition means *other than, with the exclusion or exception of:*

No one was there except me.

Adapt / adept / adopt

Adapt and **adopt** are verbs. The first means to *adjust* something or *make it suitable:*

Like a chameleon Sean can adapt himself to his surroundings.   *student journal*

Adopt means *accept:*

The resolution was adopted 5 yes, 2 no, 1 abstention.   *committee minutes*

Adept, by contrast, is an adjective meaning *proficient:*

My older brother is adept at getting the blame placed on my shoulders   *student paper*

Advice / advise

Advice is the noun, what you do when you **advise** (verb) someone about something.

What did they advise? Was their advice reasonable?

Affect / effect

These two words are confused perhaps more often than any other pair in the English language, probably because their spelling, pronunciation, and meaning are similar. To use them properly, remember that **affect** is normally a verb and **effect** is—usually—a noun. To **affect** means to *influence:*

Nothing the Shah can do will affect the outcome.   *newspaper story*

Effect as a noun is simply a *result* or *consequence:*

The effect of inflation on the family budget is a matter of national concern.   *news magazine*

Less frequently **effect** is used as a verb, where it means *cause, accomplish,* or *bring about:*

The passage of the Red Sea was effected by a strong wind, which, we are told, drove back the waters.   *S. T. Coleridge*

Already / all ready

Already means *by this time* or *prior to a given time:*

The coffee was already brewing by the time I rolled up my sleeping bag.   *student paper*

All ready, on the other hand, consists of two separate words, each of which functions independently. **All** means *everybody;* **ready** shows the state of preparedness:

We were all ready for the supreme test [we—all of us—were ready].   *student paper*

Among / between

The distinction here is that **between** is used with two (*divide the money between Glenda and Joan*) and **among** is used with more than two (*divide the money among all the committee members*). Lately, though, **between** has become an acceptable alternative to **among** in the second instance; in other words, *divide the money between all the committee members* is also acceptable to many readers.

Anybody / any body / anyone / any one

Anybody and **anyone** each act as single nouns:

Is anybody home?

Anyone needing tickets for Tuesday's game, see Tom in Room 331. *bulletin board sign*

Separate the words when **any** is used as a modifier:

Any body not claimed by relatives was immediately buried or cremated [**body** is a separate noun and **any** modifies it]. *newspaper item*

There are three clerks here, any one of whom can help you.

As / like

These two words are perfect examples of words about which there is a fierce debate. Both can be used either as conjunctions or as prepositions. Let's take conjunctions first. Everyone accepts the use of **as** (*as if, as though*) in clauses of comparison:

He leaned forward as if he were about to faint.

Many—most?—writers would accept the use of **like** in the same situation:

He leaned forward like he was about to faint.

But not everyone agrees, as the furor over Winston cigarette ads made clear ("Winston tastes good like a cigarette should"; "What do you want—good grammar or good taste?"). Still, you are probably safe in allowing **like** to encroach upon the territory of **as** when they are conjunctions.

As prepositions, **like** is often permissible where **as** would not be. This sentence would be proper, therefore:

Dave played first base like a pro.

But lately **as** has found supporters, even such impressive ones as Ernest Hemingway:

He was built as a swordfish. . . .

Nevertheless the encroachments of **as** into the territory of **like** are not as large as the encroachments of **like** into **as.** Despite Hemingway's practice I would advise you, for the time being at least, to stick to **like** in these latter cases.

Awhile / a while / while

Awhile is an adverb meaning *for a while* and written as one word: *Please stay awhile.* The noun **while** is often accompanied by the determiner **a**: *a while ago, for a while longer.* **While** is usually a conjunction expressing time, however: *Nero fiddled while Rome burned.*

Beside / besides

Beside is a preposition that usually means *by the side of* or *next to:*

Beside the tombstone was a small floral wreath.

Both **beside** and **besides** can mean *aside from:*

Can't you offer any other excuse beside(s) that one?

But **besides** can also act as an adverb, in which case it means *moreover:*

Besides, the price of meat has been going down recently.

Between: see among

Cite / sight / site

These three homonyms have quite different meanings. **Cite** is a verb meaning *refer to, quote:*

Be sure to cite all the information which relates to your case.   *legal form*

Sight and **site** are nouns. The first means *a view, something seen* (*a beautiful sight*); the second means a *place or location* (*a building site*).

Compose / comprise

To **compose** is to *fashion* or *create;* **to be composed of** is *to consist of, be made or constituted of.*

The book is composed of a series of essays.

To **comprise,** like **to be composed of,** means to *include* or *contain.* Avoid *is comprised of* when you mean *is composed of, consists of.*

North America comprises (consists of, is composed of) Canada, the United States, and Mexico.

Different from

Although many people use *different than* in speech, the form to use in writing is **different from** (no one objects to the latter, but many people object to *different than).*

Effect: see **Affect**

Either / neither / any / none

Use **either** to mean *one of two;* **any** means *one of several:*

Either job sounds interesting [of two].

Any dated receipt will be sufficient [of several].

Use **neither** to mean *not one of two* (**neither** = *not either*); **none** means *not one of more than two:*

Neither your first nor your second proposal is satisfactory.

None of us knows the answer.

Note that **either, neither, any,** and **none** normally take a singular verb.

Etc.

This abbreviation for the Latin *et cetera* ("and so forth") should be used only with lists and statistics, not as part of a normal prose sentence. If a sentence lists several items, mention them all. If you close a sentence with **etc.,** readers might think you are just too bored to finish. Write this:

I packed some clothes, three books, and my tennis racket and headed home for the weekend.

Not this:

I packed clothes etc. and headed home for the weekend.

By the way, since the *et* of *et cetera* means *and,* don't use *and etc.* or *& etc.;* that's like saying "and and so forth."

Except: see **Accept**

Extra

Be reluctant to use this word to mean *very,* as in *Her tacos are extra good;* some people object to it in formal writing. Words like *unusually, especially,* or *very* are probably better choices.

Famed

Many readers object to the indiscriminate use of this word as an alternative to *famous*—stick to *famous.*

Farther / further

Farther is generally preferred as the comparative of *far (Houston is farther than Dallas).* But **further** is gaining acceptance too, in both writing and speaking. Of course **further** can also be used in reference to additional quantity or degree *(further information, to discuss further).*

Fewer / less

Fewer refers to nouns that can be counted: *fewer people, fewer cars.* **Less** applies to nouns that are not counted: *less energy, less bread, less attention.* In other words, **fewer** applies to number and **less** to quantity or degree.

Fine / good

Often used as adverbs in speech *(He talks good, he talks fine),* these words are really adjectives, and in most writing they should be employed only in that capacity.

Good: see Fine, Well

Irregardless

This word is sometimes used, mistakenly, in place of *regardless.*

Its / it's

Its, without the apostrophe, is the possessive neuter pronoun *(everything in its place).* **It's,** apostrophe included, is the contraction of *it is.*

Kind / sort

Both of these words are singular in form and usually take singular demonstrative adjectives: *that kind of day, that sort of temptation.* The hitch comes when the noun associated with **kind** or **sort,** such as "day" or "temptation" in the preceding examples, happens to be a plural noun. In such cases, the demonstrative adjectives are sometimes in the plural to agree with the noun *(these kinds of days, those sorts of temptations),* but they should not be plural unless **kinds** or **sorts** is used: *this kind of day* or *these kinds of days.*

Incidentally the variants *kind of* and *sort of* as synonyms for *rather—It's kind of windy today—*are best restricted to informal writing.

Lay / lie

The most famous trouble words of all? The only solution is memorizing the difference—or looking it up here if you can't remember. First decide which meaning you intend. Do you mean *to recline* (intransitive)? Then you *lie* down, or the bundle of wheat *lies* in the fields. Yesterday the wheat *lay* in the fields, and after thirty days we can say it *has lain* there for a month. But if you mean *to place,* with an object implied (i.e., transitive), then you *lay* down your umbrella. Perhaps yesterday you *laid* it down on the table, where you *have laid* it many times before.

In sum, the two verbs are **lie, lay, (have) lain,** and **lay, laid, (have) laid.** I think you can see why they are so often confused: the past tense of one and the present tense of the other are identical *(lay);* the meanings are similar (although you *have laid* your umbrella on the table, it may not *have lain* there long); and when followed by the word *down* the two are pronounced the same way *(lay down, laid down).* So the only alternative is memorizing the distinction.

Lead / led

Since *read* (present tense) and *read* (past tense) are spelled alike but pronounced differently, some writers think they should use **lead** for the present tense and **lead** again for the past. But the correct past-tense form is **led.**

Less: see **fewer**

Like: see **as**

Loose / lose

Loose is the condition of being unrestricted, free, not tight: *a loose garment, a loose doorknob.* **Lose** is a verb meaning to no longer possess: *Did you lose your keys?*

Moral / morale

Moral is a lesson *(the moral of the story)*; as an adjective, it means *ethical,* having to do with right or wrong conduct. **Morale** is a spiritual or psychological state *(their morale remained high).*

Neither: see **Either**

None: see **Either**

Okay / O.K. / OK

You know what this expression means, but be reluctant to use it in formal writing.

Past / passed

For the verb *to pass,* the **past** tense is **passed.** And that last sentence illustrates the point here: the verb form is **pass, passed, (have) passed;** the form of the adjective, adverb, and preposition is **past** *(past tense, past due,* [*go*] *past the first stoplight*).

Principal / principle

A **principal** (noun) is a person who runs a school. This person will succeed only insofar as he or she is guided by certain clear **principles** (the noun meaning *code of conduct, fundamental truth or assumption*); absence of such principles could be a **principal** (adjective meaning *main, primary*) reason for later failure.

Raise / rise

The easiest way to know which of these verbs to choose is to see whether the verb will have an object. If it will, in other words if the verb is transitive, the proper verb is **raise, raised, (have) raised,** which means to *make something go up or appear:*

To decrease heat, raise handle to upper notch.   *instructions for charcoal grill* [note *handle* as direct object of *raise*]

If the verb is intransitive, in other words if it has no object and means simply to *move upwards*, **rise, rose, (have) risen** is the right choice, as in these lines from the poet S. T. Coleridge:

A sadder and a wiser man
He rose the morrow morn.

Real / really

Real is an adjective meaning *genuine: a real diamond.* In writing, **real** should not be used as a substitute for the adverb **really;** i.e., write *a really big prize,* not *a real big prize.* (Better yet, use *very* or perhaps no intensifier at all.)

Shall / will

For both speech and writing the old distinctions between when to use **shall** and when to use **will** in the future tense are fast disappearing. At one time, **shall** was supposed to be used in the first person *(I shall go).* In practice the use of **will** to express all forms of the future tense is now just about universal.

Sight, site: see **Cite**

Someone / somebody: see **anyone / anybody**

Sort: see **Kind**

Suit / suite

You can wear a **suit** (noun) if its style **suits** (verb) you. But **suite** is used only as a noun: *a suite of rooms.*

Their / they're / there

Pronounced alike, these three words have quite different meanings: **their** is a possessive adjective *(their bicycles)*, **they're** is the contraction for *they are (they're coming)*, and **there** indicates place *(put it there)*.

Till / until

No difference between these—use them interchangeably—except **till** would be unusual at the beginning of a sentence.

To / too / two

To is the preposition *(go to bed)*, **too** means *also (you come too)* or *excessively (too heavy)*, **two** is the number *(two days)*.

Try to

The expression *try and,* often used in speech ("Try and catch me"), should be replaced by **try to** in written English.

Used to

Because the *d* and *t* sounds are so alike, we drop the *d* sound when we say these two words. But in writing always make sure the *d* is included; i.e., avoid a construction like *We use to go to the movies more often.*

Well

This adverb is often replaced by the adjective *good* in conversation: "How's your car running?" "Pretty good." In writing **well** has the prerogative—*feeling well, sleeping well, painting well.*

Who's / whose

Who's is the proper contraction for *who is.* Keep *whose* as the possessive adjective—e.g., *the golfer whose clubs I carried.*

Will: see Shall

Your / you're

Your is the possessive adjective *(your room)*; **you're** is the contraction for *you are.*

Glossary of Grammatical Terms

> The greater part of this world's troubles are due to questions of grammar.
>
> *Montaigne*

This glossary includes definitions of key grammatical terms which writers need to know or may want to know. Many of these definitions are condensations of longer discussions appearing elsewhere in this book.

Active voice: see **Voice**

Adjective, adjectival An adjective is a word that modifies, defines, or specifies a noun, as in *thin boy, gorgeous day, this dictionary,* or *my family.* To say that it modifies a noun is to say that it changes—modifies—our idea of that noun *(thin* boy, not *fat* boy or *tall* boy or just plain *boy*). Adjectives therefore help a writer be more precise. Parts of Chapters 1, 2, and 6 will aid you here, especially the sections on being specific (pp. 36–38) and on using modifiers (pp. 342–349).

A good test of whether or not a word is an adjective is to ask yourself if it can be compared by changing its form. A *thin* boy, for example, can be compared to another boy and thus be called the *thinner* boy. If still other boys are involved, he might be the *thinnest* boy. These comparative and superlative forms are often signaled by an *-er* and *-est* ending or by *more* and *most* when the adjective is three or more syllables *(more gorgeous, most gorgeous).* The comparative and superlative forms of a few adjectives are

irregular, and you simply have to learn them individually: *good/
better/best*, for example, or *bad/worse/worst*.

Sometimes we recognize adjectives because they occupy a
position in the sentence that is typically an adjective position.
Consider, for example, the sentence, *The crowd seemed apathetic.*
We recognize *apathetic* as an adjective because that position —
the word following a linking verb — is usually filled by an adjective. (Try putting in a verb or a noun and see if the sentence
makes sense.) Also, of course, we know that *apathetic* can
be compared—*more apathetic, most apathetic.* See p. 342 for more
information. The same principle holds true for words that
cannot be compared but that fill the same positions that other
adjectives do. In the phrase *a brick wall,* for example, *brick* acts
as an adjective modifying *wall* even though we cannot add an
-er or an *-est* to it. Such words are called adjectivals.

There are many kinds of adjectives:

> **demonstrative adjectives** designate or point out a specific
> item (*this* notebook, *those* chairs)
> **descriptive adjectives** provide description (*busy* street)
> **interrogative adjectives** ask or question (*which* door?)
> **possessive adjectives** indicate possession (*our* house)
> **predicate adjectives** form part of a predicate and complement
> a verb or verb phrase (She was *ecstatic*.)
> **relative adjectives** introduce subordinate clauses or phrases
> (the girl *whose* mother is a journalist)

Adjective clause   An adjective clause is a dependent clause
used as an adjective, modifying a noun:
> They're looking for an employee *who can speak Japanese.*
> The woman *who was sitting in front of me* was wearing a red hat.

Adverb, adverbial   Just as adjectives modify nouns, adverbs
usually modify verbs. Consider the sentence *She walked rapidly to
the door. Rapidly* modifies the verb *walked,* it refines our idea of
that verb (walks *rapidly,* not *slowly* or *sedately*). Adverbs usually
have the ending *-ly;* the comparative is formed with *more* (*more
rapidly*), and the superlative is formed with *most* (*most rapidly*).

Adverbs can modify other parts of speech besides verbs. They
sometimes modify adjectives: *He gave the poem an especially careful
reading* (*especially* modifies *careful,* not *reading*). They can also

modify other adverbs: *The reception room was decorated very taste-fully* (the adverb *very* modifies the adverb *tastefully*, which in turn modifies the verb *was decorated*).

Occasionally other words not normally considered adverbs act as adverbs. Example: *Let's go Thursday*. Usually *Thursday* would be a noun, but here it tells when and modifies *go*. Words used in this way are called adverbials.

Adverb clause   An adverb clause is a dependent clause used as an adverb, in other words, to tell time, place, manner, or what-ever:

> Let me know *when you get there*.
> He left *without her seeing him*.
> I'll go with you *unless you decide to stay home*.

Agreement   The term *agreement* is simply a way of expressing the relationship that ought to exist between one word or phrase and another closely connected word or phrase. Three kinds of agreement are important for our purposes: agreement of subject and verb, agreement of pronoun or possessive adjective and antecedent, and agreement of demonstrative adjectives with the nouns they modify. The first two are discussed in Chapter 6. Suffice it to say of the third category that a demonstrative adjective should be singular if the noun it modifies is singular (*this table*, *that painting*) and it should be plural if the noun it modifies is plural (*these tables*, *those paintings*).

Antecedent: See **Reference**

Appositive   A word or phrase with the same function as another word or phrase and intended to further explain or de-scribe it is called an appositive.

> My brother, the *Kansas* freak, has his door closed and his stereo
> turned up to 9.   *student journal*

The phrase between the commas is the appositive. It has the same function as the subject noun it describes — i.e. *brother*. To find out if a word or phrase is an appositive, all you need do is eliminate the word being explained and its modifiers, then see if the appositive can take its place. If it can't, then it's not an appositive after all. Our example sentence still makes sense if the appositive fills in for the subject:

> The *Kansas* freak has his door closed and his stereo turned up to 9.

Article   Three familiar little words — *a, an, the* — are known collectively as articles. *The* is a definite article and *a* and *an* are indefinite articles. See **Determiner.**

Auxiliary verb   An auxiliary verb is one that helps to form a verb phrase expressing voice, mood, and tense. Forms of the verb *to be, to do*, and *to have* are the most common auxiliaries: for example, *she **is** buying, she **did** buy*, or *she **has** bought*. Other frequent auxiliaries include *can, get, may, might, must, need, ought, shall, should, used, will*, and *would*. See **Verb, verbal.**

Case   When we discuss the syntactical relationship of a noun, pronoun, or adjective to other words in a sentence (see **Syntax**), we are discussing case. In English there are three cases: **subjective** (or **nominative**), **objective**, and **possessive**. To find out which one a certain word is, you must ask questions like, "Is the word a subject? A direct or indirect object? A possessive?" Most problems of case occur with pronouns. When you have to choose among *I/me/mine, he/him/his*, or *she/her/hers*, case is the chief factor in deciding which form to use. See **Subject**, **Object**, and **Possessive** or Chapter 6, p. 326–332.

Clause   A clause is a word group that contains a subject and a predicate. Take this sentence:

> Even though we left at four, we still didn't get to LaGuardia until after the plane had landed on the runway.   *student paper*

This is a single sentence, but it contains three clauses, because there are three subject-predicate combinations, *we + left, we + didn't get*, and *plane + had landed*. Only one of those three clauses could form a sentence by itself, however. You can convert *We still didn't get to LaGuardia* into a separate sentence and it would not seem strange. Therefore it is called the **main clause**, or the **independent clause**. The other two clauses cannot stand by themselves in this way. They need a main clause to latch onto, and they are therefore said to be **dependent clauses**. Notice that length has nothing to do with determining which clauses are independent and which are not, since the second dependent clause here is longer than the independent clause. The crucial distinction is whether the clause can form a sentence on its own. (See Chapter 2, pp. 70–86.)

Clauses are often confused with phrases. Just remember that a group of related words must have a subject and a predicate to be a clause. Thus the words *on the runway* in the example sentence should be termed a phrase, not a clause. The words are clearly related, but they contain no subject or predicate.

Within a sentence clauses can take the place of nouns, adverbs, or adjectives. In this last case they are often known as **relative clauses**, because they relate to, or modify, nouns. Such clauses are often introduced by relative pronouns, like *who, which, what,* and *that,* or by relative adverbs, like *where, when,* and *why.*

Comparative: see **Adjective**, **Adverb**

Complement   As the word implies, a complement is a word that fills out or completes—in this case, fills out or completes a predicate. If your sentence contains a verb that usually has a direct object, that object is a complement to the verb. In the sentence *Mark threw the football,* the word *football* is a complement: it fills out the predicate, which in this case consists of the last three words. Similarly, if your sentence has a linking verb, the noun, pronoun, or adjective that completes the predicate can be termed a complement: *She is **a real professional.** They appeared **foolish.***

Conjunction   A conjunction is a word that joins: it can join words (*you **and** I*), phrases (*after the sunrise **but** before the rain*), clauses (*Sue was angry, **although** she kept her cool*), or sentences (*I left the party early. **Yet** I can't say I was really tired.*). Some of the most common conjunctions are *and, but, or, nor, if, because, since, although, as, unless, before, after, when, for,* and *while.*

Contraction   Contractions are words in which all or part of an unstressed syllable has been eliminated: *cannot* becomes *can't, did not* becomes *didn't, she is* becomes *she's.* An apostrophe replaces the eliminated letters. We use contractions quite often in conversation. Therefore writing that reflects conversation or tends toward informality makes liberal use of contractions.

> Florence's hoteliers *aren't* as greedy as some of their Peninsular colleagues — but *they're* in there pitching.   *Fielding's Guide to Europe*

More formal writing or speech, on the other hand, tends to avoid them. For instance, consider a sentence from Lincoln's Gettysburg Address:

> But in a larger sense we cannot dedicate, we cannot consecrate, we cannot hallow this ground.

How would this sentence have sounded if Lincoln had used *can't*? In your own writing, be careful about using contractions in research papers or other serious works; they tend to make writing sound informal.

Demonstrative Demonstrative adjectives or pronouns (*this*, *that*, *these*, *those*) point out or indicate *which* of a class of things is referred to (*this* camera, *that* one, *those* over there).

Determiner Determiners include articles (*a*, *an*, *the*); demonstrative, possessive, and indefinite adjectives (*those cards*, *her cards*, *some cards*); and words referring to number (*one*, *two*, *first*, *second*). Determiners occupy an adjective's position and do an adjective's work, but they do not have an adjective's form — for example, they cannot be compared.

Double negative Two negatives are not usually used in the same sentence. You write *I know **nothing** about it* (one negative) rather than *I **don't** know **nothing** about it* (two negatives). The idea behind the custom is that two negatives make a positive (affirmative), just as when you multiplied two negatives in seventh grade mathematics and got (or should have gotten!) a positive result. Taken literally, *I don't know nothing about it* would mean *I do know something about it*.

Ellipsis An ellipsis is the omission of certain words, usually from quoted material. Three spaced periods (. . .) mark the deletion.

Gender To ask about the gender of a word is simply to ask whether it is masculine, feminine, or neuter. English makes comparatively little use of distinctions of gender, except in things like the pronouns *he/she/it* and *his/hers/its*. The older custom of using alternative forms of a word to show sex, as in *blond* (m)/*blonde* (f), is disappearing. Similarly, few people would now distinguish between *mediator* (m) and *mediatrix* (f) or *poet* and *poetess*. On the other hand, most writers still use the alternative forms *actor* and *actress*. In between come the more complex decisions. Is it *chairman* or *chairwoman*, or *chairperson* for both sexes? Does *congressman* describe just the job, with equal application to both sexes holding that job, or should the title vary (*congresswoman*, *congressman*) with the sex of the incumbent? Tread carefully here (and see pp. 333–335).

Gerund   The ancient Greeks believed in the existence of creatures called hermaphrodites — half man, half woman. A gerund is an hermaphroditic kind of word — half noun, half verb. In function it is a noun; it fills a noun's place. For example: *Overeating is my worst temptation*. The word *overeating* is quite clearly a noun subject. But in form it resembles a verb, because it has a verb ending (*-ing*), can take an object (*overeating pasta*), and can be modified by an adverb (*grossly overeating*).

Idiom   An idiom is a phrase that has a certain agreed-upon meaning for users of the language but which cannot necessarily be understood from the individual words in the phrase; for example, *to rain cats and dogs, to be on Cloud 9, to paint the town red*. Other examples are:

> Why is it always someone else's fault? [the *-'s*, signal of possessive case, here added to the adjective—a grammatical deviation]

> A good union knows how to drive a hard bargain. [How do you *drive* a *bargain?*]

Idioms are used in very specific ways to mean specific things; instructors sometimes have to call a student's attention to phrases that are not idiomatically correct, as in this example from a student paper:

> The U.S. should not ring its hands in despair.

If we take the words literally, it is probably as easy to *ring* your hands (like a bell) as to *wring* them (like a wet dishrag). But the proper idiom requires *wring*.

Infinitive   Like gerunds, infinitives (*to* plus the present form of a verb, the stem of the infinitive) resemble verbs but often act as nouns. Greta Garbo's famous wish "I want to be alone," contains the infinitive *to be*. *To be* in this sentence takes a complement (*alone*) as a verb would. Yet by function it is a noun, in this case a noun that is the direct object of the verb *want*. Note that the distinction between gerund and infinitive is often one of form but not function: *I like to be alone* (infinitive); *I like being alone* (gerund).

Interjection   Interjections are words that express an emotion or give a command, like a simple exclamation, but that are not related grammatically to the rest of the sentence in which they appear:

> She is in her grave / And *oh!* the difference to me. *William Wordsworth*

Other examples: *Ouch! Ah! Alas!* and *Ha!* The familiar "four-letter words" are often, technically, interjections.

Intonation   Intonation is a general term describing the sound qualities peculiar to a language: its patterns of pitch (tone — high or low frequency of sound) and of terminal juncture (e.g., the way we link *n* and *g* in a word like *ring*). Intonation determines whether a sentence is a statement or a question.

Intransitive: see **Verb**

Modifier   A word or group of words that qualifies, or modifies, another word or group of words is said to be a modifier. Included in this general category are adjectives, adjectivals, adverbs, and adverbials. Also included are phrases or clauses that act as adjectives or adverbs. See the entry for **Clause,** and also Chapter 2, pp. 70–93 and Chapter 6, pp. 342–350 for more information.

Mood   In English there are three moods, or forms, that a verb assumes to express the manner in which the action or state takes place: the **indicative**, the **subjunctive**, and the **imperative**. Most sentences are in the indicative mood (which includes many tenses — present, past, future, and so forth — see **Tense**). Both questions and declarative sentences can be in the indicative mood. The subjunctive mood is used in dependent clauses to express: 1. something hypothetical or contrary to fact (*If I were rich . . .*, *If only I could get up earlier . . .*), 2. necessity (*It's essential that he know the truth*), 3. wishing or willing (*I wish you were here*, *I insist that you be more attentive*). The imperative mood, finally, is used for commands: *Wash the dishes! Let's go! Be careful!*

Noun, nominal   Like most other parts of speech, a noun can be identified two ways, by its form and by its function. In terms of form, nouns are words that can be made plural by adding -*s* or -*es*: *train, trains; crutch, crutches; box, boxes*. I imagine you are aware too of the many exceptions, either words like *barracks* where singular and plural are the same, or words like *man, ox*, or *memorandum* which form plurals in unusual ways (*men, oxen, memoranda*). Another way to identify nouns is the use of an apostrophe and -*s* to show the possessive case. In a phrase like "the dean's office," the addition of -*s* to *dean* shows that the office belongs to (is in the possession of) the person designated by the noun *dean*.

As for function, nouns fill several kinds of slots. They can be subjects (*The waves slammed against the dock*); direct objects of verbs (*She sent flowers*); or indirect objects of verbs, usually shown by their position before the direct object and by the implied presence of *to* or *for* after the verb (*Larry gave* [to] *his fiancée a ring*). Nouns can also be appositives (*His new toy, the Honda, is a dangerous one*); complements (*Their oldest appliance is a refrigerator*); or objects of prepositions (*Good luck on the exam*).

There are many categories of nouns. **Common nouns** are general, nonspecific (e.g., *constitutions*), while **proper nouns** are specific (e.g., the *U.S. Constitution* — note the capitalization of the noun when it is used as a proper noun). **Abstract nouns** are ideas or qualities (e.g., *socialism, mercy*), whereas **concrete nouns** are objects (*window, mosquito*). Moreover certain words, phrases, or clauses can act as nouns and are therefore called nominals; gerunds and infinitives, for example, can be nominals (see p. 429).

Noun clause   A noun clause is a dependent clause acting as a noun; for example, consider this sentence: *My only wish is that we arrive safely*.

Number   This term, in the grammatical sense, merely indicates whether a noun, pronoun, or verb is singular or plural in form. See Chapter 6, pp. 332–336.

Object   Objects are nouns or nominals that are affected by the action of a verb, indirectly or directly, or that follow a preposition. Here is a sentence illustrating all three:

> The drunk gave the *cop* [noun as indirect object] a shaky *wave* [noun as direct object] of his *hand* [noun as object of preposition *of*].   *student paper*

Participle   A participle is a verb form used as an adjective or adverb. It is also used to form certain tenses. A **present participle** ends in *-ing* (the form also used for gerunds) and is used in progressive tenses: *is going, has been dancing, will be arriving*. A **past participle** relates to the past or a perfect tense and takes the appropriate ending (*-d* or *-ed* for regular verbs): *written proof, locked door, had finished, will have eaten*. Past participles are also used in the passive voice (see **Voice**).

Parts of speech   Grammarians have traditionally divided the English language into eight parts of speech: nouns, pronouns, verbs, adverbs, adjectives, prepositions, conjunctions, and interjections. For more information, see the entries for each.

Passive: see **Voice**

Person   To describe the person of a pronoun means to show whether it refers to the speaker(s) (**first person:** *I, we*), to the person(s) spoken to (**second person:** *you*), or to some third party (**third person:** *he, she, it, they*). Verbs show person only in some tenses, for instance, *I jog, you jog, she jogs* (present tense).

Phrase   A phrase is a group of related words that, unlike a clause, lacks a subject-predicate combination. There are many types of phrases, defined by function: **noun, verb, adverb, prepositional, gerund, infinitive,** and **participial** (see the entries for these or related terms).

Possessive   The possessive is a case, sometimes called the **genitive** case. Possessive pronouns and adjectives include *my, mine, his, her, hers, its, our, ours, your, yours, their, theirs,* and *whose*. Possession is also shown with an apostrophe or apostrophe and *-s* after a noun: *the boss' secretary, the dog's bone.*

Predicate   A predicate consists of a verb plus all of its objects, modifiers, and complements. An easy way to identify the predicate of a sentence or clause is to first find the subject and all its modifiers; what remains is the predicate, since all simple sentences and clauses can be reduced to the formula S[ubject] + P[redicate]. See Chapter 2, pp. 68–70.

Prefix   A short, usually one-syllable form added at the beginning of a word changing the word's meaning is called a prefix. Familiar examples include *non-, un-, re-, con-, mis-,* and *ex-*. Prefixes are bound forms—that is, they must be attached directly to a word, sometimes with a hyphen. Advertisers have had some fun experimenting with prefixes lately — remember the UNcola?

Preposition   One of the eight parts of speech, a preposition is a connective, or linking word; it usually has an object, as in the phrase *into* [preposition] *the garage* [object]. The most common prepositions are *in, into, from, of, with, to, by, for, on, at*—there are many others. Sometimes two prepositions are used together, like *because of* or *due to*. Some words, like *but, before, since, after,* and *for,* can be either prepositions or conjunctions, depending on how they are used. For example, in the sentence *We have not heard from him since Wednesday*, the word *since* is a preposition. But in the sentence *Of course I'm angry, since you won't listen to me*, the same word is a conjunction. (See **Conjunction**.)

Pronoun   A word that can be used in place of a noun or noun phrase is called a pronoun. Pronouns show case (*he*, subject; *him*, object; *his*, possessive) and number (*I*, singular; *we*, plural; *mine*, singular; *ours*, plural). They also show gender (*he*, *she*, *it*) and person (*I*, *you*, *he*, *she*). In general pronouns perform the same functions as nouns: they can be subjects, indirect or direct objects, complements, or appositives. What makes pronouns different from nouns is that they need *antecedents*, nouns that they refer to and replace. (See **Reference**.)

Pronouns are sometimes categorized as **subject pronouns** (*Tom went, although **he** didn't want to*); **object pronouns** (*Give **it** to **her***); **reflexive pronouns** (*You shouldn't criticize **yourself** so harshly*); **indefinite pronouns** (***Anybody** can sing*); **relative pronouns** (*The book **that** she chose is a bore*); **demonstrative pronouns** (***That** surprised me*); **reciprocal pronouns** (*Love **one another***); and **interrogative pronouns** (***Who** will be elected?*).

Proper names   Proper names (nouns and adjectives) are specific names of people, places, institutions, and so forth: *President Roosevelt, St. Louis, University of Colorado*. Proper names offer us our one sure chance to determine how a word will be pronounced. You can spell your name *S-m-i-t-h* and pronounce it "Jankowski" if you want. The people of Des Plaines, Illinois, have all agreed that their town is to be pronounced "Dez Planes," the entire French phonetic system notwithstanding.

Reference   We noted in Chapter 6 (pp. 332–342) that pronouns must agree with their antecedents. Reference is a term to describe this relationship: each pronoun *refers* to an antecedent and therefore must be the same as the antecedent in person (first, second, or third), in number (singular or plural), and in gender (masculine, feminine, or neuter).

Reference can also mean the naming of sources. If a statement in one of your papers has the word *Reference?* written next to it, and if there is no problem of pronoun reference, what your instructor means is that you should have named the sources— the books, articles, or people—who gave you the information upon which your statement was based.

Relative clause, relative pronoun:

Sentence   This topic is a large one — so large that all of Chapter 2 is devoted to it. If sentences are defined as grammatically complete expressions, they must have both a subject and a predicate. They must always be capable of standing alone; in other words, they cannot be dependent clauses (see pp. 68–72), even though dependent clauses have both a subject and a predicate. The verb of a sentence predicate must also be complete in itself. Compare, for example, *I went home* and *I going home*; the former is satisfactory as a sentence, but the latter needs an additional word — *I was going home* — to be complete and acceptable.

There are many types of sentences. A **declarative sentence** states something and is followed by a period (such as the sentence you are reading). An **exclamatory sentence** shows force or emotion and is followed by an exclamation point: *Help! Go away! I can't believe it!* An **interrogative sentence** asks a question and is followed by a question mark: *What did you say?*

Sentences are also classified as **simple, compound, complex,** or **compound-complex.** A **simple sentence** contains only one subject and verb (that is, one main clause): *We are going.* A **compound sentence** contains two main clauses (which have subjects and verbs and can each stand alone): *We are going, but they are staying home.* A **complex sentence** has a main clause and a dependent clause (the latter cannot stand alone): *We are going, unless it rains.* Finally, a **compound-complex sentence** has more than one main clause and at least one dependent clause: *We are going, but they are staying home in case John arrives.* Chapter 2 explains these distinctions in greater detail.

Subject   A subject is usually a noun, nominal, or pronoun about which something is stated or asked. The complete subject is the simple subject plus all the modifiers associated with this noun, nominal, or pronoun—see Chapter 2, pp. 66–68. To put it another way, we can reverse what we said about predicates: since any simple sentence is S[ubject] + P[redicate], you need only subtract from a sentence all those words that form the predicate. What is left is the subject.

Suffix   Just as prefixes are short forms that are attached at the beginning of a base word, so suffixes are forms that are attached at the *end* of a word. Examples: *-ing* (*going*), *-s* (*loves*), *-es* (*boxes*),

-ed (*hoarded*), *-er* (*mixer*), *-ly* (*properly*), *-able* (*pardonable*), *-tion* (*consideration*).

Superlative: see **Adjective, Adverb**

Syntax Syntax is the study of the relationships between various words and/or phrases within a sentence. In other words, for the sentence *I am going to the post office*, we might note that the arrangement consists of subject (*I*) plus verb (*am going*) plus prepositional phrase (*to the post office*). We might further observe that this particular arrangement is required by our language. We cannot say *I to the post office am going*, or *Am going I to the post office*, even though these forms might be acceptable word order in other languages. To study this arrangement of the words within the sentence is to study aspects of syntax.

Tense Verbs can change form in order to enable us to specify when the action they describe is taking place (was taking place? will take place?). If we use the verb *to give* as an illustration, we think immediately of three tenses: present (*give*), past (*gave*), and future (*will give*). Further refinements of tense let us show less common tenses by using the past participle plus a form of the verb *to have*: thus present perfect (*has given*), past perfect (*had given*), future perfect (*will have given*), and conditional perfect (*would have given*). We might note also the progressive tenses, which require an *-ing* form of the verb plus another auxiliary verb: *has been giving, is giving, will be giving, would be giving*.

Transitive: see **Verb**

Verb, verbal Again we encounter a part of speech that can be identified by form or by function. In terms of form, verbs are words that show a distinction according to time, or tense. In the case of the verb *to run*, for example, the present-tense form is *run(s)*, the past-tense form is *ran*, and the future-tense form is *will (shall) run*. When combined with auxiliaries, verbs can show many other time relationships, as in *has run* or *will have been running*. In one specific instance—third person, present-tense —verbs also change their form according to number (*she runs*, singular; *they run*, plural). *Run*, by the way, is one of the many irregular verbs; regular verbs use the suffix *-ed* like *act, acted* (see Chapter 6, pp. 350–354).

As to function, verbs are the essential parts of predicates. If there's no verb, there's no predicate; no predicate, no sentence.

Predicates can of course include many other words, phrases, and clauses besides the verb, but the verb is essential — it makes the rest of the sentence work.

Verbs are often divided into **transitive verbs**, which can take a direct object (e.g., *throw*, *lift*), and **intransitive verbs**, which do not take an object (e.g., *exist*, *sit*). Some verbs can be used either transitively or intransitively.

Because verbs are often combined with other auxiliary verbs to show very complex relationships, you might want to look at the entries for **Mood**, **Tense**, and **Voice**, and perhaps also at the verb-related sections dealing with **Complement**, **Predicate**, and **Sentence.** Chapters 2 and 6 are your best resource. Take special note also of **linking verbs** (pp. 344–345).

Verbals are words derived from verbs that have verb-like forms but act as another part of speech. See the separate entries for **Gerund**, **Infinitive**, and **Participle**, which collectively can be called verbals.

Voice   The relationship in a sentence between the subject and the action of the verb is described by the term **voice**. That is, if the subject is performing the action, we say the sentence is in the **active voice:** *He drives the car.* On the other hand, if the subject is being acted upon — *The car is driven by him* — the voice is said to be **passive.** (The active voice is preferable in most instances—see p. 93.)

Index

437